MW01120373

—EVERYBODY—
Everybody
Is
A Somebody

JBI: Jacob Bergen Insight' is not a version or translation, just what the original Version (KJV) suggests in a particular passage. Please use only as the author's thoughts in a paraphrase manner.
JBI will often include the words of the original (KJV).
More JBI Thoughts

I often use big words, and to some they are not as understandable as the little to the point words that I could use. I do not do this to show off my word skills, but to open the door to encouraging those who like the depth of reading to dig a little deeper once again from where they have been, and to encourage those of you who like more of a shallow read to go deeper as well.

However, I usually try to include a defining word in brackets [and or other words, for the big word] so those who like a shallower read to be able to do that without using the dictionary and or Thesaurus, and this is to open the door to other synonyms which take the thoughts and themes into an even greater understanding of what I mean to say.

EVERYBODY:
EVERYBODY
IS
A SOMEBODY
"When All Is Said And Done"
Jacob Bergen

TTOTH Publishing

Discover other titles by Jacob Bergen
It's Jacob! My Name Is Jacob! What's Yours?
Authorhouse (Formerly 1ST. Books Library)
(April 26, 2002)

The Mandate
(June 21, 2006)
Xulonpress

Twin Towers of The Heart
September 11, 2016
CreateSpace (Print)
Amazon (E-Book)

Bridging The Gap
April 2018
CreateSpace (Now KDP—Print)
Amazon (KDP—E-Book)

Next Book Expected—In The Year 2022—Lord willing

"Searching For A Heart of Gold"

(All are E-BOOK, Paperback, [The Mandate is also Hardcover]
Available at Amazon, Kindle &Many Other Sites
Contact: [***Preferred Contact]
77TTOTH77@gmail.com ***[Preferred Email]
jcbbergen@gmail.com ***[Preferred Email]
twintowersoftheheart@gmail.com
bridgingthegapjb@gmail.com
Twitter
https://twitter.com/jacobbergen77
https://twitter.com/jcbbergen
https://twitter.com/TwinTowersHeart
https://www.facebook.com/public/Jacob-Bergen

DEDICATION

We need to appreciate life and its giver.

"To Him who can keep us from falling,
Be Glory, Honor, and Praise, Now and Forever."
(The Bible Jude 24-25; JBI)

Determining truth is worth committing our time to follow; in my humble opinion, God's Word, The Bible, needs to be our principal aim in life.

My prayer is to kindly write words relevant to readers in all categories of this world. The work that God placed in the heart of this writer, and the blessed hope in this heart, can be a forever thing in the eyes of God.

My wife Mary Ann is my soul mate and friend, and she deserves and has my appreciation. She allows me the needed space and time to carry out what it takes to share the heart of this book; be it reading, writing notes, articles, or books. (Jacob Bergen)

Four sons and their wives, twenty grandchildren, two great grandsons, friends, strangers—these, each are part of what gives me the strength to write. Thoughts of things that happened; thoughts of things that will happen today; thoughts of things that an unseen tomorrow will bring; these are part of why I write.

Writing—What A Joy!

FOLKS, I am not writing anything new, but I am only bearing reference to what has been written long ago, from somewhere around the beginning of our physical time on earth. As time proceeded, that *"Old Commandment,"* often misunderstood, and treated as though it were too dark to see the light of truth in it, it became alive and new because it came as a major beacon of light in the *"New Testament."* This Light was Jesus, and all that He could be to help us see more clearly the way that lay before us in a new reality, through 'Grace.'

If we claim to be enlightened by Christ, and have hate in our heart towards others, we remain in darkness. If we love Christ, then we need to love those who wrong us. If we claim Jesus as our leader, we have been forgiven a great debt; we need to pass on this forgiveness to others who wrong us. God The Father has always existed, and The Holy Spirit with Him. Jesus was and is also in this endless existence, but we just did not consider Him as He was, but we see Him because He came to show us the path. [These are my Jacob Bergen Insights (JBI) about 1 John 2 7-14 KJV]

I'm not writing to *'tell you what to do and how to do life.'* Most people know all about the 'just,' of doing life. We all need reminding about the things we once experienced, the things we may have let slide from our day to day. So, I write, hoping as we read, and or me as I write, we will throughout the time of reading or writing be reminded of those things that are not as fresh as they once were, and let those things grow within us again. The guideline I use is the Bible, and I pray that the illustrative examples I use will challenge us to look again at what life once was, to see if the examples of the past will allow us another peek at how things can grow successfully towards the tomorrow we want to experience someday—To Be With Jesus; To See Him As He Is!
IF THIS IS WHERE YOU ARE AT,
PLEASE READ ON.

TABLE OF CONTENTS

Being Different, Does Not Mean We Are of Less Value!

The vicissitudes [ups and downs] of life may affect [impact] all of us differently; I say 'may,' because there are many situations in life which many people handle the same way as others manage them. However, I still believe I have a certain character that is mine and mine alone. You may have to look hard for the difference I have which the next person does not have. Even if it is only one 'minute' [little] item of the makeup I have, which no one else has. If I can make the difference no one else could have made, life is worth the developments of life I have faced and will yet face because of my makeup. It may seem as though many people must have all the same characteristics as someone else in the big world we live in; I may be wrong, but I 'like to think' there is something different in me, in which only I can say "I made a difference in a certain person which would never have happened, had I not been born!"

How often have I judged someone else for the diversity [assortment] of their character, maybe their looks, maybe how they speak, maybe how they react to the hard times they encounter.

One time when I was a teenager, I remember being in the backyard of my cousin in Ontario, Canada, and we were looking at a girl over the fence, from some distance away. To my way of observation she was quite attractive; when I looked over the fence for a better view, I was somewhat disappointed by what I saw [my fault, not hers]. I knew nothing about her character; I never found out because we never formed a relationship.

In around 1980, my relationship with God was not what it is today. My wife asked me to go to church with her, and I did; it was a Baptist Church. I say this with no discredit. I began to listen to the sermon, I was not impressed with the preacher's demeanor, manner, character, or appearance—but something he said stayed with me for a time. I can't remember specifically what he said, but it had some impact on me. I cannot say that what he said, at the time, effected my coming into a relationship with Jesus Christ [God]. It may have done so in a way only he [this pastor] may have had a part in for me.

Life, seems we can't live with it, and we can't live without it! Someone said, women, you can't live with them and you can't live without them. Women probably say the same about men.

My desire for a relationship with my Creator was nearer now [I did not yet know it at the time]. Yes, my wife had asked me to go to church with her. She knew I was not outwardly impressed with the Baptist Church [she grew up in the Baptist Church]. She said, 'pick the church and I will go there with you.' Having been raised somewhat in the Pentecostal Church, my bent was to look for something like it. I looked in the newspaper, by accident [ya, right] I came across the Downtown Calgary Full Gospel Church. I hadn't attended church for 16 years, but I still had my Old Bible; I still have it. Even though I had been a long way from a relationship with God till this time, I took my Bible to this Full Gospel Church April 5, 1981; turns out it was Holy Ground for me. God knew what 'He' was doing [Surprise]?

As the preacher walked to the podium, I said to myself, 'this ain't going to be much!' He was a smallish man of stature; on this basis, I formed an opinion on which I believe God turned the tables on me. Had the preacher been Samson or Gideon, a 'Mighty Man of Valor,' I would have fallen to my knees in repentance to God for having strayed from Him [I guess?]: Or not!

God works in mysterious ways His wonders to perform. The preacher came to the lectern and asked us to turn to Psalm 40; I did. However, my eyes moved across the page of my Old Bible, now, somewhat tattered, and I landed on Psalm 41: 4. "I waited patiently for the Lord; He inclined unto me and heard my cry. He brought me up also out of an horrible pit, out of the miry clay, and set my feet upon a rock, and established my goings. And he hath put a new song in my mouth, even praise unto our God: many shall see it, and fear, and shall trust in the Lord. Blessed is that man that maketh the Lord his trust, and respected not the proud, nor such as turn aside to lies."

I came upon Psalm 51: "Have mercy upon me, O God, according to thy lovingkindness: According unto the multitude of thy tender mercies blot out my transgressions. Wash me thoroughly from mine iniquity, and cleanse me from my sin. *For I acknowledge my transgressions*: My sin is ever before me [*I acknowledged God again on April 5/1981*]. Against thee, thee only, have I sinned, and done this evil in thy sight: that thou mightest be justified when thou speakest, and be clear when thou judgest. Behold, I was shapen in iniquity, and in sin did my mother conceive me."

—This Pastor remained my Pastor for 18 years. —

INTRODUCTION

People and Purpose,
This Is The Theme

The Mid-Eighties offered me the opportunity to experience Writers Conference at Three Hills, Alberta, Canada; established authors, novice authors and wannabes, blended with a good array of speakers: Publishers, Editors and Authors who'd had successful writing careers. I was 'green,' but had a heart for affecting people with written words. I benefited by gaining an understanding of what being a successful writer is about. What constitutes success?

Now, some thirty years removed from Writers Conference, living life in what I think of as normal, has changed. Had I slept after this event and only woke up yesterday I would have suffered the shock of a lifetime! If I only watch the newscasts of the day for an hour of any day it is sufficient time to realize that life, ticketed as what many people once considered normal, is impossible to return to. Oh, how things have changed. Try reliving what you once had and see where it gets you in todays world.

I am thankful for much of the change. If I look at life as it presents at times, from a personal perspective, or selfie mode, I may think the 'good old days' have us beat. I am from an era which presented life more securely in addressing the Moral Code of Ethics from a standard, affixed to a belief system with an origin submerged in God as being the ultimate truth. Time hasn't changed how I see morality; it appears loyalty to change in this arena is so easy today; everything seems to be acceptable today. The debate on the issue's rambles on ferociously for some, for others, these are non-debatable issues. Morality and Tolerance are more closely related today.

At times, the shadows of blockage consume us, blinding our gateway to understanding differences between 'right and wrong' [as judged by whose standards?] For many folks, one person's right is another person's wrong; another person's wrong is another person's right. Harmony on anything is near impossible because life has changed so much. Life as we know it changes rapidly. So, what hope is there for tomorrow?

When I say our understanding darkens to where we don't see the difference between right and wrong, I do so from the set position to which I hold dear. Everything had a beginning. This beginning is God. Nothing I know of ever came out of absolutely nothing. The understandings of life as we knew them, have adjusted over the years to learn about things we did not always know about life.

As I see it, 'simplicity' has left the playing field. Something or Someone [and I Capitalize Someone because it seems more logical to understand that Someone was responsible for the initial creation of anything] had something we cannot see with our natural receptors [eyes in this case]. Someone had something we cannot understand without trusting. This Someone had our best interest in mind somewhere back in the eons of time, when the concept of 'us' was planned out. Something or Someone had *Eternity In Their Heart* so we could have the Best of Both Worlds: Physical and Spiritual. Using 'their,' may signify a difficulty; it does so for most people, as we think of the relationship it has to 'One God!' God pictures out as Father, Son [Jesus], and The Holy Spirit of God! Will I totally understand this during my tenure? I'll say this, 'it is challenging to fully grasp' Someone Who is so Perfect and Complete. Yet, He became Human without losing the Godhood only He possesses.

Is it conceivable [imaginable] to think 'nothing' can be described by adjectives to make 'nothing' any clearer? We may call 'nothing,' absolutely nothing, the ultimate nothing, Nada, but the synonyms of 'nothing' are, "not a thing, not a single thing, not anything, nothing, nil." Attempts to clarify 'nothing,' only pose a conundrum [problem] when we attempt to make 'nothing' more than it is, 'nothing.' The other best description of 'nothing' I found is 'zero.' One thesaurus suggested using the word boring as an adjective for 'nothing.' Boring is a state of mind that suggests it is a lack of something. Is this our stance?

The opposite of 'nothing' is, "something, something or Someone." This presumes [discerns, discovers, or divines] a prior state. Is it possible that an inanimate or lifeless entity can achieve a second living cell? Another living cell always has to be available for reproduction to be possible. Does non-existing matter ever produce another living entity? This always bodes [prefigures, suggests, or foreshadows] the question, "Who made God?"

Don Richardson, the author of *Peace Child*; *Eternity in Their Hearts*; *Heaven Wins*; has been studying the Muslim world for a long time. He and his late wife, Carol, spent 15 years among the many Sawi folks, a Stone Age tribe of Irian Jaya. Where did the thought *Eternity In Their Hearts* come? [Don Richardson]

From the context Don Richardson writes from in the book *Eternity In Their Hearts*, he found the beginning of the 'hope of anything' [something, not 'nothing] to be a living entity, not a dead nothing entity. The Bible tells us Jesus is The Blessed Hope; Jesus is what Don Richardson gave the Sawi, a Stone Age tribe of Irian Jaya. The first words of Mr. Don Richardson in *Eternity In Their Hearts* goes like this, "Tell us, Nicias, what advice has the Pythian oracle sent with you? Why has this plague come upon us? And why did our numerous sacrifices avail nothing?" [We know more about 'Plague' these days [Covid-19].

The understanding of the heart, if you would, was in the dark ages until the light tunnel opened up to them through the ministry of Don Richardson, to the Sawi, a Stone Age tribe of Irian Jaya. Many other folks with the same mandate, showed 'this way' to others on life's journey. As we look around us in our day-to-day it often seems like we are fighting a losing battle of irrationality or craziness. When someone, seemingly out of nowhere commits a violent act, and the people who knew them are asked about them, the response is often, 'they were just regular people, neighborly.'

How can this be? Somewhere along the way something went wrong. It is as if these violent offenders were still living in the dark ages, as if they did not understand the benefits and or the consequences of life—the benefits of right living and harsh consequences for wrong living. Were these folks in a column that left them more worthless than the rest of what we may call the normal world? Or, were they from another planet? Someone said, "It is a jungle out there." "Doesn't anybody care anymore about the sanctity of life?" We may look at life and say, "I don't Think So!" We live where 'eternally offered valuations' are rare. 'There is nothing in the light tunnel of Eternity.' There is a long light tunnel we could call earth because earth is the preparatory, introductory, or opening remarks for any conversation about Eternity. Earth is the prelude to death and what comes after death. Steven Hawking said, "asteroids pose major threat to human and alien civilizations."

There have never been, nor will there ever be any absentees on the list of birth records of history, who experienced nothing, or will experience nothing after they experience their final breath. Many are the pointers showing us a passage we can travel leading to the light at the end of the tunnel. If we pay any mind to history, we'll see pointers which God highlighted at the beginning of the record of Genesis. 'Genesis,' written long ago and highlighted often since then, at the hands of farmhands, scholars, prophets, preachers, missionaries—shows evidence there is more to existence than what we see on this planet in the physical sense. Many believe there is something beyond this reality!

There are many educated people in our world. The world is packed with every conceivable educational facility. We teach and we preach to one another. We say, 'this is the way we need to go.' After surveying the multiplicity of gods who accomplished nothing, The Athenians were of the opinion there was another God out there somewhere. There had to be, how else could life be rational. So, they built an altar to The Unknown God: 'The One' they knew had to address their lack of answers, but they soon forgot Him too.

Way leads to way. History leads to today. Introduction leads to the rest of the book. Each thought leads to another. One good deed leads to another. One good leader can lead to another. However, this is not always the case, people forget. We often return to the garbage dump looking for something of significance. Sometimes we find it, most of the time it is just smelly old garbage. The garbage dump often offers sustenance for the less fortunate.

To fit what we experience into a reverted, lapsed, or past model of what we had, this is impossible. What never changes when our day-to-day changes so drastically? What never changes when our tomorrows are so different from our yesteryears? Our approach to Whom we will serve or acknowledge as the only entity worthy of our complete unadulterated obeisance or respect, this never changes; so much so, that we will give our lives to Him, for Him, and other people; this never fluctuates. What never shifts? Our propensity or bent to place ourselves above all else, this never varies in the mega sense of what humankind will offer to the Unknown God. Be He God or not, we wrestle with this for the perpetuity [eternity] we think we are ensconced in, hidden, or concealed in as if we were in our self-made 'paradise—' it seems nothing ever changes.

Pointing forward with intensity and heart—this is my intent. If we do not heed the good lessons of the past, our future fades or blackens. Our successes look good until they turn sour. We look for help. *The Unknown God*, is He Unknown or Ignored?

In *The Road Not Taken*, Robert Frost says,
"Way leads on to way."

What I lived yesterday is all that yesterday had for me, except what my future held for me, based somewhat on how I planned for the future and how I lived life in the yesterday which existed then. I say somewhat because I am not entirely the master of my fate. Someone got me started; they are responsible for this.

However, in the big picture of time and eternity past, Someone or something, I guess [based on the Big Bang, which must have been a gravitational force which must have overruled nothing], planned for my arrival on the architectural drafting board [hypothetically], outlining all that was to be: *To Be Or Not To Be, That Is The Question!*

What was the color of the first cell brought about by an invisible force of gravity from nowhere to create this huge bang up scenario we call *The Big Bang*? Are colors more than just a perception on our part? Do colors form because of an objective truth or are they just a figment [pigment (play on words)] of our imagination: the subjective fantasy [emotive] we think will brighten our day? When I begin a research of black and white, they tell me they are not colors, just an assumption, speculation or perception.

If I point forward with my own smarts, thinking they will carry the day, it leaves room for defeat, failure. My claim of doing it '*My Way*,' with no help ever from anyone, is a failed attempt. We need not think too hard to realize we did not create ourselves; 'no,' poof, and there we were, or were we? We would need to be God to be ever existent out of nothing or gravity. We would be self creating entities. Think About It! The gravity or seriousness of this scenario leaves us with the question, "how did nothing get here?" Who or what had the gravity, and significance to create that first cell? We spin our wheels in a quagmire with no one to place us on solid ground unless we reach our arms up and out to the saving grace of The Eternal Being Who would have to be God, to help.

Adam preceded us. His-Story says he consulted with God! The rules of life for Adam came from this conference. The end of the story was not in sight for him. As *way led to way*, people entered. Adam was first in Scene One of human existence. In Scene One, Act Two, God gave us a woman for lonesome Adam. The rest is history. The Rule, 'do as I tell you,' was broken in a coalition between Adam and Eve. The rest is history. We all know what breaking the law gets us. If we think we can beat the Law of Gravity we should try jumping off the Empire State Building. "No, don't do that, it will kill you!"

Finding the Beginning leads to needing God to finish 'The Story.' If this isn't the case, everything, including us, is still Nada, nonexistent, 'nothing.' One race was created, The Human Race. As people multiplied, their character, human features, and all the rest took on different features, composites, or complexities—leading to differing displays of our complexion. We are still running around aimlessly. God knew we would break the first rule—not obey. So, He built a genetic factor into our DNA. This tells a huge story. This was for our complexion to be set apart by differing pigmentation and character [I have no factual evidence for this, I can do no experiment to prove this, it is just what I call JBI (Jacob Bergen Insight)].

People did not listen. Their first test in The Garden of Eden was a failure. Sin birthed in the Garden of God because people chose not to listen. Hence, everybody followed the lead. Everybody concocted their own ideas, differing about anything and everything. Hence, we end up with differing belief systems from those initially intended. We have Two Testaments in The Bible, The Old Testament, and The New Testament; each possessed, and still have their space in history, past, present, and future. The future we consider as 'today' will someday be our past.

I foresee a motion-picture declaring my heart for people everywhere in *Everybody: Everybody Is A Somebody*, along with a presentation I conceive to be the truth of what God intended to be our mandate from the Beginning. If Adam could not listen and obey what God minded [prepared], as *The Road To Travel*, so we who are a part of the physicality of Adam because of the genetics of his humanity would see us travelling *The Road Not To Be Travelled*, then where was the hope? *The Road Less Travelled* is the *Road God Laid Out To Be Travelled.*

Our lives pan out differently. Each of us come to the end of one path and begin another. We are not always satisfied with the new road we are called to travel because each of us make our own choices. Will an eternal satisfaction still be a fulfilled promise for us if we choose our own path when the end scenario of all of life as we know it, is over? What does death leaves us with? We can follow the course of 'the rule of life' as God set it out to be, this is by our choice. Hope is not gone while we live, we can still have God!

Life has a way of not turning out to be the way we think it should have turned. We may have thought it should have been better because we are such great people. We often wish we could have a do-over, one we think of as a comfort zone. *Gone With The Wind* paints a clear picture of this. One TV Show portrays well what this Do-Over looks like—*Extreme Makeover*. When we are no longer satisfied with our present overall state with life, "What Then?"

In her novel, *Gone With the Wind,* Margaret Mitchell captures a main idea; the world of the old South (the past life) is gone: *Gone With The Wind*. Margaret tells of an old woman, Grandma Fontaine, who with a barbed tongue, talks about the overthrows and distresses of the Civil War. Grandma Fontaine exclaims, "The whole world can't lick us, but we can lick ourselves—by longing for things we 'ain't got' anymore, and by remembering too much."

As long as we imagine too vivid a picture of the past as the best of 'the best' we get, nursing our wounds with these reflections, we will never move into the better future we could have.

There comes a time to dress the wound, bind it up with faith in God's providence, and let the healing begin. It reminds me of Vince Lombardi's words to his defeated football team, "Okay— Sack up your guts; let's get going."

Are we different? Yes. Are we thereby less?

Or,

ARE WE DIFFERENT? YES, BUT NOT LESS!

Is Everybody Really A Somebody?
Me Thinks So!

EVEN GOD IS A SOMEBODY

YOU ARE APPRECIATED!

Welcome to my world!

My prayer is to be something vital to someone along the way as we journey together on many of the roads of life. Some of these are the side trails which are part of the interchanges of living, and the thoughts and questions which are a part of the whole story. As we go through life together, you might learn from me. However, if I haven't learned something from you, this whole matter of writing this book and the others I have written, have been "Exercises In Futility!"

Changing channels with a remote control is easy on a TV. Changing Chapters from the beginning to the end of a physical book, has no remote control, we need to "run the gamut.'

As we venture together through this book, each Chapter will have a specific theme, which the Chapter Title should suggest. As we move through *Everybody: Everybody Is A Somebody*, the intent is, that each Chapter will transfer us easily into the next Chapter, through to the end of the book, because of the subheadings and the pointers I use. The approach to each Chapter changes as we move from *Part One*, to *Part Two*, to *Part Three*, to *Part Four* and finish up in *Part Five*. The theme remains to be an introduction to each Chapter.

This comes before each Chapter begins with its Title.

In *Part One* It will be *The Approach Shot*
In *Part Two* it will be *Believe It Or Not?*
In *Part Three* it will be *The Neutral Zone*
In *Part Four* it will be *There Is No Neutral Zone*
In *Part Five* it will be *Understanding The 'REAL: The Visible! And The Invisible!*

Each chapter should end by leaving correlating thoughts of the earlier words of the Chapter. These thoughts will usually be headlined with the following Highlights:

Looking Back To See
And
What Did I See, and What Does It Say To Me?

Tell Me A Story: Okay!

One day I walked into Vacuum Township, where people of every sort dwelt in their own niche. These folks lived close enough to almost touch each other; nary a word was spoken between any one of them, not even a glance of recognition was offered to make any effort to get acquainted. It was as if it was a dream; we all know what dreams are like. We dream about stuff such as reality allots us whilst we sleep. When we awake to think about the dream, we see how unreal it was in so many respects. If dreams were reality we would surely be living in a mess.

In some remote corner of Vacuum Township, a 'No-Man's-Land' as such, one neighbor happened to glance over as if by accident, saw the other neighbor notice the glance and said 'Good Morning and offered an 'I have not seen you before;' 'same goes for me said the other.' 'I have lived here for what seems like a lifetime; I thought I was indeed living alone in this world, as if in a Vacuum!'

As they had never talked before it was tough to initiate a conversation because each of these folks were oblivious to each other, for that matter, oblivious to life as well. However, the next morning both of these neighbors once again said "Good Morning." One said to the other, "It Is A Beautiful Day!" Every day the conversation became more relational. There seemed to be a camaraderie forming. Life was Good in Vacuum Township.

The clatter of friendly banter quickened. People on either side of these two folks took notice and wondered where these folks had come from. They got into the mix, following through to becoming more aware of life, people, and their surroundings. As time went on, the place in which each person thought was a 'world of their own,' became a community of people who began to have a heart for the welfare of their fellow person.

While living as if in a world of their own, no-one knew the worth of the other. No-one knew they were all equal, even though they all seemed to have the same kind of houses, the same everything. As time went on each person began sharing their feelings. One person said they loved to bake bread, and so they began sharing this bread with their neighbors. Another said they loved to barbecue; they invited the rest of the folks to share a meal with them. The flicker of a flame became a wildfire.

Before this time no one had ever noticed one neighbor was of this culture, another was another culture and so on. 'The thing is' everyone was on the same page now; everyone was equal to everyone else in this community. As long as everyone stayed right where they had always been, life was good, really good, I guess, because nobody knew any different.

One day a few of these folks ventured beyond where they had ever traversed before, outside of what seemed to be an impassable invisible border; they saw there was another place they had never seen, another place where more people lived side by side; no one there knew anybody else; in the same way as it had been in Vacuum Township. There was a big difference here, these folks lived in much larger houses; they had many more luxuries; it showed that there was more in life than what these initial dwellers were experiencing. Their houses were not 'ticky tacky' row houses.

American folk/blues singer-songwriter and political activist Malvina Reynolds, best known for her song writing, wrote and sang *Little Boxes* and *What Have They Done to the Rain*—among others. I like *Little Boxes*. It fits well here. Pete Seeger and others sang this as well; they also had good success with this and other folk songs. '*Folk Songs*' seem to bring folks together into a companionship which fits for me, better than '*Rock Songs*' do. We owe credit to many of the writers and singers of these *Folk Songs* because of their heart for togetherness. Realize with me please, we need individuality, but our hearts for the world around us needs to be one with 'open arms' attached in some way.

So, back to the folks who had explored beyond what they had known to this point. They attempted to connect with these new folks [new to them], but they were promptly put in their place [as if to say, get back into your little boxes]. They were told to leave and never venture out from where they had been. They were told they did not belong here; they had no business trying to assimilate [mix] with them. The folks in the New Neighborhood liked the way they were living, unhindered by people who seemed to be less [lesser in value than they thought they were]—they wanted to stay this way. So, they excitement died down. These folks who ventured out to explore, were discouraged, went home and once again became what they once were, isolated from everybody to live in their own world, never again to reach out and touch a world outside their own!

Turns out this story was only a dream: Or Was it; is it?

Many folks say, 'Life Is Good,' living with an open door approach; arms reaching out. Often, we don't know how to welcome each other. We the people live within the built-in offerings we have. Can we know *Everybody: Everybody Is A Somebody*! What would the world look like if we all appreciated having the same ingredients for living; this must be 'something;' it's got to be more than a dream!

At least our Creator thought so!
We might glean something as we *Go The Distance*.

Joan Baez's song, *Forever Young* also fits well here. If we all remained *Forever Young*, to where we have not yet become so set in our ways, *What A Wonderful World This Would Be*.

Folk songs were part of the integration of the hippie culture, which was responsible for much of the hallucinogenic drug culture movement, yes, but they produced songs with meaning akin to poems like Robert Service penned. I frequent Gospel songs. They take me to another community of life, one which points me to *Another World*, one where the difficulties of this life are no longer even part of the makeup of life 'in this zone.' we might begin to notice this place as we move along into *Everybody: Everybody Is A Somebody*. We are just beginning a journey of words to help us.

Each of us within our individuality, have stories which could, if shared, enlighten and assist the rest of us in living [doing Life], just a little more fully. However, while keeping our 'individuality,' let us not forget we were put on this earth to be a part of a Community Culture, each of us to some degree or another, while never becoming more valuable than anybody else in this world.

We may each achieve to differing degrees, but we all have blood coursing through our veins which we may sometimes need to allow for us to bleed for someone else. Compassion needs to bleed from within us for our world. Jesus already gave His Physical Blood for us to have access to the place [Heaven] I talked about. We need never give this blood, nor could we ever in the same way [although some people have given their blood as a physical sacrifice] [like soldiers in wars] give our lives for others like Jesus did for the salvation of the souls of others. Yes, Jesus asks us to be like Him, but we will never be Him!

Reading the works of others is enlightening. I am reading a book called *The Luggage of Life* [by Frank W. Boreham]. This morning I came across a word, a set of words in fact, which brought me to a stopover in time, for a purpose. Please hear them with me.

"In childhood's golden hours, we, all of us, squandered a vast amount of sympathy upon Robinson Crusoe. And in later years we have caught ourselves shedding a silent tear for the sorrows of poor Enoch Arden, imprisoned on his 'beauteous, hateful isle.' In imagination, too, we have paced with the beloved disciple the rugged hills of Patmos. We have even felt a sympathetic pang for Napoleon in his cheerless exile at St. Helena. And all the while we have clean forgotten that we ourselves are each of us cast upon lonely, sea-girt islands. We are each one of us hopelessly cut off, isolated, and insulated. Unlike the heroes of Defoe and Tennyson, we shall never sight a sail. Our beacon-fires will never bring down any passing vessel to our relief. It is forever. At our very birth, we were chained, naked—to our rock in mid-ocean; and no Perseus will ever appear to pity and deliver us. The links of the chain by which we are bound are many and mighty." [by Frank W. Boreham]

'Sea-girt,' this thought stopped me in my tracks. Please look at the simple description of 'Sea-girt:' 'surrounded by the sea.' While writing *The Luggage of Life*, Frank Boreham uses the word sea-girt differently in the perspective he has on his mind than I might. Mr. Boreham suggests we are born naked, this is true; somehow intrinsically [basically] and or hypothetically chained to a rock surrounded by the sea [of life] like sea-girt suggests, as if we have but one mandate; to be servants of life and being. I am not too far into this book so I will only use his words to present my case, not to extend what he projects here.

John Donne suggests every soul is a part of a continent. If we fail to look for background in every sentiment one person may own, against the thought another person may house, we may get misplaced on a sea-girt island without a hope of sighting a sail manned by a rescue crew for our survival. If our brain is in seclusion, unexposed in spirit to reach out to others, we are all in trouble. The stories others relay to us in various ways, often have life changing impact on our life's journey—more than we may know.

John Donne alludes or refers to us as being linked to someone else in relationship to the whole of the plan of life. "Make No Mistake:" There is a 'Value-Added Plan' in place for each of us when we are born. Frank W. Boreham may give us a mental imprint of hopelessness, as if we are forced to be individually locked away on a Sea-girt Island; if we chew too long on the following words he chooses to use.

"And all the while we have clean forgotten that we ourselves are each of us cast upon lonely, sea-girt islands. We are each one of us hopelessly cut off, isolated and insulated."

Wait for it! Wait for it! John Donne speaks in terms of relationships; Mr. Boreham speaks in terms of individuality or separation. Mr. Boreham suggests we are each of us so individually isolated, so invaluable to God, even He has no compassion for us as if on our own we are incapable of understanding the hugeness of what we are in the sense of what we showed up for in the beginning. Each of us delivers our market value to the world by the choices we make. To be available to others so they have opportunity to achieve everything open to good moral decisions, is part of our task in life.

"And by far the mightiest of these insulating factors is the mystery of our own individuality. Each several ego is dreadfully alone in the universe. Each separate 'T' is without counterpart in all eternity. In the deepest sense we are each fatherless and childless; we have no kith or kin. When God creates a person, He reveals the form [or model]. Heaven builds no sister-ships. We may build relationships of friendship and fraternity with other island dwellers across the intervening seas. We may hear their voices shouted across the foam and read and return their signals; but this is all. The most intense sympathy can never bridge the gulf. No man can enter into the soul of his brother man.

I was in the isle, says John. And he says it for us all. In all the chief matters of life says Amiel in his Journal, we are alone: We dream alone; we suffer alone; we die alone. We are all islands, says George Eliot in one of her beautiful letters to Mrs. Bray; each in his hidden sphere of joy or woe, our hermit spirits dwell and roam apart."

"There is nothing more solemn, says Dr. Alexander McLaren, than that awful loneliness in which each soul of man lives. We stretch out our hands and grasp live hands; yet there is a universe between the two nearest and most one—and perhaps Matthew Arnold said the last word when he said:"

"Yes, in the sea of life enisled; with echoing straits between us thrown; dotting the shoreless, watery wild; we mortal millions live alone.

We have shed our tears over the terrific solitude of Robinson Crusoe and of Enoch Arden; in return, Robinson Crusoe and Enoch Arden urge us to weep for ourselves. For their partial, temporary solitude, was as nothing compared with the absoluteness and permanence of our own." [F.W. Boreham]

"Everybody: Everybody Is A Somebody"

Accountants will let us know fairly quickly if we are in "The Red," or in "The Black," when they open the Company's Books at Tax Time. Someone said there is nothing so sure as "Death and Taxes." This carries a lot of weight, from a purely human or earthly perspective, this has a degree of merit. Add in The Spiritual Factor and the story becomes one of "Value Added Benefits," vs "Coming Up Empty" *"When All Is Said and Done!"*

Throughout the duration of *Everybody: Everybody Is A Somebody*, the story of "Death and Taxes" unfolds in multiple ways. It presents to an extent of time and commitment we need to offer voluntarily. Not one of us can be coerced or persuaded through intimidation. This book is not about nailing someone to the cross and manipulating anyone to bend their knee to God. This will not work. Submitting to God, Jesus, is what comes from the heart when we come to the end of ourselves, knowing we are lost without God.

Everybody: Everybody Is A Somebody is all about expressing what God is all about, by looking at life as we know it, with a Look Over The Horizon of Life at the next part of our journey, one which is more than physical humanity offer us.

The theme of this book is simply: *Everybody: Everybody Is A Somebody*. We were born of "Equal Worth." God never made one fit for people of greater value, and another pattern for second class citizens, those with less to offer than those in the other mold. Someone said, *"We Are Different: Not Less!"*

We are different from each other. I do not believe there are any carbon copies. We do not all look alike. We do not all talk alike. We do not all live alike, but we all live! We build worth for ourselves through different means, while living life—some through hard work—some through lotteries—some through inheritances. These and others increase our physical worth, allowing for some folks to accumulate more stuff, but our Human Inherent Value came at birth. When God does the Taxes at Years End [His planned time to wrap up this world as we know it now], this is where we will know if we used the life we were given at birth to its full capacity. At birth, we were all equal because God so loved the world, He gave us everything we needed to get to the next life. The access route is called "Choice."

History tells us Adam preceded us. His-Story says he consulted with God! The rules of life for Adam came from this conference; the end of the story was not in sight for him. As *way led to way*, people entered: Adam first, in Scene One of human existence. Scene One, Act Two, God gave us a woman for lonesome Adam, the rest is history. The Rule, 'do as I tell you,' was broken in a coalition between Adam and Eve, the rest is history. We all know what breaking the law gets us. If we think we can beat the Law of Gravity, jumping off the Empire State Building would prove differently. "I do not suggest anyone should try this to find out!"

Finding the beginning leads to needing God to finish The Story; otherwise, everything, including us, is still nada, nonexistent nothing. One race was created, this is 'The Human Race.' As people multiplied, their character, human features, and all the rest took on different features, composites, or complexities, leading to differing displays of our complexion. God knew we would break the first rule and not obey Him, so He built a genetic factor into our DNA, this tells a huge story. This was for our complexion to be set apart by differing pigmentation and character [I have no factual evidence for this, I can do no experiment to prove this, it is just what I call JBI (Jacob Bergen Insight)].

I invite you to explore the life we were given at birth; to be different from each other, yes, but not less than the next person!

Everybody: Everybody Is A Somebody is for all of us to get a good look at, so each one of us can make a difference! If we read nothing else in this book, we need to take note of this, God says,

"We Are Different: Not Less!"

You Can Take This To The Bank!
For God so loved the world, that he gave his only begotten Son, that whosoever believes in him should not perish, but have everlasting life. [John 3:16 KJV]

PART ONE

THE LAUNCHING PAD.

The Opening Hole.

Hole Number 1, 445 yards, par 4 (Tea Olive): This slight dogleg right plays uphill and has a deep bunker requiring a 317-yard carry off the tee. The bunker has a tongue in the left side, so anything that enters the front of the bunker might be blocked by the lip. A bunker is left of the green, which falls off sharply at the back and to the right. AUGUSTA, Ga.

The Masters at Augusta, Georgia is one of my favorite PGA Tournaments. The Opening Hole is just the beginning. More challenges await us at "Amen Corner" as we Forge Ahead and Follow Through,

IF you are a Golf Fan,
Say AMEN!
Otherwise, Please Continue Anyway.

In The Bible The Apostle Paul said something like this in a certain passage of scripture,

"It does not bother me at all if I repeat myself from time to time. I do this intentionally, so as to have a better chance of getting you my "Pupils," to get the message I am trying to get across to you!" [JBI Insights]

I do this from time to time. I will try to mark these as "IBID." In short, "IBID" means I said it in another place.

Part One—The Launching Pad.

The Chapter Preamble In *Part One* will reflect on a mention of Golf, something like the following, but not exclusive to Golf.

In Golf: The golfer wants to hit the ball as close to the hole and the surrounding Putting Green as possible with the least amount of strokes to garner the lowest score they can achieve: A Hole In One, Eagle, Birdie, and Par; beyond this they go into the deficit scenario: Bogey, Double Bogey, Triple Bogey ETC.] However, when the golfer deliberately hits the ball toward the Putting Green on their second or third stroke, typically from the fairway, we call this their *Approach Shot.*

In Tennis: An offensive shot, allowing a tennis player to transition from the baseline to the net, hitting either a forehand or a backhand, this is also called an approach.

In both of these sports they are reaping or creating the best preparation point to achieve the highest success. Winning over an opponent, or simply being the best they can be to be the most productive at making life better for someone else, naturally [as in human nature], they also wish to post a better lifestyle for themselves. This is the Final Goal!

Life is a Picture of Grand Design. We each receive the 'Gift of Life' through the birth process, allowing us to use those capabilities to form positive strategies or approaches towards life. Not everybody has usage skills equal to another person, although with proper training and or preparation, many of us can learn to do most anything. Even when we cannot imagine the value of what we possess as things and ideas coming into our formative mental arena, we are as important as the next person!

Some folks are unable to grasp this concept. Simplicity is their gift or forte, this is where they are at. What they become may be some of the irregular, fluid, or uncertain qualities they were born with, as they choose what life to live; these may outline or framework their position. Their natural individuality does not determine them to be losers. Limitations, and we all have some, these are not other people's business for determining our state. The Equality of Birth Equates our worth.

The Approach Shot

1st Chapter

Advancing, Achieving!

What King, going to make war against another king, sitteth not down first, and consulteth whether he be able with ten thousand to meet him that cometh against him with twenty thousand? [Luke 14:31 KJV]

No King or leader of any country goes into action without first preparing and surveying his chances of winning before he advances. [Luke 14:31 JBI]

Pursue A Passionate Perspective, Progress Positively.

No other game combines the wonder of nature with the discipline of sport in such carefully planned ways. A great golf course, both frees and challenges a golfer's mind. [Tom Watson on Brainy Quotes]

I commit to keeping my pledge to life while searching for the right vantage point on my horizon, to hear what my Creator will say, making sure I know how to answer Him when He speaks; while I often think differently than He thinks. This is often a challenge!

In my spirit I hear The LORD say, "do what I have laid out for you as your mandate" [Jeremiah 29:11]. "Make My Message as clear throughout the advancement of your day, so that the folks you run with will grasp the baton of focus on Me, and My will for them."

For I know the thoughts I think toward you, saith the LORD, thoughts of peace, and not of evil, to give you an expected end. [Jeremiah 29:11 KJV]

The move I make towards others may not be for a current situation; it may be an insert they will need as preparation for tomorrow; it will be apropos or applicable. Please, Please, wait for it! I will not be late. [RE The Bible—Habakkuk 2: 1-3 JBI—Jacob Bergen Insight]

Chapter 1
THE OPENING VALUE: BEGINNINGS

The Blueprint of Life includes a consciousness factor for us to control the adverse issues we sometimes put aside, as if not having sufficient importance. We decide moment by moment how we will manage life for ourselves. If we mess up early in life we can make it up later. The reality is, we do not always get a second chance. Everyone has individual characteristics. However, does everyone disburse this capacity of purpose to others throughout their lives, to keep positive actions birthing more positive actions? Good question.

Connecting humanity with a purpose to meld or fit everyone into a relationship with God in the person of Jesus Christ, one in which all of us will know who He is, and what He has made us to be, is a goal worth pursuing. If we approach living in our compass range in any other fashion, emptiness seems to result from our attempts. We need to radiate compassion, community, commitment, loving-kindness, and human understanding in our determination to promote relational peace—this is pictured as my heart's goal.

John Donne made famous the saying, "No man is an Island, entire of itself; every man is a piece of the Continent, a part of the main; if a clod be washed away by the sea, Europe, is the less, as well as if a promontory were, as well as if a manor of thy friends or of thine own were; any man's death diminishes me, because I am involved in Mankind; And therefore never send to know for whom the bell tolls; It tolls for thee." [Meditation XVII, English clergyman & poet (1572 - 1631)] (IBID)

Other writers, and for that matter, other people "PERIOD," have important input to share with the rest of the world. *The Luggage of Life* set me on a course to where I had to "Stop, Look and Listen" to what these others had to offer me at a given time.

"In childhood's golden hours, we, all of us, squandered a vast amount of sympathy upon Robinson Crusoe. And in later years we have caught ourselves shedding a silent tear for the sorrows of poor Enoch Arden, imprisoned on his 'beauteous, hateful isle.' In imagination, too, we have paced with the beloved disciple the rugged hills of Patmos. We have even felt a sympathetic pang for Napoleon in his cheerless exile at St. Helena. And all the while we have clean forgotten that we ourselves are each of us cast upon lonely, *Sea-Girt Islands*. We are each one of us hopelessly cut off, isolated, and insulated. Unlike the heroes of Defoe and Tennyson, we shall never sight a sail. Our beacon-fires will never bring down any passing vessel to our relief. It is forever. At our very birth, we were chained, naked—to our rock in mid-ocean; and no Perseus will ever appear to pity and deliver us. The links of the chain by which we are bound are many and mighty." [by Frank W. Boreham] [IBID]

Sea-girt—the simplest definition means we are surrounded by the sea. We could, and we likely would, if we knew the song, fall back on the old song, *Oh, Lonesome Me*, written and recorded by Don Gibson and Chet Atkins in 1957. There are more ways than one to use the word 'Sea-girt.' Frank Boreham, in *The Luggage of Life*, presents the picture differently than I might. He feels we are like as if born naked, and we are, but he sees us as if being shackled to a rock on the sea of life—having but one purpose, and that being, in a state of servitude to life. I use his story simply to create a theme for my purpose, not necessarily to lean heavily on what he believes.

John Donne implies we are all part of an island. If we fall short in realizing the context of each person's lives we send the message that we are more important than they are, so please do not bother us with your stuff—as if saying we like being 'Sea-girt,' not knowing we are the ones needing to be rescued. If our understanding is in isolation, obscure or hidden from reaching out to others, we are the problem.

The narratives others convey to us in a variety of ways, can have life altering influences on 'our life's journey.' If we only knew! He suggests we are all connected to someone else in liaison to the plan of life before us. "Make No Mistake:" There is a Value-Added Plan in place for each of us when we are born. Frank W. Boreham seems to suggest to us a picture of hopelessness, as if we are pressed to be confined on a Sea-girt Island—all alone!

And all the while we have clean forgotten that we ourselves are each of us cast upon lonely, *sea-girt islands*. We are each one of us hopelessly cut off, isolated, and insulated. [IBID]

Wait for it! Wait for it! John Donne speaks in terms of relationships; Mr. Boreham speaks in terms of individuality or separation. Mr. Boreham suggests we are each of us so individually isolated, so invaluable to God, even He has no compassion for us; as if we, on our own, are incapable of understanding our worth in the sense of what we showed up for in the beginning. Each of us delivers our market value to the world by the choices we make; to be or not to be available to others, so they also have the opportunity to achieve everything open to good moral decisions.

And by far the mightiest of these insulating factors is the mystery of our own individuality. Each several ego is dreadfully alone in the universe. Each separate 'I' is without counterpart in all eternity. In the deepest sense we are each fatherless and childless; we have no kith or kin. When God creates a person, He reveals the form [or model]. Heaven builds no sister-ships. We may build relationships of friendship and fraternity with other island dwellers across the intervening seas. We may hear their voices shouted across the foam and read and return their signals; but this is all. The most intense sympathy can never bridge the gulf. No man can enter into the soul of his brother man.

I was in the isle, says John. And he says it for us all. In all the chief matters of life says Amiel in his Journal, we are alone: We dream alone; we suffer alone; we die alone. We are all islands, says George Eliot in one of her beautiful letters to Mrs. Bray; each in his hidden sphere of joy or woe, our hermit spirits dwell and roam apart. There is nothing more solemn, says Dr. Alexander McLaren, than that awful loneliness in which each soul of man lives. We stretch out our hands and grasp live hands; yet there is a universe between the two nearest and most one—And perhaps Matthew Arnold said the last word when he says—yes, in the sea of life enisled; with echoing straits between us thrown; dotting the shoreless, watery wild; we mortal millions live alone.

We've shed tears over the terrific solitude of Robinson Crusoe and of Enoch Arden; in return, Robinson Crusoe and Enoch Arden urge us to weep for ourselves. For their partial, temporary solitude was as nothing compared with the absoluteness and permanence of our own. [F.W. Boreham] [IBID]

At the moment I am and have been all day long engrossed or riveted on [as if in the Presence of God Almighty] the word *Sea-girt* as if my dependency for surviving this life and getting on into the next depends solely on me. If so, I Am In Big Trouble! What others offer of their individuality and personality is of immeasurable, infinite, or of endless importance in these, what I foresee as the 'Last Days.' I can be a 'product of value' to someone who may be lost out on the *Sea-Girt Island*, seemingly without hope of rescue. Oh the picture some of these other authors of books have embedded in my spirit for life.

If we fail to include God in the landscape of lives or on the waters of the seas of our journey, like someone being born as a functioning human, while shrinking moment by moment into an oblivion of nothingness in eternity, all it leaves us is nothing to show for our lives in this Eternal Sense. It is challenging to surrender to God's purpose.

Open The Door To Value

While thinking in terms of equality, [fairness], I grow thematically as does the stem of a tree [plant] growing upwards from the roots to the fruit on the branches, to this question, "Am I ready to live with an open-door policy in my own life; offering it to people of all stripes; as it mixes with the truth of human integrity?"

Equal admission, free access, generosity, smiling, reception, warm-heartedness—these revolve around The Open-door Policy.

Some workplaces present people with an open-door policy to management; they say, touch basis with us anytime; this may be the mantra. In many places, not all, the drift is, there is a process to follow to grow any form of approach to the higher-ups, the bosses. The door is often closed, and it is difficult to pry it open to be on an approachable level with management.

Is an Open-door Policy good or tough? Queries abound concerning this policy. Initially, the concept is outstanding, and suggests there are no caveats, qualifications, and or warnings to be mindful of before we venture past the guard's [secretary's] desk. Open-door policies are great in principal. However, is their upkeep as easy to support with heartfelt meaning, as words are to say?

Recently, some countries opened their doors to immigrants; this is a good thought, but one coming with a huge commitment. After a while, the experience is not always thought of as pleasantly, because of the commitment factor. When we go over the list of countries promoting [or once promoted freely] open borders, we realize a list looking like this, India, Australia, France, Spain, The UK, Canada, Saudi Arabia, Germany, Russia, and the United States of America.

While browsing the list, searching for 'the juicy peach' [Wow] of these countries, physically and subjectively [feeling based], are we thinking about the views they once provided? Some of these countries are rethinking their policy regarding open borders. What we think as our commitment to a cause often develops a component of distance, because of the cost of the relationship.

Some walls crumbled or were voluntarily removed at one time. Some folks think the walls need to be reconstructed to shut down the Open-door Policy. Why is this? Perhaps it amounts to a lack of allegiance to our fellow person? As I think about this attitude towards the concept of openness or the lack thereof, I am reminded within my heart of hearts, part of my being, the part which I alone can see or feel, may be prompting me to share myself with someone who needs a hand-up.

To decide regarding openness, the variables or unsteady state of being committed to the cause is more of an event than it was once. It is easy to understand we are living in precarious times. How does the subject of personal and corporate openness affect the importance level we perceive or consider in people?

Stock Market Issues

The Stock Market embraces considerable diverse markets in securities. There is a market for corporate securities and government securities, and there are differences between them and how they are traded on the exchange. Corporate Securities are tools for generating capital from the public.

I possess no capacity for detailing every imaginable segment of the Stock Market. I cannot accommodate too much distance in this volume for the nuts and bolts of it entirely. Simply speaking, companies try to get listed to sell shares of their valuable commodity in the public market, in this way they have funds for reinvesting their capital to become more valuable entities; getting bigger corporately; it is all about making a greater profit.

The public gets involved in buying stocks and bonds, and while they buy it at what they deem is reasonable value, they intend to gain money along the transaction. This is a vicissitude [up and down] situation which depends on world conditions. It boils down to everybody gambling money they have, while hoping to get those Four Aces or a Royal Flush. There are winners and losers in the gambling scenarios. Now "The Coronavirus" is affecting things.

The stock market makes up several distinct markets in securities. The most significant difference is between the market for corporate securities and the market for government securities. Corporate securities are instruments for raising long- term corporate capital from the public.

What is Security? Was the 'Berlin Wall,' this picture of security for what became the greater communist East Germany, rather than being an integrated personhood; once all German Citizenry; some having Democratic ideas and some people having more socialistic or communist leanings. After WWII the Soviets, as their proportionate part of the booty of victory over the Germans in the war, became the driving force of what was the part of Germany having different views than did the Democratic portion of Germany. East Germany had a populous of socialists, yes, but there were also many people living there holding the Democratic Viewpoint of living life, as opposed to the Communistic Community View. After WWII, the USSR [Union of Soviet Socialist Republics] exerted more pressure on The East German people [East Berliners], and life became a hodgepodge mess of 'who belongs where.' This is the nature of life, no matter where it is when people do not feel secure living together with one another in some kind of unified manner so as to allow others to choose their own destiny. Each country should be allowed to set the parameters or borders of what they will allow, and not allow, as the right way to live. In the just said context our present freedoms are in jeopardy.

There is one Moral Code of Ethics set out to be the Right Moral Code for all humankind to abide by. God [or a nonentity] sets these parameters. The consequence of breaking this code is, God has a wall between the eternity He adopts, and the path the devil led us down in the picture we see by the time of Adam and Eve in The Garden of Eden when they went it on their own. For now, let's concentrate on earthly things, how they jointly [cooperatively] or covertly [secretly, stealthily] relate to the spiritual aspects of life!

What is the ultimate purpose of our existence—in our personal term of life? Question—is value objective or subjective? If any, what is the gap between the two? Is value simply a matter of monetary worth? Worth, is it calculated by using a financial calculator? Question—is worth calculated by something or Someone bigger than physical means? Question—is worth calculated by what we practice, depending on how much we practice? It often feels like we are under the gun of working our way to acceptance rather than living with a freedom of community.

Questions, questions, and more questions! While observing the harsh standards of the realness of the measuring system we utilize through the status quo, at what pace are we evaluated or devaluated? Is there a more impartial [fairer] measuring rod than the status quo? Who is President of the status quo?

Market value is the amount for which something can be sold in a market. It is often contrasted with book value. Who sets market value? Who decides what the market can bear? Is it those who are only interested in higher profit margins as opposed to allowing everybody fair access to a life free of hardship?

Who sets book value? Is it the status quo? How far back in history should we go to find a system differing from the one we live with every day of our lives, one which we will live with while waiting for the 'big when' to drop out of the clear blue sky to afflict us more than we can often endure.

Value is a huge commodity. When we consider a product, we might look at it as a two-piece entity, goods, and services. Each is a separate entity. Might we consider which is greater—goods or services? Did the product appear out of thin air? Does any product, entity, or thing appear out of nowhere? Magicians try to make us believe this to be the case, generally, we know better. Do we really? If it is magic, is it real?

11

When we consider these thoughts we face an ever-present issue when we appraise something or someone. Even currency faces this assessment, it is not just money when we consider what money we are talking about. Are we discussing Canadian currency, American currency, European currency, Asian currency? Each of these perform differently in their own country.

Gold is the product we extract from the ground. Is it more important than the labor of those who worked strenuously to bring it up for market value where we evaluate it in the monetary sense? Gold has and always will create a euphoria, rapture, jubilation, or a sense of high worth in the eyes of us humans—why?

When we open our eyes to something physically attractive, like the woman God created, or the women who just showed up in the evolutionary [not my choice] sense, we take notice. Sometimes we say WOW! Beauty (is in the eye of the beholder) is something which wows us. Many minerals we mine cause us to experience eye-popping moments as we see dollar signs instantly growing in our mindset. The same doesn't hold true when we pick up a handful of dirt.

Most of the time when we pick up a handful of dirt we just think, 'this is dirty,' now I will need to wash my hands and the clothes it contacted. Dirt never quite matches up to high carat gold, or diamonds in the rough. However, there is huge worth in the dirt. Just ask the farmer. The farmer can tell you all about the importance of the dirt on his land by the efforts he takes to bear fruit from his acres. I often laugh to myself when I see people in their whites, working in the dirt [TV, Movies].

As we consider these commodities we need to consider water, air, electricity—the list may seem endless when we consider the list of things we call entities, merchandise, possessions, and time. It seems easier to appreciate product worth more easily than 'service-value' [unless it is sports related].

Let's keep our mental frontlets in focus. A frontlet relates to Judaism. A frontlet or phylactery is two small, black, leather cubes containing a piece of parchment inscribed with verses 4–9 of Deut. 6, 13–21 of Deut. 11, and 1–16 of Ex. 13; one attached with straps to the left arm and the other to the forehead during weekday morning prayers by Orthodox and Conservative Jewish men and sometimes it is an amulet, charm, or safeguard against harm or danger.

The scriptures can guide us through our day. In the sense of what I am writing about I suggest it is not actually about physical product and its value, but the value of human life. Relating to the product and the value of it is simply an example to use as a picture to grasp the story more easily.

Services are the duty we owe to life. Service is what vendors provide to customers when they retail cars, flooring, appliances. The service they sell us needs to present integrity in an equal sense as a product they vend, sell, hawk or trade. The manufacturer must honor the wares they pass on to the consumer.

Oil and other things, those coming from the ground are not minerals, they may not be as physically attractive to us like the mineral such as gold, silver, bronze, diamonds, but they hold huge worth. However, just think of the euphoria someone feels when they discover oil on their land—Black Gold.

Blood, sweat, and tears—how does this rate? Blood, sweat, and tears are basically the products of plain old hard work. Blood, sweat, and tears do not just appear out of thin air, they take us once again to Creation or its counterpart—The Big Bang. God, at the exodus of humankind from the Garden of Eden, said people would need to exercise the blood, sweat, and tears scenario [services] to get the goods [Equity, Fluidity Liabilities].

Plato, one of the Great Philosophers of history, fought hard to salvage the position of the essentials of humankind. Our qualities must carry integrity to weigh out effectively. Plato believed our individual choices have nothing to do with whether something is true, good, and beautiful. We never gain objective values when we are unsure we agree with someone on an issue because we differ from each other because of our formative years. Perception can lead us in two directions—true or false.

By looking at a Japanese Blow Fish [Fugu] one might perceive and assume it is edible by just removing the skin, the head, and the guts, and slapping it into the frying pan—just like one would do with any other fish. If you are unfamiliar with preparing the Fugu, Blowfish, Puffer Fish, and you bite into the first scrumptious looking morsel, this could be your last meal. Perception in this case can be subjective, based upon a feeling everything is all right, but there needs to be objectivity involved in this evaluation or proposition.

Is value objective, or subjective? What is the gap between the two?

In the scenario of the Blowfish, the absence of objective truth is in the gap; life and death are the consequential options. You may have innocently gone fishing and caught a Fugu and expected to top off your day with a delicious meal of Fish and Chips. There is nothing wrong with all the good feelings you had about this adventure, but ignorance of the truth in this matter can be costly. The greater cost in this picture may be the cost of a life lost, and the funeral expenses, compared to the price of a good meal.

Often we can judge importance within the eye of the beholder scenario without facing dire costs [if you are married, watch out for this 'eye of the beholder' thing]. In this fish story a person may think it is much cheaper to catch their own Blowfish, prepare it themselves and enjoy this delicacy at a much less expensive monetary expenditure [like eating any mushroom in the world of choices]. If they knew the truth, the whole truth, and only the truth, about the preparing and the cooking of this pufferfish, they could save huge dollars. A Fugu prepared meal in a Japanese Restaurant could cost upwards of one-hundred dollars.

Everybody: Everybody Is A Somebody could be a strength, as it is in the Golden Rule, if we set what the market can bear with impartial [objective] standards, opposed to profit margins.

So, what is The Golden Rule? This is a great question, and it depends on who you ask. My favorite resource is God, through what He says in the Bible. Next to this and further down the line I come close to saying Thesarus.com is my next favorite resource. There is somewhat of a battle for me here as well because Google is also high on the list of my favorite human resources.

When it all comes down to the bottom-line on this subject, any morally uncorrupted search resource will always be high on my list of Go To Search Places.

Because we live in an 'anything and everything goes society,' largely because of tolerance issues, I find it difficult to pinpoint exactly how to answer certain questions. Right about now, somebody will ask me what I mean by a Morally Uncorrupted Search Resource, and that, possibly in an intense manner!

Everyone has their own opinion on what is morally acceptable. It is hard for anyone to give anyone else an answer to this question in the world we all live in. Each answer generates another question, guaranteed! I am not isolated about this comportment [attitude] of tolerance we face about moral or immoral correctness. All I will say on this issue for the moment, is, I have a starting position for all the answers of life based on what I said already. My favorite resource is God, through what He says in the Bible. This differs from what many others use as a starting point on these topics. Herein lies the whole problem in this life regarding how any of us can ever finish a conversation about these things.

While trying to be diplomatic, while maintaining the rule of life I learned from people who journeyed this life before me, I realize they also had their starting points. Even then, in the history before each of us arrived, no one ever agreed on a 'one starting point system' of everything which came before us. If we use The Genesis connection as the Beginning, we use the Bible as the Beginning of The Story, God's interpretation of life as He tells it. If we use 'a genesis theory,' we leave the books wide open because there are too many pages to fit into any one observable resource [book]. The resource pool of life is huge—who can conquer it? Some mysteries are answerable, so it seems—others require only faith.

Questions: What a conundrum [mystery]. While looking back to my question, 'What Is The Golden Rule,' I look at Dictionary.com [Thesarus.com] and this is what I see:

1] a rule of ethical conduct, usually phrased "Do unto others as you would have them do unto you," or, as in the Sermon on the Mount, "Whatsoever ye would men should do to you, do ye even so unto them." [Matt. 7:12; Luke 6:31].

2] "any philosophy," guiding principle, or ideal of behavior, as in a discipline, pursuit, or business:

These definitions contain both scenarios, God's side, and every other position—either or finds coverage under this definition. When I type 'The Golden Rule' into Google, I get a list of options, just a meager beginning of the proponents or lists of similar possibilities of the Golden Rules people have about seemingly every entity of existence, Faith, Buddhism, law, dog training, The Bible, Christianity, driving, accounting, and there are many more.

Because none of us can change anybody's mind about anything, it seems we cannot even use God as the determiner of what is right or wrong. I use God as my determiner, as do others. Some people we struggle with, may just not use God in these things. I am confident there is no other final entity which we can use as an alternative, except this guiding principle [mentioned in the dictionary definition], which will assist people to make a difference in someone else's life—now and or for eternity's sake. Let's look for a moment at the Theory of God and His Golden Rule.

1] a rule of ethical conduct, usually phrased "Do unto others as you would have them do unto you," or, as in the Sermon on the Mount, "Whatsoever ye would men should do to you, do ye even so unto them." [Matt. 7:12; Luke 6:31].

This is great, but it may be just 'a little bit incomplete' by itself. We need to add just one more thing to this definition of the 'Golden Rule' scenario: [Matthew 22:36-40]:

"Thou shalt 'love' the Lord thy God with all thy heart, and with all thy soul, and with all thy mind; the second is like unto it, thou shalt 'love' thy neighbor as thyself."

Often, people do not readily get the message right away, or ever! Life is all about God and people. Some of us think it is all about us individually. The God scenario says we need to come to Him when He calls, and He does call. Now, we can love Him like He says we need to for us to get to the rest of the story right. There is no conundrum, or mystery here. We need to believe God exists; turn our lives to Him in relationship; then we will better understand that He is all we will ever need.

I try to inform people about God, and how to have a relationship with Him, one which allows for our every need to get satisfied. This is God's Golden Rule; it has only one starting point— God. Evolution is another entity with a Golden Rule, it is the other side of the God only side rule. It is the flip side of the coin, the heads or tails story; you can have only one or the other when someone flips the coin and says, 'heads or tails.'

In the Dictionary.com [Thesarus.com] definition I began with, the Evolution side fits into the second option:

2] any philosophy, guiding principle, or ideal of behavior, as in a discipline [persuasion], pursuit, or business:

'Any,' this word can be bothersome, it leaves the door wide open to an anything goes scenario. Does this mean any philosophy, any guiding principle, any ideal of behavior, as in discipline, pursuit, or business, will do fine? This idea leaves out the mega-important factor, one which can make anything else work, a 'starting point!' The leading command Evolution espouses or adopts, kind of looks like this, 'any philosophy or belief system will do fine, as long as it does not include A Designer Theory!'

Evolution has a Golden Rule, it differs from God's Golden Rule. It ventures out into the deeper waters of confusion to use the 'survive and reproduce scenario' as a version of God's Golden Rule—what is good and bad, and what is right and wrong. Evolution realizes they need to address humankind, or human culture with a means of survival in this meta-confusion of a creative work; reference to itself or to the conventions of its genre, and the self-referential universe we are all a part of. Evolution suggests a Golden Rule without satisfying thoughts of a Designer related theory.

Maybe it's just me, but as I study the resource materials of other belief systems, I often stumble through while trying to find a starting point which suggests a non-subjective, objective moral truth, opposed to subjective [meta, individual, independent, feeling related or emotive] moral truth. No matter what anybody espouses [advocates, champions, preaches], whatever else we call it, it is a belief system. I cannot fathom why anybody would champion a cause if nothing was gained from it. It is difficult to attach eternal precedence to something if money is the only physicality or reality resulting from it; not objective truth. Money will fail us when we die.' Distancing ourselves too far from objective truth widens the gap between truth and error.

We need to determine whether the God synopsis or outline for morality [right or wrong] is viable [workable] in all experiments, but we need to go further. Whether someone believes in God or not, we need to look to see if the God scenario, presented as the eternal beginning and end of all eons past or future, is also good for our present living situation. Let's ask ourselves if there is any likelihood the God concept stems from ethical values to present His objective moral platform. We need to use the same standard of objectivity on every belief system. Let's not forget Occam's Razor. Simplicity is better than complicated for determining a better shot at 'Truth!'

INTERMEZZO!

[This is a short connecting instrumental movement in an opera or other musical work, a short rest!]

"Lord: How are they increased that trouble me! Many are they that rise up against me. Many there be which say of my soul, There is no help for him in God. Selah. But thou, O Lord, art a shield for me; my glory, and the lifter up of mine head. I cried unto the Lord with my voice, and he heard me out of his holy hill. Selah. I laid me down and slept; I awaked; for the Lord sustained me. I will not be afraid of ten thousands of people, that have set themselves against me round about. Arise, O Lord; save me, O my God: for thou hast smitten all mine enemies upon the cheek bone; thou hast broken the teeth of the ungodly. Salvation belongeth unto the Lord: thy blessing is upon thy people." Selah. [Psalms 3; KJV]

SELAH

DO NOT RUSH!

Grab a Break and a Breath!

Selah—an expression occurring frequently in the Psalms, thought to be a liturgical or musical direction, probably a directive of the leader to raise the voice or perhaps an indication of a pause.

Web Examples for Selah:

First is the famous "Selah," which we used to hear pronounced with great solemnity when the Psalms were read. Who Wrote the Bible? — But here comes the Selah and the voice is hushed'—I will speak of other things. [Washington Gladden]

At least God is a Source from which we can claim a sense of right and wrong, opposite to the 'nothing' scenario from which Evolution fashions The New Golden Rule of Evolution 2.0. I always begin with God; observe the other offerings and try to balance them against the God idea—everything else comes up empty. Many scientists have crossed over from the No-God Side to The God Side because of common sense evidence for and against from the other side. Confusion will remain supreme regarding life and existence because people think they are in control.

There is no mega or meta-confusion [confusion because of principles ever moving forward and back to grasp a wider meaning of the subject, like I do by getting synonyms to go deeper into my story] on the God Side Scenario, because He never changes. What He claims now, He claimed at the outset, for today and what remains forever after today in the eons of eternal time. Why? Because this scenario presents God as eternal, the beginning [starting point] and the end [The Final Answer]. However, subjectivity conquers our evaluating proponents, emotively, when we try to assess what we feel God is trying to get across to us. Evolution's theories are ever shifting.

In the God scenario of the two primary participants of the ever-questioning public opinion regarding all universal existence, we can explain meta-confusion or the lack of it by stating God plainly says we must work towards acceptance of Him, worship and respect Him, apart from any other choices or contenders. We must love God with our complete heart, all that we have. The second component of this simplicity is, we should do the same too, with, and for our neighbor, and everybody is our neighbor. We need not search beyond the fact God is who He says He is, this is the faith principle of simplicity.

Conscience: ethics, morality, principles, scruples, integrity; how can we explain it if it came out of nowhere [nothing]? When God the Creator created people, He permeated their mentality, and mindset, with a moral and or ethical acquaintance with the truth we can call our conscience—right and wrong. How can a Big Bang justify this out of nothingness? Accidentally? Life calls for solid or objective worth to receive physical and spiritual sustainability to prevent the reduction of life out of the now or the eternity many of us hope for when 'our now' is over and done with at death.

If God is merely a figment of the imagination for the Christians [believers], you know, you have heard it, weak minded people who hold no sense of reality, then there is no objective moral truth anywhere; we are still drifting about in some unbelievable immoral soup in a sea of nothingness. Makes sense! Right! If subjective [feeling based] morality can get us through this life successfully into the next life many are expecting to get to, there is no stability in any theory of existence. [I also have some property I can sell you in Florida. I feel you should buy some real soon before it sells off completely]. Many are the cons people have fallen for in regard to this property for sale in Florida. We know what the reality is, it is swampland!

So, are we this fickle? Mega and meta-confused [needing continual explanations to justify our selfishness]. Are we befuddled or changeable with every new explanation? Are we as though we are an accidental spin-off of a planet of possible multi-universes? Or are we one messed up universe, which no one can satisfactorily or reliably claim measures up to the simple explanation: "In The Beginning God?"

Adam and Eve came out of the gate with a meta-mentality [self-referential], looking for a change from the simplicity of obedience to God, to the 'selfie-mode, safe-mode' and beyond. It's like they were dissatisfied with simplicity. God in His great love for Creation, wanted to build it for eternal satisfaction. He allowed them to choose whether His architectural drawing was structurally sound.

In the wee hours of the night just passed, I listened to a sermon by the son of the man who was my Pastor when I was young. The message James preached was *A Message from The Head of The Church*. This Pastor of FWC was not talking of his own position of leadership as the Head of The Church he is privy to. James was acknowledging The Someone who made it possible for him to subsist with the opportunity to recognize objective truth. This guides me on a little further to a point he made about people who think and advocate the supernatural or miraculous ended when the Last Apostle died. He spread out a scene as if it were one of the Last Apostle lying on his deathbed, expending or allowing to exude or project from his body the last vestige or trace of healing power to help many to be pain free to live life to the full; before he himself expired.

And so, when he passed the great line-up of people who came to this man for the healing of their bodies, he came to a dividing point, like when someone draws out one domino in a row of dominoes ready to continue along continuously. If the Last Apostle could no longer perform this God appointed task, it seems according to some folks, God could no longer perform miracles [the supernatural].

Some say, if this is how it is, "God Is Dead." What substance is there then for people to rely on anything to help them through the conflicts of life, if "God is Dead?" God is not dead! God is still the architect of building a life and a new life into His creation! We can have a new life and a purposeful existence if we accept the invitation of Almighty God to continue to come to Him for the issues we confront, this is the role of The Supernatural, this is part of the miracle God will give to any who come unto Him.

The Golden Rule is so vast; others have The Silver Rule, and some folks have The Platinum Rule. When it comes down to thoughts of how we should treat our neighbor, we try to agree with each other about everyone being important enough to be included in a life worth the living. I try to look at life from both sides. Am I part of the answer or a percentage of the problem? The way I interpret it is, The Golden Rule of Evolution 2 comes as a picture of participation in The Golden Rule Effort from a group principle. As I understand it, they are saying we need to concur on what ethical or moral principles can rightly be accessed by everyone in the group [The Whole World].

Is everything which does not actually physically or emotionally hurt someone else okay? In The Golden Rule of Evolution 2 we all need to agree with what other folks consider immoral. Does this need a makeover so we will think it is okay to practice what God has always said was wrong?

I agree everyone may practice what they feel they wish to practice within the confines of 'starting point morality' if it does not hurt the next person, based on God's rule of purity. We all have the rule of choice. So I ask, 'what is the definition of hurt?' I ask, 'does it simply mean everything is all right under The Golden Rule of Evolution 2, providing we do not punch someone in the face or kill someone?' When I check the thesaurus, I find many other words attempting to define hurt. Please look with me at the list:

Aching, agonized, battered, bruised, burned, contused, crushed, damaged, disfigured, distressed, grazed, harmed, impaired, lacerated, marred, mauled, miffed, mutilated, nicked, offended, pained, piqued, scarred, scraped, scratched, shook, shot, sore, struck, suffering, tender, tortured, warped, wounded, all torn up, busted-up, in pain, indignant, put away, resentful, rueful, sad, stricken, umbrageous, and unhappy.

How do we participate with these things within the rules of present-day humanity in a world of tolerance 'at all costs?' We do not know the end of the story until we live to the end of the story. If we follow the God Principle for life and living in the Golden Rule, we will survive, if we rightly employ the right starting point. We are 'nothing' in life if we never began at some definite time. Is this an individual issue? Am I responsible, and to Whom, for implementing The Golden Rule as outlined in God's plan? Or, as The Evolution Golden Rule 2 suggests, is this a group issue, one where The Golden Rule must be a part of conceding potential immoralities because of our right to the subjectivity [feelings, or emotive sensitive] scenario?

Eliminating the God-Side Only scenario leaves us with an open book of 'nothing' to show for our existence. This again, always leaves us floundering around in a sea of turmoil—until the outcome, end result, will be the Road of Travel [reality, said and done]. I may always be in jeopardy with someone because of what I believe.

Antonyms of Hurt—happy, healthy, perfect, pleased.

While looking at The Golden Rule, no matter which version, I see hurt is still always in the picture. Complete healing is never within our grasp until we give credence or credibility to God Alone. The opposite of hurt is out of reach in the picture of us wanting to see the completion of the task to where there is no one ever hurting anymore. Evolution and all the other counterparts of opposition that frame themselves against God and His Rule, do not have a leg to stand on, if it is evolution based, everything came from 'nothing.' If it has some correlating link to God's Rule and they leave out the rest of God's will and plan, they still have no leg to stand on because God's plan demands complete commitment to God and His rule, plan, purpose, and or promise to receive the benefits of God's promises in the everlasting sense.

The you scratch my back and I will scratch yours option never leaves us with a solid foundation for life, it is ever changing as people move on unsatisfied with what they had yesterday. Why? Because feeling based reality is no reality. Feeling based or subjective principles are wishy-washy. If you do for me, then I will feel satisfied maybe, and do the said same for you.

Synonyms for reciprocity: cooperation, exchange, substitution, payment, amend, reparation, satisfaction.

Chapter 1 is the foundation for all I wish to build in the rest of *Everybody: Everybody Is A Somebody*. I will retrieve things from *Chapter 1* to keep on keeping on.

What does it look like when we line up two paths of choice about The Beginning [John 1; 1 John 1] of everything which ever was or will be? God's path is one thing, all opposing paths, quite another thing. One path is to Jesus, through objective truth; other paths lead to all the other gods of subjective truth choices. *The Value of The Beginning* is a huge issue within our quest for the answers of life.

Jesus said, "I Am the Way, The Truth and The Life; no-one can come to God in any other way" [JB1]. This option presents only one way, all other options make their point by saying Jesus is just a good man, not God, just one means of attaining a varied heaven.

In the Jesus as Son of man, Son of God, and as the whole of what 'God is' scenario, there is only one path opposed to the many paths to the heavenly setting many folks declare to be 'the way, the truth, and life everlasting.' Jesus is the Object [objectivity], the only context, the Truth of it all.

When we look at all other options for the heaven of eternal life, and yes, every one of them say they are the only way, it gets more confusing because they all borrow some of what God says and expand their points by using a subjective approach, which is based on emotion. All other religions move from their pivot point of works to attain salvation and or some heaven. I cannot fashion my presentation here to suit everyone; I cannot expect everyone to agree with me; I can only present my case from a beginning, Genesis, or starting point presenting the most commonality or harmony for allowing for a universe dependent on an originator, not on a 'nothing' concept. Every other belief system hangs onto a "By Chance Theory" for our Genesis.

"Initially, God created the heaven and the earth. And the earth was without form, and void; darkness was upon the face of the deep. And the Spirit of God moved upon the face of the waters. And God said, let there be light: and there was light. And God saw the light, that it was good: and God divided the light from the darkness. And God called the light Day, and the darkness he called Night. And the evening and the morning were the first day." [Genesis 1]

Differing manner of people will read this book:

—People on the opposite side of everything opposing their belief, these folks may not read far enough in this book to garner an understanding in which more than one kind of person exists on this planet; everyone can choose to believe what they wish.

—People open to listening, watching, and trying to understand another person's belief long enough to check reliable facts long enough to read this book; these folks may find there is a truth in this world which supersedes all other perceived truth.

—People on the same page as the author might say Amen!

Prepare to Launch!

We have been in the rocket sending business for many years. The list of first orbital launches by country, go like this,

1] [Sputnik 1, a Satellite; Sputnik PS a Rocket] Baikonur, Soviet Union (today Kazakhstan) 4 October 1957.

2] [Explorer 1, a Satellite; Juno I a Rocket] Cape Canaveral, United States, 1 February 1958.

3] [Astérix a Satellite; Diamant (A) a Rocket] France at CIEES/Hammaguir, Algeria 26 November 1965.

At some starting point we encountered the Genesis of an idea where we could launch rockets into space to reach the heavens, not Heaven itself. Another effort to reach Heaven was launched many years before, at about 3500 BC. The Tower of Babel was the site; this 'Rocket Idea' was the brain power of the day; this was somewhat archaic to what we have today because technology increases more rapidly today than it did back then [Genesis 11 The Bible]. Give them credit for our progress on space exploration, or not, this is a big question. We could credit them for progressive thinking, it was not The God Only Side thinking; Babel Fell Flat on its face.

The singing group ABBA released this song in the USA just over forty years ago, April 1978. This was at one time one of my favorite groups. *Take A Chance On Me* reverberates or rings in my ear as I write these words. As I always do when I write I let thoughts come into my head, thoughts with a relationship with what I am writing about.

As I am presenting these closing words of *Chapter 1*, it has me thinking of offering us a look at what was in the Heart of God when He first designed people. Might God have used words like,

As you are making your way through life when things may not be going as smoothly as you would like them to, might you *Take A Chance on ME?* You might say, "no, I don't think so." But God, being who He is, having created us because He loved us, might have said,

"Perchance, if you have a change of mind, know this, I will be the first in line."

"Take a chance on ME!"

If you simply need someone to help you through the tough times, let Me know. I Am just a holler away.

If you are wandering about with no place to go, feeling so low you don't know which way is up, look up to where the birds fly, *Take A Chance on Me*! If you change your mind from thinking there's nobody out there, thinking you have to do it on your own, *Take a chance on Me*! Put Me to the test. If you want Me, you will find Me!

"O lord, thou hast searched me, and known me. Thou knowest my downsitting and mine uprising, thou understandest my thought afar off.

Thou compassest my path and my lying down, and art acquainted with all my ways. For there is not a word in my tongue, but, lo, O Lord, thou knowest it altogether. Thou hast beset me behind and before and laid thine hand upon me. Such knowledge is too wonderful for me; it is high, I cannot attain unto it.

Whither shall I go from thy spirit? Or whither shall I flee from thy presence? If I ascend up into heaven, thou art there: if I make my bed in hell, behold, thou art there.

If I take the wings of the morning, and dwell in the uttermost parts of the sea; even there shall thy hand lead me, and thy right hand shall hold me.

If I say, the darkness shall cover me; even the night shall be light about me. Yea, the darkness hideth not from thee; but the night shineth as the day: the darkness and the light are both to thee.

For thou hast possessed my reins: thou hast covered me in my mother's womb.

I will praise thee; for I am fearfully and wonderfully made, marvelous are thy works; and that my soul knoweth right well.

My substance was not hiding from thee, when I was made secretly, and curiously wrought in the lowest parts of the earth.

Thine eyes did see my substance yet being unperfect; and in thy book all my members were written, which in continuance were fashioned, when there was none. How precious also are thy thoughts unto me, O God!

How great is the sum of them! If I should count them, they are more in number than the sand: when I awake, I am still with thee—." [Psalms 139:1-18]

Search me, O God, and know my heart: try me, and know my thoughts: And see if there be any wicked way in me and lead me in the way everlasting. [Psalms 139; 23-24; KJV]

The Value—The Bottom-line

—Realization, everyone has distinctive characteristics.

—Query, does everyone transmit [transfer or handover] the same capacity of purpose during their tenure?

—Is value the ultimate purpose of our existential [fact of existing] term of life?

—Is value objective, or subjective?

—What is the gap between the two?

—Is value simply a matter of monetary worth?

—Is worth calculated by using a financial calculator?

—Is worth calculated by something or Someone greater than physical substance?

—Is worth calculated by what we do, and dependent on how much we do for a cause?

—At what rate are we evaluated or devaluated by the harsh standards of the reality of the measuring system we see employed by the status quo [existing conditions] of society?

—Is there a more impartial [fairer] measuring rod than the status quo? Who is President of The Status Quo?

Market value is the amount for which something can be sold on a market, often contrasted to book value. Who sets Market value? Who decides what the market can bear? Is it those who are only interested in higher profit margins as opposed to allowing everybody fair access to a life free of hardship?

Who sets the book value? Is it the status quo? How far back in history should we go to find a system any different than the one we live with every day of our lives, a systematic approach which we will live with while waiting for 'When?'

The Value Of The Beginning

Value is worth the time to explore, when we want everything life has to offer now, and for the eternity we will experience after we take our final breath on earth as we know it now!

The Approach Shot

2nd Chapter

Forge Ahead, Follow Through!

Master, which is the great commandment in the law? Jesus said unto him, Thou shalt love the Lord thy God with all thy heart, and with all thy soul, and with all thy mind. This is the first and great commandment.

And the second is like unto it, Thou shalt love thy neighbor as thyself. On these two commandments hang all the law and the prophets. [Mathew 22:36-40 KJV]

I'll never know all there is to know about you; you will never know all there is to know about me. Humans are by nature too complicated to be understood fully. So, we can choose either to approach our fellow humans with suspicion or to approach them with an open mind, a dash of optimism and a great deal of candor. [Tom Hanks on Brainy Quotes]

Though this is not a golf quote it holds true as an insert in our lives. It can act as resourcefully as does The Approach Shot in the game of Golf. If we follow a devotional concept [something we are devoted to do regularly] to build the certainty of a belief or an invaluable concept into our lifestyle to better handle life, we are in good stead.

Follow A Devotional Viewpoint; Continue with Certainty.
Know People Intently!

As we 'Forge Ahead,' let us think in terms of "Foraging,' because this put us in a search mode to where we are hunting for the Food of Life which will keep us alive Forever!

Chapter 2
IS THE GOLDEN RULE POINTLESS?

In Chapter 2, there's a continuation of the Game of Life. The insight of experience shows us how to play the game. Confusion has a way of interrupting our lives every day on a moment by moment basis. Too many voices can cause our uncertainties about life.

This is not just about creating a successful life pattern for ourselves. 'IF' and 'AS' we forge ahead and follow through on our intentional habits of good life planning, it can never happen without an intentional knowledge about people, those folks we know and those we can only see from a distance. Our closest connection outside ourselves is likely always going to be family. Next, our reach may be towards our neighbor. From here the world can be our field of play. Wow! There is no end to where this can lead us.

The priceless construct of knowing our foundation cannot crumble over time, leaves us with the assurance all is well for Eternity. We have no way of understanding without believing One God was and still is in charge of all of history past, our present, and all our tomorrows; this is Faith's example!

Faith does not present blindness such as we see when we look at someone who physically can't see when their eyes are wide open. Faith is a trustworthiness upon Someone who does not need to see with eyes wide open, rather, they see with their Heart! Someone who has Faith like this can move mountains of doubt!

Belief systems use a measure of some entity to advocate their presentation of the rationality of their conviction of faith. It does so to strengthen their position regarding the Genesis of all Geneses [Beginnings]. We may flounder on this foundation or platform, each in our own belief system, as we try to convince people about the God we champion. In this our multifaceted and or multiethnic society we may struggle to know how to come to grips with choosing the One Right God.

Philippians Chapter Three [The Bible] reflects the pure delight, pleasure, bliss, and the total worth of the "Priceless Value of Knowing Jesus Christ." Another passage of the Bible says it this way, "I put up with the inconveniences [suffer] of life because God is Who He said He is, in The Person of Jesus Christ. I do so unashamedly because of what Jesus did for me on the Cross. I may suffer the loss of some things because of it, so be it!"

> For the which cause I also suffer these things: nevertheless, I am not ashamed: for I know whom I have believed and am persuaded he can keep that which I have committed unto him against that day. [2 Timothy 1:12 KJV]

If I can make this clearer for us within the confines of this book, I can lay me down to sleep in peace tonight and every other night. I can know I have a solid foundation for purporting or contending JESUS CHRIST IS LORD OF ALL, by including a multiethnic model of human worth we face many issues as to The One God scenario. What are the promises of the afterlife when we ignore the One God scenario? If any, by whose say so?

Belief systems are varied and or many, multifaceted, multi-layered, complex, complicated, many-sided, and multidimensional. This picture often displays at the forefront of each of us who with our own belief system, endure our lives on what seems like we are on separate planets, as if we are separated by another Berlin Wall, dividing us from each other. I will not try to sieve [filter] these out to indoctrinate you with my belief system, so it says I am right, and you are wrong, to be as if 'care less' about the emotions others own.

This stated, I cannot be true to what I have grown up believing, by placing 'crossings paths' or bridges over junctions to some other belief system. Unless I look at all belief systems, separated into two columns: Column One being "It Is All About 'God,' Not Me;" the other column being, "It's Not All About 'God,' but me," I can never trust I have an Eternal Security I can bank on.

Thoughts such as these guide me through a process of determination between subjectivity [feeling based beliefs] and objectivity [Fairly based belief, yes, but based on The Infinite God scenario as the final answer]. If everybody throughout the time of their sojourn [stopover] had sorted out life like this, what a world we might have had. If's, And's or But's cannot cut mustard.

There are so many variants within every belief system. Inside Christianity [those who are Christ Followers], Christ based religions, there are varied sentiments. It seems we are running towards being Christ Followers from a different prospectus of Christs; even from another Universe; so it appears. This is a puzzle from which it is difficult to create an existing juxtaposition [comparison with a correlation] to what Jesus had in mind for us when He presented us 'The Way, The Truth, and The Life.'

As a belief system, Deism for one, has Warm and Cold Deism within their social categories. We encounter difficulties we need to overcome, while looking at the term Deism, to justify it as one belief system. I think I may just as well call white black and black, white, as I observe other belief systems, as I walk side by side with them in my beliefs.

Deism suggests a Supreme existence does not interfere in the cosmos and is principally employed by an intellectual movement of the 17th and 18th periods, which recognized the existence of a Creator on the foundation of purpose but disallowed trust in a God who links with civilization.

Christianity on the one hand, shows us how to live, by grace we are free; there is truth in this statement. Much of Christianity disintegrates from the inside out because of a grace factor which puts in peril what Jesus intended, because some say we should do whatever our little heart desires, and we will still gain all the benefits of what God has promised, even if we do not feel like listening to Him [this was The Garden of Eden philosophy of Adam and Eve].

On and on goes the narrative. The story changes with every fresh breath we use up. Every new day we wake up to, presents yet another alternative to Who and What God is. For many, God no longer lives, if ever He did. Why is this happening? Have we all ever begun at the same starting line while looking at different belief systems? Can we end at the same Finish Line? The starting pistol fires, one group runs straight ahead, another pack runs off into a field of oblivion, another assemblage veers right: Right over a cliff into an oblivion the same as others who get off the track.

Who or what is the One Entity we can, without reservation trust implicitly [completely, unquestioningly, unreservedly]?

So, someone makes a rule and we begin the race in a seemingly proper direction; soon we find the heights the of the steeplechase jumps to be different for all in the race because we do not follow The Rules of The Beginning. Imagine if there were different rules for each participant in a race. We think of the saying "Different Strokes For Different Folks" as a modicum [little] measure to get off the hook for being non-committal.

A 3,000-meter steeplechase is defined in the rulebook as having 28 barriers and 7 water jumps. A 2,000-meter steeplechase has 18 barriers and 5 water jumps. Since the water jump is never on the track oval, a steeplechase course is never a perfect 400 meter lap.

It is wise to Forge Ahead with our eyes set on the course before us. We all begin the same and we have always started from the same starting line: Birth.

Forge Ahead, Follow Through!

There was a man of the Pharisees, named Nicodemus, a ruler of the Jews: the same came to Jesus by night, and said unto him, Rabbi, thou art a teacher come from God: for no man can do these miracles thou doest, except God be with him. Jesus answered and said unto him, Verily, verily, I say unto thee, Except a man be born again, he cannot see the kingdom of God.

Nicodemus saith unto him, How can a man be born when he is old? Can he enter the second time into his mother's womb, and be born? Jesus answered, Verily, verily, I say unto thee, Except a man be born of water and of the Spirit, he cannot enter into the kingdom of God. That which is born of the flesh is flesh; and that which is born of the Spirit is spirit.

Marvel not that I said unto thee, Ye must be born again. The wind bloweth where it listeth, and thou hearest the sound thereof, but canst not tell whence it cometh, and whither it goeth: so is everyone born of the Spirit. Nicodemus answered and said unto him, How can these things be?

Jesus answered and said unto him, Art thou a master of Israel, and knowest not these things? Verily, verily, I say unto thee, We speak that we do know, and testify that we have seen; and ye receive not our witness. If I have told you earthly things, and ye believe not, how shall ye believe, if I tell you of heavenly things? [John 3:1-7 KJV]

People say, "why should I trust what The Bible says about all this Jesus Stuff?" Average people wrote the Scriptures, how do they know the truth, were they there when God Created??

My first question to the questioner is, "who believes there is an Almighty God?" Do I? Do you? If so, then ought we not 'forge ahead and follow through' with what the authors of the Bible say about this God? Has what this God said, according to the writers of the Bible, come to pass in History?

Supposedly, via the many writers of The Bible, God, said He would reach out to us as a picture of the reality of Himself in The Person of His Son. He would be born like we were, but not through human conception. Did the Son of man, The Son of God, Jesus, refer to the many things written in the past? If so, is it possible or rational to believe what Jesus said? He lived what he said!

If any of us are in the Column outlined above, the one saying, "It's Not All About God," realistically, we cannot expect these folks to be captivated by the principles of The Bible. The rules seem to change [but not really] to fit whatever is the belief about some other Higher Power than what Christ Followers believe. If it's Not All About God At All, because these folks do not believe in an intimate God, or any God as being possible for life to be what it has become, The Genesis, The Dawn, The Geneses, The Conception, The Inception—the Origin of the universe differs greatly again, as far as having a conversation where we find consensus.

Preparation in the game of golf is paramount to the success of a player's game. One set of rules applies to everyone who plays golf, the penalties for breaking the rules are the same for all.

Is it reasonable to think we can break down the whole philosophy of life, and the whole Universe, into the Two Column Idea? The Occam's Razor Principle, one suggesting the simplest approach is most likely to be the right one, is something even the many people who don't believe in God [a god] might find as being sensible enough to consider.

This is forethought to prepare for looking at how the Golden Rule can differ between us in our diverse belief systems. However, there is a consistent thread of familiarity, understanding, and or truth running throughout the Golden Rule. The whole idea of a Golden Rule concerns how we treat other people. In the biblical Golden Rule it is God first, then other people! The reverse does not work.

The Golden Rule is a moral code which says we should treat others as we would like them to treat us.

This is elementary, but on the face of it, not so easy to place into practice throughout the whole of life, society near us, and the conclave, assembly, congress or gathering of the whole universe. Let's *Forge Ahead and Follow Through* as we play through life.

Somebody said, "Rules were made to be broken." Rules and Regs. "Fizz, Fizz" [effervescence] oh what a relief it would be for us peons or servants, had Adam just said, "Yes, Yes, Yes, I will do it Your way God!" Oh, what a relief it would be for us today if Adam had not given us the indigestion of sin by disobeying the rules and regs of Creation. What if the list of regulations had been simpler? What if God had simply told Adam about The Occam's Rule Principle. 'KISS,' keep it simple. Just obey my wishes and LG, Life Is Good. Life can be good in the whole perspective!

Simplicity: "And the LORD God took the man and put him into the garden of Eden to dress it and to keep it. And the LORD God commanded the man, saying, of every tree of the garden thou mayest freely eat, but of the tree of the knowledge of good and evil, thou shalt not eat of it, for in the day thou eatest thereof thou shalt surely die. And the LORD God said, it is not good the man should be alone; I will make him a sufficient helper." [Genesis 23:15-17 KJV]

If we look back on life openly for just a moment it may convince us about the fact we do not always listen to instructions well. When we purchase a product which needs assembling, the manufacturer usually includes a How To Assemble booklet—step one, step two, step three—[most of the time]. We read it repeatedly. We still often need a good helper to assemble the thing.

Forty years ago Bayer used a TV ad jingle saying, "Fizz, Fizz, Oh What A Relief It Is." The implication was, we would find relief from our indigestion. These are words I reflect on in the jingle. While thinking on the Genesis of earthly time as I view it, I wonder if Adam and Eve had indigestion in The Garden of Eden after they chose not to follow the 'Rules and Regs' as God outlined them as we know them today. What is the saying, "Do Not Do The Crime If You Cannot Do The Time?"

A lengthy list comes to mind when we think about rules. We The People formulate good reasons for doing something we want so badly to do, even if we know there will be consequences. Reasons are fine when there is a legitimate or sincere cause at the core. When the reason we want to do something gets dicey, too uncertain motive wise, watch out. Sometimes we feel we need to over-explain the actions which seem to cause our indigestion.

What is the word I want so badly to say regarding this urge, "We The People" have to explain away the matter at hand so we do not suffer the consequences for our actions? "Come On! You Know," the emotions or disturbing indigestion we experience when something has gone South. Give me a second, it will come. Why can I not get the word out? Oh, I know the reason I cannot seem to find just the right word. This is problematic for me!

"EXCUSES!"

THERE, I SAID IT! Reasons differ from excuses, but they relate closely with each other. I believe I must journey through one of my tenacious, persistent, determined, and purposeful word studies. I believe I have good reasons. My reasoning for this is not an alibi for not delivering sufficient words or resources to occupy the pages of this volume. It is getting much easier every time I write another book to plop down a hundred and fifty thousand words as a book length for my targeted audience—I sense your trepidation.

If you are tiring of this pattern I use to get the 'Word' out there because you think I have excuses rather than reasons, you may skip a few pages. However, I will likely do it more than once as we move along. Yes, 'because' is an extension or close relative of the words 'reasons and excuses.' I will continue to be relational as I move along, without the overuse of this design, but don't hold your breath.

In the sense I am pursuing presently, 'Reason' is a noun. Depending on the add-ons we could use successfully for a reason, to extend our understanding of all the possible usages we have available, let's use nouns, verbs, adjectives. Please look at logic, sense apprehension, worry, aptitudes, deduction, conclusion, intellect, judgment, moderation, moderate rationality, reasonable, sanity, senses, soundness, speculation, understanding, wisdom, wit, and a sound mind: REASON!

[Come On Down] — "let us reason together, saith the Lord: though your sins be as scarlet, they shall be as white as snow; though they are red like crimson, they shall be as wool." [Isaiah 1:18 (KJV)]

"Come, let us reason together." We could develop interesting tidbits or humor stories around this phrase which falls into place uniquely around many of these words. Let's try these— 'sound mind, marbles.' Imagination—this is another good word, let's try it for a while. Sometimes, depending on the word and or the circumstances, and the consequences surrounding the narrative or story, I delve into a period of sadness and or even anger when I look at the whole picture of life. The coin flip scenario shows us the antonyms of some words for reason—irrationalism, irrationality, lunacy, unreasonableness, and insanity. I cringe while thinking about some consequences following us as we forge ahead, hoping to find a better tomorrow.

The upside of the coin flip from the tail's downside position is, 'Reason Wins The Day.' If we rationalize reasonably with a sane mind using common sense as we speculate or venture out into risk taking territory with understanding, wisdom, wit, sound mind with our marbles in hand, we have a chance. With this mind-set we can excuse others when they do not measure-up to our perceived standards. We 'excuse' this perceived lack on their part. No, we do not make excuses for inanity or plain out insanity. We use common sense and compassion when we encounter the folks who may not have the mental capacity [not inanity or stupidity] to rationalize things the same way as we who think we are normal do—we justify things! We do not always practice common courtesy.

When we think of the simple rule God gave us in the Garden of Eden as a guideline which would keep us from all the indigestion we face because we think we know best, we may wish in hindsight we had given the rules a chance. Though the rules were never intended to be broken, only to be used as guidelines for a successful way to live life, it seems we just cannot get our heads around the thought of rules. I was in the regular workforce for many years and situated into many job situations. Each employer had rules and regulations for the keeping: And for good reason. A lack of obeying their rules left two alternatives, "SHAPE UP OR SHIP OUT!"

Not to my surprise, sometimes to my chagrin, irritation, humiliation and or disappointment crossed me up. He, God asked, commanded, instructed, ordered, or demanded certain things of me; this was and is simply the way of life. Training in the Armed Forces makes these rules and regs come alive. These regs can cause us grief or indigestion; they usually do for the not so "Spiritual [me]."

Along with the short-stated beginning in Genesis, "In The Beginning God said,"

> Let us make man in our image, after our likeness: and let them have dominion over the fish of the sea, and over the fowl of the air, and over the cattle, and over all the earth, and over every creeping thing that creepeth upon the earth. So, God created man in his own image, in the image of God created he him; male and female created he them. And God blessed them, and God said unto them, be fruitful, and multiply, and replenish the earth, and subdue it: and have dominion over the fish of the sea, and over the fowl of the air, and over every living thing that moveth upon the earth. And God said, Behold, I have given you every herb bearing seed, which is upon the face of all the earth, and every tree, in the which is the fruit of a tree yielding seed; to you it shall be for meat. And to every beast of the earth, and to every fowl of the air, and to everything that creepeth upon the earth, wherein there is life, I have given every green herb for meat: and it was so. And God saw everything that he had made, and behold, it was exceptionally good. And the evening and the morning were the sixth day. [Genesis 1: 26-31 KJV]

If we do not look carefully at the passage which we just read, we may miss a huge factor, one of life altering proportion. We do not want to miss it—help me to realize, our position in life is one of the most important things we are here for on this planet—if we miss it, the cost or consequence can be paramount—massive.

"AND GOD SAID! LET US MAKE MAN IN OUR IMAGE. AND GOD SAID, Let Them Have Dominion," not over God, but over His creation. "AND God SAID unto them, Be Fruitful, and Multiply." Let's not miss UNDERLINING AND BOLDLY MARKING "RESPONSIBILITY" IN OUR MIND. God had some; we have some.

And The Lord God commanded the man, saying, of every tree of the garden thou [you] mayest freely eat: But of the tree of the knowledge of good and evil, thou shalt not eat of it: for in the day thou eatest thereof thou shalt die.

For the whole picture to become visible to this 'first person' and all who would be born afterwards, God placed a sense of priority in men and women. He did this [not to create a sense of more stuff is better, in as far as a person goes] to instill overall order in our lives. God designed this process, as He did in creating all the entities of creation, not just the creation of humans and not in a trial and error setup, but in a 'trust in My order setting.' We like to think if it does not work completely to my benefit, and quickly, I'll do it my way! Keep It Simple. God said Obey Me, and life will be good.

And The LORD God said, It is not good that the man should be alone; I will make him a help meet for him. And out of the ground the Lord God formed every beast of the field, and every fowl of the air; and brought them unto Adam to see what he would call them: and whatsoever Adam called every living creature, that was the name thereof. And Adam gave names to all cattle, and to the fowl of the air, and to every beast of the field; but for Adam there was not found a help meet for him. And the Lord God caused a deep sleep to fall upon Adam, and he slept: and he took one of his ribs and closed the flesh instead thereof.

And the rib, which the Lord God had taken from the man, made he a woman, and brought her unto the man. And Adam said, this is now bone of my bones, and flesh of my flesh: she shall be called Woman, because she was taken out of Man. Therefore, shall a man leave his father and his mother, and shall cleave unto his wife: and they shall be one flesh. And they were both naked, the man and his wife, and were not ashamed. [Genesis 2:18-25 KJV]

God's control over His Creation was never less than perfect. "In The Beginning God said." These are evidentiary words. Never is there any inkling of an accidental arrival of anything God said He made. What people have built is all God does not put His name on in-so-far-as Him saying this is part of My original plan.

God can put His name on it if it was ordered by Him to fulfill a purpose for what He has always known as the whole big picture plan. Everything man-made is awaiting a Big Bang Crash [Entropy: It is the general trend of the universe toward death and disorder], not a Big Bang to start life, just the completion of God's plan to bring life as we know it and as He planned it to its proper conclusion. God's Responsibility was to fashion us [create us] to fit the Universe He made for us, tell us what He expects, and the consequences of neglecting to choose the right path. Our Part, "Stop, Look and Listen," and Do. What about 'Responsibility?'

While we take another look at logic, might I ask a question? 'Is it logical to propose the following already mentioned words demanding responsibility to be the headliner for us when we sift through the reasoning scenario of every purpose we have for life?'

Please take another look at sense—acumen, apprehension, worry, argumentation, bounds, brain, brains, intelligences, aptitudes, comprehension, conception, grasp, deduction, conclusion, dialectics, oppositions, discernment, generalization, induction, inference, intellect, intellection, judgment, limits, lucidity, marbles, mentality, mind, moderation, propriety, ratiocination, rationalism, rationality, rationalization, reasonableness, saneness, sanity, senses, sensibleness, soundness, speculation, understanding, wisdom, wit, and a sound mind—'Reason!'

Responsibility is a vivid picture which looks like this, 'it is a noun, demanding accountability, blame, maturity, trustworthiness.' Relevance and application make the importance factor come alive equally as forcefully as we look at life in the many ways it so naturally stresses we look at Reality. We often flip-flop on the issues of life, those which may not look so inviting. Is it easier to go to a dinner when the 'desert' is more inviting than the 'main course?' Someone said, "How Sweet It Is!"

Actors, movie producers, singers, songwriters, and who knows how many more avenues lead us to hear these words, "How Sweet It Is." In the movie *Papa's Delicate Condition*, Jackie Gleason uses these words while he is looking over his gleanings [winnings]. When Papa [Jackie Gleason] imbibed too much in the beverage of his choice, he made bad decisions. He had good intentions, but his responsibility factor waned or faded into the background. He needed to be more 'Responsible.'

Marvin Gaye uses these words in a song by the name, *How Sweet It Is (To Be Loved by You)*. Marvin felt, the shelter of a woman's arm was so sweet; he thought it was a picture of someone who cared enough to understand his ups and downs. Did he wonder what life would be if there was no "Somebody" to take up the challenge [if you would] to be this desert for him? Was he thankful the woman in the song was not afraid of the tough parts of this job? Call it her 'responsibility,' 'call it her choice,' either way it was a godsend for Marvin Gaye. Not all responsibility situations are pleasurable enough to attach the words, "How Sweet It Is." This seems to be a need Marvin had. We all have needs. However, life is about what we do responsibly when we are in a needy position or one where life is coming up roses. Marvin Gaye was thankful someone took this responsibility for his delicate condition. Hopefully, our delicate conditions are few, not everyday events.

So, what does 'responsibility' look like—authority, duty, guilt, importance, obligation, power, restraint, trust, answerability, care, charge, constraint, contract, engagement, fault—how are we doing so far? Please, look at a few more with me, incubus, incumbency, onus, pledge, rap, subjection, boundness, holding, the bag. We could add many more related words to this list. Many of us are familiar with some of these words and not so familiar with, others having the same bottom-line meaning.

Pick a word! Pick one word which fits best for you when you think of reason, a reason, reasoning, and responsibility. My choice is a word I found by reading between the lines, searching out a purpose suiting my idea of 'responsibility.' I picked 'mission.' As I read between the lines of some synonyms above, 'trust and answerability' stood out big time for me as well.

As I checked more of the related words for responsibility, I found the word 'affairs.' I am not suggesting the disreputable affairs some folks get caught up in. Sure, if we twist things badly enough, we can even use this sense, not common sense, to fit the word I picked out of the many avenues of choice in the 'word family.'

My best choice word for 'responsibility' is 'mission.' Why Mission? Mission takes the pain [worry] of responsibility from being like an albatross around my neck to where I put my trust in someone else to help me meet my biggest need with the wisdom they have gleaned by living the life of love effectively.

Whatever makes us think the word 'responsibility' means everything is on each our own shoulders. "I have got to do this because it is 'my' job." "Me, little old me just has to do this because if I do not do this it will not get done." We come up with a horrendous list of reasons for this mentality, reasons sound so good one would think God Himself conjured them up—maybe He did!

As we read the Bible, we may realize God said, "Let us make man [people]." It is hard to understand the 'US' part of God. We may think of Him being like 'us' as we see ourselves, one person in physicality; I do. It is hard to explain this to the satisfaction of every question which surfaces when the subject of God, Who and What He is, becomes part of an undying conversation.

We might think of the word 'mission' as about someone required to give up everything they own. This includes their house, their bank account, their association with everybody they know or have ever known, their possible inheritance, their mother and father, sisters and brothers, their children. We may think of them as having to buy a one-way ticket to some little byway [an area of little detail] in a foreign and forlorn land unbeknown to the rest of us and sit there all alone and wait for God to point them to a 'Mission' affecting or changing the whole world. He may just have a small hamlet in mind.

We may not look at mission in this drastic a sense, albeit some folks do. Mission does entail or demand a responsibility of the missionary or the person who ventures out with a sense of urgency and responsibility to do their part to affect some of humanity. Yes, maybe even the whole world. Realize though, the term Missionary describes not only a person who is a God believer, a preacher of the Bible, or someone who prays to something or Someone way out in a no-man's land we do not understand or want to buy into, to achieve the mission they feel so deeply about. Many other good people are on some mission everyday to help others. We are all equally valuable simply because of our birth as a person.

To feel deeply about something, opens doors of challenge to be a part of something greater than ourselves. In the broadest sense we most often use this word missionary [mission person] as one relating to the telling of the story of Jesus. The Bible calls Jesus, Immanuel, God with 'us.' The Bible also calls Him more than this. The Bible sheds light on our present thoughts on at least two words—responsibility and mission.

INTERMEZZO

Hey, here's the thing. The more stuff we accumulate, the more time we spend maintaining it, leaving less time to feel the breath of real life which surrounds us so we can breath freely. The more stuff we have, the more other people will want what we own, and thereby they may steal our stuff, or our stuff gets old, and moth eaten, and we don't want it anymore. If we use our resources for the sake of God and others, the benefits of the life we were born with will provide for the need of others, and in the process, we will be more refreshed because we will carry a lesser burden.

The more we see, the more we want to have and horde, because we may need it someday; our mess will not reproduce anything when we store it for future use. We can love and serve ourselves and end up the same as those who have nothing in so far as material things go—in the grave. Or, we can serve God and others and our rewards will be satisfied in a job well done, God will be glorified. Other people will be touched by our love and motivated to go and do what we did to make this world a better place.

The simplicity of nature is a clear picture of the cycle of life which works best. Trust God, and everything you need will be supplied. If we watch the birds and animals for even a short while it is evident they have a good life. Yes, they face dangers we do not face in the same way, but the more we live life, the more dangers we face every day. Just watch the news for a day. Our safety and security is not so great any more. Thieves steal our identity and our bank accounts; shootings causing injury and death are more prolific today than ever before, to where the wildlife is safer than we are.

If we try to find out what God likes we will find it. If we make His purpose, our purpose, we will never lack anything we really need. So, the bottom-line is, do not worry so much about the things you cannot control. Yes, there is more than enough bad stuff out there, but there is also a whole lot of good stuff happening. Look for it! [Mathew 6: 19-34 JBI (Jacob Bergen Insight)]

Think about,
"It Is Well With My Soul"
&
"Precious Lord Take My Hand"
Selah

But the dimness shall not be such as was in her vexation, when at the first he lightly afflicted the land of Zebulun and the land of Naphtali, and afterward did more grievously afflict her by the way of the sea, beyond Jordan, in Galilee of the nations.

The people that walked in darkness have seen a great light: they that dwell in the land of the shadow of death, upon them hath the light shined.

Thou hast multiplied the nation, and not increased the joy: they joy before thee according to the joy in harvest, and as men rejoice when they divide the spoil.

For thou hast broken the yoke of his burden, and the staff of his shoulder, the rod of his oppressor, as in the day of Midian. For every battle of the warrior is with confused noise, and garments rolled in blood; but this shall be with burning and fuel of fire.

For unto us a child is born, unto us a son is given, and the government shall be upon his shoulder: and his name shall be called Wonderful, Counselor, The mighty God, The Everlasting Father, The Prince of Peace.

Of the increase of his government and peace there shall be no end, upon the throne of David, and upon his kingdom, to order it, and to establish it with judgment and with justice from henceforth even forever. The zeal of the Lord of hosts will perform this. [Isaiah 9: 1-7]

The most inclusive picture of God I can imagine is in what I see as His responsibility and or mission as it always was. He came to us for a specific time in history [Calvary, The Cross] and it was for the whole of humanity. It was a 'responsibility' second to none in one sense because God promised He would come like this. It was also God's Joy. Jesus was and still is, called Wonderful, Counselor, The Mighty God, The Everlasting Father, The Prince of Peace.

The Jewish nation, indigenous or native to the history of the Old testament of The Bible, waited for many years for the person, they call Messiah, to come and deliver them from the physical slavery to those who were on the opposing side of this their God— Messiah, Champion, Liberator, Leader, Defender, Savior, and much more. These are the titles most suitable for the expectations of many Jewish folk.

The other part of the Jewish Nation believes Messiah is more than a Liberator from Roman oppression, He is The Liberator from our inbred sin of disobedience. The original disobedience in The Garden of Eden shows us a picture of us presenting ourselves as the savior from oppression, leaving God out in the cold in this sense. The Creator of The Universe deserved better from His Creation, but 'Better' was and is an 'Absentee Contender.'

Other titles we relate to in the word Messiah, are Christ, The Good Shepherd, Jesus, King of Kings, Lamb of God, Lord of Lords, Messiah, Prince of Peace, Son of Man, Lord, Redeemer, Savior and ultimately God. Yes, God! Earlier, I said this picture is not so easily explainable except by faith. The Bible states those who come to Him can simply come by Faith. This is not an option!

When we think of the Jewish people we may confuse the term sect or group of people they are indigenous to, or those from their earliest history, to be those who thought of what it says in Isaiah 9:7, to be one where they believed Jesus was this Messiah. There was a part of Jewry collectively or communally who were and are still Jews because this is their birthright. But who believes Jesus is the awaited Messiah? The other part of Jewry is still waiting because the deliverer as they had it figured did not come during Jesus birth. Yet again, others recognized Jesus as the Messiah. How long must they wait before they will realize the huge misconception many of these good folk have been deceived by. It seems many will never grasp the truth.

Now, let's get back on track for a while with, Reason, Responsibility, Mission, [Missionary]. No matter which side of the fence we are on, be it the Jews for Jesus side, who has come; be it Jews for God as only one entity [excluding Jesus], who has not yet sent Messiah to save; Jesus is not actually God, but 'only' a Deliver, Champion, Liberator, Leader, Defender, and Savior sent by God to save Jews from the physical oppression they experience in life. Or it may be anyone who sets out on the journey I call a 'Mission.'

It might, or might not, be God related. A Missionary is a Messenger, sharing knowledge they believe they have received from a higher power or just something they feel originated within the sphere of their knowledge, or something gained through living life and studying the available resources they feel they just need to share with some part of humanity, or the whole of the world.

I tried to include every state of mind and reality, but I am sure I have missed something as I am trying to fashion My Perceived Mission around the words Reason, Responsibility, Mission [Missionary]. Besides what we believe as our sincerely dogmatic mandate in life there is a factor we cannot miss if we are serious about 'Truth' [Re the Pilate scenario]—*Everybody: Everybody Is A Somebody!* If we miss everything else, let's remember this, because Jesus came to show this to us.

> For God so loved the world, that he gave his only begotten Son, that whosoever believes in him should not perish, but have everlasting life. [John 3:16; KJV]

We may not all agree everybody is as important as the next person in the whole big picture of life, because of how they do life. We probably all think who 'we' are, what 'we' are, and what 'our' mission is, as being more valuable. When we get to the bottom-line for market share and book value, it's all about 'me,' I guess? I realize, we all need to realize, the misnomer here. The selfie world is alive and well. If it is like this, I am Out To Lunch—Off Track!

Running the track of life and meeting up with people in all categories of life, is intended to reach people of every kind, type, and category in every field of life, and show them to be important to me and to life. My goal is always "Gold," like the Olympic Athlete.

Am I competing against the field? If I am competing and contending with the field where all of us forge ahead and follow through to accomplish a 'Mission or Mandate' of and for life, and winning acclaim is the only solution which will hit the mark for the sake of Eternal Value, I am challenged to ask myself the question, "Am I Running My Race Well?"

We need to have a reason to be in the race. The race sets the rules; this race of life sets the Golden Rule as the target we need to hit. From amongst the array or collection of different people and the categories each fall into, the final analysis is, 'if there is a beginning, and it is logical to assume there is a beginning to all existence, this beginning, we most often differ on because of our beliefs, reasons, and excuses, presents two columns: Right [The Truth] or Wrong [Error]; Black and White.' So, if there is a Beginning, does it all come down to the choices I make as to how it will all come out Re The Bottom-line for me?

To have any chance of accomplishing anything of value in the short term or longer term, we need to grab the bull by the horns. We need to address the responsibility factor, which is incumbent, binding, or unavoidable for each of us running the 'Race of Life.' 'This represents all of us!' None of us are exempt from the race of life. We all have a beginning and an end. The Initiator of life actually built grace and mercy into life for those who have limited resources, and we all have limitations. Look once more at some words I mentioned more than one time,

Reason—logic, reasoning, sense acumen, apprehension, worry, bounds, brains, intelligences, aptitudes, comprehension, conception, grasp, deduction, conclusion, dialectics, oppositions, discernment, generalization, induction, inference, intellect, intellection, judgment, limits, lucidity, marbles, mentality, mind, moderation, propriety, ratiocination, rationalism, rationality, rationalization, reasonableness, saneness, sanity, senses, sensibleness, soundness, speculation, understanding, wisdom, wit, and a sound mind: "REASON!"

"Come now, and let us 'Reason Together,' saith the Lord: though your sins be as scarlet, they shall be as white as snow; though they are red like crimson, they shall be as wool." [Isaiah 1:18 KJV]

The size, scope, magnitude, or the bordered dimensions of the responsibility each of us face moment by moment are often beyond our mental capacity to grasp. There is a border, there are limitations we encounter. Why? It is because of our humanity. This limits us openly; our imperfection is evident. Do you concur [agree]? Synonym's tell a huge story. They describe 'reason.' I must decide where I place my trust in the columns of choice—objective moral truth, and subjective moral truth, these are the choices!

To be objective, we need to focus on or admit to the One First Starting Point, an impartial, neutral, fair, and independent choice, not a subjective or feeling based entity. Lining up the 'dots,' doting our "i's" and crossing our "t's," offers us a chance to realize none of us were at The Beginning of Everything. Both of our perceptions of objective moral truths and subjective moral truths are theory based, in a sense, imaginary. Some of us have a huge imagination. Who is right? Simplicity often best tells the story.

Occam's razor is the problem-solving rule saying the simplest solution is usually the right one. When offered opposing propositions to solve a problem, should we not select the solution with the fewest assumptions? The idea is attributed to William of Ockham (c. 1287–1347), who was an English Franciscan friar, scholastic philosopher, and theologian.

What makes the most sense? Everything comes from Something or Somebody? Everything comes from nothing or nobody? Either God always points us to common sense scenarios or solutions based upon what the Bible says God says, or our directive points to nothing. We all know, we know, what nothing is, or do we? Every imaginable thing we know about physicality, 'anything and everything,' came from a known source—this makes more sense as per the simplest explainable principle. "GOD," Who always was, or nothing, which never was? HMMM? "Let Me Think" about it for "three-hundred billion years!" Here in *Chapter Two*, the Title is, *Is The Golden Rule Pointless?* Please allow for my messing with you!

Now I need to wrap this up with an answer to this in a succinct, brief, or concise manner. I mentioned The Golden Rule in *Chapter One* and defined it fairly often. From those mentions I come to where we are at in summarizing *Chapter Two*, by actually saying, 'this is the point.'

If I stop here I am not describing what is the point to anything at all! Too often we get to this place and simply expect people to know what the point of life is because we may think we know.

While knowing What The Point of Life Is—because we all seem to have differing views on the subject, we are not dealing with *What's The Point of A Golden Rule?* Not everyone thinks of acknowledging the full contents of The Golden Rule as defined in The Bible in [Matthew 22: 39-40 KJV]. It is a near impossibility to find two people of similar cultures who agree on anything, let alone different cultures who agree on anything anymore—Life's Tasks!

1-I am the Lord your God.
2-You shall [never] have no other gods before me.
3-Do not take the name of the Lord in vain.
4-Remember the Sabbath and keep it holy.
5-Honor your father and mother
6-You shall not kill/murder

7-You shall not commit adultery

8-You shall not steal

9-You shall not bear false witness against your neighbor.

10-You shall not covet your neighbor's wife.

This is the Jewish Talmudic Version; The Christian Orthodox Version says the same. The first three verses simply say we are to respect God and recognize God as Supreme [we mess up big-time on this]. Verses six to ten simply say we are not to kill our neighbor, commit adultery with our neighbor, steal from our neighbor, we are not to tell an untruth about our neighbor, and we are not to desire to have our neighbor's wife [because everyone is our neighbor according to the theme of The Bible, this says we are not to mistreat our neighbor in these ways]. We have two 'Main Rules:' 'Love God;' 'Love Everybody! How difficult can this be? Well, live life with your neighbor for a while, and you will know!

Master, which is the great commandment in the law? Jesus said unto him, Thou shalt love the Lord thy God with all thy heart, and with all thy soul, and with all thy mind. This is the first and great commandment. And the second is like unto it, Thou shalt love thy neighbor as thyself. On these two commandments hang all the law and the prophets.

When we compare the Ten Commandments with these two commandments in Matthew 22, the only difference I see is, instead of seeing these commandments as an a strict list of things for which we could be executed for back in the day, if we broke one commandment, we see we are to 'Love' God First; it did not seem to be the norm back in the day. Instead of execution for breaking one law by careless action, we are given 'Grace and Mercy' to cover us if we mess up without being careful in how we LOVE GOD or our Neighbor! [Matthew 22: 39-40; KJV]

What's The Point of A Golden Rule? Learn to Love God and treat others how we wish to be treated, then life will be GOOD! So, What's The Point of A Golden Rule? The Point Is To Forge Ahead, Accept God for All He Is, and Says We Are To Be, and Follow Through In What The Bible Says About How To Get Into A Relationship With Him In This Way!

With two chapters in the books I have covered considerable territory. I have, as I always do, and will always try to do, broken apart differing concepts with words related to the heading of thought I express throughout. I will regurgitate or bring up many of the same headline words as we proceed. Some of these words are, Excuses, Responsibility and Truth—Reasons. Repetition, what is the value of it? The more I review something, the easier it is to preserve it.

Excuses or Reasons—The Thesaurus often breaks down words until they are almost equal. In this way we may look like we have a valid reason for our willful action of just not liking the entity someone asks us to be involved in. It is okay not to want to be involved in certain scenarios, but when we make too many explanations for non-compliance or refusal, it is just simply an EXCUSE. Reasons and Excuses are not "Kissin-cousins." When we give someone a 'Reason' for being unable to comply with their request, only a simple explanation is necessary.

An Example: Please come to my Birthday Party?

An Example of a Reply: I cannot come because I need to get groceries; I need to go to the barber; I need to take my child to the park! [These may all be legit] Or, they might simply EXCUSES?

An Example of our possible Reply: My son or daughter has a piano recital that day, so I cannot fit into the occasion of your Birthday Party! [This also may be legitimate] This is a REASON! A simple explanation. This is reasonable.

Tucked away in the middle, or the differences between 'Excuses and Reasons' are the thoughts, "Responsibility and Truth." Do we owe anybody an explanation for the choices we make? Is it our responsibility to be fair in our responses to people when they ask something of us? I will not even try to tell 'you' what the answer is here! Common sense can answer this when we give a serious nod or assent to "The Golden Rule!"

Responsibility and Truth are powerful words. They can inflict pain, and or they can lift a heavy burden someone may be carrying. When we try to figure out the prominence of these words in the best-case situation, we can quickly eliminate 'excuses,' because excuses are always as if creating a mystery, leaving the truth of a matter as an unknown factor.

Can Responsibility and Truth easily be "Kissin-cousins?" I wonder! I know a little bit about kissing, and there usually needs to be a 'Reason' to kiss someone. In many cases the reason is 'LOVE!' Sometimes it is not! We can break up the word 'LOVE' into many categories. Even when we break it down in the context of the ROOT SOURCE, as defined by the people who think they know, those who write our dictionaries and thesaurus's, the message is not clear as it compares to the "LOVE" The Bible talks about. The responsibility of "TRUE LOVE" is often hard to digest. Without trying to get too PREACHY, I believe it to be imperative to have a reliable source, one which give a clear directive to explain what the writer of John 3:16 meant when he wrote it.

For God so loved the world that He gave His only begotten Son, that whosoever believes in Him should not perish, but have everlasting life.

Further explanation goes like this

We love him because he first loved us. [1 John 4:19 KJV]
Let all your things be done with charity. [1 Corinthians 16:14 KJV]
And we have known and believed the love that God hath to us. God is love; and he that dwelleth in love dwelleth in God, and God in him. [1 John 4:16 KJV]
He that loveth not knoweth not God; for God is love. [1 John 4:8 KJV]
This is my commandment, That ye love one another, as I have loved you. [John 15:12 KJV]

Now, here is one of the major passages of The Bible, a set of words, many people refer to when they talk about "God's" LOVE!

Charity suffereth long and is kind; charity envies not; charity vaunteth not itself, is not puffed up, doth not behave itself unseemly, seeketh not her own, is not easily provoked, thinketh no evil. Rejoiceth not in iniquity, but rejoiceth in the truth; beareth all things, believeth all things, hopeth all things, endures all things. Charity never fails, but whether there be prophecies, they shall fail; whether there be tongues, they shall cease; whether there be knowledge, it shall vanish away. [1 Corinthians 13:4-8 KJV]

This passage refers to the highest degree love, the best description anyone could ever answer to when asked about what love means! Love is the number one rule when it comes to defining The Golden Rule. Agape Love is the best! Agape Love describes a relationship between God and man; His love for us. It also describes the love people can attain to if they are Christ Followers. This is the distinction between Agape Love and any other form of relationship we call love! Agape Love should not be described in the same way as Philia Love. Brotherly love, self-love, is similar to the feeling we have of a universal, unconditional love which out-does casual friendship and remains strong, not depending on how you treat me, so I am obligated to treat you the same.

Philia Love comes near to the thoughts of being "Kissin Cousins," however, in my opinion, it is still not the same. Philia Love comes close to Agape Love in characteristics or qualities, but it does not necessarily link to God, like Agape Love! Philia Love reaches farther into a relationship than just a feeling [subjective], it extends or stretches out to the point or degree of wanting the best of the best for another person: Related or Not!

Eros, or erotic, sensual, sexy, or suggestive love is outside of both Agape and Philia Love. Though this is the case, God created people, knowing they would need more than Agape Love in a life having a source coming from the dirt He created us from. When he said, "Be fruitful and Multiply" He gave a very specific command, one in which He knew people, 'men and women,' would experience eroticism—sexual attractiveness, sexual attraction, attractiveness, beauty, handsomeness, good looks, charm, seductiveness, fascination, and sexiness, and through this process children would be born to populate the earth He created, so they would be, to keep it simple, "Christ Followers."

Abuses—I have no time, desire, or emotional strength to address these issues here or at anytime in the near future. Depending on which side of pleasing God, His wishes and or commands we subsist on, the reality of the world of choice each of us are born with, because God gave us this right to choose; how we choose to behave in a world where it seems there are no right or wrong behaviors, and how far out of whack our desires for self have gotten to, we will live out the life we have, and "—The Torpedo's, Full Speed Ahead!" It is what it is! Please do not Judge me too harshly!

The full extent needed to understand this command the way I feel God intended it to be understood, facilitated, or enabled, was through an Agape Love process. People would love God so much, they would through an Eros, erotic, fascination for the other sex, fulfill the command "To Be Fruitful and Multiply," it would be almost like a religious rite, because God gave us the capacity to reproduce. To get this 'Reproduction Thing' totally right, the intent was to "Love GOD First and Above All Else." 'Above All Else,' these are powerful words, demanding a commitment level which we humans, without out a God Particle, or better still, God Himself living in us, face futile attempts to get it right!

So, if we want to take a snapshot of any Golden Rule someone is spouting, the passages I quoted about love are the best of the best I know of to clarify the issue. If these are not the set-in stone standards, there is a deficiency in the Golden Rule anybody is selling!

Sometimes we feel we must engage in someone else's life 'because,' according to our rules, what they are doing [how they handle living life] is not right. They may not be living life in a normal fashion. Though this may be true, and we may offer hints or suggestions, such as is the case when folks are close friends, there is still a line we should not cross until we are asked for our input. If we are not careful about this, we may take away the dignity of someone else's right to live life as they wish, by their choice. No matter how we differ with those cultures differing from us, we can be kind. Kindness has no borders, or limitations. Love and or Kindness are the open-ended commands of God—No If's, And's, or But's [Butt's].

Where someone else's life is a real mess because of the circumstances they are in, the best course of action may firstly be to just be a real friend. We may accrue or gain the right to share the truth, not necessarily 'our perceived truth,' because of having a close relationship with someone. But truth, tried and true, can still leave the person with their dignity intact or undamaged. Some folks are enablers, they continually need attentive care twenty-four-seven, otherwise they think they cannot live another moment on their own. I am not saying there are not "Special Needs Cases." There are cases where twenty-four-seven care is necessary and even life sustaining. These issues are not necessarily "One- Shoe- Fits- All scenarios."

Example: Take a situation where someone is wasting away, stress and distress are visible, and the friend needs to make a move, how should this happen. Should we say, "you are not looking well, I hope you get over it, I will Pray for you?" Or should we say, "are you okay, you do not look well?" Often, in this case people will say, "I am alright."

Some folks are private people and want to handle their own situation; I believe we need to allow them the space to do so. However, it does no harm on our part to stay close enough to observe their life at a proper distance without setting them aside to stew in their mess.

What if the person in distress replies differently when we ask them if they are okay? If they tell us they are struggling with something in whatever way they may be battling, and we say, "I hope you get over it, I will Pray for you, talk to you later," is this the right thing to do? Are we allowing them to make their own way out of their mess? Are we allowing them to remain in their distress? When they forget about "dignity," they may just be crying out for help.

Responsibility—responsibility is a huge task. When someone is crying out for help and we are just asking the right questions to get off the hook, and we say, "I will pray for you," are we doing life right? If someone responds to our question about whether they are all right, by saying, "No, I really need your help," might we say, "How Can I Help You?"

Sometimes we feel we must engage in someone else's life because according to our rules [and we may think they are equal or co-equal to The Golden Rule], what they are doing [how they are handling living life] is not right; they may not be living life in a normal fashion.

If this is how we are evaluating people, and I have been guilty, maybe I need to do a health check on my own life. As I write this book, titling it as I have, *Everybody: Everybody Is A Somebody*, I will be honest with you, "I do not always have it together in my thoughts about how someone else is handling their life." I may well need to look at myself and ask if what matters most is, 'let the truth of love' be the bottom-line fixer.

William Stafford was once asked in an interview, "When did you decide to be a poet?" He replied, the question was put wrongly, "Everyone is born a poet—a person discovering the way words sound and work, caring and delighting in words. I just kept on doing what everyone starts out doing. The real question is: Why did other people stop?" Maybe the reason is—when we are off center everything is out of proper balance.

I am thinking of someone who is eccentric. They have a way of thinking which suggests they are an oddball—. It may be the case because of some brain function out of balance because of how they lived, or because of something which happened to them to allow for this to happen. Being eccentric may not be to say someone is wrong, messed up, or weird; some people, who by choice or upbringing are simply the way they are. It may prove to be their mandate in life. Am I the one to judge them on this?

While I am in *Chapter 2*, and Looking Back To See What I Saw, and What Did It Say To Me, I tried to nail it down. We are all born of equal, and that for A Special Life Purpose. Though we can live right or wrong by intent or by how circumstances challenge us to either accept or reject common sense, in both cases we will suffer either rewards and or consequences. However, I am not a master of the fate of how life will pan out in the Big Picture Sense, and this includes Eternity! Someone other than me controls the big switch of life. Someone said, "I AM THE WAY, THE TRUTH and THE LIFE: I believe Him! Oh, I did not tell you who this LIFE is: IT IS JESUS!

I may think, because I choose to DO IT MY WAY I am actually in charge of all of life.

NOT SO!

I ask you, *Is The Golden Rule Pointless?* After every determination has been made, The Golden Rule helps us to look away from ourselves long enough to notice life is not just about ourselves. We all began in some fashion. Each of us at one time or another. When we get to where we can rationalize, 'we will choose' Whom or what we will use as a guideline for living life, and for the chance we have in whatever the afterlife will be.

The Approach Shot

3rd. Chapter

Balance and Connection

Thou, therefore, my son, be strong in the grace in Christ Jesus. And the things thou hast heard of me among many witnesses, the same commit thou to faithful men, who shall be able to teach others also. Thou therefore endure hardness, as a good soldier of Jesus Christ. No man that warreth entangleth himself with the affairs of this life; that he may please him who hath chosen him to be a soldier. And if a man also strive for masteries, yet is he not crowned; except he strive lawfully. The husbandman that laboureth must be first partaker of the fruits.

Consider what I say, and the Lord give thee understanding in all things. Remember that Jesus Christ of the seed of David was raised from the dead according to my gospel: Wherein I suffer trouble, as an evil doer, even unto bonds; but the word of God is not bound. Therefore I endure all things for the elect's sakes, that they may also obtain the salvation in Christ Jesus with eternal glory. It is a faithful saying: For if we be dead with him, we shall also live with him: If we suffer, we shall also reign with him: if we deny him, he also will deny us:

If we believe not, yet he abideth faithful: he cannot deny himself. Of these things put them in remembrance, charging them before the Lord, that they strive not about words to no profit, but to the subverting of the hearers. Study to shew thyself approved unto God, a workman that needeth not to be ashamed, rightly dividing the word of truth. [2 Timothy 2: 1-15 KJV]

Learn The Game; Continue To Learn; Learn Some More:
This Is The Game of Life!

Golf is a game of ego, but it is also a game of integrity: The most important thing is you do what is right when no one is looking. [Tom Watson on Brainy Quotes]

Chapter 3
IS BALANCING THE BOOK OF LIFE OUR JOB?

Maybe it will be a "Chip Shot" Par Three in front of us; a lush green fairway; one-hundred yards; a shot at a Hole in One, or a Birdie. Or, maybe it is a one-hundred- and eight-yard Par Three with a huge valley between the tee and the green; trees and a gigantic slope to the right of the green; on the left, it gets no better as the green is circular with only about a fifteen-foot diameter wide. Yes, a "Chip Shot" should do the job with a pitching wedge.

Every golfer, Pro or Hacker, has loves and hates about the game, advice for others, and bad habits of their own. Many are the variations of swing patterns; each person handles their swing their own way. We are not Carbon Copies in physical makeup or in the character growing out from our soul. Cloning supposedly makes exact copies, I guess. Our world is becoming super technical; knowledge increases at such a rapid pace it can easily leave us in the backwash [confusion] if we are not careful. Knowledge is good for us to be able to sort out what life's difficulties are; how 'we think' to better life, often 'lies in misunderstandings.'

In computer science, cloning is creating an exact copy of another application, program, or object. If everybody were the same in every part of the movement of their body, we would all be robotics, as if manufactured from the same template. When coins are made, they are manufactured from the raw material [gold, silver, bronze, copper— whatever is required for a specific coin]; there are many procedures to follow, until each coin is properly fashioned.

People, creatures—and everything in the created universe [or in the Big Bang Scenario, evolved to become something different, through every process it takes] all have certain variables or instability factors [due to changes in the environment due to].

One of the key factors of functionally for finally getting our golf shot right and hitting the ball so it will go near to where we think we are aiming, is to begin from a set of rules from which we can learn the right habits to getting it done. If our balance, foot placement, crouching stance are right, and we connect properly with the ground under our feet, Voila; "The Eagle Has Landed, Maybe."

Communication must have a foundation, an unmovable support system, unquestionable when dealing with the advantage of life. Communicating is essential when dealing with our banker, stockbroker, insurance person—when dealing with things where the rubber meets the road. If we understand life and or our financial day-to-day, even when a fuller understanding of what the future may hold in terms of how life will change with none of our say so [the unexpected], we have a better assurance of our future.

Subjectivity or feelings-based entities do not garner as much assurance as things based on stable or unchangeable facts: Objective things. Empirical, observed, practical established and applied marks of change as proven through history are more sensibly unmovable; they point us to an avenue of objectivity [fairness which can stand alone]. Ostensibly or supposedly sound ventures can leave us fearful and unsure of an investment of time, financial undertakings, or other physical and or spiritual endeavors.

The short of it, when comparing objective to subjective, is this, 'objective words out [points]' to grip an 'object' in our mind, not because we are formulating an image, but that we can fixate the object, because we can physically grasp this object—it is there, it is not blowing in the wind. An object is something we can physically hold or touch—solid like concrete.

When we are subjective, the setting is the exact opposite of objectivity. Shortening 'subjective' to look at it as if speaking about a subject, is something we cannot point to [word out] and say, 'there now,' is what I am speaking about. There is no 'there' to hold on to. It is blowing in the wind. Everything we declare to be true is all in our head unless there are facts which then makes it objective.

An objective declaration is entirely neutral. It is not affected by the presenter's prior experiences or preferences. It is provable by eyeing up statistics or completing accurate calculations. When it comes down to making rational decisions, those which our lives depend upon, we need to attack objectively, not flippantly.

A subjective testimony might be flavored or embellished to enhance our story. If the facts are included so we can see the reality because we present provable facts, the testimony proves to be viable, like an object is viable. When we present only our views or opinions, we are without a foundation which can stand the test of time. The test of time proves many a theory wrong, and sometimes right!

Might it be better to watch out for things coming from someone who knows all about the future? Might our future be more insured, giving us a better assurance of the endgame results, if we learn more often than jettisoning our theories onto the table others are eating from? To worry about what is out of our control, just drives our blood pressure sky high, and begins an ulcer which may grow out of control in time. Every day already has enough issues to keep us as busy as we need to be. We get up early, come home late, and often wonder, "Did I Get It All Done Today?"

Hey, Just Sayin!

But seek ye first the kingdom of God, and his righteousness; and all these things shall be added unto you. Take therefore no thought for the morrow: For the morrow shall take thought for the things of itself. Sufficient unto the day is the evil thereof. [Matthew 6:33-34; KJV]

Dictionary.com declared 'Existential' to be The Word of The Year for 2019. What does it mean to be existential? They say it means, "of or relating to existence:" Example, "Does climate change pose an existential [existent or existing] threat to humanity?" They go on to say existential means, "of, relating to, or characteristic of philosophical existentialism; concerned with the nature of human existence as determined by the individual's freely made choices."

This plays into what we were discussing in the objectivity and subjectivity portion above. God created us to be perfect; He described the beginning in 'words' we have not yet understood. Or maybe we were fashioned by a random explosion, the which we have no way of knowing at the beginning, because it came from non-existence—neither of these left us in a perfect state because of the 'choice' factor mentioned in the definition of 'Existential.' God gave us 'choice;' Evolution gave us 'Ka Sera Sera,' "Whatever Will Be Will Be." God said we were people made from dirt, Evolution says we were nothing, then maybe monkeys— 'Who Knows?'

'Existential,' motivates us to ask questions concerning the source of who we are and expects, if you would, for us to seek out the purpose of why we are existent at all. Everything lies in the scope of the many challenges we encounter on a moment by moment basis. We are reminded we can make choices one way or the other in life—how we will live effectively to survive or be destroyed by anything from a pistol to an asteroid. How do we answer the questions of life! Objectively or subjectively? Just being 'People' is no easy task!

What does it mean to be eccentric—off center? Well, sometimes it seems like eccentric means to be abnormal, unnormal, or out of 'balance' with reality—like the eccentrics are wrong and the rest of us are right! However, eccentricity may simply be a trait some folks suffer, endure, or 'consider' perfectly normal, as maybe we should also do, or are challenged by in some other manner which lives in a reality differing from each our own individuality.

We may think of ourselves as being more well-formed mentally than are the eccentrics. 'Balance'—what a tale telling thing or objective this is when used correctly. This leads us to neutrality regarding equality [fairness]. Just think for a moment about people who have an equilibrium problem, like vertigo or the like, balance is a problem. I have been there. If we do not know what exercises to do to get on 'balance,' back to where the balance is normal again, it can be scary because we think we are 'on our way out!' We address this sense of 'balance' in this Chapter, *Is Balancing The Book of Life Our Job?*

Syntactic adjectives—are linguistic, semantic, acceptable, allowable correct, morphological, phonological, syntactic, well-formed. How are we judged in the picture these words suggest? Who is the judge in this wide-ranging thought? I am not applying for the position—are you?

Trekking Purposefully Through Stock Options With An Essential View of Truth, Will Be Paramount To The Success of Any Venture. Stock options are important when it comes to how we wish to build our Stock Portfolio in the financial sector; make the wrong choices and our stock may plummet and or disappear. What may have been an Up Arrow producing huge dividends, may suddenly become a Down Arrow, creating financial bankruptcy. Options are choices and or selections we make which can enhance our portfolio or diminish or mar our set of options.

Think again if you think the words 'Stock Options' only refer to financial situations. We store the dollars we accrue or accumulate in banks or we may reinvest them for even larger gains. We have storehouses to hold our booty for usage on another day. We wait for some other container to come and take them off to market where the marked-up product will pass on to someone else who needs what we have passed on. They establish the goods someone else purchases to become fodder for personal use or consumption. The story just gets bigger; the narrative does not narrow down, it just moves along into another scenario, one which may come out as just a tale to produce a laugh, or it may produce a spiritual narrative. What are some of the spiritual options or descriptions, accounts, or subscriptions, we allow into our scenario?

Mystical, Divine, Unworldly, Otherworldly, and or Physic— the spiritual archives we attribute to what we consider untouchable with our fingers like 'cash,' come across as differing pictures. These are the Faith-based items running amuck amongst the people of the whole world; this is an awfully big place in which we try to make sense of it all! I suppose we need to be careful what we wish for when we build our Stock Options. When our Bucket List gets too long, it also becomes more difficult to manage, so we increase the debit side of two columns—debits and credits, and for what? Well, most often we do so to increase our bottom-line, and what is our bottom-line? It takes our time, energy, resources, and too often it takes our peace of mind to generate a satisfying Bucket List.

Indispensable Content sums up our total substance or existence in these words: Core, crux, essence, income, profit, reality, basis, conclusion, determination final decision, fundamentals, last word, loss, main idea, main point, meat and potatoes, name of the game, net, nitty-gritty, nuts and bolts, point, sum and substance, and what is it all about anyway when we take our final breath?

No matter what game we play while living, *Clue, Monopoly, Checkers, Chess*—some games leave us clueless till the end; some games allow us an accumulation of property in fantasy or in reality; some games have us checking our progress to see if we are making any progress towards the Endgame; some games are the most challenging, and not always the easiest to play. Today, Reality Shows run amok.

In Chess, when the bell tolls, it is Checkmate. However, there is what they call a Tie, or a Draw in Chess. Even when this happens, it is usually because one player, the one who has forced the other player to be on the defensive, is really in one sense the winner. I know, the reality of the Endgame is, both players get a half point. I have often heard a tie is like kissing your sister, which is different than kissing your spouse. The excitement level varies somewhat between these two scenarios.

Back to the Chess game—simultaneously, we need to accredit the player on the run with a great measure of ingenuity or resourcefulness because they averted a loss; they still came out not being on the losing end of the game. The stock options of life allow for us to be cognizant or perceptive enough to move the players of the game around successfully enough to allow for the success factor of the endgame to be a sweet delight. Who does not want delightful nourishment or delightful endings?

> Endgame defined: [noun] The final stage of a game such as chess or bridge when few pieces or cards remain. Example: "the knight was trapped in the endgame."

Be it Physicality or Spirituality [and here we are back to "Two Columns" again], these are the essentials to accomplish the gain of our dreams, no matter what else or whatever else we believe them to be. We all need to sift some things out to accomplish great things. When we work with our stock options [spiritually speaking], Finishing Well—is the gold at the rainbows end. Could it be something like the carrot on the end of the stick? Could be, when someone finally removes the stick, we get the carrot?

Most of what I have written falls into this concept or context of two columns, or "either or choices in life" which pan out as either right or wrong. Today in our world of tolerance issues [I believe we need to consider other folks our equal] we need to be exceptionally careful how we present each word, phrase, thought, action, event, reflection of history, spirituality—because it may offend someone's idea of what is right or wrong morally and in every other sense. *Twin Towers of The Heart, Bridging The Gap, The Mandate, It's Jacob! My Name Is Jacob! What's Yours?* and some of my unpublished works all seem to present thematically on whether an issue is Right or Wrong—Two Columns.

Oh, if only life was as simple as we often envision the past to have been. A dollar bought a lot of stuff in the nineteen hundreds. Research tells me, when a person "brought home the bacon [the paycheck]" in 1900, they could buy a pound of bacon for fourteen cents a pound [today, it would be between 4-7 dollars a pound]. An average wage for a male farmhand in Canada in 1909 was about $35.00 a month including room and board. For a female it was about $20.00 a month including room and board, about a dollar a day for a man, and about $0.60 a day for a lady; room and board included.

In 1962 I earned 60 cents an hour, $4.80 a day, $24.00 a week, about a hundred dollars a month; thirteen hundred dollars a year: Gross earnings. The Midtown Buffett in Winnipeg, served an "All You Can Eat" Buffett for ninety-nine cents: Go figure! Well, we have broken this wage rule. The average wage in Canada in 2018, depending on where you live, is between about forty-thousand dollars a year, to sixty thousand a year—without room and board. This is about 3500.00 per month, about twenty dollars an hour at the forty thousand per year mark; about thirty dollars an hour at the sixty thousand a year.

My wife says she wishes we lived in *The Little House On The Prairie*, and *The Waltons* days. In retrospect they look inviting as we look at our world through dark glasses; unable to see the light at the tunnel's end. It is easier to see what we had and call those the Best Years of Our Lives, than it is to see any good in our Future Shock Days. A friend wrote a book called, *The Best Days of Your Life*: This is a relevant theme to live by.

Memories often look so inviting, but they are not always the reality we want. We may look back to a time when things seemed affordable because what costs a hundred dollars now, may have cost a dollar. However, everything is relative; according to just the average wage of today compared to the average wage back then, if a person made a dollar a day, then, this equates to about one-hundred and fifty dollars [give or take a few dollars here and there] for a day's work today.

The thought of living on memories, beginning today—throughout eternity, what would this look like? Back in the day, people managed well enough. However, back in the day they did not know how much the introduction of new knowledge would change how we would need to live life ahead of where they were at the time.

Oh, but the memories—memories of a wage earner coming home from a twelve-hour day to a family at home who loved them so much—with dinner on the table—children sitting around the table with Mom and Dad and Grandma and Grandpa to a homemade meal, not canned beans, a pizza ordered in, KFC from Colonel Sanders, or a handy meal with a Skip The Dishes phone number at the ready. Then after dinner and before an early bedtime they may sit around the radio and listen to some archaic rendition of *Ma and Pa Kettle*. What a day it would be—or maybe not? Maybe not, because of all the conveniences we have spoiled ourselves with to look after Little 'Old' Me First.

Yesterday I thought, where can I go with this book; I have nothing left in my human resource pool. Today is a New Day, and today the windows of Heaven opened up and my mind was fresh again. I had a good night's rest; a good wife at my side when I woke; I had my coffee with my wife in front of our electric fireplace, and we talked freely about anything; it was not work in the work-a-day world as many know it. We are in the plus seventy range; we are tired and retired as we look at the comparisons between today and the Good Old Days. But, once again the Lord was "Faithful" and opened up a few more words for me to pass on. What would I do personally if it had not been for "MY LORD?"

Most of the time I know without a doubt God will fill in the gaps for me when I find myself depleted in my own strength. He will fill the gaps for me at the appropriate time—this I know. What a difference a day makes when everything is coming up roses. When there is a lighted tunnel prepared for me to walk into, one adjoining to paradise, with paradise just a few steps away; what a difference a day makes. In times like these I am chomping at the bit; I am ready to conquer supposed unconquerable lands.

What a difference a day makes when I walk out the door to bask in sunlight rather than the onslaught of a rainy day with gloomy skies on the horizons. What a difference a day makes when I go to the Post Office and there is an unexpected windfall waiting to be picked up. What a difference a day makes when the words flow on a page as I turn page after page four-hundred words at a time, and I tally it up to a great number of two-thousand or more words—sometimes a whole chapter [3000-4000 words] on those exceptional days.

What a difference a day makes on days like this for me. You may have days like this, only you may not be a writer [you may be my reader]. Your vocation will likely differ from what mine was and is now. However, you also will likely have days like the one I spoke about—everything about as good as it can get. Those are wonderful days and I am very thankful for days like this: "Aren't We All?"

You probably have times when you are especially thankful to and for someone who simply made your day. If you did not have such a day, life may not be great in your mind. "What a difference a day makes" when we cannot find even one thing to be thankful for. Maybe we are not looking in the right place to see the benefits out there, without which, we may have died—literally. Just because we cannot see the pluses happening, we could be thankful for those we can see, even if the reason to be thankful is not in place in the present moments we see.

What a difference a day makes. I recognize not every day is a banner day if I only look for the especially great gift, beautifully wrapped with ribbons; all just waiting to pop out when I open it, with a special voice booming out at me, "Surprise, This Is Your Lucky Day, you have just won a Million Dollars." Or someone pulls up in the driveway with a glossy new car and hands you the keys and says, "Drive Safe, this is yours."

What A Difference A Day Makes

We all know, through the course of a lifetime not every day has been the same as the last—yesterday, and or history in our past lives. Dare I say it, not even one day throughout the journey of life, has any of us lived as though our days were "ditto marks" of any day of the past. Each day and the seasons of time they represent are as if out of orbit to us now for actual usage. Besides the memories of them for assistance in deciding for today and our future, they are as lost to us for those character-building moments of life.

If life presented us chances of employing the "ditto" scenario to determine the best place in our lives, the one we sometimes cherish as a thought to relive, "What a difference a day would make" to adjust the day of doom we feel we are going through. Sometimes when we are in these distressful moments we crumble. Oxford Dictionary understands "ditto" to mean, "the same thing again."

Some of the synonym's for ditto are—repetition, duplication, replication, rerun [and we all know what reruns are on TV], duplicate, replica [as in say a redo of an old ship; like a replica such as Noah's Ark, so they say; a point of interest is, no one seems to have made a replica of Moses's Ark; a basket in the water amongst the bulrushes], copy, echo—ditto; indicating what someone already stated, when applied a second time is a ditto mark. If one person folds their arms or legs, everyone else in view does the same; this is the picture we can make sense of to define ditto. We may all have a few memory filled situations we would like to 'ditto,' like some rich person we would like to see share their wealth with us—their bank account transferred to ours—Ditto.

Even in *Groundhog Day* not every day was the same, although it began the same with the alarm clock ringing early in the morning. Then each day opened up new people and new opportunities to make a difference. Bill Murray, as it seems he always had, has a way of lightening the moment by making a difficult moment for someone else in the movement from a problem to a solution, come out not so bad. Along with *Groundhog Day* I am thinking about *What About Bob*, the movie.

What if every morning at 6 AM, my alarm clock [one which I have not used for many years, because I had an alarm clock in my head] blasted out *I got You Babe* and the announcer chirped *Rise and Shine*, wouldn't it bring memories of repetition to mind?

Groundhog Day: What good came through the process of the story in relationship to trying to sort out the two columns of life and living through some processes of the repeat scenarios we live through in our lives till we get it right? Is there anything to be learned through Circular Reasoning—Groundhog Day?

How many years have we been listening to preachers telling us about God and how Jesus died to save us from ourselves; seems it goes in one ear and doesn't for a moment, stop long enough over a cup of cocoa to realize I need to stop and listen to the words. Over, over, and over, it gets repeated, but fewer people are buying it. *Groundhog Day*: Over, Over, and Over! How often a year does the groundhog pop their head up out on this farmers field in a day. Then on one particular day we are supposed to take special notice; it will accurately forecast the weather pattern for the future. 'What Do You Think,' is this pretty far fetched?

With a picture of eternity in our mental scope for the sake of worth, would we classify *Groundhog Day* as one of the greatest philosophical films, or is it just an easy picture to watch, one which gives us a few laughs? Triviality or nothingness; what can this do for me in a world of frustration and confusion? The TV Series, Monk, with the words of the theme song which allows us to see what this world looks like, says, *It's A Jungle Out there*, [by Randy Newman]. It looks like this,

Misunderstandings and mix-ups about one thing or the other have a way of disturbing our lives and messing up the best laid plans of our future and those we have on a minute by minute basis. It appears we are living in an uncaring world, where it seems no one is doing anything about the air quality, and the water we drink, but Mr. Adrian Monk says he does. He says he worries all the time; this is evident as we watch the show; Monk is a regular visitor in the psychiatrist's office.

Mr. Monk says, if we paid attention to what is happening all around us, we would be worried too. Largely, I think we notice the perceived and actual dangers of the world as it is out there, and our concerns seem to go unheeded. So we kind of 'zombie out' and carry on as if it will all work out okay, even if we do not note the warnings which say, 'we cannot keep doing it like this.'

INTERMEZZO!

"And there came unto me one of the seven angels—and shewed me that great city, the holy Jerusalem, descending out of heaven from God, having the glory of God: and her light was like unto a stone most precious, even like a jasper stone, clear as crystal; and had a wall great and high, and had twelve gates, and at the gates twelve angels, and names written thereon, which are the names of the twelve tribes of the children of Israel: On the east three gates; on the north three gates; on the south three gates; and on the west three gates. And the wall of the city had twelve foundations, and in them the names of the twelve apostles of the Lamb.

And he that talked with me had a golden reed to measure the city, and the gates thereof, and the wall thereof. And the city lieth foursquare, and the length is as large as the breadth: and he measured the city with the reed, twelve thousand furlongs. The length and the breadth and the height of it are equal. And he measured the wall thereof, an hundred and forty and four cubits, according to the measure of a man, that is, of the angel. And the building of the wall of it was of jasper: and the city was pure gold, like unto clear glass. And the foundations of the wall of the city were garnished with all manner of precious stones. The first foundation was jasper; the second, sapphire; the third, a chalcedony; the fourth, an emerald; the fifth, sardonyx; the sixth, sardius; the seventh, chrysolyte; the eighth, beryl; the ninth, a topaz; the tenth, a chrysoprasus; the eleventh, a jacinth; the twelfth, an amethyst. And the twelve gates were twelve pearls: every several gate was of one pearl: and the street of the city was pure gold, as it were transparent glass. And I saw no temple therein: for the Lord God Almighty and the Lamb are the temple of it. And the city had no need of the sun, neither of the moon, to shine in it: for the glory of God did lighten it, and the Lamb is the light thereof. And the nations of them which are saved shall walk in the light of it: and the kings of the earth do bring their glory and honour into it. And the gates of it shall not be shut at all by day: for there shall be no night there. And they shall bring the glory and honour of the nations into it.

And there shall in no wise enter into it anything that defileth, neither whatsoever worketh abomination, or maketh a lie: but they which are written in the Lamb's Book Of Life." [Revelation 21; KJV]

Someone said, "rules were made to be broken." This happens for me when I watch *Groundhog Day* [and *What About Bob?*]. Triviality or a time of respite or relief comes over me and I laugh through things which seems too burdensome—The News Media's version of what they feel we need to know to get us through the day. Triviality or nothingness, what can this do for me in a world of frustration and confusion?

It is like I was living in a world where I was experiencing great difficulty over the issues of life to where I thought I could no longer live life anymore. Then I reach past myself to meet a clone of myself in an ethereal world, one where I have come for help [such as in a video called Simulacrum]. If I were in this world facing myself as if I were a clone of myself, I would be asking questions of myself as if it were just in my mind I was doing this, but with an otherworldly sense, as if I were facing a real other person: This would be scary. However, knowing I had a clone of myself and knowing each day another clone would take my place, I could take risks knowing there would be no consequences.

Groundhog Day is like the concept of a perpetual or endless life where every day would come back at you just like the day before, and the day before—forever repeating itself. There would be no originality because today was just another yesterday. However, "what a difference a day might make" as we see we could make a difference with the knowledge of those yesterdays to make today better, changing the pattern to make a new tomorrow the challenge of perseverance!

If in this scenario, like in *Groundhog Day*, there were one particular pleasure you wanted to live on into infinity, you could do so by just repeating each day as you would like to live it, 'what a day this would be.' You could avoid every bad entity because of this power of knowing you could begin tomorrow at 6 AM again and sing *I Got You Babe*. I got this; Deja vu. No, Deja vu is just the feeling of having lived the same day repeatedly.

If it were a pleasurable day one was reliving, it would be great. However, had life been a life of misery the story would pan out differently. The reoccurrence of a day, which was not a good day, but bordered on being what some call a day from hell, this does not look like a banner day? This day of perpetuity, a state of lasting forever, would be Hell!

For Phil Connors [Bill Murray], it was really not a recurrence of yesterday, it was just a recurrence of a new beginning in which it began the same, but the caveat or warning was, he needed to adjust his life as it was, to making his life the best for what others could become if they just had a second chance. If Phil [Bill Murray], chose not to alter his life as it was, the scenario of recurrence was a picture of an endless life of same old, same old.

This is where we often live when we get down on something, discouraged about an issue or do just not understand life—without having had a prepared recovery plan in place for these moments; these times come upon us all. All we can see is, the stuff we are living through is everybody else's fault. If everybody else would just change how they are living and focus all their attention on little old me, then life would be the best it could be; then I could live on in perpetuity, endlessly on this theme of life because this would be great.

It is much more comfortable to understand life when it does not include the array of problems we encounter, the pains we experience, physical or emotional, or if life does not offer us challenges appearing to be so immense not even GOD CAN HANDLE THEM—if there is even a God! These and many more are the issues Christians, Casual Believers in God, and or Non-Christians face every day across this immense globe of ours, and we think it is all about us.

What stimulates us to ask the seemingly unanswerable questions; differ with each other along the issues of life; throw up our hands-on whatever faith we might have possessed, or thought we may place our lives in? Might it simply be we do not understand because we have not been taught early enough in life, God exists. He, God, does have a plan for each of us. It will offer enough sustenance for us to survive this life; endure this our sojourn, and maybe even actually love this life enough to enjoy the best it could offer to the fullest degree.

Groundhog Day tests Nietzsche and Deleuze, and their rendition of recurrence. This biosphere of theirs and the reappearance of the matching entity is wrong because Phil Connors can pose it in a dissimilar fashion each day and cause unlike things to happen. *Groundhog Day* presents for us a far more human variety of everlasting recurrence. Connors typically muddles through it all.

Sometimes Phil is less optimistic, sometimes more; he does finally reach a state of change as he is driven by real concern, and in this moment he is freed from the reappearance theme of the story. Phil was living with baggage, hurting himself and innocent people in his day-to-day. As if by some divine intervention, Phil caught sight of the solution for the problems he had.

A lady named Luce Irigaray can give us the right keys with which to reach the world with a change factor to make a difference in our day and make a difference in the lives of the people we meet. This story reminds me of the theme of "The Golden Rule." We will be talking about this in other parts of this book, *Everybody: Everybody Is A Somebody*. Luce Irigaray wrote a book called *Sharing The World*. If I could find the EBook Version, which seems to be non-existent, I would buy it, because it seems to tell some of the story in her words, which I am trying to say here in my words.

Irigaray seems intent on promoting the relevance of others. She basically presents her thoughts in a feminist fashion, which usually looks rigidly opposed to the traditionally masculine mindset often prevalent in some societal sections of life. Promoting the significance of people is paramount—on this I agree.

The Golden Rule

Thou shalt love the Lord thy God with all thy heart, and with all thy soul, and with all thy mind; the second is like unto it, thou shalt love thy neighbor as thyself: that's it. [Matthew 22:36-40]. On this I can never improve.

What a difference a day makes when I understand there are rules in place to make room for the rights and freedoms of all people to live and let live a morally dignifying human life. Not every day is an exceptional day if I only look for the boundless gifts packaged for me with ribbons and all the trimmings, just waiting for special little old me. Sometimes Breaking The Mold [cast, or pattern] means the same as Rules Were Made To Be Broken.

Publishers Clearing House and other "you are the big winner" settings, always present us with a glossy look at what life might be like in a world where problems do not exist. If only my excellence in life was boosted by a windfall, a jackpot greater than I have heretofore experienced—my value would increase—or not?

We may look at the rich and famous, thinking they have the plenty we feel would be enough to make a difference—at least for ourselves. Often, the windfall scenario looks so good; if we just won the lottery, think of all the good we would do for others; this is a great concept, but how much of this mindset transfers into the 'others' category in the reality of real life out there?

Rules—every lottery or contest I know of has rules needing to be followed to get to the bottom-line. "What is the bottom line you ask?" It's always about winning. Do I win the money, and how much? Do I win fame and fortune? Is there a skill testing question to answer before I get the prize? Is it an easy math question or will I have to list the names of every President, Prime Minister—of every nation in the world? What are The Rules?

Rules, what a conundrum, problem, or challenge we raise when we mention the word. People say they do not want to go to church because there are too many rules. Or when you ask someone if they would like to go to church or some church event, they ask, "Are there any rules, or dress codes?" Do people ask if there are any rules when they go to a Rock Concert? Often they just go crazy here!

How often, when we approach someone we know is a sports fan, and tell them we have extra tickets to some sports venue, and we ask them if they would like to join us, do they ask if there are any rules to follow before they consent or jump up to receive the invitation with open arms? Oh, they will know there are rules for the players of the game to follow. They will know all about the penalty box and or the penalties attached to an infraction of the rules of whatever game or venue they are consenting to go to with you; funny how the rules change for us when they fall in our favor. Dean Martin sang a song called, *Ain't That A kick In The Head*. Rules God has, "Ain't it a kick in the head," [all our plans are shattered].

When someone asks us to join them for a dinner engagement at a restaurant, and we are unfamiliar as to whether or not it is an upscale place or a casual dining place, it is usually appropriate and expected for us to ask what the ruling is as far as the dress code goes. Most often we do not put up a fuss—the benefit to ourselves is a pleasurable experience. I could go on and on to include every event known to man and lay out the groundwork and or the ground rules of each venue or event, but none of us has sufficient spare time on hand at a moment's notice.

For most folks, and there are exceptions I will not venture into for now, rules are a part of plain old living life. We do not get up in the morning or whatever time we get up, without following one set of rules or the other, even if it is just using the washroom, facility, commode, toilet—or just out behind the barn—as it goes sometimes for some folks. In some countries the rules of use are not as proper as we in the modern world adhere to them.

Rules were made to be broken:

Who thought up this line anyway?
What's My Line?

Questions—we all have doubts; it seems we suffer them all the time. Here and now I will assume the first question: "In the beginning, were rules made to be broken?" I take this question carefully, to be politically correct, this is expected in the market of life. I say the market, and by this I mean The Market Place of Life. If we are not totally on track in the Politically Correct Arena we are immediately confronted with tolerance issues. Are we excluding anyone; marginalizing anyone; insulting anyone; defaming anyone; devaluing anyone?

As I call for my question, and before I answer my question, I wish to insert or interject some thinking, like *What's My Line?* I present myself openly and as fairly as I can, hopefully and prayerfully. By intention I try not to force my line on anyone, but I simply try to work from a set point of The Beginning. From this starting point of reality we fall in line or we divide to form two lines. It simply makes sense, any and every narrative, report, or event has a Starting Line.

Marathons, horse races, races towards any political office, races to be the best athlete of any genre, to be the best partner in any relationship, the best overall employee of any firm, or just the "Employee of The Month," the best person on the planet—these and more all have a plumbline and or starting point [a beginning] for setting a balanced approach for the next step to achieve any venture. If there was never a beginning there would never be an end to any physical endeavor. Within the compass of our finite minds we can never define an "Exacto" tomorrow [eternity]. We know about so many things, better left alone, but tomorrow: HMMM.

I realize I have not yet given an answer to my question, or even asked you what you think. Before I do so I want to put out some source; maybe I should put out some Ground Rules! For many years now the game show industry has been part of our culture in a big way. It may be difficult to affix a time for The First Game Show Ever. However, whenever it was and whatever it was, you can bet your boots the Rules of The Game were spelled out; this makes me think *The Spelling Bee* was one contestant for being the first in line from the starting line of time for the event. According to my research on Google, The Inaugural Broadcast of *The Spelling Bee* was May 31/1938.

One Game Show I wish to bring back into the picture here is called, *What's My Line. What's My Line?* It ran on the BBC beginning in 1951. It was a simple panel game show. Contestants with unusual occupations signed in, performed a mime of the job they do, then they fielded yes-or-no questions from four celebrities aiming to work out the contestant's job. Questions answered with a 'no,' caused the next celebrity to pick up the investigation; ten 'no' answers meant the panel lost and the contestant won. Little skill was involved on the contestant's part besides recognizing when they had an unusual enough job to stand a good chance at stumping the four wise people, or those who so perceived they were wise. This was the just of it all. It was all about asking questions to discover what mystery lay behind the contestants pose, composure and or presentation.

Mystery, what an intriguing concept. Does the beginning of all-time present mystery? Well, if we are still asking questions after all this time, be it billions of years, or even just somewhere around ten-thousand years, the mystery still exists for many of us. This number is not the big issue in my mind, although it is huge in many facets of determination for the answer.

I was talking about *What's My Line*. I was doing this so as for us to grasp reality. For us to come to any conclusion about anything, something needs to be stated, something needs to be determined about the statement; questions need to be asked to arrive at conclusions; once certain conclusions are analyzed by a panel or group of others, someone will come to the final conclusion—The Final Answer. With the show I am writing about, someone comes out the winner.

Where we have a winner in a contest involving more than just one person we also have losers. The loser does not necessarily suffer the loss of money, personal standing, or credibility; they just did not have the best Final Answer. It is always good to acknowledge the fundamental worth of other people as per their right to be as important as their counterpart in humanity. Each person can bring out their best value to living life with and for their neighbor.

Who is our neighbor? Once, in The Bible a legal expert asked Jesus, this question. It seems this person was trying to justify their own position. The caveat or proviso for knowing who our neighbor is and if we have done all we can to help them in and through their dark days, this takes little common sense. Everyone is our neighbor.

The whole process of determining anything comes down to how we follow the rules of the game [the game of life], and or if we follow the rules or not. If we follow the rules we have a good chance of coming out on top. If we ignore the rules we will lose and or be disqualified from the game or entity. There is a Rule of Life: Like it or not. If we break the rule, we will suffer dire consequences. In the day-to-day present, in the earthly future we strive for, and after both of these expire [death], there is an eternal or endless future.

This eternal future depends on how we feel about one belief system or the other. For those who are atheists, belief in God is not an issue, so as far as they are concerned, God's rules do not apply to them in any equation about the rules of life pertaining to those who believe in God and obey what He says. If we think we die and this is all she wrote, 'End of Story,' this does not conclude a final answer because it is just what we believe. If we think everybody goes to some heaven when they die, where God rules, or one where God does not rule, then we need to evaluate the facts to determine the Final Answer. Too often we cross paths with the final answer to settle an issue, but enough is never enough: So it seems.

Can We Balance The Book Of Life?

Misunderstandings and mix-ups about one thing or the other have a way of disturbing our lives and messing up the best laid plans we have on a minute by minute basis.

Someone said, "Rules were made to be broken."

It is timely to think about God when we are young, and always remember Who He is, When He began, Where He is, What He is, Why He is, and How He can affect or touch our lives. If we forget these things as we grow older, we may lean towards the pleasure of things other than God, this can spell disaster—any direction away from God is unprofitable eternally.

As long as the sun comes up every morning, as long as the moon and stars shine at nighttime, as long as the rain clouds still come to water the earth to grow what we need, and as long as the Rainbow still hovers in the sky after a good rain to remind us the Promise of God is reliable for all eternity, we need to think about what got us here.

The promise of many days before us, these can be good ones as we take time to remember our Creator. As time goes on we grow older, yes? Different parts of our body seem to reverse in our bodies, our body parts wear down because of a natural process and we often accelerate the process by the way we treat our bodies; by the lives we live out. Many are the warnings we are not following regarding the rules of our beginnings.

People on every side of life tell us things are not as they were when God created a beautiful Garden in which we would never need to face the difficulties we find ourselves in today. As it works out, we guessed we knew better than God and we conked out about life. Our first mistake was a Big One; life digressed from there onward.

Vanity of vanities, saith the preacher; all is emptiness.

And because the preacher was wise, he still taught the people knowledge; yea, he gave good heed, and sought, and set in order many proverbs. The preacher sought to discover acceptable words: and that which was written was upright, even words of truth. The words of the wise are as goads, and as nails fastened by the masters of assemblies, which are given from one shepherd. And further, by these, my son, be admonished: of making many books there is no end; and much study is a weariness of the flesh. Let us hear the conclusion of the whole matter: Fear God and keep his commandments: for this is the whole duty of man. For God shall bring every work into judgment, with every secret thing, whether it be good, or whether it be evil. [Ecclesiastes 12: 8-14 KJV]

Hey, have you ever thought of how many volumes have been written to tell us how to survive? How many volumes are composed every year telling us how to remain healthy? How many records are written to tell us how to have all the joys of life? How many books are written telling us how to win? Many books are written to tell us how to get rich? Many books also tell us how to die if we are tired of living and or are getting too fragile to live life as it was originally intended to be lived! There is no end to someone trying to show us a better road to travel than the one we are travelling. We may think we do not need this advice, sometimes we may not need advice, but sometimes we need an adviser. We all need help sometimes; the problem is, we may not realize it till it is too late.

> And further, by these, my son, be admonished: of making many books there is no end; and much study is a weariness of the flesh. [Ecclesiastes 12:12 KJV]

Often, when I am reading a book I read a certain distance into the many pages before me and I realize I can summarize what the rest of the book will be saying. The words might be many and varied, because of how in-depth the thesaurus's, dictionaries, encyclopedias—break down the words to come at us from many positions. This is not a bad thing because life is full [like full to the brim of a cup of coffee] with so many genres, categories, sorts of lifestyles, ethnicities, backgrounds, and choices.

So, why do we write and or communicators spend so much time writing and or telling people how to get through this life with the best possible of all the differing means we have to travel life? Are we just spinning our wheels? Do we realize we may be wasting our time? Are we wasting our time getting the word out?

The other day I was as if calling back to myself about much of what I have just said. At the same time I am facing back at myself to see if I was doing the same thing I was thinking just other people were doing. I realized again, what I have often seen before, I am no different than anyone else. I look at the title of a book; it excites me when the theme seems to suggest what fits my life's position. I have interest levels, as do you; they may differ, but often we share the same interests. We may not always come to the same conclusion about what we read; we might feel we know the rest of the story already, so why bother.

As I began this book I was thinking of the value of people of every genre—however, I wish to look at the term 'value' as we move along. When I delve into or begin a new book I look at the length of it; I read some of the introduction; I look at some credits other people give the book; I check out the Table of Contents; I notice some of the Chapters of specific interest to me; sometimes, after I take a peek at the end of the book, I flip over to *Chapter One*, and I begin reading the book.

At the outset, I am gung-ho as I find the nuggets I can cash in for Great Value in some part of my life as I move along in my read. At first I find it fruitful to make bookmarks which I propose to backtrack on for further study or another read through of certain sections. My reading habit tends towards the EBook format. At one time I read only paperbacks, so did we all. I always underlined or marked up the things which interested me in varying ways—using highlighters of a variety of colors.

At any venue or location in the book I need to decide if I need to do a complete read through to get all the nourishment I need to get to move on in life to cover the reason I began the book. I have hundreds, probably more than a thousand books on my Kindle; many of these I may never read. All these caught my interest level, so I bought them and still buy them for different reasons. Sometimes I buy books because I feel they can help me with an issue. Sometimes I buy them because of something I am writing about, because the author has written something along the lines of my interests. Because I write with a different initial context and with different words and thoughts, I want to acknowledge their input into my life, so I buy their book to say, "Thank You." This gives them a book sale.

There are two ways to read a book—to get through it fast, or to gain from it with a slow paced read. Just to say WOW, I read the book, puts no feather in my cap. I benefit personally from most books, both ways as I flip through after a time of digging at the beginning until I either realize this author has nothing much to offer me, or I get to a place where I think I need not read anymore because 'I get it!' I have many more books on any subject, which I need to read, want to read, and would find great pleasure in reading. The problem is, I not only need to read pleasurably, I need to read for resourceful purposes. I also need to use my time writing books.

When I am serious enough about a book to make sure I glean and digest every morsel, I take a long time. I may spend an hour or more on just one word, a phrase, a page; once something gets my attention, I use Google to the 'Nth. Degree' to discover everything I can about the things which got my attention on this given page. I take what seems like forever to get through these books. These for me are the most pleasurable books to read. I Am "Mr. Muller" [I like to mull things over; please do not confuse me with Mr. Mueller]. I am a digger; well, actually, so was Mr. Mueller. I dig so deep a shovel is not enough for me, I need a Backhoe to do the job. Google is my Backhoe.

People say if you want to be noticed in this world, "Rock The Boat; Break The Mold." Our world today experiences terrorist related events where someone or some groups are trying to get noticed; so they rock a community—with senseless damage and killings. This is not how we need to react to our hatreds or dislikes about how life is playing out everywhere we look.

How do we balance the books for the now we live in and for the Eternity we will all experience? None of the belief systems of this world will ever change anything without us beginning at the beginning of life and adhere to the rules laid out there. It matters not so much about how we got into this belief system if the foundation is faulty. If we never follow the rules originating with the first Entity Who made the rule, we will never have a clear or organized existence in this life—we may always be satisfied to live without God!

Freedom Fighters, the movie, is quite an eye opener. Until someone stands in a place of vulnerability and ready to make a difference in the lives of those who cannot easily stand up for themselves, nothing ever changes for the better. If someone does not get it right, life will never be lived for "better or worse," like the old marriage contract laid out the rules of marriage. If we, yes you and I individually and or corporately do not get it right, Hell on Earth will continue to heighten to a degree even greater than we see all around us in every facet or plane of life.

A young teacher inspires her class of at-risk students to learn tolerance, apply themselves and pursue education beyond high school.—Anonymous.

Freedom Fighters [The Movie] opens our eyes to what we may not want to see. Once we see life in the manner or mode of the terror it lives out in *Freedom Fighters*, we may be challenged to play a greater role to facilitate change. I am not advocating tolerance of the level of anything and everything is allowed. Change the laws on morality and life will miraculously look after itself and the world will be a better place; the perfect heaven we may think will just happen because we are such beautiful people: Ain't gonna happen!

We need to be tolerant with right and wrong defined to follow God's Golden Rule. But tolerance does not necessarily mean what we with our subjective wants or feelings for a newer experience than we have had, think we need to add into the laws originally written in stone [The Ten Commandments]. You will forgive me for my predisposition or tendency to follow God's Rule of Thumb in The Ten Commandments, as the Rule of Life; this should not be a big issue: But It Is! Oh yes, I too, often wish our life were created so breaking the rules would not constitute suffering the harsh consequences.

In 1994 uncompromising or committed Erin Gruwell of Long Beach, California begins her teaching job at Woodrow Wilson High School: teaching freshman and sophomore students. Two years earlier the schooling system brought in a program of a voluntary combination of students: Mixed races and cultures. Some existing teachers balked at the idea, as it seems, it Rocked The Boat, Broke The Mold of teaching which had kept the school in safe mode, as they considered safe mode to play out. The academic standards took on a new look, one which saw many students come into the system who may never graduate or even be well-educated unless the teachers fell into line on the voluntary program instituted.

Even though Erin chose the school purposefully, she finds herself hard pressed to maintain order, because she was not ready for what appeared before her this first morning she walked into her classroom. The students had learned severe ethical codes of caring for their own, but the codes were not those which normal society [whatever this is] usually followed. Many of her students are in gangs, most know somebody killed by gang violence.

The Latinos detest the Cambodians, the Cambodians hate the blacks—etc. This is not a pretty picture to walk into on your first teaching assignment here or anywhere else. The only person the students hate more is Ms. Gruwell, why, because she was about to try to Rock Their World. She was trying to Break The Mold.

There is a world of ways in which people will break the mold or style of life we consider normal. Alexander Fleming did so when he found the cure for Penicillin [The Movie *Breaking The Mold*]. People will do almost anything to come up in the face of "The System" because they are rebels: Sometimes with a cause and at other times without a cause. Yes, there are many ways to live outside of the cast or the shape of things; how they generally are; some are admirable as the results of their rebellion prove worthy—The *Stone of Destiny* is another movie of this sort.

If we never have Eternity In Our Hearts [I am thinking of *Eternity In Their Hearts* by Don Richardson here] we will likely never get our Portfolio of Life lined up in such a fashion to have chosen the absolute best Stock Options for completing a Successful Journey. When we live life in an off-centre manner we miss the mark. We need to keep our eyes on the goal. When we watch sports it is not too hard to realize the players on the field or court, have a concentration level in mind—they keep their eye on the goal!

> I envy not in any moods
> The captive void of noble rage,
> The linnet born within the cage,
> That never knew the summer woods:
>
> I envy not the beast that takes
> His license in the field of time,
> Unfetter'd by the sense of crime,
> To whom a conscience never wakes.
>
> Nor, what may count itself as blest,
> The heart that never plighted troth
> But stagnates in the weeds of sloth.
> Nor any want-begotten rest.

I hold it true, whate'er befall.
I feel it when I sorrow most.
'Tis' better to have loved and lost
Than never to have loved at all.

[Tennyson, Alfred. The Poems of Alfred, Lord Tennyson: In Memoriam A.H.H. Amazon. Kindle Edition.]

I need to run my own race, not yours, but we do run much of the race in tandem, together; not to beat or win over each other as in a competition, giving a prize to the winner, but to compliment and or assist each other in finishing well! Love is the key to this endeavor. There is a place for those who are off-centre or eccentric; somehow, in the balance of life, this too fits in somewhere; this is not the easiest for us to come to grips with, but are we the Final Judge?

What Did I See, and What Does It Say?

Is Balancing The Book Of Life Our Job?

If we are familiar with accounting practices, we may better understand it is not always as easy as it may appear to "Balance The Books." We need to reference the available legal means or laws of the land to find out which deductibles are allowable—this varies because of the place we live. Each country or place we live might have varying definitions of what is allowable when we are trying to balance the books. The larger the entity, corporation—the tougher it may be to "Balance The Books." Accountants in these areas need to take training to manage the affairs of others. Registered Accountants need an even higher degree of training: The costs in time and money are huge.

However, The Books Can Be Balanced.
God Will Balance The Books of Time,
In His Time!

I ask again, "*Is Balancing The Book Of Life, Our Job?*"

It may be for each of us for our own lives in the things we can control, but in some of the other situations it may be better if we mind our Own Business—First!

The Approach Shot

4th Chapter

Appearance vs Reality

It came to pass, when they were come, he looked on Eliab, and said, Surely the Lord's anointed is before him. But the Lord said unto Samuel, Look not on his countenance, or on the height of his stature; because I have refused him: for the Lord seeth not as man seeth; for man looketh on the outward appearance, but the Lord looketh on the heart. [1 Samuel 16: 6-7 KJV]

I don't just want to be known for the way I dress. I want to be known for how I play, how I treat people, and how I am as a role model. I don't just want to be, "he dresses cool" or "he dresses crazy." You're going to have lovers and haters. I want my golf game to be the main thing. [Rickie Fowler]

Golf is the infallible test. The person [man] who can go into a patch of rough alone, knowing only God is watching them [him] and play their [his] ball where it lies, is the person [man] who will serve you faithfully and well. [PG. Wodehouse]

WYSIWYG
Is This Really The Case When We Look At Another Person?
Is There A Difference Between The Look and The Heart?
Appearance
Reality

Chapter 4

BOOK VALUE REALITY: WHAT IS REALITY?

I use the mind picture of a golf hole—like many other games, the multiple aspects of the game of golf which can relate to us are so interspersed with overall life itself as we "PLAY THROUGH." At first thought I would use these words, "Play Through" just to represent a picture of our journey of life, and the many turns it takes as time passes us by so quickly.

In "Golf," the term "Play Through" has a more definite reference point. It is somewhat like when one doctor makes a referral for us to see another doctor because it will speed up the process of us moving forward in life as we know it; to be in a position to see the greater good accomplished for the good of the whole game of life. In golf, when one player by themselves, or a group of players playing quicker than the group ahead of them, are held back because of the slower group, a standard courtesy is usually offered to the faster group by the slower group—it is the invitation given by the slower group for the faster group to "Play Through."

Usually the slower paced golfers will wait at the tee for the faster group and tell them they are welcome to "Play Through." This relieves the pressure on the slower group to play faster than they can play while still maintaining every opportunity to have as good a score at the end of it all. We are not all built in the same way. Some folks can play through life at a fast pace and keep all the tools working efficiently so everyone else keeps their proper pace for finishing well. Many are the determining factors placing each of us at different intervals during our term of life, even when we start from the gate at the same place and time. For some folks, health issues come into play; these are severe hindrances in our race of life. Seemingly innumerable issues change the rules for each of us.

The First Glance—what does the first glance look like for us? First Impressions of people about other people we see for the first time we see them, can be the 'Biggest Mistake of Our Lives,' then again, it may not be a mistake. Any of us, at a specific time, 'present ourselves' in different ways—for different reasons. Does this first impression allow us a look at the 'Reality' of what is on the inside of this other person. Will we base our affections and or opinions about this person we may be seeing for the first time, based on their appearance? I wonder, how many of us are 'not guilty' of judging or analyzing because of the first glance?

I love The Masters Golf Tournament; Amen Corner is one highlight for me. Holes 11, 12, and 13 can have their drama; these holes can be challenging. However, these are not the only holes on the course. Flowering Crabapple, Hole #4 may present a challenge as well at 240 yards. It is only a Par 3, but can we say "it is only" a Par 3? This hole has two vicious bunkers [sand traps] on the front of the green, these present dangers and challenge.

So we look at this hole carefully when we stand on the tee box; we consider the wind factor; we consider the pin placement; we give Hole #4 a good look to determine what club will handle the dangers and the challenge to get a hole in one, a birdie, or a par. Do we even consider settling for a bogey [one over par]? Just giving the hole a good look does not do the job, it is a matter of all our actions being handled right to get the best result.

Could life itself expect of us the same sense of duty when we look at another person so we can expect the best results for them and ourselves? Have we ever even considered how Jesus looked at these situations when He was on this earth? Do we consider how Jesus would look in physical appearance if He were physically on earth today? Would Jesus give us the 'evil eye' of disapproval or would His theme of Grace continue?

How fickle are our commitments to life, other people, and yes, ourselves? I am thinking in terms of an analogy such as my screen saver in Microsoft Windows 10—Bubbles. My screen saver comes on about seven minutes after I have processed anything on my laptop. As the bubbles float across the screen, I visualize how easily these bubbles would burst if they were actually real bubbles coming out as I blew into the bubble pipe I had as a child—the pipe with the soap solution in it. How easily are bubbles burst?

Sometimes, when I am in a gloating mode, and someone says something to me in response, I may think, "Do Not Burst My Bubble!" We may feel the homegrown rules we live by are good enough, even when we take an honest look at the character we present, we can see there are deficiencies. When we are confronted by someone regarding our attitude we may either say or think, "Do Not Burst My Bubble!" [Do not try to change me!] Or, it may fit a situation where we are exulting or basking in a Glory Moment when someone advertently or inadvertently says something which does not burst our bubble or let the air out of our balloon, but initiates a false sense pride within us, like as if patting us on the shoulder, giving us the nod. How fickle are our commitments to life, other people, and yes, to ourselves?

Trekking Purposefully Through The Books of Reality, With Rational Balance and Truth, Makes A Difference. Purpose: Requires The Definition of A Goal Or Cause.

Is it even possible to have a purpose without a goal in mind? Pantheism says The universe exists for itself, without cause or purpose. Nothing existed before it which could have been its cause. Nothing exists outside it that could be the source of its purpose.

I am not writing specifically to dispute, debate or argue with all the "ISMS" we see about us worldwide. However, it is easy to see our agreement level with each of these does not balance out as coming from the same source—one with another. As I have looked at life from both sides now, I have never seen or experienced anything in the cosmos or any part of the universe which was there without a purpose or cause. If anything is unprovable, can anyone prove otherwise? The principle of logic goes a long way towards helping our understanding if we adhere to logic in its fullest descriptive sense.

Booking Options for accommodations and conveniences of all sorts, are many. We book appointments for doctors, lawyers, dentists, meetings of a huge variety of entities—but we live life helter-skelter with our own agenda, often without booking an appointment with the Maker of eternity for the life we think we will have after death. "Dust to Dust," "Ashes to Ashes," and then what? Reality speaks in both harsh, and gentle ways, at differing seasons.

There is no end to the variety of books which abound. For every idea someone concocts, there is a need to write a book. I do not think this a bad idea, except to say, the more ideas that surface, the harder it is to come to consensus or harmony on the one essential ingredient required to form the logic we seek to understand how we got to exist. I may dig my way through new books on my shelf, or I might just skim through them to grasp a quick view of the context—wondering why I bought the book, because it is useless to me.

'Book Value' is, as I understand it, an entity which does not show up in the retail sector; it is a factor we use on a balance sheet to determine for tax purposes, how much credit I have against what an entity cost me to purchase, attain, or secure in whatever manner or for whatever purpose I realize it. Book Value scales out [measures] the value of a company, frequently mentioned to us as accounting value. When we price out any item, do we even think about what it cost someone to get it to market?

It may be easier to draw-up a balance sheet for the financial efforts of life than to fashion a balance sheet for our physical, spiritual, ethereal—components of life outside of the financial arena. Reality, Rational, Balance, Truth—all factor into the equation of 'Book Value'—be it financial or our life issues. The main topic or context of Book Value is whether it represents the Truth—in the final or the bottom-line break-down or analysis.

Once we determine the truth of an entity we can determine the market value of the item. Market Value differs from the Book Value because it represents what said item will demand on the Open Market. What about where we live; where the rubber meets the road; in the grocery store; at the gas pump—or at the gates of Eternity, where not a one of us finite, limited, restricted humans will have a part in judging our book value, or what our market value achieved. Whoever or whatever it is that began life, and our universe, will be the Accountant Who will determine what my life amounted to, and the Whom I gave it up for while living this life.

The task we face as we live life, you know, how will we be making a difference during our term of existence, is this a toss up? What does life look like when we stand outside of the picture or scenario we live in; when we stand outside of the box to take a serious look at what is inside this box [ourselves]; when we stand at God's "Tee Box?"

We may have to break the lock and take a peek into the chest of goodies inside. We may see one thing from the tee box and experience another at the "Green" level or other placeholders for where we have shot our ball. Do we need x-ray vision to grasp it all? Do we need a lot of help to take such an introspective look at what we are and where we are traveling headlong towards our final end?

In one end and out the other is the norm when we enter the tunnel of life. We start here and we finish there, wherever there is. When we think of German [Wurst] Sausage a German Proverb tells us it has two ends. Where does a person start and where is their finish line? Life gets confusing as we think about the many cultures of this world; we may wonder about how we can balance the differences we see in the other cultures from those of what we grew up with. Most countries with any amount of affluence or material comfort are targeted as refuge sites by the many immigrants living a meager existence where they live now.

Real life differs from Wurst Sausage, we do not have a choice as to which of the two ends we begin and end at. In retrospect or remembrance of the things in life which have caused us grief, we may wish we had started at a different place in the life we have lived, to have avoided some of the big mistakes we made. However, such is not what our Maker pointed out after we chose not to take Him at His word about the life which He had planned out for us if we said yes to His wishes.

When we line up the options of life side-by-side as to whether or not one entity began everything which was or will be, who and or what will be our individual choice? It will come down to choosing Whom we will serve in this life; it will determine where we end up. Does Pantheism and or its "ISM" counterparts or competitors have it right. If so, what's the point of life? I guess we just keep doing what feels good! It does not matter if we do good; there is no such thing as Good; there is no God—I Guess. This is the thought of many "ISMS," the likes of which there are many.

While looking over other options for the heaven of eternal life we find a concoction of the many who claim they are the only way; confusion clouds our judgement. Most options beg, borrow, or steal some of what God says; they diversify or spread out their base points by using the 'subjective approach,' based on sentiment, spirits, visions, dreams they have, and or feelings.

I cannot style my theology here to suit everybody. I cannot expect everybody to approve my conclusions, I can only present my case from a beginning, Genesis, or starting point presenting the most cohesion or agreement for allowing for a universe which is dependent, reliant, or needful for the help of an Originator: Not A Nothing Concept. The way I see it, every other belief system hangs onto a By Chance Theory for our Genesis.

Initially God created the heaven and the earth. And the earth was without form, and void; and darkness was upon the face of the deep. And the Spirit of God moved upon the face of the waters. And God said, let there be light: and there was light. And God saw the light, that it was good: and God divided the light from the darkness. And God called the light Day, and the darkness he called Night. And the evening and the morning were the first day. [Genesis 1]

Statements of 'perceived truth' leave us in a quandary or dilemma, always searching for the attainable—in the bottomless pit. The precious worth of our acquaintance with proven relationships, reliable ones, allow for us to experience an assurance suggesting we are safe; our world will not come crashing down on us in a moment of time. I am not talking about the physical world all around us, it is precarious, but a world in which we know our eternal future is in good hands. This requires the Faith which is in the right column.

Belief systems, in and of themselves are feeling based unless they prove to be true through the lens of an eternal perspective. Everything we know has a beginning; we need to remember this. While this is paramount or the primary entity in every search, it can keep us in a never-ending search—like trying to find the bottom of a bottomless ocean. Are Value Calculators this essential?

Unless we find and are able to trust the one objective source with the measure of success we can depend on forever, we cannot say we have physical proof. Every one of us, Evolutionists, Atheists, Creationists and or Christians are in a never-ending physical, verbal, or temporal [time-based] battle for control in The Genesis of All Time. Time had to have had a beginning; time as we know it will have an end. So, what should we do to solve the problem? We need to find the courage to trust the beginning beyond time as we understand it.

In *Chapter Five* we will chase after more about Market Value—the amount for which something can be sold on a market: Often contrasted to book value. Who sets Market Value? Who decides what the Market Can Bear? Is it those who are only interested in higher profit margins, as opposed to allowing everybody fair access to a life free of hardship?

Who sets the Book Value? Is it the Status Quo? How far back into history, should we go to find a system any different than the one we live with every day of our lives, and will live with while waiting for "WHEN?"

The universe exists for itself, without cause or purpose. Nothing existed before it that could have been its cause. Nothing exists outside it that could be the source of its purpose. [Pantheism]

Jesus said, "I Am the Way, The Truth and The Life; no-one can come to God in any other way" [JBI John 14:6]. This option presents only one way, most other options make their point by saying Jesus is just a good man, not God, just one means of attaining Heaven

On the Jesus as son of man, Son of God, and as the whole of what God is scenario, there is only one path, as opposed to many paths to the heaven many folks declare to be "the way, the truth, and life everlasting." Jesus is the object [objectivity], the only context, the Truth of it all. From this simpleton [me], this is what I believe!

We Need A Touch Of The Master Builders Hand: His Handiwork?

Awareness—What a huge concept! Question: Are We Aware of Our Existence? Are We All Really Aware of Our Existence? The capacity or size of purpose is exceptionally evident—Someone or something handled our Initiation Into Life.

Purpose Requires A Definition, The Defining of A Goal.

Let's assess for a moment, if we would, "is it even possible to have a purpose without a goal in mind." Pantheism says this, "The universe exists for itself, without cause or purpose. Nothing existed before it that could have been its cause. Nothing exists outside it that could be the source of its purpose." This is a picture of a box, a Closed System.

As I have looked at life from both sides now, I have never seen or experienced anything in the cosmos or any part of the universe which survived without a purpose or cause. [IBID]

The sun, moon, and stars each have a purpose. This means they have a causal beginning. If they existed for themselves there would be no need for people. If people had no purposeful cause, existing for themselves and themselves alone, they would not require the need for the sun, moon, or stars—people would be self-sustaining. I think no one would die. I ask, what would people call living? Living and or dying would not matter at all! "Splain it to me Lucy!" This is what Ricky, on the *I Love Lucy Show* said when Lucy had done something off-centre, off-the-wall, or something displeasing to him. Often we venture through life too fast to grasp the need to recheck the purpose we began our journey with.

When we take the time to look at the life we know, from each our own perspective of our upbringing, from the way circumstances have changed the perspective we were taught, and we see it from every angle, the picture we see is huge. There are more rules in life than we care to accept or adhere to, this I know for sure. One rule links to another, so it is hard to pull rules and or disciplines apart and say one can stand or exist without some part of the other. We follow some rules voluntarily, without argument. Our bodies are ruled by a few necessities, such as eating and sleeping; we do not mind this. If we challenge these rules for too long, we will feel the blows of ignoring proper eating and sleeping habits.

Eating and sleeping go hand in hand. These are a part of the Laws of Nature. Who or what handles the Laws of Nature? Who or what initiated the Laws of Nature?

God did not create the laws of nature; the laws of nature are a part of God. To get an understanding of what God is, think of Him as the laws of nature. You are halfway there. Now, add love to the laws of nature, and you are 3/4 of the way there. Now add a way to live and keep enough room for a train load more understanding. Now you know what God is. We need to remember God created this universe, so it belongs to Him. He runs it by His rules and not ours. Anyone who can create a universe which includes living humans, knows how to run it [Herman Rhodes—I changed a few words].

The Characteristics of God and The Laws of Nature: 1] The Laws and God Are Both Absolute Truth. 2] Both The Laws and God Are In A Spiritual Realm. 3] Both The Laws and God are Unchanging. 4] Both The Laws and God Exist Throughout The Universe. 5] Both The Laws and God Were First In Order. 6] Both The Laws and God Cannot Be Added To or Taken Away. 7] Both The Laws and God Are Eternal. 8] Both The Laws and God Can Be Proved (if you are smart enough to understand proof)."

I kinda like how Herman Rhodes explains these thoughts about the Laws of Nature. Are they politically correct in every way the Bible speaks of things about God, who am I to say, the Bible tells the whole story? However, I am taken aback by these words written here by Herman Rhodes.

While reading these thoughts, I thought "How Awesome" God is. God is truly "Above All!" Kudos to you Herman for sharing your thoughts so neatly. Within a Selah Time [Pause], if I take the time to hear what the words are pointing me to, I can hear whispers of what the whole of Creation is speaking to the whole of what time is all about. I often hear more than whispers. I often hear a booming voice. No, I do not hear an audible voice sounding like a loud thunderclap. Some people say they've heard an audible voice, who am I to say. I have never heard an "audible called at the line of scrimmage." [For The Football fans] I realize not everyone is a sports fan, and I do use some sports analogies, but even those who are not sports fans might understand the gist of what I say here.

God Is Life and Above All: God Is Enough

Above All speaks to a capacity, dimension, quantity, mass, or breadth of a measuring tool, device, or other means which often leaves me wondering if I will ever understand what it means. Most often these few simple words of the song, *Above All*, speak volumes [a play on words for me, as I am a writer]. Let's look for a moment at what it means when we speak about Volumes, or when we speak Volumes. We are not just addressing something or someone singularly [individually]. Someone said, "The World Is Our Classroom." When I hear this I feel an extension of importance arise in my spirit regarding these words.

The synonyms for Volume here are in a noun form, an entity, or a thing, and they look like this: Capacity, amount, figure, number, quantity, size, total, aggregate, body, bulk, compass, content, contents, dimensions, extent, mass, object, cubic measure—and there are many more related word, but these will bring my message across. Briefly, the antonyms or opposites of "Volume" "are, letter, individual, one."

The reason I extend or lengthen thoughts of the word volume, is so we can at least try to grasp the scope of my intent in this, *Chapter Four: Book Value Reality: What Is Reality?* Definition is imperative for us to best be able to answer the questions. It pays to establish a plan to help others see the perspective or standpoint from which we extend or spread-out our philosophy, whatever it may be. We ought to have a fixed point from the past to find a beginning of all things. Without a fixed point we are left flapping in the wind of time without a field to land on.

Added to this we should have a fixed position on the end of or culmination of all things as we believe this to be. Then, to bring validity to this in each our own belief system, we should compare these beliefs to other mainline objective based value systems we have in place before us in the community we call the world. Our best understanding comes full circle when we have the bird in the hand. The relevance of what we gain exists not when the cheque is made out in our name, but when we go to the bank for the cash, and the cash is there waiting for us to do as we would with this bounty.

Individuality speaks of exclusivity, singularity, and could extend towards selfishness: "It's all about me!" This is a peek at the opposite of "Volume [inclusivity]." Although God is one, He freely expresses Himself to us so we can more easily understand Him if we open our eyes and ears.

Yes, God is One, but He is also "ample" in His stretched-out capacity towards us; He is a Spirit; but He is by no means selfish, although He is exclusive in His purpose for all life throughout all time as we know it and into the Eternity we may not grasp. Genesis One tells us "The Spirit of God moved upon the face of the waters." Right at the beginning of Biblical time as some understand it, we are told how God executed the purpose He had throughout the infinity of His existence.

We can see the individuality of purpose here, but in another sense, we can see God is not a loner, individual in purpose, only to present Himself as "only out for Himself" with an "all about Me mentality." Alongside all of life, God is *Above All*, in every sense because He is and always has existed. "He is The First and The Last, The Beginning and The End." Again, though this is true, He says, if we believe in Him, give ourselves to Him, we will someday be like Him [not be Him], because we will finally see Him as He is. "Our Value" is a priority with God—these thoughts are real!

Let us make man in our image, after our likeness: and let 'them' have dominion over the fish of the sea, and over the fowl of the air, and over the cattle, and over all the earth, and over every creeping thing that creepeth upon the earth. [Genesis 1:26 KJV]

—Unto us a child is born, unto us a son is given, and the government shall be upon his shoulder: and his name shall be called Wonderful, Counselor, The mighty God, The everlasting Father, The Prince of Peace. [Isaiah 9:6, KJV]

These pictures help us imagine the position of the worth God wanted for us in The Garden of Eden, but we chose not to accept the Superior Value of God's all-knowing Character. I see God The Father, The Son [Jesus], and The Holy Spirit of God projecting to us an invitation to have full access to all He planned for us. How sweet it is when we are invited to the "Inaugural Ball;" well not the one we think of as in the election of The US President; you know, just the special invite to a special moment in life!

Volume look like this: Capacity, amount, figure, number, quantity, size, total, aggregate, body, bulk, compass, content, contents, dimensions, extent, mass, object, cubic measure—and there are many more related words, but these will get my message across. Briefly, the antonyms or opposites of Volume are, letter, individual, one.

Every plan, if it has a specific purpose, must also have definitive and or detailed boundaries if it is to complete its purpose as planned or initially orchestrated. The boundaries may be hard to understand because some folks say we are not limited. It may be all right to think and say we can do anything we put our mind to.

However, logic and or common sense has the means to tell us there are some things we do not have much of a chance at becoming even when we are really open-minded and or liberal thinking people. Even though every one of us on the path of life may wish to be the President Of the United States of America, there can be only One President. Boundaries force us to see this is not only a limiting reality in one respect, yes, but it actually also frees us to be in the big picture of what we were scoped out to be in the overall plan of life, without thinking we have to do everything—causing us undo grief.

So, I believe that within the life we live and call our mandate for life, each one of us are restrained from being anything and everything we may wish to be. This is a picture of boundaries we should not try to reach past. We need to find our niche or calling in life and stay within those boundaries. This requires we follow guidelines and or rules. We have already discussed rules to a considerable degree, but it does not hurt to be cognizant of them on a moment by moment basis; they present us with a benchmark.

I am not suggesting we should have no vision to reach past where we are at; if this is the plan of God! What I am saying about boundaries does not mean we should limit ourselves to being only Poor Little Old Me. In context, this may spread itself out as if detailed for specific wish or dream on our Bucket List. Often, we have too many items on our Bucket List and we suffer the consequences of it; sometimes in hazardous ways. Priorities can be huge helpers if we adhere to following the rules of doing first what is most important.

We cannot claim we are living out God's Rule on the one hand and blatantly, deliberately, or obviously disobey what is His plan, as we expect glorious success on His path. If we leave out a proper relationship with God, His will and plan will not fit into the box we have created for Him to fit into. God is to Voluminous or Huge in purpose for all of Creation. He will do it His way; God does not Flip-flop on His overall plan.

> So shall my word be that goeth forth out of my mouth: it shall not return unto me void, but it shall accomplish that which I please, and it shall prosper in the thing whereto I sent it. [Isaiah 55:11 KJV]

To have a leg to stand on, God's plan demands complete commitment to Him and His Rule, Plan, Purpose, and or Promise. Without this we may fail to achieve enough to receive the full benefit package in the everlasting sense. Sure, when we fail to follow the rule, God is gracious and forgiving when we realize we have strayed, and we ask Him for forgiveness and help. However, a flighty, variable, unreliable, and the dishonest plea from us just to get off the hook, can in-fact be hazardous to our health—physically and spiritually. Commitment, with the expectation to reap the full rewards of the promise given, requires us to repent or be sorry for our less than complete commitment, and do an about face.

A you scratch my back and I will scratch yours option never allows for us a solid foundation for living. Society today is ever changing as people move on discontented, unfulfilled, and dissatisfied with what they had yesterday. Why? Feeling based reality is no reality. Sensation built or subjective principles are wishy-washy. "If you do for me," then I will feel satisfied, maybe, to do the said same for you. This may work for a while, but it never carries the day. God does not operate by these rules.

Synonyms for reciprocity are cooperation, exchange, mutuality, reciprocation, trade-off, switch, barter, substitute, remuneration, satisfaction, amends, compensation, indemnity, recompense, restitution. What pictures do we see regarding compensation and Restitution? In compensation, we receive from someone, and in restitution we extend our self to giving by helping to fix something we had a part in damaging.

We need others to offer or contribute reciprocity and or mutuality, for us to fulfill a plan or purpose. As we have just looked again at the synonyms for reciprocity, we can readily see we can accomplish nothing on our own. We may suggest we did something all by ourselves; in the immediate sense this may be true. However, when we break down everything which got us to where we suggest we did it all on our own, it should become obvious; if someone else had not done this, that, and the other someone else had not done this or that before that—we would not be here at the moment to do what we thought we did "All By Ourselves." Some interchange of ideas or some other entity preceded the reality of our moment in the spotlight.

Reciprocity and its buddies, cooperation, exchange, mutuality, reciprocation, trade-off, switch, barter, substitute, satisfaction, indemnity, recompense, restitution—are nouns which determine a certain reality. A noun facilitates or eases us into a situational word, the sense of which governs or limits us within the context of the story of reality. Nouns deliver the terms of existence for all things—people, objects, sensations, feelings, etc. There is no unswerving verb form for the noun 'reality.' We come close to offering up a verb when we say we realize something—actively.

The noun needs the verb to do anything. The noun by itself is just a thing. A knife is a thing, a word is a thing. For a knife to present its best face it needs to do something, it needs to cut something else, and someone needs to do the cutting—a person—another noun. A word is a noun, but when we add an action to it, it says something in spoken or written ways. A word speaks loudly in so many ways. We can lay the word "Love" on a scrabble board and it speaks volumes when we put reality to work in the lives of two people who have formed a lasting relationship. We cannot say "poor little old me" had to do it all alone. Do you see it all coming together? Love at work looks somewhat like cooperation, exchange, mutuality, reciprocation.

Compensation [restitution]—we can receive compensation from someone—or pay restitution to cover a wrong someone encountered—we compensate [a verb] them. Nouns and verbs relate continually to help make the world go around. When we pay it forward, we may ensure we have a good attitude about life.

Making amends sees us outspreading ourselves to open-handedness in finding a solution to something we had a part in destroying. When we reimburse someone for a loss we caused, we are giving back. What a beautiful picture of living life in relationship. Relating nouns and verbs in relationships: How exciting could this be? Maybe small things do amuse little minds.

All along the way we are creating effective purpose. The more I look into the Bible, and what it speaks all the way through the sixty-six books making up the Bible as we have it, the more I get past what seem to be 'The Rules' we balk at occasionally. I see a picture of the relationship: God with us and us with God. What a beautiful picture this is. Yes, we are servants, but according to God, He thinks of us as Friends.

As we stretch out our lives from the past, we do not know [before we were born, in God's personal time], to the past we know, to the realization of what we have today in the present and go beyond the present to the future we do not know or understand, we find what we know is not enough to satisfy our wants or needs for the tomorrow we do not know. This is where Reality comes into the picture before us to allow us to set, establish and or fashion a course of living helping us to find the tomorrow we crave.

Book Value Reality: What Is Reality. It is easy to fashion a Chapter title sounding good; one offering a solution to the temptations to go it alone. There is a temptation to Go It Alone without God—ineptly, inadequately, or partially. But many things come into play as we open ourselves to a serious look at adeptly, adequately, or completely, to give reality a free hand to work in each our individual lives, and the lives of other people. What are the mysteries reality may hold; what we think it may hold as we struggle through our own strength; this is the bridge we need to find, explore, and then cross over to get our satisfaction about 'reality?'

If we never consider the thought that reality has an 'attachment,' an extreme benefit—why bother setting a plan to search for it. It is not a matter of trying to figure out if reality has any merit attached to it, this is a given. Reality attaches its own costs, based on how we observe to do life. We can try to fashion a course which will give us the pride factor we think we need to boost our egos. Reality will spread out the costs based on the false sense of security which boosting our ego will present. The Good Life is not necessarily best attained by taking the road less travelled, the lonely one, because the visible wear and tear is missing.

When we take the road less traveled, we will experience challenges differing from the road most travelled, in the right sense of usage attached to both roads. The road most traveled gives us the option of taking the paths others carved out for us, making it easier to get to our destination. Sure, we will still need to travel the path; experience the pains and the joys of the journey for ourselves; this is the cost of Reality. This process increases the application of our lives to ourselves, but with the purpose in mind of being a part of increasing the value of the people around us as we 'make the journey together.' Many years ago now I had a first-hand experience which showed me the reality of just what I have been talking about.

Now, what about the "Road Less Travelled?" On one vacation I took I stopped at Marble Canyon in the Kootenay Park of British Columbia. I had often passed by it on the highway, but I had never explored the tremendous beauty of the handiwork which God has displayed here. As I walked the path which kept me climbing higher and higher, I related to everything having a meaning. I always look for what God is trying to say through the things He shows me on the physical level.

When I first stood at the bottom of the path leading to the mountaintop, I thought to myself, it would be nice to get there, but it seemed as though it was an impossibility. As I walked the path, I realized it was possible to negotiate the climb. Instead of having to grab onto trees, and ledges on the rock surface to make what seemed to be a hazardous ascent, there were actually steps rustically carved into the mountainside so I could make the climb more easily. It made me think for a while, 'Life is a breeze,' this is not always so.

Climbing usually has me out of breath quickly. Even though it was a steady grade to walk, I did not find it strenuous. Someone had made it easy for me to get to where I could see the beautiful spots; I could have gone right to the top. Someone else made a path on which I could walk until I got to where the mountaintop was not so high anymore. It was becoming a plateau, which was attainable. You might have been there yourself. You might have seen how the water has carved its way through the limestone rock to create beautiful sculptured shapes into the mountainous terrain. It may have spoken to you.

I would like to share with you, what it spoke. I realized it was a picture of how God leads us through our Christian [our walk as Christ Followers] journey. When God saves us, we are at the bottom looking up to the high plateau. We probably may think it impossible to get there unless someone makes a path for us to follow. I walked up the mountainside with more ease. It became evident that it could have been much tougher. If the designer of the path had not wanted to put as much effort into it, he, or she, could have just gone up and down it a lot, so the people who would come later could see there was a path. Here, we would be gripping for trees, rock ledges, and whatever else we could do to make the strenuous climb. However, what actually happened was, other people made it easy for us to envision reaching the top.

It was a laborious task for someone else, but it was a cinch for me. People in the work of God help us get through life. When God salvages us from the ruins of sin, other people make steps along the pathway, so we have a hope of making it to the top. These people can go under the name of: Pastor, Evangelist, Teacher, Apostle, Parent, Son, Daughter, or maybe Friend. As they begin to be like the water which comes from the top of the mountain, they carve out ledges for steps so we can make the trek. These people teach, show by example, and cause us to avoid some of the dangerous drops by making a path around the tough spots. They make the climb easier because they give us only as much as we can handle at the moment.

Some people make the climb too hard, giving us too much to carry. By so doing, we break down under the load. This is why we have caregivers, not slave drivers. Jesus said,

Come unto me, all ye that labor and are heavy laden, and I will give you rest. Take my yoke upon you and learn of me; for I am meek and lowly in heart: and ye shall find rest unto your souls. For my yoke is easy, and my burden is light. [Matthew 11:28—30]

Every so often I came across a bridge. If someone had not built a bridge, I would not have gone any further. But someone built a bridge so I could carry on, ever reaching for the top; yes, there were limits, but they offered opportunities to reach the top.

Christ builds the bridge; usually He uses people to be the needed instruments of service. At some point, we may just go along as the observer, and the learner. But with each step we take we also tell or show someone else they have a chance of reaching the top.

My trip to "Marvel Canyon" [Notice The Change From Marble To 'Marvel'] made me realize again, God did not place us here to be showpieces. Even the handiwork of nature is not just a viewpoint: It continues to reproduce. I just realized again this morning, now many years later, everything which is built into life, houses, cars—and yes, even we finite humans, came out of the ground, as per what we read in Genesis of The Bible. All the minerals, trees—came out of the ground. So when God created the Universe, He did know what He was doing.

Surprise, Surprise, Surprise!

INTERMEZZO

In this reflective 'SELAH' TIME, I stop my editing for a few moments [whatever amount of time this is,] and I worship God for Who He is. I read some scripture to put God at the very top of my thoughts. In this Chapter Intermission I found the Song *In His Time*, on You Tube, and sang along; this song had been in my spirit for a few days already, in preparation for this time of editing. I close my eyes and sing as if singing to God!

To everything there is a season, and a time to every purpose under the heaven: A time to be born, and a time to die; a time to plant, and a time to pluck up that which is planted; a time to kill, and a time to heal; a time to break down, and a time to build up; a time to weep, and a time to laugh; a time to mourn, and a time to dance; a time to cast away stones, and a time to gather stones together; a time to embrace, and a time to refrain from embracing; a time to get, and a time to lose; a time to keep, and a time to cast away; a time to rend, and a time to sew; a time to keep silence, and a time to speak; a time to love, and a time to hate; a time of war, and a time of peace.

What profit hath he that worketh in that wherein he laboureth? I have seen the travail, which God hath given to the sons of men to be exercised in it.

He hath made everything beautiful *In His Time*: also he hath set the world in their heart, so that no man can find out the work that God maketh from the beginning to the end. [Ecclesiastes 3: 1-11; KJV]

Verse 11 speaks to me to say, God "Has Made All Things Beautiful In His Time;" not in my time; not the time I use for 'ME. What it amounts to here is I need to have the kind of Faith which says, "LORD, I Trust You Implicitly!" Right Now!

The song, plays out like this, "*In His Time*." The just of it says, "*In His Time*—" Then the writer expresses words which say this to me, "Everything He Made and or Makes, Is Beautiful!" "*In His Time*—" Then, I hear thoughts which say, "As you show me the way to go, and as You teach me, assure me You Keep Your Promises!" The wrap is, "*In His Time*." Find the song and sing along. I try not to rush back to working this Chapter.

The Following Will Still Be Here After I Worship GOD!

If Adam and Eve had listened to God in The Garden of Eden; chosen to eat of the Tree of Life, instead of the tree of Knowledge of Good and Evil; life would have been different for us. We would not have had to scrimp and scrape to get by, to get what we needed, and yes, our wants would have differed greatly. Make No Mistake About It, we would have done Life differently. Life would not have been about the pride of doing things alone and our own way. Yes, it might have been different: "But It Ain't Yet."

The waters of Marble Canyon are always moving along. Sometimes they come up high to shape the rock up high. Other times, the water recedes, so it can work on the rock that is lower in the chasm. Caregivers are just as we read about in Proverbs 4:18: "She is a tree of life to them that lay hold upon her: and happy is everyone that retaineth her." The caregivers I am referring to are like this because they light the path by being instruments in the hands of Jesus. I would just encourage you to keep your eyes open. God may just try to say something to you. He is always talking, but sometimes many of us are just not listening. I just about did not listen when He said, "Stop here at Marvel Canyon for a while." Why did He even take the time to ask me to stop there? Well, it was my fault. On my way home from Invermere, B.C. I asked Him to speak. Once again, He was faithful, and He spoke. "For He, that hath mercy on them shall lead them, even by the springs of water shall he guide them."

The life of a Christ Follower is the best thing my Creator ever thought of. If everyone who was ever born had lived it, life would be a paradise. This concept became The Impossible Dream when sin entered into the picture. To have a dream without ever seeing any hope of its fulfillment is not an inviting scene. The Bible compares life with a runner running a race. This is the most accurate description of my life. Sometimes it seems as if I am running and running without ever knowing where the finish line is, or if there even is a finish line.

The Road Less Traveled explained—well, there are many experiences I have travelled—physical roads, spiritual roads, and subjective or feeling based roads on which I took a path other folks have traveled. Often these roads were not so clearly marked out and prepared, for the moment I was in. Sometimes, for me, it was *The Road Not Taken Before*.

Part One—The Launching Pad

I was born in the small town of Steinbach, Manitoba, Canada. I lived the first four years of my importance, on a farm. I should not have been around long enough to write this book, except for the healing power of God, when I was young. However, God wanted me to be an example for someone to learn from so they could be illustrated for another part of humanity, in their saga.

I was also raised in a family where struggles were a part of everyday life. Then I extended to where I had women troubles, money troubles, and the same troubles you had. One of the woman troubles I experienced was when I was about twelve. I was just a shy young lad who could hardly look someone else in the face without turning red as a fireball. One day, one girl in my neighborhood called me on the phone. When my sister, 'of all people,' told me there was a girl on the phone for me, I headed out the door and down the alley as fast as I could maneuver the obstacles in my way. It was not toward her house. It was in the opposite direction. Call me crazy, but yes, "I missed an opportunity;" as Lady Luck would have it, or not? My sisters did not hesitate to tease me; yes, I blushed all the way down the alley.

I am married now, so some things must have changed. If memory serves me correctly, Jacob of The Bible had woman problems too. The names and situations were different; the usefulness for historical or spiritual purposes did not differ in the least. God used incidents about the women in my life [mostly the woman in my now life] to fashion me for purposes useful to Him.

Some people have glanced at me to see what I am like. Yet others, have looked and thought, "He is a cheat, a liar, a deceiver." Another segment of society may have seen me as the person from whom they could learn a positive lesson. Though I have done many rotten things, I have done right things. All these are set out as part of the learning process.

I was young once. I had hopes and dreams. I sang in the church and I did some speaking when I went out on the evangelistic field with my pastor. I had hoped to go to Bible school and become a preacher: 'It Never Happened.' My discouragements caused me sixteen years of wandering from the presence of the LORD. Jacob Israel had hopes and dreams when he left home to find a bride. Things did not pan out like he had hoped for. He was not walking in the presence of the God of his Fathers. He had his down times.

I have taken the time to contemplate the scenario of my short story. I will put it on a hypothetical video for you. As my life began, I see myself as being as if it were a car headed off in a direction away from God. Sometimes my parents were behind the driver's seat, so the forces of self-destruct did not take all the disastrous turns I might have taken on my own. I jerked the wheel away from them and hit a few trees. However, they would gain control, and pull the car back on the road again. It was a good thing there was always somebody available to help. When I review some of my life, once again as often is the case, I find myself Very Thankful to have had those others in my life. I could not have done life without "YOU!" 'You People,' are travelers who are still here, some far and wide away in locations I know nothing about; maybe even people I never knew in ways only God knows. 'You People' Are Important To Me! Some of these important people have died, but I think of them too.

I became a Christ Follower when I was twelve. However, I did not let Him [Christ] have complete control of me, there were still a few bumps in the road now and again. I began serving Christ, but I was young and did not always stay on course. I ignored the advice of the LORD at times and got a few off-road experiences.

I guess I thought if I couldn't be perfect when God was in my life, He must have done something wrong, for that to happen. I thought I would manage life on my own. In 1965 I began a sixteen-year hiatus, I took a sixteen-year detour. Wish I hadn't; wish I had stayed the course! As if driving a car, I picked up speed, hit a few trees here and there [hypothetically], I had a few fender benders [hypothetically], and rolled the car [true in a sense, my friend was driving my car and rolled it]. However, that did not stop me. Although everything was going against me, I kept speeding right along. In 1981, sixteen-years later, I came to a place where I was as if heading 150 mph toward a crevasse. I could see it now. I knew I had survived many dangers, by the grace and mercy of God!

Do you remember the old James Dean movies? The fifties were exciting times. I remember seeing movies where the young people would play chicken. Sometimes it was to impress the girls; while in other instances, it was just to prove to each other who was the bravest. I can see them now as they lined up at a certain distance from the edge of the gorge. They raised the R.P.M. of the engines, and I see two teenagers ready to play chicken.

Part One—The Launching Pad

The idea is for both to race toward the edge of the cliff. The first one to put on the brakes is chicken. I was never physically involved in this demonstration of my manhood. It was a picture of this magnitude, which I saw for myself in 1981. There was no stopping me now. However, when I came almost to the very edge of the gorge, something within me said; "You had better put on the brakes right now, before it is too late to stop." [Hypothetically]

If I had not listened to the word of the LORD, which said, It is time for you Jacob to "Stop The Car:" [I am thinking of the Ikea Commercial]," I felt I would have been at a point of no return. Until this point in time I had incurred damages. It was as if I had ripped out the under carriage of the car when I came screeching to a halt at the edge of the cliff. It was as though I were teetering at the edge of what could have been a bottomless pit. I felt trapped in the car, pushing all my weight to the back, so the car would not go over the precipice. The next move was up to the Master Driver whom I had ejected from the driver's seat sixteen years earlier. It was He, who distributed the weight to allow me to exit the car and plant my feet on solid ground again. Once I was safe the car went over; I saw the wreckage it caused.

"Back To Present Reality!" When I took a trip out to the mountain's years later, I understood how great the danger had been. I worked my way down a steep slope to get myself as close as I could to the edge of a certain cliff. I wanted so badly to see right over the edge and get a look like the eyes of an eagle would see. I wanted to see what was at the bottom of that gorge. Suddenly, something within me said, "You had better not get any closer, trust Me. If you move in for a closer look, you will be at the bottom of the gorge, and you won't see anything ever again, in this life!"

I took the advice of the still small voice within me, and I stepped back. From here, I could be sure that I could continue to appreciate the beauty [*In His Time*] of all that was at the bottom of that crevasse. It was beautiful; there was also danger. I learned of the danger which can present itself when one gets too close to the edge. Some people like living on the edge. I am not that adventurous. As I sat on some logs near the edge of this beautiful gorge in the Rocky Mountains I thought, if this is the scenario I was in just before the LORD got my attention in 1981, I was in serious trouble. Like most of us, trouble may often have been our middle name.

If I listed some irreparable wreckage caused by me being out of control, first on the list of importance was, I missed the best God had prepared for me. Another thing I could not repair was the broken relationship I had with my first wife. A child was involved in this marriage. Many other things were lost because of the years I spent speeding around in my old jalopy [so to speak]. If my life had stopped there and nothing else had taken place in my life, I could have been thankful that God spared my life. Still, living on from there without having something to replace the losses, would have been tough. God builds us with the need to have relationships.

The LORD has restored my relationship with Him. He has given me back a relationship with a woman, the name has changed, but He has once again blessed me with a good wife. I did not run away when she phoned! We're nearing fifty-years together.

We have married children, grandchildren [all getting too big, no small ones anymore] and two great grandchildren. I have felt the blessing of the LORD while writing. The preaching goal of ministry seems gone. But He has replaced it with something that I love to do, "I love to write." What lies ahead for me, I do not know, but one thing I know for sure is, "IF" God has repaired and rebuilt my life, and He has, He will not quit until my race is finished.

This thrills me. One big question I had, that I have found the answer to, is this, "What allowed for the changes which took place in my life?" Some people never stopped praying, people like my parents. Joining them was a host of other people called friends. Added to this list were a few shepherds who prayed for the sheep who had strayed. Hopeless as it may have seemed, they kept on the prayer line; they called out a few AUDIBLES at the line [again, a football analogy] to Him that Matters most: God The Father, in The Person of Jesus Christ The Son, through the work of The Holy Spirit! Believe It Or Not; Like It Or Not; this is the way it is in my life and has been now for many years: "I Kinda Like It That Way!"

I Am Looking Back To See "IF"—
"IF" You Are Looking Back To See—
"IF" I Am Looking Back At You—
Or
"IF" You Are Looking Back At Him Who Is Able

Now unto him that can do exceedingly abundantly above all that we ask or think, according to the power that worketh in us, Unto him *be* glory in the church by Christ Jesus throughout all ages, world without end. Amen. [Ephesians 3:20-21 KJV]

Now unto him that can keep you from falling, and to present *you* faultless before the presence of his glory with exceeding joy, to the only wise God our Saviour, *be* glory and majesty, dominion, and power, both now and ever. Amen. [Jude 1:24 KJV]

This is the picture of those who do not believe and live as though God Is Able: "Their idols are silver and gold, the work of men's hands. They have mouths, but they speak not: eyes have they, but they see not: They have ears, but they hear not: noses have they, but they smell not: They have hands, but they handle not: feet have they, but they walk not: neither speak they through their throat. They that make them are like unto them; so is everyone that trusteth in them." [Psalm 115:4-8 KJV]

The LORD, changes everything: "Tremble, thou earth, at the presence of the Lord, at the presence of the God of Jacob, Which turned the rock into a standing water, the flint into a fountain of waters." [Psalms 114:7 &8 KJV]

"I will restore to you the years that the locust hath eaten, and ye shall eat in plenty, and be satisfied, and praise the name of the LORD your God, that hath dealt wondrously with you: and my people shall never be ashamed." [Joel 2:25&26]

The whole scenario of my life is like a row of dominoes. It was because of prayer; God could pull out one domino so that the rush of dominoes to the edge of the gorge would stop. If someone had not pulled one domino, my car would have gone over the precipice, and I would have gone with it. In *Chapter 11* we will talk more about Dominoes.

A little while ago, I spoke of the gorge I visited in the mountains. On both sides of the crevasse were huge logs people had arranged. They were the remains of what once was a bridge over the chasm. I have been in and out of many life settings, some real and some hypothetical; no matter, "There was a whole lot of Reality in the mix of it all."

Over time, something tore down this bridge in the mountains
of Panorama where I looked over the edge into the gorge I talked
about. I do not know how they even built this bridge over troubled
waters, but the water below had taken away whatever support once
held the structure. Water is a lifeline, but it also has destructive
forces. What Christ has done in my life, is to become, "The repairer
of the breach." The Mandate, Gods Mandate, Is My Mandate! "Now
unto the King eternal, immortal, invisible, the only wise God, be
Honor and glory forever and ever, Amen." [1 Timothy 1: 17 KJV]

What Did I See, and What Does It Say?

We have traveled a long road. Every word in this Chapter
was necessary to get on to the Rest of The Story. We may think we
are *Masters of Our Own Fate*: REALLY? We can look closely at
Reality, and all that has transpired in each of us, each on our own
journey, yet not totally on our own, but only ours within the process
of life which always includes others. So, in this sense, we are not
Masters of Our Own Fate! Because of this I feel we need to take a
second look, a third look—at our lives to where life for us began in
the presence of God before we were born. To fathom an existence
in Someone's Heart before the reality of birth—I Just Say WOW!
How great does this make us feel?

"Before I formed thee in the belly, I knew thee; and
before thou camest forth out of the womb I sanctified thee, *and*
I ordained thee a prophet unto the nations." [Jeremiah 1:5 KJV]
This might just be talking about more than just to Jeremiah.
Maybe this is how it is for each of us; we are all God's product,
each of equal value.

For thou hast possessed my reins: thou hast covered me
in my mother's womb. I will praise thee; for I am fearfully and
wonderfully made, marvellous are thy works; and that my soul
knoweth right well. My substance was not hiding from thee,
when I was made secretly, and curiously wrought in the lowest
parts of the earth. Thine eyes did see my substance yet being
unperfect; and in thy book all my members were written, which
in continuance were fashioned, when there was none. How
precious also are thy thoughts unto me, O God! How great is
the sum of them! [Psalms 139; 13-17 KJV]

"But when he who had set me apart before I was born, and who called me by his grace," [Galatians 1:15 KJV]

And now the Lord says, he who formed me from the womb to be his servant, to bring Jacob back to him; and that Israel might be gathered to him— for I am honored in the eyes of the LORD, and my God has become my strength—. [Isaiah 49:5 KJV]

"Even as he chose us in him before the foundation of the world, that we should be holy and blameless before him. In love." [Ephesians 1:4 KJV]

There are many verses in The Bible that speak of how intimately God has been involved in our lives, long before we showed up, when Mom heard that first cry for help in the hospital or wherever we were born. We needed help then and we are still crying for help; sometimes we do not admit it; sometimes we have not realized we are more dependent than we can figure out right now. However, the time will come for all of us where we will know we needed God's help—I pray we do so before it is too late to do anything about it!

And this is the writing written—Thou art weighed in the balances, and art found wanting. [Daniel 5: 25-27 KJV]

Weighing or evaluating is important to figure out book value. We have been this looking at in *Chapter Four*; this has been more about us coming to understand how "Little Old We" are important to how life turns out for someone else. Yes, each us has huge extended reach, we just need to realize it and use our given Book Value in the Reality of the Life we are given, within the context of it—This is Reality! In *Chapter Five* we will be dealing with, Finding Valuable Market Value?

I Get It! —Do I really? [fully understand] Each of us is as important as the other person who seems to shine as though they are the only person of value.

Question of The Day—Do we all shine in our own way, as though we matter? Or is our light so dim that no one even sees us?

Basic, Characteristic Worth; The Practice of Worth.
This is a process to work within!

The Approach Shot

5th Chapter
Our Target and Pin Placement

For which of you, intending to build a tower, sitteth not down first, and counteth the cost, whether he have sufficient to finish it? Lest haply, after he hath laid the foundation, and cannot finish it, all that behold it mock him, saying, This man built, and could not finish. [Luke 14: 28-30]

I loved hitting a low fade to a back-right pin with the wind howling from the right. Few guys [people] could get it close because they kept it low by just putting the ball back in their stance. Playing the ball back turns you into a one-trick pony you can only hit hooks. [Lee Trevino]

I believe the target of anything in life should be to do it so well that it becomes an art. [Arsene Wenger]

Golf, What An Amazing Game; We Tend To Think A Lot About What People Think About Our Game, When We Ought To Think More About How We Can Contribute To The Team Effort Of Life!

Chapter 5
FINDING EFFECTIVE MARKET VALUE?

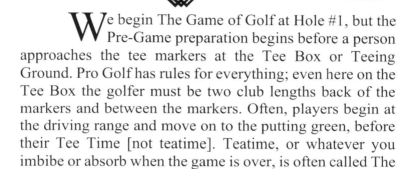

We begin The Game of Golf at Hole #1, but the Pre-Game preparation begins before a person approaches the tee markers at the Tee Box or Teeing Ground. Pro Golf has rules for everything; even here on the Tee Box the golfer must be two club lengths back of the markers and between the markers. Often, players begin at the driving range and move on to the putting green, before their Tee Time [not teatime]. Teatime, or whatever you imbibe or absorb when the game is over, is often called The Nineteenth Hole.

On the rare occasion I go golfing anymore, the idea to go golfing in the first place, comes to mind; before I get my clubs out and check over my bag to see if everything is intact—clubs are clean, I have enough tees and balls. I think for a while about some issues I often have about the functions of my game: Swing, stance—generally, how I will approach that first shot of Hole # 1; this is where there are usually the most people lined up, waiting for their tee-off; here I want to put my best foot forward—show them what I got, or most times, I want to show them I am prepared for my game that day. If this was the first time I ever played, it might not be pretty.

So, when does our preparation for life begin? What is more important, the Prep or The Game? Someone said, *You Can't Have One Without The Other!* Frank Sinatra said something about this when he sang about *Love and Marriage*, saying you needed a horse and a carriage to get out there and move on in life. If you are single, you operate with different rules, but still, rules are always there; but to get somewhere you can do so with just a horse and not a carriage. Well, this is only in the Short Term, in the big picture, The Long Term, everybody needs somebody else to make life work: *You Cannot Have One Without The Other*!

It may not be easy to determine our importance factor—we may need to check the demographics or the horizons of whatever area we are scoping to access. We need to know the pin placement of our general target for living. We can draw many comparisons for living life, by the things around us.

If we knew we could not fail, what might be our perspective—no matter what the target of our goals. Eleanor Roosevelt said, *What could we accomplish if we knew we could not fail?* When I search this phrase, I find the thoughts of many people on this subject. If I knew I could not fail, what would I endeavor to accomplish for the needs of humankind, this is a huge playing field.

The priceless value of knowing our foundation cannot crumble or disintegrate over time leaves us with an assurance all is well for the Eternity we have no way of understanding without believing that ONE GOD was and still 'Is In Charge' of all of history past, our present, and all our tomorrows: This is Faith as we know it.

Every belief system measures out the presentation of the rationality of their conviction of faith to advocate their position regarding the Genesis of all Geneses [beginnings]. We stagnate on this foundation of each our own belief, again and again. We do so because of the trust factor we can never seem to come to grips with. Who or what is the One Entity we can, without reservation, trust implicitly [completely, unquestioningly, unreservedly]? What one source or resource will suffice?

Philippians Chapter Three [The Bible] talks about the pure delight, pleasure, bliss, and total worth of the *Priceless Value of Knowing Christ [Jesus].* The Bible shows us there are reasons we need to know Christ; there are priceless merits in doing so, and it takes much preparation to do the job. Though it is a job, it is not a job: Does this make sense? Your homework is, 'work on figuring it out; if you need help, ask someone who can help you!' People get lost travelling to new places because they do not ask for directions.

I put up with the inconveniences of life because God is who He said He is, in The Person of Jesus Christ; because of what Jesus did for me on the Cross: For this I am not ashamed. If I suffer the loss of some earthly things, SO BE IT!—"For I know whom I have believed and am persuaded that he can keep that which I have committed unto him against that day."

Everybody needs someone when it comes to 'doing life.' There are no lone rangers in life. To live life efficiently, I need you and you need me! "Capeesh" [Do We Understand This?]

If I can make this clearer for us in *Chapter Five*, then I can lay me down to sleep in peace tonight and every other night, knowing I have a solid foundation for purporting or contending that JESUS CHRIST IS LORD OF ALL.

Chapter Five is pivotal. A pivot is the axis or swivel on which we hinge, like a teeter-totter. Here I am soaking up what I have been saying in the in the previous Chapters.

Chapter One: The Opening Value: Beginnings.
Chapter Two: Is The Golden Rule Pointless?
Chapter Three: Is Balancing The Book of Life, Our Job?
Chapter Four: Book Value Reality: What Is Reality?

As we remember from where we have come in this book; where we have come from inside the Book of Life; it is imperative to know there is a Beginning to everything. Solomon said it like this:

> To everything there is a season, and a time to every purpose under the heaven: A time to be born, and a time to die; a time to plant, and a time to pluck up that which is planted; [Ecclesiastes 3:1,2 KJV]

For the moment, I will not write the whole of Ecclesiastes 3; however, the rest of the story of life continues picturesquely, and we may leave it with you at another time. But for the moment we need to remember, without a beginning, without an attached value to 'this' beginning, why bother to exist at all? Without a beginning there is no existence of any sort, besides the One Who began our existence from within His Infinity or boundlessness. Our hope for the future dims if no one shares what they deem to be the truth. Someone said, how can they know if someone does not share.

What's The Point of A Golden Rule? The universe and everything in it, could never have come as far as we have, nor could we continue to survive without The Rule of Life: Not "A" Rule of Life! But "The" Rule of Life." Some prospector said, "There's Gold In Them Thar Hills." This saying dates to the California Gold Rush Days in 1849; it can bring us to a place of opportunity, but not without following the right rules; not just the promises of a false rainbow, the one that does not produce gold at its end.

If we walk out the door of our house at whatever time we do, to go to work in our car, driving in whatever way suits our fancy, if we keep it up, guaranteed, we will discover there are rules. Extend this into every part of life in the society we live in and we will soon discover there are also rules for how we live life. My guess is, Golden Rules are imperative to successful living in every society. They may vary somewhat according to what we believe if they vary from the Biblical Golden Rule.

What is interesting is, no matter which great culture we hail from, one rule remains the same for all, if we have a spiritual belief system in place for our individual lives, The Golden Rule is the same in context or content, they just differ in what they express, to say the same thing. I could list all the cultures and belief systems, but it would take too much space in this moment of the present. However, the simplest words often tell the story best. These words are plain enough for a child to get it!

Do unto and for others, what you expect as goodness and kindness towards yourself.

What does this direct us to? Is it not logical to have a source; one source for all? Moving forward into *Chapter Five*, me thinks that the basis for eternal success lies within something we might call 'Realization.' Alongside this, we need to come to a position of 'Acceptance;' everything and everybody had a beginning. *Chapter Three*: "*Is Balancing The Book of Life, Our Job?*" *Chapter Four*, "*Book Value Reality; What Is Reality?*"—these open up some avenues of life that if followed to one Principle Source, will give us the same hope, and justifiably so. What is the market share of every belief and everybody, and by what Rule?

What does the number five mean in the Bible? The number 5 is noteworthy in The Bible, and for many other reasons: People have five fingers on one hand; five toes on one foot; we have five senses: Seeing, hearing, tasting, smelling, and touching [nothing said about Common Sense here, although, if we break down the five senses we should come up with Common Sense]. This number five in The Bible leads us to see the number five as a picture of Grace [in Christian belief Grace is a portrait of the unrestricted, undeserved, and welcome favor of God, as established in the salvation of sinners and the delivery of God's blessings].

Mysteries: We are challenged with plenty enough mysteries on a moment to moment basis every day. The Bible challenges us with at least five more mysteries: Father, Son, Spirit, Creation and Redemption:

> And without controversy great is the mystery of godliness: God was manifest in the flesh, justified in the Spirit, seen of angels, preached unto the Gentiles, believed on in the world, received up into glory. [1 Timothy 3:16]

The Thesaurus gives us a few synonyms for the word mystery—puzzle, enigma, conundrum, riddle, unsolved, question, question mark, closed book, poser, and secret. This may be a misnomer or an inaccurate designation here because The Bible tells us all about God and what He has done and what He Promises us for the future. A Mystery—a secret in the NT, according to Strong's Concordance, speaks of the guidelines of God, as once being unseen by us, but now opened up to us in The Christian Gospel. If we search for truth, and listen with an open mind, we will likely find truth. The Bible speaks of God as not being far from any of us [Act 17:27].

Yes, I agree that to the many folks who have not studied The Bible and formed a Personal Relationship with God in The Person of Jesus Christ, much of The Bible appears to be a mystery. However, God has not left His followers [Christ Followers] in the dark.

> But we speak the wisdom of God in a mystery, even the hidden wisdom, which God ordained before the world unto our glory: which none of the princes of this world knew; for had they known it; they would not have crucified the Lord of glory.

> But as it is written, Eye hath not seen, nor ear heard, neither have entered into the heart of man, the things which God hath prepared for them that love him. But God hath revealed them unto us by his Spirit: for the Spirit searcheth all things, yea, the deep things of God.

> For what man knoweth the things of a man, save the spirit of man which is in him? Even so the things of God knoweth no man, but the Spirit of God. Now we have received, not the spirit of the world, but the spirit which is of God; that we might know the things that are freely given to us of God.

Which things also we speak, not in the words which man's wisdom teacheth, but which the Holy Ghost teacheth; comparing spiritual things with spiritual; the natural man receiveth not the things of the Spirit of God: for they are foolishness unto him: neither can he know them, because they are spiritually discerned.

But he that is spiritual judgeth all things, yet he himself is judged of no man. For who hath known the mind of the Lord, that he may instruct him? But we have the mind of Christ. [1 Corinthians 2: 7-16 KJV]

I realize some things in The Bible and in life itself as we know it, are hard to come to grips with. We can know of everything that matters. The Bible as we generally know it, comprises sixty-six books; the author count is forty-plus; some folks question this number. The people we see as the authors of The Bible seem to have heard from God—was it audible [clear as in them hearing a physical voice]? I believe God's voice was audible for some people; there are other means of hearing from God—Angels were one of them.

God did speak to these and many more people over our time of sojourn on this earth. History has spoken; today, life itself speaks to us; God speaks to everyone. Had God always spoken in a manner that people heard a booming voice and they could say, "I heard from God today?"

The Bible is The Word of God; it will guide us into an eternity we may not always understand. Much of this is a mystery to us because it is a puzzle, because too many folks have too many ideas about what God meant when He said, "This, That, or The Other!"

I am working on my fifth book for publishing purpose, you are reading it now! I was inspired to write it before I plunked down the many words I have written so far; my inspiration came through 'five' words that came into my mental capacity one day: *Everybody: Everybody Is A Somebody*. Did God speak in a voice such as you would speak with to me if you were you talking to me about something? NO! Do I think I was inspired to write this book in this way by God? Yes, I get inspired to do a lot of things; some are just things I am involved with every day. Inspiration for things we do or hope to do is part of who and what we are.

Because of the relationship I have with Jesus Christ, God, I am inspired to do certain other things such as writing. I am not so special I outshine anybody else because of the inspiration I had and have to write books. We are all special in the eyes of God. We all need to have a personal relationship with God to go to His House in the end. The invitation to do so is open to everybody.

Chapter 5 has me thinking of the 5th Hole in Golf. This is a play on formatting a theme of learning about God, about life, and people. I see the 5th Hole on the golf course as being like Wednesday is in the layout of the five days we generally think of as the working week [in todays world every day is a working day for someone]. On the Golf Course, there are two nine-hole groupings: Holes One to Nine, and Holes Ten to Eighteen. Hole number Five is the middle hole of the first nine holes.

As Wednesday is thought of as Hump Day, I put an importance factor on Hole #5. There is no Hump Day in the Bible so rest easy; there is no Hump Point in my book [Part One and Part Two have Five Chapters, and that's by design].

In The Beginning of Time as we know it—[Genesis], when God formed and spoke our Universe and everything in it into existence, He Kept It Simple. He said—and the evening and the morning were the First Day [not a Saturday, Sunday, or Monday] and so on through the week. As to the seventh day He did not say, The evening and the morning were the seventh day. The Seventh Day was Different—Work Ceased—It Was Time To Rest! There were no names for the days on God's Calendar.

> Thus the heavens and the earth were finished, and all the host of them. And on the seventh day God ended his work which he had made; and he rested on the seventh day from all his work which he had made. And God blessed the seventh day and sanctified it: because that in it he had rested from all his work which God created and made.

It particularly interests me how these three verses of Genesis 2 [1-3] are spoken. 'The' is a Definite Article, so this speaks as if saying, This Is For Sure. Seventh, speaks as if to say that The Work Is Over; now, I just want you to enjoy Me. I want you just to enjoy My company as I will enjoy My time with you! I think to myself "What A Wonderful Day!"

This is the day that The LORD has made.
This is the Wonderful Day Of Life!
The challenge for all of us is to remember:

GOD BLESSED THE SEVENTH DAY!

I just listened again to the song, *What A Wonderful World* as sung by Louis Armstrong. I hear the words about seeing green trees, red roses, and I see a picture of them growing and blossoming for us all; I see blue skies and white clouds; I see a day blessed, and a night that is sacred because it offers me rest from that hectic day behind me; then there are the colors of The Rainbow to enhance that blue sky; I see people going by me; shaking hands with each other, with those Five Fingers God gave them; saying Howdy, but they're saying I LOVE YOU!

"So, I Think To Myself, My, What A Wonderful World."

The Ten Commandments contain two sets of five commandments: The First Five relate to our relationship with God; The Last Five relate to our relationship with each other.

All the preliminary stuff such as The Approach Shot; The lengthy set of words before this point, all culminate in what I call *Part One*. The wrap on *Part One* is much aligned around value.

Part One: The Launching Pad

Chapter One: The Opening Value: Beginnings
Chapter Two: Is The Golden Rule Pointless?
Chapter Three: Is Balancing The Book of Life, Our Job?
Chapter Four: Book Value Reality: What Is Reality?
Chapter Five: Finding Effective Market Value?

Awareness—what a huge concept! Question, "Are We Aware of Our Existence, Really Aware?" The capacity, power, and motive of our purpose should be very evident—Someone or something handled our Intro Into Life. As I observe the feelings many people have on the topic of existence, it is evident, each person in their own belief structure, believes they have it right! Until we can seize hold of this message we leave ourselves lacking in our viewpoint or of the full scale potential each of us has to attain God's full purpose for us; if it is God's purpose we are concerned about. If we are alive, we know our existence, unless we are in La La Land.

I have looked at life from many sides; I have noticed nothing in the universe or any part of creation which is deprived of a drive or reason for existence—can anyone demonstrate otherwise? The sun, moon, and stars each have resolve; this means they have an underlying inauguration or an appointed beginning. If they occurred for themselves, people would not be necessary. If individuals had no source or determination for themselves, they would not need the sun, moon, or stars.

Though we ramble just a little from time to time, let's not forget, we are still considering market value. I will discuss this with more intent as we move along. I try to bring understanding to what I write with inserts, allowing us to form a picture. Yes, "A Picture Is Worth A Thousand Words;" we have heard it a thousand times, but to my way of thinking it will never lose value.

The words, "I saw Beautiful Scenery as I drove through the mountains of British Columbia, Canada, The Rocky Mountains," are great and descriptive words. However, they still leave me wondering if the description is as good as the communicator is trying to make it look like. Beauty is in the eye of the beholder. Take a 'still shot,' better still, a 'Video Shot' of what you saw and present me with a messaged photo of the same on my cell phone or tablet; what would I chose as the better portrayal of your trip through The Mountains of British Columbia, the World-Renowned Rocky Mountains? This is a No-Brainer Question: Think About It!

Some time ago I saw a film called, *That's What I Am*, it is a great movie from which to understand how we all fit into the landscape of 'Life Alive,' not the scenery of life itself, but how we all fit into any important live motion picture of life— words alone will never carry enough strength to narrate the whole story. As we survive life, if you would, with one another, through the ugly and the beautiful, let's not only see The Ugly. Too often the Ugly stands out like a sore thumb. This is unfortunate. Too often, what is most evident to us at first glance, are the flaws we see in other people; in this framework we make evaluations about What People Really are!

That's What I Am portrayed many people, but three people stood out for me as the key components: Mr. Simon, A Teacher wrongly attacked for being something he was not, says without explaining himself to justify himself in any way, how wrong everyone else was—he just said, *I am a Teacher, That's What I Am.*

Following this we have A Student, Stanley, Big G Minor, who, after some of the 'ugly' stuff he was hit with, declared, "I Am A Singer, That's What I Am." Stanley could have been hurt to never rebound to any value, but he simply told us What He Was. There simply was no 'quit' in Stanley.

Another student, Andy Nichol also faced the adversity of trying to fit in, and after some of 'The Through It All Moments,' he says, "I Am A Writer, That's What I Am." Andy is a part of a group of three lives that could have ended in the scrap pile of life, but he elected not to be derailed by the unfair onslaught of others. Andy knew no meaning for the word 'quit,' nor did the other two folks.

Moses was confronted with the challenge of leading a horde or a mass of people out of 'bondage' [and this covers enough content to fill a lifetime] into the "Promised Land;" he asked God, *Whom shall I say sent me*? Moses was worried about what people would think about him and his God, and what they would do to him if he did not perform up to 'their' expectations. God's reply was, "I Am, I Am that I Am!" "That's What I AM!" This needs no explanation. This is simply the WYSIWYG picture.

God said, "I AM;" "I do not need to explain that to anyone. Just look around yourselves at creation and people; if you do not see My hand at work in life and all that it holds, I Can Not Help You!" I am not putting words in God's mouth here. I am just asking us to look at life as if we are looking through the eyes of God; with the desire and expectations God has for us. [Thoughts Re John 3:16]

Words—do we just take them to mean what everyone else thinks them to mean, because those who think they know best, tell us what these words mean? Take the words "Sacred, Holy and God," put them in your thesaurus and see how they fit into the picture of the One Who declares Himself To Be, the All Sufficient One, [The One Who Can Handle Life with us if we really want that.]

Sacred: Cherished, divine, hallowed, religious, revered, solemn, spiritual, angelic, consecrated, enshrined, godly, numinous, pious, pure, sacramental, saintly, sanctified, unprofane, venerable—. Does this fit when trying to understand the "Almighty," the "First Word and The Last Word?"

When we look up the word Holy we have an extension of 'Sacred:' Please look musingly at the following.

Holy: Divine, hallowed, pure, spiritual, believing, clean, devotional, faithful, innocent, moral, "perfect," blessed, chaste, consecrated, dedicated, devoted, devout, faultless, glorified, god-fearing, godlike, godly, immaculate, just, Messianic, pietistic, pious, reverent, sacrosanct, sainted, saintlike, saintly, sanctified, seraphic, spotless, uncorrupt, undefiled, untainted, unworldly, venerable, venerated, virtuous, are equal to Holy.

I realize that many words describe things we need to reach for in our lives, but when I see the word 'perfect,' I am taken aback. Who but The Great I AM! Is PERFECT. Each of us in our own perspective of perfect, differs hugely from what perfection actually is. Perfection aligns effortlessly with Holiness. When we hear the word Holiness, relating to Someone, we should be able to relate immediately to Someone outside of the earthly.

As I stretch out the path of this journey of *Everybody: Everybody Is A Somebody*, and how it relates to 'how I think' of all those folks who do not think the same as I do, I may be called on the carpet for how I may view those opposed to my views. What is the market value of goods and services in the earthly sense? What is the market value of life in the spiritual sense?

We buy something for one price; we often use said goods to manufacture items to go on sale in a finalized format as something else because we have combined differing items to be a part of the whole of another; sometimes not recognized for the individualized product we used to fashion said item. We count our cost to produce said product to find book value, and then comes the crunch—how much is it worth on the open market?

The story of God gets so confusing as we ask questions about God. It is hard to fathom God as one who walked among us, in times past; He still does so today. Ludicrous, absurd, nonsensical; we may think: God With Us Now? Who He is, What He is, Why He is, What can He do, Why does He not do—and the list lengthens as we continue to ask questions not always justified to ask of Someone who is 'All in All!' "God is A Spirit and those who worship Him [those who worship Him understand this] must worship Him in Spirit and in truth." "The Spirit [part] of God moved upon the face of the waters" [Genesis 1]. God said, "Let us make man in our image" "In the beginning was The Word;" "The Word was God;" "The Word became flesh [Jesus], and dwelt among us." [John 1]

INTERMEZZO

Seek the peace of the city whither I have caused you to be carried away captives and pray unto the LORD for it: for in the peace thereof shall ye have peace. For thus saith the LORD of hosts, the God of Israel; Let not your prophets and your diviners, that be in the midst of you, deceive you, neither hearken to your dreams which ye cause to be dreamed. For they prophesy falsely unto you in my name: I have not sent them, saith the LORD. For thus saith the LORD, That after seventy years be accomplished at Babylon I will visit you, and perform my good word toward you, in causing you to return to this place.

For I know the thoughts that I think toward you, saith the LORD, thoughts of peace, and not of evil, to give you an expected end.

Then shall ye call upon me, and ye shall go and pray unto me, and I will hearken unto you. And ye shall seek me, and find me, when ye shall search for me with all your heart. [Jeremiah 29: 7-13 KJV]

While writing this Chapter, I see mega pictures of God's desire to share a relationship with us, one which will cover the bases from home plate, to first base, on to second, to third base, and then safely back to Home Plate: Please forgive the Baseball Scenario.

The priceless importance of knowing our foundation cannot crumble or disintegrate over time, leaves us with an assurance all is well for the Eternity we have no way of understanding without believing that ONE GOD was and still 'Is In Charge' of all of history past, our present, and all our tomorrows—This is Faith as we know it.

To everything there is a season, and a time to every purpose under the heaven: A time to be born, and a time to die; a time to plant, and a time to pluck up that which is planted; [Ecclesiastes 3:1,2 KJV]

During this Intermission I am thinking through the wonders of God—all I can say is,
"WHAT AN AWESOME GOD I HAVE!"

Someone asked the question, "Could God make a rock so huge even He could not lift it?" My Answer is NO! If God even stooped to this level to prove Himself as GOD, He would not be God, the Rock would be the God, and if the Rock did the same, and made a Rock bigger than itself, it would not be God—ETC. If all we ever do is to think of God as a physical being we will never get the answer right. This said, God was in full mode in the person of Jesus Christ on this earth; this was so He could show His Relationality, His Connectedness with us mere mortals; those whom He calls friends. His Grace, Mercy, Kindness, Love—show us He understands our frailty—God does care for us! "I suppose, I wonder, and I surmise about our actual view of God when it comes to really understanding us as He says He does; you know, as if God had skin on just like us?"

Put God in search bar in Thesarus.com and the search goes to 'god' not GOD, as the single One and Only First Cause of all humanity. Please look at the words used to describe 'god' [GOD].

> God: Allah, Jehovah, almighty, Yahweh, creator, deity, demigod, demon, [devil, fiend, evil spirit, fallen angel, incubus, succubus, hellhound, rakshasa] cacodemon [little devil, devil, fiend, hobgoblin, goblin, elf, sprite, puck, bugbear, cacodemon], divinity [divine nature, divineness, godliness, deity, godhead, holiness, sanctity, sanctitude, sacredness, blessedness], idol, lord, maker, "MASTER?" [in many of the others], numen, power, providence, soul, spirit, totem—[Now we get to more of the unconscionable thoughts to link with the following—Devil to God, go figure:] Absolute Being, All Knowing, All Powerful, Divine Being, Holy Spirit, Jah, King of Kings—. It is hard to get our heads around a God like this.

Someone said, "put that in your pipe and smoke it!"

If the beginning of all things—gravity, time, and space were capsulized into that one cell entity of all time, as some of the scientific theories suggest, what would it look like? What in reality would it be? Animate or inanimate? Me thinks it would be singular, made up of either nothing or something? Would it be an 'It?' Would it be a 'nobody,' or a 'SOMEBODY?' Would it be daft? Would it be Intelligent? Or would this entity be he or she?

Never was God's sense of total control over 'His' creation set to be less than perfect. "In 'The' Beginning—and God said," are words evident throughout 'The' Bible. Never is there any inkling of an accidental arrival of anything God said He made. What people have built, is all that God does not put His name on in-so-far-as Him saying this is part of my original plan. God can put 'His' name on it IF it was ordered by Him to fulfill 'A' purpose for what He has always known as the Whole Big Picture Plan. Everything man-made is awaiting a Big Bang Crash, not a Big Bang to start life; just the completion of God's plan to bring life as we know it and as He planned it, to the proper conclusion.

God's Responsibility was fulfilled by determination, but more than this. To build or form us [Create Us] to fit 'the' Universe He made for 'Us,' responsibility alone could not cut it, it had to be something that was part of what GOD IS! He tells Us what He expects and tells us 'the' consequences of neglecting to choose 'the' right path. Our Part—Stop, Look and Listen, and Do. Is this that hard? Can we know Him? Do we know Him?

In the previous two paragraphs I have used single quote marks [''] to emphasize a few examples of "Determiners." What are determiners? Determiners identify, recognize and spell-out things so they become truly clear in so far as telling us that "this is it," "you can count on this," and "This Is The Gospel Truth." 'Each' person is responsible to be 'a' "Determiner" of their own future by their choice of whom they will serve in this life. If we make the wrong choice in this life as to who is seated at the "Head of The Table of Life," we will never sit at God's table when this life as we know it is over. Do we have the same parameters of choice as Adam and Eve did? Were Adam and Eve special in the eyes of God? Yes! They were created for a special purpose in and for the Big Picture. However, IF we read scripture correctly, so were we!

Determiners satisfy our need for greater detail. Dictionaries define determiners as the adjustment of the many words we need to make the big picture small enough for us to grasp the things we struggle to get to our brain.

Determiners differ from pronouns. A determiner determines how to present something, like when presenting 'a' guest-speaker to 'an' audience. 'An' is indefinite, or unsure about who they are presenting this 'specific'—to 'an' 'audience,' or 'a' 'guest-speaker.'

Personal and possessive pronouns are not used as determiners. [I, you, he—personal]; [mine, yours, his, are not determiners; although 'His' according to the MS Word grammar checker says that 'His' is a determiner; go figure]. The indefinite articles 'a,' 'an;' and the definite article 'the' are used as determiners.

Determiners are in place to use before a noun to tell us if we are talking about specifics, something of a precise nature. If you would, let me do a little play on words thing. Take the word "Determiners," and divide it into two other words: "Deter and Miners." I am using the word "deter" as if I would want to keep from improperly valuing the noun to become less "specific than the sentence it is in is trying to imply. Example: Johnny can loft, fly, launch 'the' kite he got for his birthday, [('the') kite is specific, he got it for his birthday]. Another example of being a less specific determiner is, "Johnny might be able to fly, loft, launch 'a' kite on his birthday [see how the use 'a' instead of 'the' makes a difference. Using the right determiner adds to the story]." The more notability we can determine in a product, the more viable it is.

Now, I wish to use the second part of the word "Determiner:" "Miner." A miner is digging, drilling, sifting, panning for something: Coal, gems, gold. If we look at the example of a miner searching for gold we can see another example of value. Why is gold such a valuable commodity? Is it because it is so physically attractive—like a beautiful woman or a handsome dude? No, when gold is purified by fire to the nth degree, it is pure and perfect—like what God makes us when we accept Jesus.

A miner may be looking for gold on someone else's property, and they may find gold. If they have the rights to mine on the property they can keep the gold. If they do not have the rights to mine for gold on a certain property, any gold they find would not belong to them.

If we had the rights to mine 'the' gold Johnny found on the property he purchased, we can determine the greater value of the gold Johnny found. If Johnny did not have the rights to mine for gold on the property, and he dug up some gold on the property, he would lose-out on the value of the gold. Again, when we say 'the' gold Johnny dug up was of huge value, that it had huge market value, we define it as being 'Specific.'

Neil Young released *Heart of Gold* in 1972. He talks about being a miner for a heart of gold. He put effort into searching for just the right heart to have for life's significance. Neil and I are about the same age and went to the same school in our early years. I went to Earl Grey School in Winnipeg, Manitoba in 1953; Neil Young attended Earl Grey Junior High in 1963. I was 7 when I attended; Neil was 18 years old when he went to Earl Grey. He started his first band while there, "The Jades." Neil connected with Crosby, Stills and Nash, Joni Mitchell, The Guess Who—and guess who I was: Might I say, "Just Little Old Me," or did I just have a life that differed from Neil Young and 'the' others, yet still being equal!

No connections I have had, add any relevance to or for me because Neil and I were at one time in the same place. I have met other notable people during my life in some of my work capacities, but this does not make me a "Somebody!" These simply create points of interest to look at to see how we all travel different paths but retain the same built in worth; we just use what we were given, differently; this determines book value and market value.

My value, my 'Market Value,' and costs related could have been better had I lived life in the best vein of life, as if it were a 'Vein of Gold,' to determine market share. Did you think I was just relating to The Financial 'Stock' Market and Value! "Points of Interest—" these may determine how much our accumulated physical worth amounts to as we or someone else tries to define who and what we are appraised at. Interest gleaned from investments determines how much we gain materialistically. Things we invest in people's lives, for people worth, determines our 'Market Value.'

Life and death does not matter so much as to 'who we know,' but "WHO" we know when scoped-out or placed in the picture of eternity. As I look at the universe around me, and all that it contains, including people, this is what enhances my existence on this earth. Jesus said in Mathew 22: 36-40, we are to love the WHO, GOD, in all that He is, above all else in this universe. This is the first and most important Rule or Law of Life.

The second Rule or Law was to love our neighbor [everyone else] just as much as we love ourselves. This is tough, but sometimes I think it is because we have messed up on the First Rule: GOD FIRST! Until we realize how messed up we have gotten in life by our own rule, we will likely not realize we need God.

In Jewish history [as written in The Torah] there were [are] 613 laws; if we broke one of them, we may as well have broken them all. This is why every year a person had to make an animal sacrifice to atone or make up for the wrong done by them. Jesus here in Mathew 22 gives the implication that even the Ten Commandments come second to the Two Commandments listed here. The sacrifice on The Cross of Calvary, where Jesus paid the ultimate price, is enough to cover us for eternity: If we accept Him as our "First and Last, Beginning and End;" [Re Mathew 22 36-40].

God does not look down from The Lofty Heights of His Great Throne in Heaven, thinking, 'those with the most money, property, or notoriety will be more valuable to Him on this earth.' The Bible houses a story of comparison to those who were rich in earthly stock, with someone who had no earthly stock of any great worth. Someone who gave everything they had for His Kingdom on earth, actually had the greater heavenly worth. We find that story in The Bible when we search out the story of The Widows Mite.

And he said unto them in his doctrine, beware of the scribes, which love to go in long clothing, and love salutations in the marketplaces, and the chief seats in the synagogues, and the uppermost rooms at feasts: which devour widows' houses, and for a pretence make long prayers: these shall receive greater damnation.

And Jesus sat over against the treasury and beheld how the people cast money into the treasury: and many that were rich cast in much. And there came a certain poor widow, and she threw in two mites, which make a farthing. And he called unto him his disciples, and saith unto them, Verily I say unto you, this poor widow hath cast more in, than all they which have cast into the treasury: for all they did cast in of their abundance; but she of her want did cast in all that she had, even all her living. [Mark 12:38-44 — KJV]

God searches out just the right heart for us to have as a part in life. God determines the path we ought to walk on to get the best results; we choose which path we will travel; while trying to get the best market stake [not steak!] for the least cost. Sometimes we do not seek to experience life for the best-balanced cost; we go to extremes to waste life to get the most emotive satisfaction.

We use a detailed determiner, so folks can know what things or persons we are centering out for presentation. Other determiners are, 'this, that, these, those;' these are demonstratives because they demonstrate something or someone. Some possessive [possessive adjectives, describing a noun or thing] determiners are, 'my, your, his, her, its, our, their—.' There are more general determiners. I will not do a Grammar Class right now. I just want us to get an overall understanding of life. Everything in life as it maintains its own course, as in the solar system, each planet automatically tracks on the same course all the time. Who determines these wonders?

Please understand what I am saying in *Chapter Five* about The First Cause of life itself, the earthly results of life itself; these are largely determined by our choices—please understand the breakdown of how we do life. Many are the out of control items which crop up in our lives. People, who for reasons I cannot explain to everyone's satisfaction, do not seem to get a fair shake from God. According to the many folks who say, IF there is a God, why does He not fix the poverty situation, and a host of other situations in this world, the questions always seem to go unanswered.

Can science conclusively determine how life began and who or what got it going? IF it can, we may establish a Market Value to and or of the entity that science declares to be The Most Important Entity of all history. It is probably near impossible to list all known declarations of the items [THE BEGINNING] in this conversation —books, recordings of every genre, discussions, speeches; this said, be it 'Science or Its Counterpart,' if there is one, or the antonym of this, we would have to call this entity 'The Original!' Originality is hard to pin down when it comes to all the questions flying about anytime origins are discussed. It always comes down to the theoretical or the hypothesis; the theory of so many variables open to undergo experimental treatments in the laboratories, or the schools of thought. There seems to be no end to the schools of thought existing, regarding the Original Cause, or schools of thought on which is the only possible truth.

Is there such a thing as a Counterpart of Science? If we get closer to SCI-FI or SF [Science Fiction]—as it is in the world of Sean Carroll [Caltech theoretical physicist], this may be possible. There are people in this world with an imagination bigger than the number of multi-universes that are suggested by Sean Carroll.

The more we get into the world of Metaphysics, where we wonder about every conceivable theory about every conceivable entity or thing that may ever have been blasted into reality, or created, the more we get outside of The Occam Razor Principle.

Before I get ahead of myself, let me give you a snapshot of the two things I just mentioned: Metaphysics and The Occam Razor Principle. Until we come to grips with the Reality of there only being One Beginning, we will be disputing with one-another until "Hell Freezes Over!" I cannot fathom Hell Freezing Over—unless I think about Propane Gas, it is so cold it burns the skin. I know, I tried it! [Another Time, Another Story]

Metaphysics is the division of thinking [philosophy] which observes the central landscape of realism, truth, and or reality. It includes the relationship edged by mind and matter, between stuff and value, between opportunity and fact. The word 'Metaphysics,' has its origin in two Greek words, which when bonded together literally mean after or behind or among the natural: 'Metaphysics.' This is history, past, present, and future, in the 'non-physical' world. The Sciences and the Spiritual fit this picture. The differences we have in these areas is often near insurmountable, although we know that anything is possible—The Bible tells me so!

A 'counterpart' is something of equal value, running parallel to that of something else. I ask myself if there is a counterpart I could expound upon to that of market value. I can only think of the two as simply being a picture of Reality. If we put up a sign with huge lettering and it reads "Market Value," it would not matter if it were in our living room, in the desert, or in the mountains; if we put up a huge mirror in front of it, it would reflect an exact picture or a duplication of what was in front of it: A Counterpart.

The Market Value of two people is the same with their worth as a human. However, each person may come to having a higher or lower physical worth in accumulation factors. Each person may generate a different looking equality to that of another person than I can, because of the limitations I may have compared to them, but still, the value we are because of our birth puts us all equal. We are equal in this sense, in the evaluating process that God uses. Any gains [long term or short term] we achieve here on earth will be cast at the feet of Jesus at the end of the story because we are to be in this life to Worship God. Any crowns we gain, we will cast at His Feet.

There is a TV Series called *Counterpart*; about a man having what they call a Counterpart, however, in the truest sense of the word, the series does not truly represent the definition of the word "counterpart." The man in the TV Show has his 'Other,' yet, this other has different traits or characteristics than does "The Original Man" in the show. In one part of the show someone says, "I have learned to deny almost any truth." What is the truth we know about our neighbor? They live on one side of the tracks and I on the other. They have a million-dollar shack and I have a rental I pay just over five-hundred dollars a month for. Are they in better stead than I am? You be the judge!

Because the position we are at right now is the end of *Part One*, I would like us to remember that the greater portion of *Part One* is value centered on an understanding of the stock market and terms that relate to this. Though the 'Stock Market' I speak of in *Part One* is materialistically focused, I hope that the concept of the 'Personal Worth' each of us should pursue, points us to a greater worth: "An Eternal Worth."

Terms like commodity, short term gain, long term gain, bottom-line, market value, balance sheet, assets—are initially relative to the earthly stock market. As we look at these, I hope these will translate into greater value presentation in so far as helping us to understand, these terms fit rather well into the Spiritual Realm of our present life and the life we hope will be our eternity.

What Did I See, and What Does It Say?

When I determine to look back over this Chapter, I look to see if I have muddied the water of life for my reader or made them clearer, so all that matters most is visible. Jesus cleared up the value issue in these verses.

For the kingdom of heaven is like unto a man that is an householder, which went out early in the morning to hire labourers into his vineyard. And when he had agreed with the labourers for a penny a day, he sent them into his vineyard. And he went out about the third hour, and saw others standing idle in the marketplace, and said unto them; Go ye also into the vineyard, and whatsoever is right I will give you. And they went their way.

Again he went out about the sixth and ninth hour and did likewise. And about the eleventh hour he went out, and found others standing idle, and saith unto them, why stand ye here all day idle? They say unto him because no man hath hired us. He saith unto them, Go ye also into the vineyard; and whatsoever is right, that shall ye receive.

So when even was come, the lord of the vineyard saith unto his steward, call the labourers, and give them their hire, beginning from the last unto the first. And when they came that were hired about the eleventh hour, they received every man a penny. But when the first came, they supposed that they should have received more; and they likewise received every man a penny.

And when they had received it, they murmured against the good man of the house, saying, these last have wrought but one hour, and thou hast made them equal unto us, which have borne the burden and heat of the day.

But he answered one of them, and said, friend, I do thee no wrong: didst not thou agree with me for a penny? take that thine is and go thy way: I will give unto this last, even as unto thee. Is it not lawful for me to do what I will with mine own? Is thine eye evil because I am good? So, the last shall be first, and the first last: for many be called, but few chosen. [Matthew 20: 1-16 KJV]

Does Market Value react differently in one demographic than it does in another demographic. Are we who have much in the countries of Canada, The USA, Europe—better than any others who may be begging on the streets of Calcutta, where Mother Teresa worked joyfully to minister to the folks in these dire straits? God has no counterpart; we who are humans, have equals. Everyone on earth is our equal; what differs in each of us is how we react to the Words of Jesus. God is not partial to the person with many resources, and the right skin color [differing in how we look at people of a differing race than our own sometimes]. Partialities and impartialities are huge demonstrations of part of what constitutes being a Christ Follower. Sadly, because of our right to choose a preference on theoretical, objective, and spiritual philosophies, and the biases involved, we do not always present well.

Weighing or evaluating is important to figure out book value. We looked at this in *Chapter Four*; this has been more about us coming to understand how 'Little Old We' are important to how life turns out for someone else. Yes, we are each of a huge importance to life, we just need to realize it and use our given Book Value in the reality of the life we are given, within the context of it: This is Reality! In *Chapter Five* we dealt with, *Finding Effective Market Value?*

Market Value—The amount for which something can be sold on a market often contrasts with book value. Who sets Market Value? Who decides what the Market Can Bear? Is it those who are only interested in higher profit margins, as opposed to allowing everybody fair access to a life free of hardship?

Who sets the Book Value? Is it the Status Quo? How far back into history should we go to find a system that is any different than the one we live with every day of our lives, and will live with while waiting for 'WHEN?'

Just this morning my wife and I were surmising the high cost of everything and how the products to help people with life in the many ways this presents itself, have what we think of as "Market Value," and to allow for the highest "Profit," the margins are often as high as five hundred percent more. This seems hugely wrong when we think of the many folks who cannot afford to pay the high prices to live life above just surviving.

PART TWO

WHO BELIEVES WHAT?

AND

WHY?

Maybe, I or We, need to be a rocket scientist to figure it all out. At the beginning of space exploration, much of the knowledge base of today was unknown. In comparison, one might say we were "flying by the seat of our pants" in the beginning, based on the technology in our present resource-pool. In the beginning of space exploration, rockets were inferior in comparison to the rockets of our day, so, the dangers may have been greater as well.

The first rocket which could fly high enough to get into space was the V2 missile, which was first launched by Germany in 1942. The first rocket which actually launched something into space was used to launch Sputnik, the first satellite, on October 4, 1957. The rocket that launched Sputnik was a R-7 ICBM rocket.

Today's [2020] Offering is, The Space Launch System (SLS), is, a US super heavy-lift expendable launch vehicle, which has been under development since its announcement in 2011. It is the primary launch vehicle of NASA's deep space exploration plans, including the planned crewed lunar flights of the Artemis program and a possible follow-up on a human mission to Mars. SLS replaces the Constellation program's Ares V launch vehicle of 2005, which never left the development phase.

Rocket Scientists have made considerable advances since 1942. Sometimes, I think I have made considerable advances in the knowledge base of life, 'and I have;' however, as I compare myself using the vernacular [language] of the scientist, rocket or otherwise, I want to crawl into a small hole and hide. 'Smarts' come in a huge variety of categories, but they do not come in packages of greater Human Worth, as in one person's quality of inception being less than another persons. Higher degrees of knowledge carry a higher degree of "Responsibility" to get it right and pass it on "Rightly!"

MULTICULTURALISM
MULTICULTURAL
MULTICULTURE

Multiculture: This word, as I write it, seems to be a conundrum. Many thesauruses hesitate to tackle giving a definition and or description of this word; rather, their decision is to direct me to their alternate—multicultural and multiculturalism. Wiktionary is one of the only brave enough souls to tell me what 'multiculture' means [countable and uncountable, plural multicultures]. A culture is made up of many heterogeneous [varied or diverse] elements—a multicultural society or collective. Wiktionary tells me that 'multiculture' is a noun.

Maybe I, or We, Need To Be A Rocket Scientist To Figure It All Out!

In April 2019 Merriam-Webster added six-hundred and forty new words to their "Smart Book [my concoction or defining presentational phrase for dictionary!]" My penchant or fondness for learning while I am writing, led me to discovering that McGraw-Hill has a learning program called *Smartbook 2.0* under a heading called *CONNECT*. However, when I used these words, "Smart Book," I was unaware of this idea.

So, when I want to use the word 'Multiculture,' I am not too far off track from the adventure that Merriam-Webster uses to enhance our knowledge base by continually adding 'New Words' into our lives. Hey, IF, or AS we go back in time, we had a lot fewer words in the vocabulary of the day; maybe it is okay to be adventurous in our play on words. Just think, did the abundance of words make things different for the better!

Multiculture, displays a picture of diversity. Within the diversity in which we all live, we are on a continual journey and yes, often in a battle to deal with the whole scenario of "How Can We Cope" with the diversity we face each day? How can we remain true to the Constitution of each our own "Countries Constitution, or Bill of Rights" when America, Europe—and yes, even Communist Countries are feeling the pinch of this Conundrum?

All cultures want to have more of a say to be able to propagate or spread their culture. These folks want to mix evenly with the culture of the folks whose land they come to. Each of us, in our own country laid out ground rules for what we wanted our country to look like; the things we would and would not allow, as part of our constitutionality [penalties and fair play]. Should people from other lands and or cultures be expected to abide by these guidelines or be rejected as being unfit to be called a legal citizen of our country? With the proliferation of immigration, we have opened the doors for people to become part of us, each in our own country, to begin to fashion the rules and regulations for integration into the country any one of us are part of by birth.

As we explore what lies ahead in Part Two of *Everybody: Everybody Is A Somebody,* I wish to use *The Approach Shot* idea of Part One, but call this snapshot theme, Believe *It Or Not,* for Chapters Six—Ten, to form a Gateway Principle before each Chapter officially tells the story of their Chapter of The Part of Life that each of us contends with.

Believe It Or Not

6th Chapter
The Gateway of Hope

Truth is: I will never know all there is to know about you, just as you will never know all there is to know about me. Humans are by nature too complicated to be understood fully. So, we can choose either to approach our fellow humans with suspicion or to approach them with an open mind, a dash of optimism and a great deal of candor.
[Tom Hanks—Brainy Quotes]

Hope: The Final Frontier

Do We Believe This?
Is It Possible In This Life?
Or Is It

"WHYCELIH"

"Why Hope You Could Ever Live In Hope?"

Can We Trek Purposefully With Hope From A Standpoint of Truth, To Aid the People We Encounter?

Chapter 6
EVOLUTION FIGURED IT OUT: OR NOT?

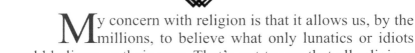

My concern with religion is that it allows us, by the millions, to believe what only lunatics or idiots could believe on their own. That's not to say that all religious people are lunatics or idiots. [Sam Harris; Brainy Quotes]

Truth or Consequences—Truth garners the ultimate possible worth or value, producing actions; consequences describe or picture out the results of truth or error reasoning. There is seemingly no end to the number of debates which have failed to placate, conciliate, soothe, calm, mollify, appease pacify—the whole audience: Some attend for value related purposes, for the value of truth; others for entertainment value.

Question and Answer Events are often entertaining for the audience: Or Not!

When the basis of our communication is built upon an unquestionably sound foundation, we can better understand real life; we may not feel life as subjectively [feelings based on emotion or unstable things]. Empirical, proven, and practical evidence is more sensibly unmovable, pointing us to the avenue of objectivity [fairness, which can stand alone]. Statements of perceived truth leave us in a quandary or dilemma, here, we are always searching the bottomless pit for the possible or attainable salvation we crave. We the people seem to be on a never ending search for satisfaction.

The prized wealth of our understanding or acquaintance with associations which demonstrate themselves to be reliable, allows us to have a deep assurance of safety. Creation will not implode or explode in a moment of time. The present, physical and spiritual world plays a huge part concerning our eternal future, this needs to be in good hands; this requires a rightly aligned Faith. Finding this 'Faith' is our 'Homework!'

Belief Systems always present us with not only a conundrum, or puzzle, they also present us with a challenge. Belief systems in and of themselves are feeling based unless they are proven to be true through the lens of an eternal perspective. Everything we know of has a beginning and we always need to remember this. While this is paramount or the principal entity in every search, it can keep us in a never-ending search; like trying to find the bottom of a bottomless ocean. Are 'value calculators' essential? Are all 'value calculators' out to present Truth?

Unless we find and can trust the one objective source with the measure of success we can depend on forever, we cannot say we have physical proof. Both Evolutionists and or Atheists, Creationists and or Christians, are in a never-ending physical, verbal and or temporal [time-based] battle for control as to 'Who' or 'what' is The Genesis of all time. Time had to have a beginning; time as we know it will have an end. So, what should we do to solve the problem? We need to find the courage to trust the beginning beyond time as we understand it—I stress a 'Beginning Entity,' not a 'nothing entity!'

Many are the reasons and excuses we generate or fashion to suit our subjectivities and or favoritisms. Here it is again, 'isms,' what are they and where do they get us. Isms are creeds, doctrines, beliefs, ideologies, and philosophies. All of these are all relevant in the right perspective if we keep the context of life in its rightful place. What is the context of life? Love God first and keep His Words deeply ensconced or tucked away within us so they will flow out of us when He asks us to come to the aid of others [Mathew 22:36-40].

This takes us back to reasons and excuses. Reasons suggest sensible, appropriate, or fitting narratives for why we cannot perform an action someone asks us to do for them. Excuses [evading something based upon feelings; I do not want to do something someone asks of me], these are entirely different approaches for replying to a plea for help. However, to ask someone to 'Excuse' me from fulfilling their request based on a valid reason, only one reasonable explanation—this balances out on the side of a 'Reason,' opposed to an excuse. When a request for aiding someone in a task generates a list of reasons, it leans towards being an 'Excuse' for simply not wanting to help in whatever way the 'Asker, Requester, or Petitioner' is suggesting their need for assistance rests.

When I reply to others and God with an array of both reasons and excuses, what I am doing is over rationalizing because of the many issues involved in complying or submitting to God and others with a heartfelt "YES, I will be glad to do that for you." I need to yield myself to be what God wants me to be, if at all possible—a servant. Don't get me wrong, this is not yet a done deal for me. We all have some distance yet to travel on these issues.

When it comes down to where the rubber meets the road I still have issues yielding myself to extend proper feelings to towards people who believe differently than I do. I may be thinking, and in some respects rightly so, if it does not line up with The Bible, then your potential decreases in my books. In the varied distinction department, in this case, my response may be wrong. Our differing belief system have nothing to do with our intrinsic right of passage; regarding our worth. We may decrease our effectiveness at living life all by ourselves by our wrongful and or immoral lifestyles.

Even then, we can see a resolution to this problem by being repentant, penitent, or remorseful for having strayed from what the original course of life laid out as the rightful way to live. People who have lived wrongly and do not believe in God can mend their ways to still be of great significance to the world around them. Even though someone does not believe in God, God still leaves the door open for them to become believers. The non-believer also feels they have a case to be made—one of equality to that of the believer.

Grace and Mercy are huge extensions of God's love for all of humanity, all of whom He considered persons of parity with each other, long before they showed up on this earth. God, knew us before He even created the physicality of the universe and everything else we do not classify as personhood. Christians [Christ Followers], those who are believers in God and the person of Jesus Christ as described in the Bible, do not have an exclusive on God's love and their value as people.

A while ago I asked the question, "are value calculators unusually essential?" I was not thinking about the elements or fundamentals of this tangible, temporal, present world we live in day to day, where people judge our value to life and to themselves, based on what we own, do, or are born as to enhance ourselves on the open market; although these value calculators are alive and well. A perfect example of this is the "Caste System" of India.

What is a Caste system? A caste system is a physically grouped platform and or foundationally built set of rules, saying, 'our birthright' is greater than yours because—. Roughly speaking, it means that in some cultures if your parents are poor you will be poor too. This belief is the same if you are rich; if your folks are rich you will be rich.

The more I use certain definitions to determine the worth of another person God created [I know not everyone believes in God], the more I make myself the Judge of all else: People included. When I make myself the Judge I am actually putting more responsibility on myself than I can carry on my shoulders for the duration. I may think it is my job to do so in this spiritual sense, but The Bible does clarify this as the job of JESUS! If we are in a position of being someone's boss or supervisor in the workforce, there are certain responsibilities a boss has to judge the worthiness of an individual to the company, based on their performance—remember to stay in context.

Please look at a "Believe It Or Not" by Denis Diderot.

It is especially important not to mistake hemlock for parsley, but to believe or not believe in God is not important.
[Denis Diderot (1713-1784)]

I never knowingly encountered hemlock anywhere. Now, since I have seen a picture of hemlock, I may have seen it without knowing what kind of plant it was. Now, since I have searched out reference to it, I will look carefully at any wild plants I might wish to eat out in the wild, if my hunger pangs are in full gear. Hemlock comes in two definitions: Poisonous and non-poisonous.

Poison hemlock (Conium maculatum: The root is carrot like) is deadly. Ingest a small amount and your "Believe It Or Not" questions will be answered prematurely when you face your maker after this your last breath. It may be worth our while to explore some nature facts before we plan a 'Survivor Trip' where we need to live on what lies before us on this adventure.

Aethusa cymatium [Fool's Parsley] is thought of as a cousin of Poison hemlock (Conium maculatum); it should not be on our list of "Incredible Edibles." It is poisonous, not quite to the degree of "Cousin Conium maculatum [Poison Hemlock; also a somewhat carrot like root]. Apparently, both of these smell awful.

On the contrary, Queen Anne's Lace, also a member of the same family is the Incredible Edible you may wish to look out for on your planned Survival Adventure. It has healing properties, smells good, and it can be a survival diet you can stomach. Be warned, just because they are almost twins in appearance, they have diverse natures in their temperament. Queen Ann's Lace is known as being a wild carrot.

Family ties are great relationships when looks is not the only characteristic they share. Like the hemlock and the family ties it has, family ties and or relationships within the people grouping are not always open enough to tell by looking at them from the distance outside of a personal relationship, to be the same within the nature and character arena.

Some carrots are edible, some parsleys are edible, some people are congenial and pleasant, others are not so manageable. When someone offers us something growing in their garden [from the earth or from their family garden where distrust and a whole lot of other stuff is growing] we might be justified and or fair in our questioning them on the integrity they are offering or lack thereof. Can we 'Believe It Or Not,' this is the question?

Let's not mistake the importance of the differences between hemlock for parsley when looking for edibles. Let's not mistake the importance level between believing in God and not believing in God when it come to Eternal value!

We are in *Chapter 6, Evolution Figured It Out: Or Not?* During my research for this Chapter, I came across the interesting facts I have described. We get away with some mistakes we make, for a time because the severity of the consequences of the mistake are not a matter of life and death. Some mistakes have immediate life or death consequences. Some mistakes may not have immediate life or death penalties but may have the same end result—the loss of the Eternal values. The values of being a Christ Follower [based on the tenets (beliefs) of what God says in The Bible], those which apply eternally, these are sectioned into 'God's Rules Package,' not ours. When we make the rules things look different!

Mr. Diderot had his opinion; the results are in; he died in 1784. Denis said, "to believe or not believe in God is not important at all," I beg to differ.

Depending on the topic, the combatant's strength of truth, subjective belief, facts or perceived facts, and the ability to debate in truth or their desire to humiliate, one debater in a debate may have the last laugh. The other may feel the disdain or scorn of the audience or the world—what's more important? It should never be our intent to tear someone apart for their belief system. Rather, we should dissect a topic to discover if there is a strong enough foundation to uphold a singular perceived truth during all time and the eternity before us. To rip someone apart for how they have come to believe what they believe, whatever that is, borders on cruelty.

The statements of other folks which I quote betimes are not meant to be in a column where I am belittling them. I would intend to invite folks with the belief system differing from mine to be ready to give a defense for what they state categorically, and be ready to hear my thoughts, and visa versa. Life is short! Too short to make enemies of those we do not understand. I will not say I have it altogether in my head all the time about this issue, and I will not claim I never make a mistake in this arena during my residency.

Awareness—What a huge concept! Question: "Are We Aware of Our Existence?"

For five chapters up until this point here in *Chapter Six*, we have been trying to concentrate on value and how it relates to the lives we live. We muddle through, or better still, hopefully we work proficiently through the challenges we face in the material world to put ourselves into the position of managing our life situations. We do so to better raise our families and teach them how to look out for themselves and their offspring as they grow further into life. As if this is not enough of a challenge, there is another challenge we face—Spiritual and Eternal options.

I suggest the word 'options.' None of us are forced to accept what goes against the grain of what we have been taught or believe through any other sources which life offers. However, above and beyond the material elements of living, as important as they are, values fit every one of us in another sense—the Spiritual Sense. We might want to call the 'spiritual sense,' the 'personal sense' because this matter hits or approaches us all at one time or the other whether we like to admit it or not.

As much as we wrestle through the struggles of the material elements of life we also wrestle through the sense of possibility each of us has within the choices of the life pertaining to what we think of as ethereal [delicate or heavenly]. When we think of this part of life, the related elements, 'such as do we have to include God in this part of the choices we make,' puts us into delicate situations on the emotive or subjective side of our lives.

When someone or something perks our attention to this part of the significant system resources of God's eternal plan for those who follow Him, we cringe or pull back. Often we say this is a private matter, and it is, but one day God will make it an open matter. For choosing which side of two columns we will live our lives in, the choice most often comes too quickly or too easily.

If, or rather when we look seriously at this situation, this issue should not surprise us. We just need to look at ourselves to realize we are built with an emotively sensitive nature. Did God make a mistake? Did the automatic system of evolution get it wrong? Could one or the other, which ever one was the ultimate originator, not get it right—what is right? What Is truth?

What value do we hold in ourselves? What value do we hold of others? What value do we hold of the beginning of all time and how it might affect us? What value do we place on the rules of life, The Golden Rule? Can we handle the bookwork of the spiritual aspects of life?

Do we reproduce at a marketplace which is fair and just within ourselves, so other people will be the beneficiaries? Does the book value of the reality of life, truth and or consequences, come into our thinking capacity when we work through the challenges of getting through to the other side of the time and space we have allotted to us? These are questions we may try to avoid or skirt around while we enjoy life in the fast and furious lane.

We will answer these life questions when we have to punch out the time clock at the end of our 'Final Day'. Easy, what is easy? What would Easy-Street look like anyway? Easy Street would have been if we would have begun life cloned to be like God, not having to make the tough decision because they would be automated—if you will. Our originator would be so proud—whomever or whatever they or it were. What 'they' or 'it' determined, would be the 'truth incorporated,' but we would just be robotics.

Today I just finished watching the movie *The Shawshank Redemption* [again] and one part of the story particularly caught my attention. Nearing the end of the movie we see how Andy Dufresne, one of the main characters, actually tunneled through a concrete wall of the Ohio State Reformatory, Mansfield, Ohio, which served as the film location for the Shawshank Redemption movie. Andy scratched away at the concrete wall until he etched out an escape route from the prison. I saw no steel rebar in his escape route of concrete. Because the prison was about a hundred years old I saw concrete which was soft and crumbly enough to work through—how construction specifications have changed today.

Strength is a tremendously significant factor for any material or theory to be classified as fit for a building project. Physically constructed or the project of building a belief system and purporting or claiming it to be truthful and safe for ever, we could call this the sustainability factor. We need to have the right strength, sometimes no less and no more, to accomplish the task. If we were created, formed, or simply appeared out of nothing, would it be us who could glean our needed strength to handle the term of existence set out for us? The picture is much different if we were created by choice, by a loving and caring heart, by A Creator: God.

Foundations use concrete. Strength is necessary for effective weight bearing to work. Working through belief systems, ideas, and facts, requires more cautious planning. The right belief system is set to last for an eternity, skyscrapers are not expected to last for an eternity. Just think of all the towers torn down in New York City and elsewhere, so newer, and perceived safer complexes could rise up in their place.

Concrete strength has multiple qualities, like density, compressive strength, flexural strength, tensile strength, and modulus of elasticity. Some buildings require more or less PSI [Per Square Inch] strength. To know the exact strength needed, many factors need to be determined depending on the size of the building. In every day concrete work, professionals usually go for a compression strength of 7,500 psi. When mixed with water, concrete sets and toughens during settlement. This is a chemical process known as hydration. Water reacts with the cement in concrete and makes it stick together, resulting in a strong material similar to stone.

As in the physical construction of the skyscrapers we have today, so is the importance of the proper foundation in building any belief system to stand the test of time. If we use the same standard of preparation and testing for durability in determining which perceived truth is objectively true and which is conjecture or feeling based [subjective], we have a starting point that leads us to a consensus or harmony with moral and spiritual beliefs. Like I said at other times, none of us were where the beginning of time began so we are all on the same page: Faith and Trust.

Faith and trust are extreme virtues or qualities to entrust or give over to someone we do not know well. When we do not do our homework, faith and trust can become like an albatross, heavy burden, or millstone [a huge chunk of concrete] around our neck. This pictures a serious problem, a hard one to deal positively with. [Think of Hemlock].

At present I am thinking of gangland narratives. Are the measures they enacted to make a point, sufficient food for thought? We do not know everything awaiting us in life. When we come from a fixed position on entropy [the worsening condition of mankind and life itself] it is out there for all to see, the whole universe is realizing the forcefulness of this worsening condition as opposed to the belief we are evolving into a betterment or improving condition of universal advancement.

I am thinking for a moment about the weight of concrete and relate it to the millstone around the neck situation. As I do, I see that the Chicago Gang's style of dealing with the issues they encountered, the ones that did not fit with their view of managing life, these were harsh back in the day. Whether fitting someone with cement shoes or a Chicago overcoat was realistic or not, the concept or notion it was reality, clearly reveals an outcome having only one conclusion, or we may call it the 'Final Answer' to a problem. The Final Answer, what a concept! When our priorities in life are intact The Final Answer will suffice for our eternity.

How does this fit into our day to day where we meet many cultures of people? We decide whether we will accept them as equals to each our own culture. Do we separate ourselves from people at arm's length? If so, is it not equal to fitting them with cement galoshes? They are as if dead to us, non-existent. They are to us as if they were never born.

The mentality of Cosa Nostra or Mafiosi was and likely still is one of sustaining a belief system they grew into from ancestral roots. From what I glean or gather from watching *The Godfather*, I see Rome, Italy was a huge part of the backgrounding scene for lifting a banner high for all to see that life needs a controlling factor to survive, it is the survival of the fittest that matters. These gang leaders, groupings of people often had strong religious beliefs, possibly differing from ours.

Christianity, which always seems to break into at least two columns, usually Catholic and Protestant, is the largest religion; the second largest is gaining ground rapidly: Islam. As I look at this picture I see a central compass point working from the North Position. A mindset or belief system gains ground here to suggest there is a dangerous position coming to the fore, a fight for control.

In the early days of AD, opposed to BC, Rome moved up to be "DA Man [The Man]." Rome was setting the pace as being "The Rule." We see it in the Cosa Nostra grouping, and I see it in the Rise of Islam, control at all cost; yes, the rule must be.

The battle for being "Numero UNO (a Spanish term)" [The most important member or entity in a grouping, oneself, expressly in the fashioning of one's own interests] has always been a part of the historical picture of humankind. This seems never to have died, there often seems to be no hope on the horizon which we call 'The Now;' it will never drop off into oblivion, so it seems. Selfie mode, Numero Uno, is muchly a part of todays culture. We see it everywhere, especially in the picture of cell phone use. What saddens me here is that children have no time to just be children, cell phones have overtaken that special time of child growth.

I do not say these things to suggest there is no hope. In the 'Now' we live in, there are Pre-set Rules [rules have always been part of life]. We often envision a lack of hope because of rules. However, there is yet to be another day, one where there is hope, eternal or unending fulfillment of what we hear is "The Blessed Hope, Jesus." Much of the time when we speak of spiritual things, the word "Jesus" dulls the conversation quickly. It is okay to talk about "God" in a generic or general sense because He is so many things to so many people. The differences between one person's God and another person's God are too often so unrecognizable, it is even hard to call "it" or "Him" God.

152

Dangerous are the days we live in as we look for a brighter hope somewhere over the rainbow, somewhere just over that new horizon which seems to include so many options. In my 2018 book *Bridging The Gap* I spoke often about Horizons. *Looking Over The Horizon* was the Pre-Chapter Caption. Tolerance [I believe in acceptance in the right context] exponents or advocates demand we adopt a multifaceted, multi layered, complex [opposed to the Occam's Razor approach], complicated, multidimensional, or multi-cultured or multicultural approach, where every belief system is part of the objective truth [factual], Moral Ultima [I suggest ultimate means ultimate], the one and only truth.

When we break apart all the components or workings of each religion or life choice we find there is no satisfactory beginning for everyone's belief; nothing seems to fit properly for everyone. When I look at the birthing process, how any of us began physically, and think of a visual to get my head around, I do not want to imagine there were over two people responsible for my beginning—besides the Initiator of all time, Who put me on the drafting table of time to fashion the possibility of 'me.'

I cannot fathom it taking more than one man and his contribution of sperm into one woman, for my birth. The idea is unconscionable [how many pieces does it take to make a single cell?]. Hard to imagine, yes? If this were the way of it, I could not respect parenthood. I would have to wonder who my fathers were and why did there have to be so many to make little old me?

This is the 'thought mode' we have if we feel that everything came from nothing and that logic is not a requirement for a birth to come about. Somebody needs to provide the single initial seed to allow the conception of any process to have an objective resource to complete the job of creation of the project.

Is the birthing of life the birthing of a nation? A beginning has set rules that allowed for life to come alive for a person to flourish enough to become nations. At the beginning of all time, no matter which belief system any of us had, only one entity could make it all work. One Somebody, and that by choice, made it all happen. This Somebody, and I capitalize this Somebody because "This Somebody" had to be "DA MAN," the main cog in our whole understanding of The Universe, Humanity, and everything related to anything we think we know!

To lower Himself, yes, Himself, because never has a birth not originated from a male gene, sperm, or fertilization process; this is 'Part One' of birthing—no secret, 'right?' Yes, a female gene or egg is also necessary. However, there has to be a giver [male sperm] and a taker, a receptacle for the gift [the female contribution]. The sperm is the fertilization of the egg and this allows for life to begin. To accept being less than God in the physical for a moment in history, to make possible the concept of becoming nations of people who would acknowledge Him for the love it required for something of this magnitude to happen poses the question, 'was it a bang?' Right about now we have a "Bang Bag" of questions, ready to explode. Oh, how the questions ring in my ears about now.

How dare I say God and what He says in the Bible is the "Final Word and The Final Answer." The ills we are plagued with in becoming inclusive of the idea that everything is okay as long as we decide it is okay and all the confusion of sexuality in the many forms it takes on, is a huge issue of concern in our present world. One entity is the fertilizer and the other entity is the ground that receives the fertilizer so the soil will be productive. Two male cells combined will never bear fruit. We need God and a Creation to make a blending we could call something made in the image of itself, a live entity. One live entity, an eternal One, is the best simple explanation, 'Call Me Crazy!'

We have become so self-minded; we do not want to think outside of this box. Circular thinking is an issue of Evolutionists accusing the God-believer of this when we talk about origins. They say Christians begin by saying that the Bible is the Infallible Word of God and carry on from there to go around in a circle like a merry-go-round to end up back at saying this is so because the Word of God The Bible says so, or I say so: Circular Reasoning.

Circular Reasoning goes kinda like this—we sometimes use circular reasoning inaccurately or unreliably while we differ in our opinions, which necessitate the support of a visual layout, which has parameters. This may put us outside the context we are implying, while entering another context. It may not necessarily be a different context of the whole scenario but one which may show us the possibility of being better recognized than the interpretation to be confirmed. A table saw buzzes circularly at high speed, it consistently makes its rounds as we move the board into the blade.

When we use a skill saw we may have a board on a table, and we move the saw over the board to do the same thing as using the table saw, to cut a piece of wood. However, there are differing pieces of wood. If we have the right saw for the job it is easier to cut each piece, depending on what kind of cut we need to make. In one situation we move the saw and in another situation we move the board. What do they say, "Different Strokes For Different Folks?" This does not mean we change the context [cutting the board] to suit everybody in their own niche, but we do need to adapt our approach to fit the intended need or use.

A carpenter will use a mixture of different saw types, while cultivating their craft. We looked at table saws, and skill saws, but there are many saws. I looked on one website and it named 26 saws all carrying specific job descriptions. Some saws are stationary, where we need to bring the piece of material to be worked out, 'to the saw:' The Table Saw and The Band Saw. The Table saw is for straight cuts. While the Band Saw also makes straight cuts, it can make curved cuts and has different purposes than a table saw and many other saws.

I like the "Coping Saw." When I think in terms of coping with an issue, this one sounds unique. Just like when we need a specific word for a specific need someone may have. Another neat saw is "The Fret Saw." The Bible tells us not to fret or be anxious about anything, not to fret about evildoers, not to fret about tomorrow, because tomorrow will have enough other things to contend with. The Fret Saw, I kinda like it! There is a wide range of hand saws and there are numerous portable saws, each having unique qualities all designed for certain situations tradespersons encounter on the job. I think about this when I am thinking about "Circular and Linear Reasoning."

In the temporal time-based, chronological, and historical sense, and in the spiritual sense, sometimes we go to where the problem lies to fix problems by building bridges with a variety of physical, spiritual, and other ministry related tools. At other times, the problems come directly to where we live and knock on our door; these are the ones we are often unprepared for. If we will meet a problem where it exists, we are usually better prepared to help alleviate the problem. It is like working with the materials on a job site, we have stationary tools and hand tools.

INTERMEZZO

Coping

Coping is widely descriptive; coping is basically a helping hand to get over a roadblock which tries to deter or halt our progress. While coping with an issue, the issue may not necessarily get better in the short term. However, a person who copes with a problem which they would rather not have, has the greater potential to grow stronger because of the tenacity they have for not giving up. The difference between coping and giving up is simple when we give up we quit trying. When we cope with an issue we keep trying despite the circumstances, we may have a better sense things will get better at some point!

Coping—confront, endure, get by, handle, suffer, survive, encounter, struggle, get a handle on, hold one's own, make a go of it, rise to the occasion. If we take each definition to the nth degree it almost seems we are pitting the positive against the negative. Take confront it means to oppose or accost. Look at handle, it means to manage an issue. Confront and handle seem almost as if being opposites [accost—manage?]. Then we have, "rise to the occasion;" this gives me a reason to hope things will get better if we do not give up! [Call Me Crazy!]

> Cast thy burden upon the LORD, and he shall sustain thee: he shall never suffer the righteous to be moved. [Psalms 55:22 KJV]
> Casting all your care upon him; for he careth for you. [1 Peter 5:7 KJV]
> Fret [Re Fret Saw] not thyself because of evildoers, neither be thou envious against the workers of iniquity. For they shall soon be cut down like the grass, and wither as the green herb. Trust in the LORD and do good; so shalt thou dwell in the land, and verily thou shalt be fed. Delight thyself also in the Lord: and he shall give thee the desires of thine heart. [Psalms 37:1-4 KJV]

SELAH—Take a moment to reflect on God's Goodness!

When we argue round and round like being on a merry-go-round, it is as if we are praying for a chance to trap someone by assuming our initial point is true, presuming the answer we give them is real and true. We often attempt to evade the burden of at least trying to prove one of the grounds or premises we use in an argument by basing it on the prior acceptance of the conclusion to be proved, [Ex "You have no choice but to believe what I say because I say it is true, based upon the Bible"]. So, the fallacy of begging the question is a methodical tactic to avoid actually having the means to prove what we are saying is the truth.

The person who encourages a dispute in the discussion by using a circular structure of argument to block the further progress of the argument, is using Circular Reasoning. Why? We do this to undermine the capability or credibility of the defendant to ask legitimate critical questions in reply. This pattern often takes away the right of the person we discuss with to have an equal opinion; whether it is fact or objectively based or simply subjectively, or feeling based. If we fight through debates just so we end up the winner, based on the tactics we employ, as opposed to trying to get at the truth, we are not winners.

However, if through discussion, we are trying to determine something is or is not the unquestionable truth, we are forced to use Circular Reasoning or admit that everything is theory based because none of us were on the inaugural platform of initiating said truth, or on the Maiden Voyage of time itself. As a Christian [Christ Follower] who believes what the Bible says to be The Truth, The Only Truth, and Nothing But The Truth, I believe people have always been in the heart of God. All people are foreknown from before time and creation as we know it to be present. What makes the difference for time and eternity is whether any of us accepts God in Christ Jesus as the only Way, The Truth and The Life.

Christians most often use Circular Reasoning. I do, and maybe you do too. I have been in a log jam of scenarios and or thoughts about how to work through these issues of reasoning, logic, truth, error, and fairness to my opposition. Herein lies the mystery of how to articulate these hard in stone issues. I have no problem with what I believe, and I will not accept a neutral position just to please others. At the same time, I do not wish to be heartless about the feelings or beliefs others have a right to articulate.

Circular Reasoning is not the overall big bad guy some of us make it out to be. I wonder if I can make some sense on this matter for the not so exclusively educated in the scholastic sense. There is a tendency in society to continue on a question and answer diatribe [harangue, tirade, or attack on every answer for every solution that someone gives]. I began by intending to use the word "simpleton" to describe people who do not attack all answers for every solution. Upon review of the word, I said no to this word because I do not wish to demean anyone, but to enhance the path of truth. Simpleton and halfwit are part of a huge array of put-downs.

As I am thinking about 'Bad Words' and their destructive characteristics, I think about who decides what is good and what is bad. As I was looking for just the right words to use in the previous paragraph I also thought of the word 'simpleminded.' Again, I said no, because like a simpleton it demeans more than it encourages. Never, never, ever is it right to demean and tear down the person when trying to make our point. The Circular Reasoning line of discussion has its place, depending upon with whom we are dialoguing, and for what purpose.

Circular or Linear, what will it be? What should it be? One person will say circular while another will say linear. One person will say white is the only color that matters. Another person will say black is the all-important color to center out. Then, as we look out over our world, and when we see the 'rainbow' after the rain, it is appropriate to admit there are more colors than black and white. There are more factors of importance than what I think or what you think. There are more important people in our world than Me. Might there be more important people individually in this world than any of all of you other people than me out there.

I wish I could have watched as the Big Bang exploded to present a promise as big and true as the rainbow after the rain [reign, sovereignty]. The rainbow is a picture of a promise that the earth we know would never be destroyed by water again. Is it not unique or exceptional, what the rainbow speaks to us comes after the threat we will never see the light of the sun again? When we experience a deluge of rain, it washes away a lot of things, yet, in the big picture a clean-up occurs, and fresh new growth comes again to refurbish the earth. This is part of the "Promise of God."

What was the color of that first cell brought about by an invisible force of gravity from nowhere to create this huge bang up scenario we call "The Big Bang?" Are colors more than just a perception on our part? Do colors form because of an objective truth or are they just a figment [pigment] of our imagination—a subjective fantasy we want, to brighten our day? When I search out "black and white" I am told that they are not colors, just assumptions, speculations, or perceptions.

You realize I am surmising, speaking hypothetically from my perspective, being somewhat casual [calm] [not causal, formative, or developmental] in a cynical way, of some offerings of explanation to the wonders of life we experience every moment of every day we live. In some of my previous words I direct my comments in a more developmental manner because of my desire to form a cause with more solidity [a Creator and or Designer] than does a cause that is not casual because it looks more accidental than planned.

We can casually accept something from nothing, "The Big Bang" because this seems to have become the norm—life without a cause; just being a "Just Because I Say So Scenario." People who hold opposing beliefs to mine are just as important in the big picture of life as I am. Just like the picture I spoke about of the Godfather Gangland placebo or sample of people who were and are part of the whole of Creation, there are differentiations of right and wrong scenarios we need to deal with. If we were not at the beginning of the universe and or eternal time, how close can any of us come to proving anything, except by 'Faith!' How close can we really come to explaining Faith without trusting in one entity to be all it needs to be for us to feel we have completed the task of gaining total understanding of life and the universe we have been placed in?

If we had no eyes there could be no explanation of color. We cannot feel color like we can feel a blade of green grass. We cannot feel color like we can feel the black dirt beneath our feet as we walk through a rich, earthy field a farmer takes great pains to maintain. We can feel the raindrops falling on our heads; we can feel the water to determine its temperature, but we cannot determine if it is clear, or explain to a blind person what the difference is between color and clear.

We all know what 'a hash' is. No, I am not talking about hashish [hash—the resin of the cannabis plant], this is another story of the time we live in, for people to live past the scenario of pain, living, feeling the fulfillment of dulling their senses—because they think they cannot live with their circumstances without the drug.

When I refer to 'a hash' I am suggesting a meal which we kinda throw together with a variety of veggies, meat and such. One recipe I found is a 'Potato Hash.' It looks like this,

Floury potatoes [Desiree (cubed)] sunflower oil, chopped onions, diced red pepper, diced corned beef, drained sweetcorn, salt and pepper, Worcestershire sauce, parsley [freshly chopped], and I suggest hamburger meat, maybe a little gravy mix, and or whatever else you wish to add according to your taste buds. The proportions depend on each our own choice.

Variety is the spice of life, use it sparingly or proportionately or you may not like the end result. It is one thing to gather all the ingredients, place them into a large mixing bowl [the size being each of our own choice], mix them together and 'micro-nuke' or bake your masterpiece or creation as such, until you are satisfied you will be able to swallow or digest the finished work. If we had no eyes, the task for this expenditure of our time would be a challenge without the help of someone who could teach us how to cook to the satisfaction of being able to endure the mixture.

If one of our other senses were also withheld from our creation, birth, or through the explosion of particles we have been taught about, I would think even common sense would be hard pressed to manage the whole process. Of course, we could eat the hash, unless of course we did not have a mouth. If this were the case, someone would need to intravenously impart the concoction they made, into our blood stream in some manner, after it was liquefied, to give us a life sustaining substance so we could continue on into the journey ahead of us!

Once it was complete and we decided we really did not want the creation we made and wanted to put the whole process in reverse to salvage each item we included in our masterpiece so it would be as though it never existed as a hash, we would have quite another story to contend with.

To parse [sort] out potatoes, corn, peas, meat—would certainly require a miracle of sorts. Once a creation of the sort I have described is manufactured or produced it is impossible to retract or return every particle to what it was at the beginning of the process [Life after death will judge right and wrong]. We could define the importance of each item we used to make the hash, suggesting they were better left in their original state [alone, not affecting another item in any way]. However, this would not change the objectivity or fact that the creation was first intended to be a sustaining entity, a necessary part of what people of importance were made to be. Once God created us to be all we could be, He had no intention of parsing the project to eliminate what He had done. God gave us the job of sorting out what lay ahead in the plans we changed because we did not choose to follow His rule of life—'A Plan!'

My recipe for hash is just that, 'my recipe.' I cannot suggest what I listed as ingredients for this food sensation, is the only way to have a great meal. Some hashes leave something to be desired because there may not be any spice added to the mix. Sometimes we do not need too much spice because the ingredients themselves add sufficient flavor without adding my favorite spice—salt. About the 'Spice of Life,' well, this is 'Value Packed' by my Creator.

Yet amazingly the Big Bang allowed for there to be a definition, explanation, or separation in every entity known to humankind, accidentally, without a plan. Even a blind person can be taught to understand feeling, but not the seeing of the eyes. They can still have imagination. I cannot understand this as well as the blind person who lives within the guidelines of what blindness offers—this is life as it is.

Visualize if you can, what life offers as differentiations and separations in every entity known to us so life can be right. There are different aspects of every conceptual and theoretical view of life: Some right and some wrong. What we can feel differs from what we can know. If I were blind and picked up a TV remote without ever having been taught what it was, it would leave me as blind as ever blind could be. As a blind person I could not differentiate between black and white. They tell us these are not colors, just assumptions, speculation, or perceptions that would mean absolutely nothing until they are explained to someone who has never seem them. But a blind person need not remain oblivious or blind to life and its source!

Helen Adams Keller, blind-deaf from nineteen months of age, had some background of the five senses of life: Smell, Taste, Hearing, Seeing, Touch [feeling]. However, much of the required understanding of life and living was not yet ingrained within her. As a 'somebody' from birth, Helen beat the odds of failure. Helen Keller is not an island unto herself in a scenario such as this. I think there may be those as well who were born blind-deaf, and this would present a greater dilemma in which to teach or train someone to be a viable or sustainable part of becoming more than we might believe is possible to become. There is no 'one size fits all' category of person who automatically reaches levels of greatness or fame. In fairness, I feel the part of humanity we are born with does not schedule us to think we are of the "Poor Little Old Me" grouping of people, leaving us short of opportunities to also attain to greatness!

This picture of Helen Keller, is one of the possibility of everyone becoming something which may appear to be impossible. Yet, it has been proven by those who are affected by physical issues of this nature—they can be overcomers. These situations differ from our birthright. We declare who we are; the market value we have, comes from refusing to quit! So often, as I have searched out people affected by physical deterrents, constraints, or limits of one sort or another, I have seen the absence of the "Quit of Spirit," or the attitude of being a "Poor Little Old Me" candidate. "Kudos to them."

There are exceptions, as there are in every scenario. Just as there are exclusions of the "I Am Not Good Enough" crowd; the refusal of those in the press of humanity who think for some reason they are excused from living life to where they attain greater market portion than they began with; there are those affected by limitations of varying kinds who give up as well.

We can feel the heart of the suns purpose as it radiates heat to make us feel good and to help the farmer's crops come to fruition. When asked what color the sun is, we say 'yellow.' Does a blind person know this, or do they fixate in their mind what yellow is, as we teach them how to get along in a world which they cannot explain as we do? What if none of us had ever had eyes, either through a big bang or because of a Creator Who wanted for us to know that everything is beautiful in its own way, without out the necessity of eyes. But everything He made was good because bad or evil was not yet on the radar of time for us finite humans.

What does life demand of a person born blind, blind-deaf—one who cannot by sight differentiate black from white: Faith. What does life demand of us who were not at the inception or initiation of that first glimpse of universal time: Faith. This is the 'Missing Link' evolutionists and all the rest of us struggle with when we begin the journey trying to explain how and why we believe what we believe because of the circumstances we grew up in and through.

Why was sight necessary either by creation and or a designer, or by a fluke of nature [Evolution]; if we did not have to make differentiations; if we had hands to feel our way through? Oh, and why were hands even necessary if life were just one big collision or collusion [complicity, agreement, or conspiracy, where we cannot even agree to disagree] of cells and atoms bouncing around playing tag with a beginning we could not relationally grasp? You know by now that for me, 'faith is the substance' of everything I trust and can believe in—God! This will always be my theme of living life!

However, I conclude here for now, based on the reality of all we see or know about everything in the universe; everything has a launch point—like a rocket launch pad as a starting line point of getting the thing out there. I have made a personal decision long ago, that for me there is only one rational or balanced answer to Who or what started the whole thing we call life. Each of us do the same by how we choose to believe what we are told, and or by how life as we know it plays out.

So, when we gather at the conference table in discussion hypothetically, supposedly, or in theory, we all come with our subjective ideas. Often, we come with the mindset which states categorically, nobody, but nobody will change our mind about how everything we see and know came to be. Some folks come with an attitude or open mindedness suggesting there may just be something of objective or factual significance they do not yet know; leaving themselves open to find the truth they have not yet experienced.

I'm open to such an experience. When I gather at this supposed Conference Table I try to listen closely, thoroughly, or meticulously to what the speaker at the time is saying. Why? I might learn something that I was not previously aware of. I listen closely with the knowledge of what I already know or think I know, because I want to know as much as it is possible to know to make life better for all of us.

I say, I listen with the knowledge of what I know because I have settled on a beginning, so have others who sit on the opposite side of the conference table of life. I have looked at both sides of the two presentations available to us. One side is God and all that He says is, based on what He says He created, and what He already spoke to the people whom He has asked to record the events of history [His-Story]. I have looked at what the folks on the other side of the equation or reckoning said and I appreciate them for their intent or resolve to make their subjective feeling known.

I for one reckon or calculate the pros and cons of the most valuable bottom-line or platform on which to plant my feet in readiness for the 'Great Launch' 'out of here,' where we all get so messed up or confused about the "Who, What, When, Where, Why, and How" of all time. I am satisfied with what God has done, but I am also looking for what He has yet planned to do for those who are settled on what He has said about the whole picture or story of life.

Because there is so much confusion and, or debate around the table, I ask this question again— 'Circular or Linear,' what will it be? We accuse each other of being faulty, defective, or out of order on these suggestions. We struggle over the direction and the distance we need to travel in any direction to find the initial objective [factual in as much as we can determine logically of by faith] value of life and the objective moral value which we need to uphold to be on the right side of the God Issue, according to His Words—Not Mine! I did not make the rules. I just try to abide by the rules I was instructed in: The Bible.

There, I said it again. I believe it all begins with God. And yes, I know, not everyone believes this. I am not neutral on this issue. I realize some folks come close to being neutral because of the tolerance issues out there. Some will confess that they believe there are many roads to God—I do not! I know, unless we come to the table with the evidence properly and truthfully presented; when the evidence demands the verdict; when the jury has come back with what they believe they have sorted out and made a consensus on; the judge will declare the right judgement for the penalty of the disbelief we horde. He meant what He said initially, and He will one day administer the judgement based on the fairness of Who He is: He is The Final Word; He is The Final Answer!

I Am Looking Back To See "IF—"
"IF" You Are Looking Back To See —.

Look back in time—try to figure out how to manage today with the things we may not as yet have learned, by looking back on the time we have lived. It is another thing to look back over the time we do not know except by trusting. However, the history of this time is written, and by whom it is recorded as fact, or not, this information is accurate to the nth degree; anything else may or may not be trustworthy without this foundation. While working in several fields of occupation throughout the tenure of my life, I have seen enough edifices which did not measure up to the standard of construction we have today. This meant for an early demise for those structures.

Conjecture, inference, or speculation always leaves us feeling [subjectivity], 'if we put our faith and trust in what history has told us, we may have it wrong'—when all that is said and done becomes the reality we have not yet experienced. This can be scary if the reality we do not yet know has an end result that is of a greatness we may not want to miss out on. Conjecture, in this scenario we may experience a 'Gap— "The Missing Link."

We may not wish to consider trusting God because it does not suit us, or it sounds too far fetched to be true: God, "No Beginning and No End!" What is the missing linkage we miss out on when life as we have it is the bird in the hand? Faith—objective faith [is figured to win the day], or subjective faith [set up for failure] these are the only two options that will cut it.

There is seemingly no end to the resources we have at the ready to sort out any problem on planet earth. We have God, evolutionists, preachers, scientists—regular folks on the street that think they know it all—regular folks on the street that 'know they know it all.' There is no shortage of resources, be they on the right side of reality, or on the wrong side of reality. Fantasy is the lack of reality. Today, we live in a world of 3D, and Virtual Reality. Yes, these come so close to what is the life we live, but they come with a huge disclaimer. They do not have their facts straight. They are just fantasy. They are exciting, fun, exhilarating—but they take us on an accelerating roller-coaster ride away from truth and reality.

What Did I See, and What Does It Say?

I love the Lord because he hath heard my voice and my supplications. Because he hath inclined his ear unto me, therefore will I call upon him as long as I live. The sorrows of death compassed me, and the pains of hell gat hold upon me: I found trouble and sorrow. Then called I upon the name of the Lord; O Lord, I beseech thee, deliver my soul.

Gracious is the Lord, and righteous; yea, our God is merciful. The Lord preserveth the simple: I was brought low, and he helped me. Return unto thy rest, O my soul; for the Lord hath dealt bountifully with thee. For thou hast delivered my soul from death, mine eyes from tears, and my feet from falling. I will walk before the Lord in the land of the living.

I believed, therefore have I spoken, I was greatly afflicted: I said in my haste, All men are liars. What shall I render unto the Lord for all his benefits toward me? I will take the cup of salvation and call upon the name of the Lord. I will pay my vows unto the Lord now in the presence of all his people. Precious in the sight of the Lord is the death of his saints.

O Lord, truly I am thy servant; I am thy servant, and the son of thine handmaid: thou hast loosed my bonds. I will offer to thee the sacrifice of thanksgiving and will call upon the name of the Lord. I will pay my vows unto the Lord now in the presence of all his people. In the courts of the Lord's house, in the midst of thee, O Jerusalem. Praise ye the Lord. [Psalms 116:1-19 KJV]

"What Did I See, and What Does It Say to Me?
This is the good question of the day."

Launching or venturing into the unknown is difficult for most people; howbeit, some folks are just gutsy enough to live in a Que Sera, Sera world: "Whatever will be will be." Some would call this faith, and others call it lunacy. Some call this trusting "The Universe" [different from trusting God], something equal to throwing everything into one basket and pulling out one object and thinking this will carry the day for eternity. Is this lunacy or not? Some see faith as part of the mix of a Que Sera, Sera world—it is closely related to or equal to throwing everything into one basket and pulling out an object, thinking this will carry the day for eternity.

Faith in God is different. When we come to the end of our own resources, and the stuff we pull out of the magic bag of tricks does not cut it, we are like an empty glass. 'Nothing' will pour into their mouth like anybody thinks will happen when they tip the glass to their lips. Nothing is still nothing. An empty glass has no value for eternal satisfaction, it can never be enough to venture out on in amongst life's adventures, but the beauty of the object—if there is any beauty in that.

To Launch or Not: That Is The Question
The Value—The Bottom-line
THE VALUE OF THE BEGINNING

We will rely heavily on this theme throughout this book.
So, Does *Evolution Have It All Figured Out: Or Not?*
The Story Continues; I Wait With Bated Breath!

Believe It Or Not
7th Chapter
Hope Extended

Truth is: Simplicity is less complicated than the lengths of our resources—devious, honest, or otherwise complicated endeavors we employ to get at the truth. [My words for Occam's Razor principle] Occam's Razor simply suggests simple explanations are more than likely to be true, than are long dialogues to prove a point. Believe It Or Not.

Truth aligns with reality at the end result of every matter. When we believe that we can get away with something that is out of line with the morality principle that God implemented to keep us all on the same page, consequences always bring the truth to the forefront sooner or later: This Is Reality!

There are complexities involved in searching out the truth of every matter because we have strayed from a "One Origin Designer Concept" [God], to a system where anything and everything goes, and this is because subjectivity [feeling based] seems more important that objectivity [fact based]. Falsehood most often breeds in musty erroneously saturated areas of desire, opposed to the satisfaction level we have with meeting our needs rather than our wants: The Simple Life.

Truth has both simplicity and complexity associated with it. Truth [reality] does not require many creations, formations, or conceptions to 'Bridge The Gap' between itself and the stories we elongate to make them 'truer.' As we oversimplify something with our drawn-out diatribes and or clarifications we find ourselves in the erroneously saturated, musty areas of the desire to please self rather than others.

Chapter 7
CHRISTIANITY FIGURED IT OUT:
OR NOT?

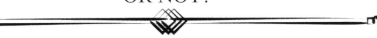

The best and safest method of philosophizing seems to be first to inquire diligently into the properties of things, and establishing those properties by experiments, and then to proceed more slowly to hypotheses [theories, suppositions, premises, and or suggestions] for the explanation of them. [Isaac Newton—Brainy Quotes]

How does 'Hope' extend beyond the borders of the frustration and confusion suggested by the areas of desire we house so securely, so we can get the satisfaction which presents the evils of the world which should be contained by steel enforced boundary walls, so as to make it near impossible to entertain the satisfaction we think immorality will bring us? 'Hope' extends because The Life Giver Promised it! The following two paragraphs come from my book, *The Mandate*; ["The Mandate" is my second self published book].

Believe It Or Not:

More of Life Than We Realize, Gives Us Hope.

"We need to be on the offensive every moment of life so we can be observant and ready to use hope to be there for us to grasp. The issue is not 'if' the promised hope will be there ready to do its stuff. The issue is 'when' hope shows itself poised to be the staying power to keep us until we complete our mandate, what do 'we' do?

I believe hope will be at the ready for all of us if we follow the principles that I have previously discussed [in *The Mandate*]. The thoughts that I have touched on from Psalms 51, Proverbs 3, Ephesians 6, are a part of the process that will allow us to move on to the next session of the four that I am promoting as relevant to the success of competition for and completion of our God given mandate." [*The Mandate, Chapter 18*, Page 239]

Most often we process 'too much information' 'from too many sources' to figure out the 'simple life.' Self evidence, or the obvious, are easily seen, the rest of the stuff is sucked down deep in some quagmire [quicksand], sinking deeper with each endeavor to explain it. Our verbose or wordy attempts to find the truth are complex: Yes? However the confusion we face is, how do we get simplicity into the 'playground' of our knowledge filled world?

Balance The Scales: Weigh Scales Have Only Two Plates, We balance One Side Against The other.

Weigh Scales—physical, abstract, or nonconcrete, are the measure of life. When we attempt to exactify [make it exact] one side of the scale against the other, [neutral, gender neutral—as in saying 'person' instead of his or her, which 'identifies' the entity] we take away the character distinctions each of us has through the process of heredity, the genetic make-up we all differ in, which the forensics of our day define for us because of DNA and RNA.

Deoxyribonucleic Acid is DNA; RNA is Ribonucleic Acid, a part of the word describing DNA. Ribonucleic Acid is a nucleic acid present in all living cells. Its principal role is to act as a messenger carrying instructions from DNA for controlling the synthesis [blend] of proteins, although in some virus's, RNA rather than DNA houses the genetic information. The DNA is The Boss, and the RNA is the boss's messenger, telling the workers how the work needs to get done [this is my description; believe it or not].

A weigh scale is the apparatus we use to measure the weight of an entity something like our body. Today these are often digital, back in the day the scale to weigh a person was a mechanical device with a plate of sorts, and a spring system and a needle to point to a number to show how much we weighed. Whose to say it was accurate. A finite mind manufactured this entity.

Another kind of scale was prevalent or common, it contained two plates, a fulcrum [a pivot bar on a hinge of sorts on which the plates were fastened], and a pointer to show the equilibrium or accurate balance as the end result. The plates were fastened to the bar, the hinge system was placed underneath the bar at exactly the center. On one plate we put whatever object we chose—the unknown weight. On the other plate we placed known weights.

Physical weigh scales are much simpler for determining the exactitude or correctness of a physical mass. Not so simple is the matter of determining the rights and wrongs of the morals we attempt to balance in life, to say who is right and who is wrong. For this, we need to know the 'center point.' One song writer craved finding this center point: They said, *Jesus Be The Center*.

Someone acknowledged a center point as the beginning. This 'Unquestionable Beginning' [in my humble opinion] was GOD! This was 'The Scale' considered by this writer, to be the 'Quantifier,' 'The Exactifier,' or the 'Exactified One!' We need to figure out unquestionably, what are the morals, or the rights and wrongs of life. This is not just a sexual issue, but it is an issue which addresses all disobediences against God's Law!

Can we exactify physicality, spirituality, and reality, without a 'One Source Beginning?' Without bowing our knee in submission to untruth, this is an almost unending task. Absolute faith in God is the DNA and the RNA of the placement of our Eternal Future. DNA and RNA decide questions of association. Forensic Scientists expend much energy to determine a beginning, one which has the objectivity [facts] to balance out our assumptions.

Can the use of multiple determiners prove the existence of God? If I claim that judges, directors, governors, masters, experts, pundits, critics—prove God's existence, I will most certainly get more than a casual argument! I know, I cannot prove the existence of God either. This said, there are many pointers we can use to make a good case for the claim of God's existence.

Learning about the origin of life in our universe, allows us a chance to understand the argument for God's existence. The building blocks of life, proteins, ribosomes, enzymes—are formed at the command of specific nucleotide, the basic structural unit of nucleic acids (DNA or RNA)] which arrange in orderly fashion in DNA and the RNA. DNA holds as many as 10 billion atoms in people. The adenine, guanine, cytosine, and thymine bases in DNA, link in a precise order, to form the genetic code in the master plan for every organism. The evidence in DNA guides and teaches us about the development of proteins; protein growth would be a hit-or-miss proposal without this. The nucleic cycle in DNA is informational.

Physicist Paul Davies expresses it well— "Once this essential point is understood, the real conundrum of biogenesis [multiplication] is clear. Since the impressive accomplishments of molecular biology, most researchers have sought the secret of life in the physical science and chemistry of molecules. But they will look in vain for traditional physics and chemistry to illuminate life, for that is a timeless situation of confusing the medium with the lesson. The mystery of life rests, not in its substance basis, but in the rational and informational rules it exploits." These thoughts surround what is said in the following link. [https://coldcasechristianity.com/]

There is a fight or struggle to bring God back into the picture of being the Designer Creator, The One and Only Source for all we know as civilization or anything else to explain what came before 'nothing.' This is not as one-sided as it became through the increase of physical knowledge. Many are the scientists, physicists—who once were convinced of the "No-God" scenario of existence, who now believe life could not have come about without God! Oh, I realize the fight is not over, not by a long shot. I know this struggle will not be over until the Return of Christ! I realize this topic falls into a minority category in the world we exist in. Our disagreements with each other on pretty much everything, and this definitely includes the God debate, is at the ready in a nanosecond of time. It is a wonder humankind has not yet destroyed itself!

We scrutinize Evolution, Atheism, Christianity, Islam, Buddhism—and the likes, to say, these are the choices we the people have—choose one, no matter which one, and you will be all right for what lay ahead eternally. If you try one and it does not meet your fancy, try another. If you are wrong about your choice, it matters not. Which we choose, No Big Deal, all roads lead to Rome; I Guess [Said tongue in cheek]. To Justify what I say about other beliefs from my own perspective, I may have to lay these, my beliefs out equally to the same scrutiny as I judge others.

Being a Christ Follower individualizes what I believe—not just what people think of as a Christian, but what people think of Christ. What I think of Christ; What are His claims; Why would I want to pick this one; why would you want to pick Christ or not pick Him as the One to beat all other choices of belief.

Can we claim anything in our universe as a Safe-Bet without the tally of expenses, or the results of the Laws of Entropy? Reality is significant as we think within the light of the possibilities we have amongst our choices, when considering belief systems, thus constructing movements—penalties or a lack thereof label the marks of truth or error reasoning.

Query and Reactive Proceedings are frequently amusing for the spectators: Or Not!

If it were not for people, we would not have needed a world, unless God stopped thinking beyond animal life and said, yes, yes, yes, who needs people? They will probably just give me a mess of trouble. Guess what? We did give God trouble. We were, and still are troublesome. Does God see us as just a bunch of messed up animals? I don't think so. God created us in His image and likeness. What is this all about? God did not need to have this world as we know it for Himself to exist, if He did not know the importance of having people to occupy the world. So, it comes down to purpose and what is the full worth of purpose!

Evolution's Big Bang had their Big Day; we looked at some of this already. This would also be of no value if the intent for the 'Big Bursting Forth' was not to facilitate people. Some folks say we came from animals and are basically animals, it's just that we are our own species of the thought. The pincers of Evolution have grasped at us for eons it seems. During my early years of schooling, I experienced this, but did not realize the full impact of this belief.

Living life always comes down to two vertical [one up and one down, with differing directions and purpose] columns of thought, lived out horizontally [parallel or similar yet differing hugely]. It pictures out like a divided highway does as two differing directions of travel. *The Road Not Taken* poem by Robert Frost, and *The Road Less Travelled* book by M. Scott Peck [MD], along with many other good writers, have broached the subject of choice—such as a divided highway. Too often, I firstly see the negative side of views opposing mine. I may put other people in a bad light. My intent is only to target the purpose and the results of the opposites under the microscope, so right wins out over wrong. Good wins out over evil. What is Right? What is Wrong? What is Good? What is Evil?

Just this morning my wife and I were talking about the justice system of Canada. This could relate equally to all countries, but this morning we were talking about a Canadian example of how the system can go awry or off-centre. Some years ago, two people concocted a purpose to sexually assault and kill young girls [this is public record], it is unnecessary to divulge the details. I could give the names of the guilty and the innocent of the story, but it will serve no useful purpose to do so; I just make note of it here as an example of how badly life goes awry when we leave God out of the story.

When sexual purpose is skewed or twisted to fit impure desire, things can go to the extreme in the wrong direction—as was the case here. The justice system allowed a plea-bargain for a lighter sentence than should have been the case for one, to make the other party in this love triangle gone wrong, pay the higher price for the booty of a crime equally shared. Please do not get me wrong, our governments are not always out with explicit or clear intent to do the wrong things or make the wrong calls. Governments usually have a right purpose for fulfilling their plans, the intent and purpose often lose their flavor or fervor because of the focus of how life began, and what was the original purpose of life.

I learned this, 'the initial purpose of life is firstly to Love God,' and second to this, we ought to, and I repeat 'ought to' love our neighbor as our self. I was taught that the second was hugely important, and that it would come to fruition if the first had its proper place in our lives. We went askew of that purpose in The Garden of Eden, and then began the recovery system of redeeming what was lost in The Garden of Eden.

This sounds much like *The Golden Rule*. It is in-fact "The Golden Rule." However, even this often gets twisted so badly, allowing for the original rule to lose its intended function: "Do unto others as you would have them do unto you." We need to know and remember; every rule has a source; every rule has a rule maker. Every rule maker must have authorization to make the rule. In this life we have governing bodies. The source we have in the eternal picture is God! We ought not aspire to judge other people; it will get us into 'big trouble.' Why? We need to live out for ourselves the things which we expect of others, otherwise we are ["What?"] Hypocrites. These thoughts did not originate with me. The rule of God is always first; our rules should sort out through His rule!

Why do we see others in a bad light, worthy of our judgement? Might it be we think we are of greater value than they are. Why would we think other people do not measure up? We are each as flawed as other people; why would we think we could not be wrong on the issues we judge. The issues of life are many, opinions about how to solve the issues are many, and people with opinion's, this is a mega-problem. What a world it might be if everybody was of one mind!

Almost every day, some of those we elect as fit to lead us in the 'right' direction, may attempt to do so with good intent, but find themselves tempted in the same way as the rest of us who are the followers. They are people like us. If they take their eyes off the ball [the original focus of the Original Law Giver, and His purpose of life's commitment to us], their humanity will splatter all over the newscasts of the world; then, how do they look as being examples for the rest of us to follow?

I just took a break from writing and looked on CNN and saw Matthew Whitaker, acting attorney general replacing Jeff Sessions, ask, regarding prospective federal judges, "are they people of faith? Do they have a biblical view of justice? Which I think is particularly important." Whitaker made the remarks at a forum where he appeared as a candidate for the Republican US Senate nomination in Iowa.

[https://www.theguardian.com/global/video/2018/nov/08/acting-attorney-general-says-judges-should-have-a-biblical-view-of-justice-archive-video]

Yes, this is what I am writing about here by asking the question in a similar fashion, 'are we using the right format for judging those we are leading along the way, or are we leading them down the garden path?' We see laws and rules in the making; we see our leaders, and we are incumbent or obligated to ask them if they are doing what they expect of us the followers. There are many who set good examples, and yet, sometimes even they make big mistakes; even they are often in big trouble. It is easier said than done to always have all our ducks in a row, I understand this, I am human too. It's easy to say, 'do as I say,' but how often do we follow this up with a subjective feeling of superiority? How often do we suggest our followers should not 'do as we do?' We expect special favors and still want the undeserved respect of our followers.

When we admit our own faults, we can see better, what the followers we lead struggle with as well. At this juncture of our own failures, we have a better chance of reacting to the shortcomings of others, with empathy instead of judgement. If we never see our own deficiencies, always seeing the failings of other people as if damnable and unforgivable, and we are not willing to change ourselves, we are frauds or phonies. These issues do not just apply to politicians, religious leaders, business leaders—this is us!

It often seems hopeless to achieve change, especially in us as individuals; the same goes when looking for a change in the lives of others. If we adjust our expectations of other folks to the positive rather than the negativity we too often display, we have begun a starting point for change. Change is hard to approach; change is hard work. If we pursue it passionately, asking the right questions of ourselves and others, we will see the reward of this hard work.

God is the best resource for these things, so I ask Him for help. If I am honest with myself, the resolution does come; although, the process is often slower than I would like. When we ask the right people for help, and we have the right motives, do we think they will cast us aside as if we do not matter, thinking we are of lesser significance than they are? Do we feel they will think we are of no earthly value if we acknowledge our imperfection? None of us are perfect: Do we think we are? Think of this picture as if we asked our parents for the necessities of life; they will probably be humane in their reply. Would they deny us the decency of compassion and understanding? Most parents have and practice the common courtesy of what fits into this love package.

If parents thought back to when they were where we are now; see how they got what they needed to become good people; would they refuse us 'our ask' if we were we asking for unselfishly motivated things? I fit into this picture just as you may. I love to see my children succeed—accomplished in living life.

Here's the wrap and the rub [difficulty] that comes with following *The Golden Rule*: Pride and selfishness do hinder enacting *The Golden Rule*.

Therefore, all things whatsoever ye would men should do to you, do ye even so to them: for this is the law and the prophets. [Matthew 7:12 KJV]

How does purpose go awry?

Both Christianity and Evolution as we exhibit them, present rights, and wrongs, as we throw them into the marketplace of life. Both have right thoughts within each their scenario but are often wrong in some areas because of the objective facts, opposed to subjective facts. Right and wrong get so mixed, good looks bad or evil and evil looks right and good. Go Figure; how have we gone so far wrong? Matthew 22: 36-40 shows us the answer to the 'why' question. How do we see God? How do we see others? How do we see ourselves? Do people matter?

People: Passion and People; is life all about God and people? Let's Head for The Hills for Awhile! Might we find some sanity for life?

The Mountains Shall Bring Peace to The People.

The Mountains: When I have considered going somewhere to ease the pain of the workaday world, there has never been a more consoling thought for me than the mountains. I am not alone in the mindset of needing a place to go when the pace of life gets so hectic it seems impossible to tolerate any more. Everyone on this planet is packaged with a cache of emotions ranging from pure joy, to what we think of as unbearable pain, physically or stress related.

Computers are a part of my world as much as they are a part of your world. We, in the modern world, technologically literate, are coherent to most other people. Some folks in third world countries may not understand so well, but even they have cell phone technology. Cell phones create a gap of separation regarding what once allowed us time for one on one, eye to eye, intentionally relational lives. I learned a new word today, 'textlationship'—we text, but rarely interact with many of these people interpersonally.

Often, when I perused computer stores I came away with a computer related entity. [I don't have this problem as much anymore because I now live in a valley where we do not have an abundant supply of computer stores]. I felt as though my spirit was lifted to satisfactory heights of relief from the workaday world. Although it was just the same illusion [*Both Sides Now* Joni Mitchell] as when I got a new toy; my momentary satisfaction was just satisfying for a fleeting moment.

Each Christmas, as I watch the children open the latest entity of their dreams, I wonder if the gift met their expectations. There appears to be no difference anymore between the dreams they have and the dreams their friends have. There is no difference in the satisfaction level each of us has, compared to that others have. If I am honest with myself, I see there is no longer as much of an exclusivity of things I have from the things you have. I see a lack of unique character displayed between one individual and another person, in my observations of their personhood.

Advertisers in the media make sure all children [and grownups, and yes, we are all still children] want the same newest toy. Wait for a while; when this toy is tarnished or broken, even a little outdated by another toy, the TLC. (Toy Loving Condition) also goes on holidays. It is my fear this is often how we treat people. After they no longer satisfy us, we discard them.

I now live in the Windermere Valley of British Columbia, where we have valley people, Alberta people, and other people (visitors from almost anywhere). No category of people is more important than the other. Each group of people has dreams or quests to satisfy their soul with something not presently residing in their lives, this is more evident every day. Wanting things is as natural as needing to eat and sleep. Some of us express our needs while others of us just go on from day to day in a quandary, not knowing what kind of a handle to put on our need.

Each of us as part of humanity has an obligation to connect with other people compassionately. Jesus did this on the cross [*The Passion of The Christ*]. I may be on another pay scale than the one of other people, yet we are all searching to fulfill our needs with physical, material entities; it may be an emotional satisfaction like none other ever experienced to date. However, when I see someone in need, I must be humane enough to affect their lives positively.

I've often looked for peace from the stuff that gets me worked up inside, while at my computer. Momentarily, I am satisfied; my mental health has improved, or so it seems. When I have sought after and found perks as fodder for a writing project in progress, yes, it has improved the mental condition that plagued me. Often, my time in front of this video time tunnel was a waste of time; other times it allowed me to *Follow That Dream*, like Elvis Presley sang about, hopefully, without an accompanying restlessness.

Much of my mountain of time has crumbled into a heap of nothing—nothing to show for the time used up, so I headed for the hills from whence cometh my help. Before we moved to the Valley, sometimes, a trip to the mountains was almost the only thing that would quench the thirst that entrenched my being.

The mountains were only a short drive away. For me it was a three-hour drive to where I found what was almost "the peace that passes all imaginable understanding." As I came down through Sinclair Canyon, and made the turn to the park gate separating me from my first glimpse of paradise, I anticipated the affirmation of a few words on a sign. Eight words on an old wooden posted sign were enough for me as I made my way into the Windermere Valley. I looked for them every time I came through the gates; often, I still do. Please, let's look at them together:

The Mountains Shall Bring Peace to The People.

These words symbolize more than a thin layer of truth. As I travel through the Windermere Valley, many cabins, cottages, and mansions are propping up in the peaceful landscape of what has always been here since God put it here, or 'some accident caused it to happen [I guess; (STIC) Said Tongue in Cheek—].' The houses is not what makes it the peace that the mountain promises.

People come here in the summer to enjoy a range of entertainments and relaxation techniques. Boating, swimming, water skiing, and a host of other adventure filled activities are a large part of the reason people come to this Valley of Adventure. Often, maybe usually, people do not even realize the real reason they come to places like this.

We all get caught up with things that keep us from what we want to do out in this big old world. Sometimes we struggle to prioritize our lives; we do not always take the time to just relax. This morning I read a devotional titled, *You Have To Relax*—Go Figure!

Except to say we need this place to get away from it all and relax, do we need a reason to come? Hey, to some folks, this is the best place on earth to hang out for a while. Many people do not have a mountain to go to; are they limited in what they do have as a place of solitude and enjoyment to go to? Even if it is some other place than what we have here, 'the mountains and the lakes,' are these folks limited? They may go to a lake or a secluded cabin somewhere. Some people pitch a tent in a field and call it their getaway.

Maybe the mountain is what we make it. You probably all know the saying, "Don't make a mountain out of a mole hill." Why shouldn't we make a mountain out of a mole hill? If it fits our circumstance, it may be right for us. There is something contained in the human psyche about this place of comfort, which we need to tackle—for many others, and me, it must be the mountains.

Deep in the heart of every person I believe we all know that this world, the universe, us, and all of creation did not just happen. All of existence has order, plan, purpose, and a creator. Look at your watch; it did not just happen. It is the reflection of mind, creativity, and power—the mind to think the idea, the creativity to design it and the power to make it, how much more your body upon which you put the watch—reflects God.

Yes, the evidence is clear, God created! As I have walked this earth on every continent in almost every nation, most people believe in God—but how do we know God? How do we find God? Does the Creator desire to communicate with His creation? As a parent desires to teach love, and even warn of dangers, how much more God wants to speak to the people, He created, to love them and guide them. But we all know something has gone wrong! [Arthur Blessitt]

Arthur Blessitt realized there is more in the complexity making up our flesh and bone bodies than 'just surviving' another hour, another 8-hour day, another 24-hour day, another weekend, or another vacation period. We call it looking out for our peace of mind; it stretches out to something more eternal than any time span we can express. When we come to grips with what 'Eternity' actually is, 'Forever,' we wonder what it will add. No matter how we perceive it—forever is a long time!

The Mountains Shall Bring Peace to The People.

My mouth waters for a place like this!

When I look at another person I should see a reflection of myself in them, as if I were looking in a mirror; it should be a lesson for the learning for me. I could be what they are. When I am in a public place or anywhere there are one or more persons, my observational receivers [eyes] are preparing to go out on the big hunt.

I am not hunting for the prize of a trophy for myself, like the big hunter on an African Safari; I just long to know what makes folks tick. The more I know about what makes another person what they are, the more I can see them in a positive perspective—the value they are to someone else. The value of every person on the planet should be a part of what keeps us going one more step; another hour; another day. If we were to value every person for their inherent worth, what a world this might be.

This mentality is not meant to be an invasion of someone's privacy, only an interest in a 'people fact-finding mission.' I guess you might call me an "Information Finding Missionary." Don't get on edge because of this when you see me; I believe that everyone else is doing the same thing, only, I confess it now. The difference between me and any other person I jostle with in a crowd, is, I may likely fulfill my calling as an "IFM—Information Finding Missionary" for a purpose different from theirs. For me, the situation I have described always includes the possibility of a story about to be vaulted into the mainstream of my life; the reason being, so we can look at life again, and see a life worth making the effort of adjusting to, to get the best ingredients into the mix of this world.

In my world, it has been the Windermere Valley, where a special place and time has always been allotted to find a time of refreshing. Right from our earliest times of traveling to the Valley, some folks have been a part of our lives, and to this date, nothing has changed. We have not nearly always done things together as something close friends would do.

There is and has been something for which we were put together; I guess it is a people thing. In this book I am now writing, the theme is 'People.' The importance of people everywhere, people of every culture, people big or little, and people with differing opinions from mine, each of us are as equal as the rest of the world, past or present, because we were all born reliant upon someone else for our survival.

At one time we took our family camping at Canyon Campgrounds in Radium on many weekends. It was always a refreshing place to be, beside the mountain waters which were more than a creek because of the energy they displayed. It was mostly R&R [Rest & Relaxation], but often, we got home more tired than when we left the R&R [Rat Race]. Go Figure.

The Mountains Shall Bring Peace to The People.

One day in August of 1991, our host in the Valley took us across Lake Windermere in their Silverline boat. We all got out and walked about, up the hill apiece, where I found myself inside of an old dilapidated farmhouse. Everyone else may just have been looking around, but not me. This place was probably 100 years old, not much to look at, but oh so valuable. What I saw as valuable in this old place differed from what the others may have seen. All of us see life as we know it round about us, with a different perspective, but it does not decrease the natural born character.

When one tours the back-wood's roads, they will see farmhouses like this. I found another house like this up by Columbia Lake just a ways past Coys Dutch Creek Ranch. Every time we talk about it my wife calls it our land (it never became ours); I have always said it would be nice to buy the property; I could fix up this old house. These two relics from the past always stand out in my mind; the story revolves around the first one. Through this window, I would like to look out across an array of people and issues to be displayed in the rest of the book. Please don't get lost. I am making a short transition here. I am leaving reality for a while, where I am about to stroll through a time tunnel. Time tunnels do not often provide enough light to illuminate our want to know things.

While looking at the old buildings scattered around the farmyard, it was easy to see it had been a while since they'd seen any maintenance. A coat of new paint could do nothing for the appearance of these old relics of the past. One can visibly see the decay that has worsened the state of the old place. The frames, once housed glass and were called windows, but now they are just hollow expressions of past glory. I looked out through this window at an array of people and issues to be displayed in the rest of the story. Paul Harvey might say: "And Now, The rest of the story."

A window can be a showplace of precious things. There are many shapes and sizes that a window can take. For example, we may find large ones in a car dealership, but I have seen small round ones, which might display dainty bits and pieces such as a set of wedding rings. Some windows house photographs of life and people of many cultures. Life is the window of reality. People are the valuables we see through windows of time.

What is it that could be highlighted in an old shell of a building that may be seventy-five or a hundred or more years old? Now, as we look on, it stands there vacant; no one wishes to live there anymore. The only life you may find there would be animal life occasionally. As I sat in this farmhouse I could focus on all the deteriorating conditions both inside and out. If this was my focus, then it is easy to find a reason for a quick exodus from this place. There was no shortage of insects to inhabit this place: But no people. The people who once lived here have long since left this inheritance to the wild. Quite an array of plant life was growing up through what once was a floor; the carpet is Moss Green: Moss and Green!

The interior designer had taken to dull colors for the most part. Various shades of gray, offset by black was the décor; in many places rust from old nails was part of the décor. The brightest colors were those of the moss green carpet adorning the floor and parts of the wall where conditions were right for moss to grow. Other colors fitting into the design were yellows and browns. The participants were a few Brown-eyed Susans off in the corner. A Brown-eyed Susan, also known as blanket flower because of its ability to disperse widely, is one of the hardiest, longest flowering native North American perennials. It grows best in well-drained, nutrient-poor soil and adapts well to sunnier locations.

The condition of the house both inside and outside was basically the same. Anything that may have been usable at one time was no longer there, or in no condition to use anymore. While sitting on the 'ground-floor,' I turned my attention to the ceiling. "Believe It Or Not," the electricity still worked. The old coal-oil lanterns no longer hung on a wall-spike, but the rooms were still illuminated.

The Master designer left the power on. While looking skyward, I saw it was the sunlight by day and the stars by night, which illuminated [this was the electricity] the house. The roof, which once covered the attic and a loft used for sleeping, had large holes in it. Through these wide-open spaces I saw the handiwork of God. On a warm summer night a person could lay back in the corner of a room and see the full moon also brightening the surroundings as if the spotlight shone to tell a story. Stories—there's no place where life's narratives go silent. [Re. Psalms 19:3]

INTERMEZZO

[Maybe It Is Time To Find A Musical Connection To Just Rest For A While In This "Intermezzo!"]

All the heavens pronounce the magnificence of God. God, through the visible expanse of the universe, invites us to join Him in relationship. God is speaking to us night and day through the grandeur of all He has created, and no place on earth is held back from seeing His handiwork. The knowledge God presents in the things He has made, is expressly known. Scientific minds are and have been for a long time been so enthralled by the knowledge the heavens declare, they are on an unending exploration to find out how it all came to be.

The sun has been given a place to call home, it has been given a platform from which to worship God in its own way. The picture of it all reminds me of a bridegroom being strengthened to run hard and fast in the race of life and time. The sun is not limited in any way throughout the universe, providing the light and heat this earth needs for people to survive.

God's law is perfect, making it possible for building a relationship with Him. I have let my mind wander and wonder as I read Psalms 19. As I read the whole passage I could have related more of how I feel when I read God's word. However, I simply wish to say, LORD, let my mouth speak of the things permeating my heart concerning the magnificence and purity of all You are, and may my life in all it is, be acceptable to You; you are the strength I need, and You are my God! [These are some my reflective thoughts of Psalms 19] Please read Psalms 19 for yourself and see what words you may wish to express while soaking up God's Word.

Selah—Break Time

While moving on from where we left off before the Intermission, I wonder, what is it that would attract a story for this bright light of the night sky in this place surrounded by mountains? As I lifted my eyes up to the hills I realized where people's help came from. The mountains promised to bring peace to the people. It wasn't the fabulous features offered up here that held my attention. What then? It was the handiwork of God. One writer put it like this:

> The heavens say publicly that God is alive, and He is highlighting his creation and His magnitude in the sky. Day after day the heavens talk to us, and every night once again they demonstrate pure knowledge. There is no verbal communication in which the voice of the heavens is not understood.
>
> The vibrations of this voice in a picturesque form, send word to the whole earth and into the ends of the world of the magnificent glory of God.
>
> He put a special pavilion in the heavens for the sun. When you look at it, it's as if it were a bridegroom coming into the exhibition area like a winner who is ready and jubilant about the task he faces. The sun comes up in one corner of heaven and completes its course to the other end of heaven. Nothing escapes the heat it generates. [Psalms 19:3 JBI]

As I remember it, "This Old House," this old abandoned house, is saying something too. The walls glare at me. The floor, which at one time may have had old newspapers overlaid with linoleum, is cold and barren of excitement; it may just have been slabs of timber, of which most often there has been a large supply in the sheltering woods. Even in its prime, this floor covering was nothing like the sheet goods we have installed in our homes today, but it once served a purpose, and all through history, purpose was always important to learn from. I pray that I will create more "Selah Moments:" R&R, just so we can take in the beauty of God.

A potbelly stove once warmed the place on a cold winter's night; it no longer beckons me with its warmth. It was rusted on a heap or it sits in a place of importance in an antique shop. It may stand there newly painted a flat black, awaiting the bid of an eager antique hunter. It may fill a corner placement of your cottage. It may bring back memories of the people of your past.

From where I sat in this old house there was no glow of hot embers akin to the chunks of tree trunks chopped into burnable sizes; coming from the potbelly stove, to bring warmth to the chill in my bones. Rubbish was all that I saw. So what kind of a story is there for me to see even now, in the spotlight of the light that shone through the skylights [holes in the roof.]

In amongst the array of deterioration I saw a crack open in my imagination, I saw a story appearing. I gazed for a moment or two, and I saw images from the past. Although at first, they were hazy, I realize these images are people in relationship to me. Relationships: How would we ever live without them and be people with the whole meaning of what we can be?

For the sake of reaching out into the heart of this book I refer to "This Old House" hypothetically, as if adjusting myself for changes in my life. Without a doubt, a picture is like lavished armloads of comfort to a hurting heart. Detailed instructions on the art of how not to have had a hurting heart in the first place, just does not make things better. When I visualize an old house such as the one in my story, I can see myself in more of a realistic manner. What I am trying to do is akin to writing a parable. Some people understand this thought: Best understood as "A picture is worth a thousand words." Writers, many years ago tell of a man who used this idea markedly enough to encourage people to cheerfully follow Him: His name is Jesus!

Now, as I allow myself to escape reality and travel in time, I take over the job as the interior and exterior decorator. The first thing I do is to fix the roof, to keep the rain out, to keep people warm and dry when they visit. A warm place of hospitality is much better than one where the shivers run through the body; like belonging to the Polar Bear Club and jumping into English Bay in Vancouver at forty below zero. I once lived across the street from English Bay, and witnessed these brave souls enduring the winter dip.

Next, I refurbish the entire interior. New panes of glass are installed in the window frames [how we look at people]. I find that the local antique shop [The Bible] has all the bits and pieces to enhance this old house. If we want to bring people back into this house [our lives], there will need to be major changes. A time may come when I may not need this old house [my body and mind], but for now I need to keep it in shape.

Then I go outside and tidy up the exterior. Much of what others have looked at in the past has not been easy on the eyes [how I have been living my Christian Life]. It takes a while, but when it is done, I stand back to have a look: Something is missing. The door is still hanging on one hinge [I am still leaving out some people as though they were outcasts]. I repair it and I go inside.

While sitting in my recliner, surveying the remake, I let warm embers comfort me. Momentarily, I have done all I can to restore "This Old House." With logs ablaze in the potbelly stove, I see this old house is now a home. The Welcome Mat invites and awaits people to enter a home full of warmth and love.

> Can one person be this lucky?
> Kissed this old gal—[house] and she kissed me back!
> The rooms were so black—but the words this old house
> spoke: "How Sweet it was." [Thoughts expressed from lyrics
by Sammy Cahn 1960]

Even though I didn't physically live in this old place, just a leg off Westside Road, I am transported to a place which relates. The things I have observed are trying to say something. From the comfort of my recliner I look through the window in my mind. I saw what was becoming more than a mystery as I was privy to the memories coming so vividly; when I looked beyond myself, to feature others.

Some reminders of a house fire that once threatened to erase this house from the landscape, still exist behind some of the new wall paneling. It was not erased, and that for a reason; instead, it was left as a reminder to all those who see it; a reminder that 'People' once called this place home. Someone has said: "A house is not a home, 'People' are." It's all about 'People.' The reason I am writing this book is so I can express these very words in amongst about a hundred-and-sixty thousand other words—*Everybody: Everybody Is A Somebody*.

I look back to my own times as a child, when I was a young person growing up into the struggles of a time and a place such as what I have been surveying; here I still wonder sometimes why I am here to go on while others did not survive their storms. Often, wind, hail, and an assortment of other disasters took their toll on our home. It was rebuilt like new every time, but the scars remain.

Even today, so many years later there are things tagged to my life with their genesis, in a picture like the one I have been imagining because I visited a relic of the past. I see the people that may once have occupied this visibly impaired old farmhouse house. Parents, grandparents, and even great grandparents; these come to view. I am confronted with the perilous times this home faced back in the day; yet they lived to tell the story. It may not have been a simple story, but through it all it was a Love Story!

In times like these something kept us going. We found the strength in a book written by a guy named Paul. He was quite a prolific writer; he always had a way of getting the message across. Although his writing dates back a long way, the things he said still ring in my ears. The encouragements he passed on never get used up. One thing he said was, "life is hard and sometimes it seems as if everyone around us has delivered the devastating blow. This kind of attack makes us confused, but we don't give up during this kind of struggle."

"Everyone wants to tear us apart, but still we are not left alone. Often, we are even physically knocked down to the ground, but we get up again and start over" [JBI]. Paul was talking about the source of the strength he used when times got tough. The source is the same as the one I mentioned a little while ago. Many folks have received the strength to move ahead because of this source: Jesus. In tough times, it pays to know where our strength lies.

There are times in the lives of every family when illness takes center stage. I am no exception. The special care required for me to recover from some of my problems must often be entrusted to someone other than myself. Who do I use as my strength today? God. It is not like I or anybody else have 'Dibs' on God's Help. Each of us can make the decision to let God be our help in times of trouble. However, it is not easy to help people to understand these thoughts. The stuff of this world gets in the way; we get confused.

When I was a baby it was not always so easy to run to the emergency ward when the children in our home got sick. One time I was affected physically by double pneumonia; no doctor's care was readily available. This was one tough time I did not yet know much about, but my folks did. Parents—what a God given gift they were then, they are gone now, but the memories remain as strong as ever.

In times like these I had someone who stood up for me before God to ask for help in making me well. My folks spoke to God for me. God got the praise. Here is an example of people helping people. This has the merit to be illuminated in the moonbeams encompassing the old abandoned house. Many such stories could be centered out for the glory of God. We were family, we became, what we became because of The LORD!

As I travel through the reality of the past, I see many precious moments, which affected my life for today. Once upon a time a little boy was in the care of the priest in the temple. He was there to learn the ways of God because the mother, Hannah, had promised him to God, if God would give her a son. She could not have a son and she wanted to do her part to be useful in life. This boy's name was Samuel. Yes, Samuel was special; he had a major part to play in history; he came to birth through some travail on the part of his mother, but he differed not in the 'Special' department! As Samuel played a major part in the story of all life, "So Do We All!"

The story says God's word was valuable in the days surrounding when he was born. The mountain was about to bring peace to the people again through a young man committed to following the leader. When we were children, we often played a game called "Follow the Leader" The person at the front of the line would go up and down the road and or field and do many things; it was the job of those following, to do exactly as the leader had done. If the leader jumped a fence, so did the rest of the pack. If the leader flopped themselves into a puddle of muddy water, so did the rest of the gang. 'Following The Leader' can put someone into the position of doing whatever it takes, to get it done.

I usually regard terms like priest, prophet, and preacher to be synonymous with someone close to God. People of that time thought so too. They came to the priest with their offerings as if they were presenting themselves to God himself. The priest was their third party. People always need someone to go to with their needs. It may be a priest, as it was with Hannah. Maybe a person would go to a prophet, as it was later the case with Samuel. These are also someone that people will go to for help. The fourth "P" is for "People," regular folks. People are "a somebody" other people will call for help. There is a transference from the Priest, Prophet, and Preacher, to what is considered 'The Regular People.'

I see that the letter P is especially important regarding the subject I am displaying. *The Mountains Shall Bring Peace To The People*. Here is another P. "And the word of the LORD was 'Precious' in those days." In the light of the existing circumstances, I don't see these words as being truly relevant until I see what God is doing despite the circumstances. If I read carefully, I will see that God is bringing up a new generation of leadership. It was through a child named Samuel that this took place. Samuel ministered unto the LORD before Eli the priest. Faced with the old, I see the new; both coming up together until the Lord separates them. On one certain day the sons of Eli died, and then on the very same day, Eli the priest dies. Can you see how God has opened the door for the new leadership to arrive? The word of the LORD became 'Precious' that day. As life positions itself before us it is not always easy to see the beauty of God's Purpose. But God Is In The Picture!

This is like the story of my old house. The old things have decayed to make way for the new house to come forth. As this old house has fallen by the wayside on Westside Road, it has opened the door for a need to be looked after. Because this abandoned house has fallen, I have moved to a new house [still hypothetically]. There were many precious moments in the old place, but it was time for the new house to be built. Just as Samuel began another era, I, too, needed to begin again in life. I realized that what was, does not always cut it. This is not to discount the past; it is there for good reason; it has often pointed forward to remind us of things we no longer do but should still do. I didn't do it with my own strength and ability. It started because someone else sat back in the abandoned house and looked through a crack in the wall, or through that window of time, and saw a familiar face. He saw that if He would go back and redecorate this old house that was now a home; He could be a part of the new building process.

The person who did this was Jesus. He came back to the earth He had created and made relationships with People. He showed the love of God. He did it purposefully. It required a sacrifice. He would be the payment for the guilt of humankind, at the expense of his life. This was done at Calvary: The Way of the Cross. He expended Himself for me. Nothing I have ever viewed in a movie has ever made it plainer than when I watched the Mel Gibson movie—*The Passion of The Christ*.

The physical part of the sacrifice is so vivid it cannot be mistaken. The prelude to his death, and the elements of the death itself make it increasingly easy to love this Jesus even more than I thought I had loved Him. I could be a part of "Precious Moments." I only needed to accept this payment as made for me personally.

Darkness appears everyday. As sure as I am the sun will come up most mornings, so sure am I that the darkness will come when the sun sets. Someone once told me I should not struggle with what I have learned when things were going well, when the times of darkness come—when I tend to doubt what I know is true.

You or I will not escape the consequences. The consequence is, there are things that cannot be done in the dark, but the hope factor tells us that morning will come and once again the opportunity to live in the light is once again offered to us. As I sat all alone in the "Pen Palace" [A cottage I rented temporarily when I first came to The Valley], at Lake Windermere, I learned of the peace that the mountain brings. During the darkness of the night, I could not grasp the beauty of the mountains in their total splendor. I know of no better place than the mountains to sink deeply into 'peace,' like I would envelop my head in a deep fluffy pillow, for a restful night's sleep.

I Am Looking Back To See "IF—"
"IF" You Are Looking Back To See—.

Much of the time, Christianity as we live it, does not look like we have it all figured out! Guesswork, implications, or theory, constantly leave us with an empty stomach, still hungry for the "Real Thing" [subjectively]. If we put our faith and trust only in what history has told us, we may be mistaken. When all that is said and done turns out to be the reality we have not yet experienced, what is the rest of the story? Unknown reality has an end result we may not want to miss out on. We may be "Missing The Mark" by not considering Jesus, because it does not fit the costume we want to wear in life, or it sounds too far fetched to be true. What is the missing linkage we miss out on when life as we have it is the bird in the hand— 'Faith!' We may look at faith objectively or subjectively; one has a solid footing and the other is sinking sand—the quicksand scenario is not a pretty one.

There is seemingly no end to the resources we have at the ready to sort out any problem on planet earth. We have God, evolutionists, preachers, scientists, regular folks on the street that think they know it all, regular folks on the street that "KNOW IT ALL—." There is no shortage of resources, be they on the right side of reality, or on the wrong side of reality.

Fantasy is the lack of reality. Today, we live in a world of 3D, and Virtual Reality. Yes, these come so close to what is the life we live, but they come with a huge disclaimer; they do not have their facts straight. They are just fantasy; they are exciting, fun, exhilarating—but they take us on an accelerating roller-coaster ride away from truth and reality. Too often Reality has been the big bad wolf waiting to devour us: It need not be.

What Did I See, and What Does It Say?
This is the good question of the day.
"Prepare to Launch!"

I love the Lord because he hath heard my voice and my supplications. Because he hath inclined his ear unto me, therefore will I call upon him as long as I live. The sorrows of death compassed me, and the pains of hell gat hold upon me: I found trouble and sorrow. Then called I upon the name of the Lord; O Lord, I beseech thee, deliver my soul.

Gracious is the Lord, and righteous; yea, our God is merciful. The Lord preserves the simple: I was brought low, and he helped me. Return unto thy rest, O my soul; for the Lord hath dealt bountifully with thee.

For thou hast delivered my soul from death, mine eyes from tears, and my feet from falling. I will walk before the Lord in the land of the living.

I believed, therefore have I spoken; I was greatly afflicted; I said in my haste, all men are liars. What shall I render unto the Lord for all his benefits toward me?

I will take the cup of salvation and call upon the name of the Lord. I will pay my vows unto the Lord now in the presence of all his people. Precious in the sight of the Lord is the death of his saints.

O Lord, truly I am thy servant; I am thy servant, and the son of thine handmaid: thou hast loosed my bonds. I will offer to thee the sacrifice of thanksgiving and will call upon the name of the Lord. I will pay my vows unto the Lord now in the presence of all his people. In the courts of the Lord's house, in the midst of thee, O Jerusalem. Praise ye the Lord. [Psalms 116:1-19; KJV]

What Did I See, and What Does It Say?

Believe It Or Not

8th Chapter

Pursue A Passionate Perspective.
Sketch One Genesis: One Beginning.

Truth is: Who Believes What? And Why? The truth is about "who" we are, and The Who [Some folks say 'what' instead of 'who'] that created us or paved the way for us to be in the existence we are occupying on Planet Earth. Let's for a moment think about the "who" we are, what we call ourselves, and the person that our parents thought we were at birth [implying ownership], and they gave us the name we carry throughout our lives [unless we change it].

When someone looks for a mate, somebody they are attracted to, what in many cases is the attraction which accelerates the process? For some it is the makeup of what the other person looks like in physical appearance, which is the first hook gaining their attention. For yet others, it may be the inner character they see in another person which garners their interest level in so far as hoping and praying that the other person will lock eyes with them long enough to know there may be a chance for a connection in the offing. These first impressions can have a lasting aftermath because of the first sketch which forms in the mind of the seeker. A picture [sketch] is worth a thousand words. The necessary words will come at the right time. The Bible story of Jacob sketches in well here.

And it came to pass, when Jacob saw Rachel the daughter of Laban his mother's brother, and the sheep of Laban his mother's brother, that Jacob went near, and rolled the stone from the well's mouth and watered the flock of Laban his mother's brother. And Jacob kissed Rachel, and lifted up his voice, and wept. [Genesis 29: 10-11 KJV]

Leah was tender eyed; but Rachel was beautiful and well favored. And Jacob loved Rachel; and said, I will serve thee seven years for Rachel thy younger daughter. [Genesis 29: 17-18 KJV] This is a Sketch, a Story worth a look. [Genesis 29]

Believe It Or Not

Chapter 8
SKETCH ONE GENESIS: ONE BEGINNING

L ove is a scary thing, and you never know what's going to happen. It's one of the most beautiful things in life, but it's one of the most terrifying. It's worth the fear because you have more knowledge and experience; we learn from people, and we have memories. [Ariana Grande https://www.brainyquote.com]

It is of immeasurable value to know who we are. Our uniqueness is important to life in a way no other person is. I suggest this makes us a special part of humankind. This said, we had no part in becoming 'Who' we were fashioned to be, but we are to a large degree able to have a part in 'what' we will become. Life situations, and people, are not so easily 'chaptered or phased' into this storyline of life growth and or transformation. Without understanding and articulating or explaining this part of the picture of life here, I will continue, leaving what I do not understand to the Entity that does; leaving me to live life to the full without carrying the baggage of guilt for that which is beyond me!

I am not the Sharpest Knife In The Drawer! I have smarts, so do you. Each of us now living, or those who lived in the past, now gone, are or were important to each our time of life! Most parents have a reason they tagged a child with a certain name. I say 'tagged,' because as we grow up into whatever society we journey through from birth to death, we may wonder "What Were My Parents Thinking" when they named me "Jacob—or whatever they named the rest of you." As I grew up I may have thought [forgive me Mom and Dad] I would have presented better with the name "Jim, Bob, Murray—," because I saw people with these names get ahead in life in a manner better than what I thought I was managing my way through life. Someone said, "What's In A Name?" This may be a more important question than we realize.

Part Two—Who Believes What? And Why?

Believe It Or Not

When my parents named me Jacob, they probably did not even realize that the name Jacob, according to the way it links back into history from the early records of the time we know, meant deceiver, supplanter, cheater—you can fill in the rest [Please Read Genesis 25-33; for here, highlight Genesis Chapter 29]. Seems I was named after my mother's father, or one of many other choice people.

As I think along these lines, my grandfather's parents probably also did not think about the history of the name, but it was the thing to do to name a child after someone in their lineage. My grandfather was named Jacob, and I got the name from this family tree. However, Jacob of the Bible was named for what he would be in the sense of his life; before he met the 'who' he would be in the rest of his life; this was for purposes hard to understand. Jacob presented a conundrum. We might add that we are much the same as was this relic of the past—will we also be relics? Good Question.

Recently, after a snowfall, I was walking through a field where we live. I was wearing shoes I should not have been wearing. As long as I was walking on the flat part of the field it was doable. However, before I was going to be able to get onto the sidewalk, I would need to manage my way down a slope. I began to walk more gingerly, kind of sideways, so as to get a better grip on the ground beneath my feet. I soon realized I would fall if I did not do something. So, I let myself take a little run towards the sidewalk, and this propelled me forward farther than I expected. On the other side of the sidewalk was the other side of the hill I was trying to navigate. So, as I had to much force to stay on the sidewalk, I tumbled down the hill. I injured myself in the process, but not seriously. Although there might have been harsher consequences, I believe God came to the rescue to prevent serious injury. I should have been more conscious of the footwear I was wearing.

Believe It Or Not: God Came To The Rescue Again!

It is positively assuring to know I have solid footing under my feet when I am walking along any path; be it a sidewalk, a path alongside a cliff, on a road, or even that the floor of my home can withstand my weight. If I were walking along a sidewalk in "Our Town," and without warning the sidewalk caved in into a sinkhole, and if I survived and I never felt enough assurance to walk on sidewalks anymore, it would change how I conducted life.

Was I walking a path near a cliff in the Purcell Range of The Rocky Mountains near "Our Town," I would be more aware of the possible dangers and I would be more watchful or cautious as I made my way along the edge that could present me with the possibility of slipping on the path and coming to the end of my earthly road. I have had situations where I walked such paths while trying to get to where the fly fishing was supposed to be inviting.

A precious resource exists in 'knowing' we have a foundation or underpinning that cannot powder up or fragment. When we have an assurance of peace of mind and of a safe journey, we are less likely to delay our journey to a distant place, or to say we do not feel an assurance all is well for this trek. There are no guarantees in life which can pledge to us that all will be well indefinitely as we live life. This is much truer when we think in terms of eternity, as far as promises made by another human go.

When one God was and still is in charge of our past, our present, and all our tomorrows, we can have this assurance of safety about eternity—this is faith as we should know it. This still means we will need to live through the conditions 'of this world' physically, facing the rough paths near a cliff now and again; God will bring us through it as we trust Him!

Belief systems all use a degree, share, and or a portion of the reasonableness of their belief of faith to advocate or promote their position regarding the Genesis of all Geneses [beginnings]. We stagnate or decay on this foundation or platform of each our own belief—over and over, again, and again. We do so because of the 'trust factor' we can never seem to come to grips with. Who or what is the One Entity we can, without reservation trust implicitly [completely, unquestioningly, unreservedly]?

Philippians Chapter Three [The Bible] talks about the pure delight, pleasure, bliss, and total worth of the "Priceless Value of Knowing Christ [Jesus]." Another passage says it this way, "the reason I put up with the inconveniences [suffer] of life is because God is who He said He is; this is so in The Person of Jesus Christ, because of what Jesus did for me on the Cross; for this I am not ashamed. If I suffer the loss of some earthly things because of it, So Be It! "For I know whom I have believed and am persuaded that He is able to keep that which I have committed unto Him against that day." [2 Timothy 1:12-14 KJV]

If I can make this clearer for us, I can lay me down to sleep in peace tonight, and every other night, knowing I have a solid foundation for contending that Jesus Christ Is LORD of All!

Heraclitus, an ancient thinker said, "You can never step in the same river twice." Life is always changing around us; God remains the same! He can always be trusted to keep His promises! We can take his faithfulness and love 'to the bank.'

Panta Rhei, "Everything Flows." The river is constantly changing and moving. If you step in a river once, then step out only to step in it again, the water that rushes past us, would be different. So it would have changed hence the quote "you can't step in the same river twice."

Distance traveled cannot be retrieved to be what we started with. What if we had placed a ditto mark in our life and we would be exactly where we wanted to be. 'What if' the 'ditto mark' was our choice for where life was the best it could be. Once the water in the river has passed where we stepped into it, retrieving the moment, or reversing it, is impossible to us; that instant, whether it was good or bad, is gone. But if we step out of the water and back in again or stay in the exact spot where the water is replaced by another batch of water, we can make a difference for the moment that has passed us by, by taking up the challenge to change our motives, attitude, and actions to make a difference.

"Everything Flows," and this, all too quickly by us. Change is inevitable—this is for sure. We should be sorry for the wrong we have done. However, we need not grieve in shame, never getting over this loss of not having done right all the time, because we made mistakes in life—everyone who has ever lived has made a few mistakes. Accept change with a quick look back, only to use as a benchmark left behind, and an even quicker look forward to where we are headed, intending to be the better person for losing the past good we 'might' have done!

"You can never step in the same river twice."

We cannot afford too quick a look over the resources that can help us move ahead and those for the good of others. We all have a part in fashioning the worth we can 'attain in life;' we had no part in the worth we were ingrained with by God, at birth!

Which will it be? Certainty or Penalties? Certainty gathers the decisive imaginable worth, thus constructing movements. Penalties define or represent the outcomes of reality or blunder reasoning. A Central Characteristic, Objectively Focused Truth provides the most benefits. Both Truth and Error Demand The Price of Admission into Life!

Worth, simply expressed as a 'word,' is 'immeasurable,' like any other word in the complete thesauri's [phrasebooks] of the whole world. The many vocabularies' languages, terminologies, or usages in which we use words, give us visualization for processing the picture or sketch of eternal purpose. The ultimate purpose of our existential [fact of existing] term of life is to express or acknowledge 'our' connection to our Genesis! How will we come to this juncture where we see enough truth, and see enough attraction in this truth, to let it make a difference in and for our lives, to increase the value we already have as human beings created in the image of God. Jacob's story in the Bible presented an attractive entity: Rachel.

As participants of life we have an innate, inborn, or a native desire to know where we came from in the overview of all that ever existed. This is obvious as we look at how people interact with others and life itself. From the 'two sides only framework' from which I most often present things, I imagine all people, 'Everybody' everywhere, have or will have a chance at eternal hope, by their choice to accept what was offered by God. 'Choice' is a huge story; it may befuddle or baffle us betimes [occasionally]. We want to nail everything down to what we can feel and see! This diminishes the impact of 'Faith' as it is defined in The Bible.

For those people who cannot figure it all out because of their mental capacity to understand the choice factor—for the stillborn, and many other scenarios, which may differ from the rest of us, there will still be an answer of hope. The fairness of the Creator or Originator of the Beginning or Genesis of every universal prospective or likelihood, will be inclusive enough of the *Everybody: Everybody Is A Somebody* statement I use as my Title, to offer hope of Eternal satisfaction. Simply, and from my 'choice' to use The God Side picture, God is omnipotent, supreme, and or unstoppable enough; He figured out our conundrums or mysteries about life, living, and fairness long before He physically fashioned people.

Let's get back to the Title of *Chapter Eight, Sketch One Genesis*: Beginnings [*The Worth of A One Genesis Scenario: One Choice Of Beginnings*]. Certainty or Penalties? Certainty assembles significant possible worth, creating changes. Penalties explain or characterize the consequences of truth or gaffe thinking. A key point, or accurately determined reality, delivers the most profits. Both truth and error require the payment of admittance to compete in life.

The Bible, in the book of 1st. Thessalonians 4, speaks of abounding more and more, progressing or growing closer to being the best that any of us can be as we pursue a relationship with this Creator God I spoke about. The entire meaning of 'value or worth' pans out in many words from which we could garner many more words to describe 'worth and value.' To lay out a graphical mind picture, etching or sketch of this growth process, let's look at a few of the descriptive words that open up this picture with extended clarity.

Account, aid, benefit, cost, credit, price, quality, rate, valuation, assistance, avail, caliber, class, consequence, desirability, dignity, equivalence, excellence, goodness, help, importance, mark, meaningfulness, merit, moment, note, perfection, significance, stature, use, usefulness, utility, virtue, weight, worthiness.

Tucked away in these words is the word 'consequence.' This is a serious sounding word, and this is just what it is, 'serious.' As we dissect this word we come up with more descriptions of Worth and Value. For us to fully understand the contexts of the many items in this book, let's look at these synonyms:

Result, the outcome of an action, aftereffect, aftermath, effect, fallout, issue, reaction, repercussion, end, event, follow-up, outgrowth, payback, sequel, sequence, spin-off, upshot, waves, bottom line, can of worms, chain reaction, follow through.

Truth or Consequences: Truth garners the ultimate possible worth or value, thereby producing actions; consequences describe or picture out the results of truth or error. We see that both 'Truth and Consequences' have repercussions and benefits.

Truth breeds impending or future action in words and realities. Knowing we will just scratch the surface with what I lay out before us all, let's set a balance and or reality of both Truth and Consequence by looking at some words that describe 'truth:'

Reality, validity, accuracy, authenticity, certainty, fact, legitimacy, principle, truthfulness, veracity, actuality, axiom, case, correctness, dope, exactitude, exactness, facts, factuality, factualness, genuineness, gospel, infallibility, maxim, nitty-gritty, perfection, picture, precision, rectitude, rightness, scoop, score, trueness, truism, verisimilitude, verity, factualism, gospel truth, honest truth, inside track, naked truth, plain talk, unvarnished truth, whole story.

From this trapline, lineage, assemblage, or collection words, we need to read the words 'worth and value' into a plot not easily definable or understood when we add the words, 'but why is this happening to me?' Anytime we state or suggest beliefs which may not be understood they way we may present them, we will encounter "But Questions." These are always challenging for the most part!

As we evaluate life concerns where the antonyms or opposites of all I mention, also tell part of the story of the whole of what I am trying to say, life gets tough. This is where 'Consequence' often tells a story we do not cotton to, or like as much, but this is a life where 'the gum we've chewed, sticks to our hands big-time when we take it out of our mouth [Jacob Bergen]; [where the rubber meets the road].

The trapline or family of words we venture into when we try to sort out the worth and value of what life lays out for us, often comes back to Bite Us on the Butt. It is somewhat uncomfortable to sit at ease [Like buckshot blast to our derriere] in times like these.

Who Believes What? And Why? The truth is about 'who' we are, and The Who [Some folks say what instead of Who] which created us or paved the way for us to be in the existence we are occupying on Planet Earth. Let's for a moment think about the 'who' we are, what we call ourselves, and the person our parents thought we were at birth [implying ownership]; they gave us the name we carry throughout our lives [unless we change it].

As I write I am treating what I say as if I were giving a lecture to create a study session within the heart or mindset of everybody. Occam's Razor is a principle of immense merit when we play detective in sorting out the facts of any matter and how to affix blame. When we use many words to evaluate, or judge anything, if you will, it may be helpful to see the big picture, but the multiplicity of words can also add to an unnecessary confusion. Who we are, this was defined at birth; what we become is up to us and circumstances.

Occam's razor (also Ockham's razor or Ocham's razor; Latin: lex parsimoniae "law of parsimony") is the problem-solving principle that the simplest solution is the right one. When presented with competing hypotheses to solve a problem, one should select the solution with the fewest assumptions. The idea is attributed to William of Ockham (c. 1287–1347), who was an English Franciscan friar, scholastic philosopher, and theologian.

Science uses Occam's razor in a kidnapping, forceful or cunning fashion, [abductive] and or in a heuristic [investigative or experimental fashion] when developing hypothetical or imaginary mock-ups. We may need to find a go between to decide on the best route to decipher a code, or the facts, if there are any facts, as opposed to the theory-based elements of a problem, such as we get when we follow the rigors or strictness an arbitrator. When we are one of the parties in the arbitration process, we may need to accept someone else's theory, and this may not sit well. Anytime someone says, 'this is the truth,' with an addendum which says, 'because I say so;' personally, I may say WHOA in this case!

Occam's razor does not always easily fit into the way science likes to do things. Science does not think of Occam's Razor as an unquestionable code of reasoning, resulting in a factual or positively unquestionable result. Science may at times falsify the results of their oppositions methods or principles, thinking they will present themselves as presenting the greater value to come to the facts of life. Each explanation of a marvel or miracle presents a near innumerable number of possibilities, and or multifaceted or intricate alternatives, like using many words to explain something [opposite to the Occam's Razor Method]. There seems to be a philosophy where 'more' is better; this is not always the case.

Someone can confuse us with failing explanations and with ad hoc hypotheses [A save my idea clause gives me more credibility; I think!] We cannot so easily prove someone wrong in discussing belief systems. Modest models are better than difficult ones to understand, because we can more easily decide not needing to decide on millions of options. This is why I say I believe in the 'Two Sides Only Scenario.'

The Worth of A One Genesis Scenario

Sketch One Genesis: *One Beginning* is the worth of objective value or one of subjective value? What is the gap between the two? Is value simply a matter of monetary worth? Is worth calculated by using a financial calculator? Is worth calculated by something or Someone greater than physical substance? Is worth calculated by what we do; dependent on how much we do for a cause?

On what basis do we evaluate worth?

Objectivity—Requires an indisputable or certain object.

Subjectivity—Requires a subject; of course, it can be indisputable or certain, but it has to be a subject based on fact and a demonstration which is an irrefutable fact, demonstrated by there being no other contenders that can match the reasonableness of the object [objectivity or moral truth] not a feeling; not a feeling about the fact.

Someone said, "The Truth Will Set You Free."
Realization—Everyone has distinctive characteristics.
Query—Does Everyone transmit the same capacity of purpose?
The Bible says this,

And ye shall know the truth, and the truth shall make you free. [John 8:32; KJV]

The whole theme of this chapter revolves around the right and wrong way of thinking, and then the process of how we live in the day to day. The day to day of our lives is where the huge challenge of survival seems to exist: Right or Wrong? How often do we assess if we are travelling in the right lane or the wrong lane?

Truth and Consequences

Truth or Consequences—these are actually two separate sketches to consider. To tell the whole story these phrases suggest, would take an eternity, which I do not have. I have a limited existence; I have many detractors or critics. Many people try to make their point in the books they write, each comes from their own starting point, one of subjectivity—revolving around feelings. Feelings are great! They may satisfy our 'want' situation. Feelings do not verify Truth.

Truth or Consequences suggest an either-or scenario. If we follow the truth, the objective truth, our end result will bring the best-case placement in the scope of our eternal position. Following the 'Truth' to a "T" in our day-to-day, in the best way we know how, to a factual right point, this may be our intent, but feelings about the truth hinder living the whole of life exactly as God intended. Remember again, my reference to the 'Two Sides Only Scenario,' and God as one side of these positions.

I am not trying to elongate or stretch out this chapter, so I end up with at least five-thousand words. Five-thousand words per chapter is usually my target, and most of the time I reach that target. However, if this is my heartfelt intent, then I will miss the boat and leave you in a worse state than is good, truthful, or right to live life to gain the eternity that God promises. I intend to break apart assumptions from facts; fact being the objective moral truth, which will bring about an end result that does not suffer the consequences in a manner we most often suggest consequences play themselves out. Sorting out differences can be frustrating to say the least.

I suggest we should think of the Occam's Razor principle as we read through this book: I am endeavoring to do this as I write this book. It is difficult to be so precise so as not to make any mistakes. Even Adam and Eve in the physical presence of God Almighty did not accomplish this precise path of simplicity which sets a clear path for us to travel.

Occam's razor (also Ockham's razor or Ocham's razor; Latin: lex parsimoniae "law of parsimony") is the problem-solving principle that the simplest solution tends to be the right one.

Adam and Eve were born into or created in or into The Garden of Eden narrative as functional beings. This story of marathon proportions was in the perspective or the viewing precipice of life—The Biggee. In and with the presence of God Almighty all around them, they made a big mistake. We have suffered the consequences ever since.

God created Adam and Eve; He presented the truth to them about the good life. He presented the facts to them through the choice He presented, by giving a command about what would be, if they did not follow His directive. This was a 'truth or consequence scenario.'

We can also rightly read this picture as being 'the truth' and 'consequences' principle. God was and is the Truth, He told the Truth, and He watched as Adam and Eve walked away from the Truth, in as much as saying "YEAH RIGHT in the face of God!" Adam and Eve did not say this [or did they?]. But the resulting consequence was, they had to leave what would have been their 'Best Day of Eternity'—and ours too!

Truth and Consequences open up two doors for us.

Truth opens up ONE DOOR for us,
"This is the way, Walk in it!"
Jesus said, "I Am the Way, The Truth, and The Life—."

Wrong things bring hurtful results; right actions bring guilt free results, not always trouble-free results. The truth presents us with 'two doors,' this way or that way; right or wrong; good or bad. It seems everyone wants the right to 'choose,' and it is a God given right! But 'choice' has baggage: Sometimes unwanted baggage. When we use our right to choose we often do so subjectively.

The narrative or epic [marathon] of life can be a 'cliff hanger.' The overture, approach, proposition, or proposal to advance into life with a success ratio second to none, was part of the Creation Story. God did His part—Adam and Eve failed to do what was hoped they would do. Well, 'hoped' may be the wrong word, God knew what the option of choice would cause. We may look at the story of The Garden of Eden and think, God made the big mistake by giving us the choice to obey or to disobey. However, if we look at the "Rest of The Story" of what giving is about, we will recant.

God loved the world He looked forward to in the Creation, in the perspective of knowing that the failed beginning in one sense was only the Genesis of what humankind would be capable of overcoming in the challenges arising for them to love like He did and continues to do. The plan was to 'give' like no other person would ever do, but God would set the bar high enough so we the people would have a high standard for living life like Jesus did when He came to physically show us the way to the 'truth' of the best in the eternal perspective. [Re John 3:16]

God gave like this by Jesus coming in the humble form of a baby, who was dependant on another for the plan of its life to go full circle. Not that God was dependent on anyone or anything, He is God and He is self sufficient. However, to show us an example of dependency on Him, God came as the son of man, as The Son of God, without losing His identity as God; this is the picture of dependency that God shows us in many places in the Bible. However, to check out every aspect of the etchings God carved out for us, this may take a lifetime.

If there be therefore any consolation in Christ, if any comfort of love, if any fellowship of the Spirit, if any bowels and mercies, fulfil ye my joy, that ye be like-minded, having the same love, being of one accord, of one mind.

Let nothing be done through strife or vainglory; but in lowliness of mind let each esteem other better than themselves. Look not every man on his own things, but every man also on the things of others.

Let this mind be in you, which was also in Christ Jesus: Who, being in the form of God, thought it not robbery to be equal with God: But made himself of no reputation, and took upon him the form of a servant, and was made in the likeness of men: And being found in fashion as a man, he humbled himself, and became obedient unto death, even the death of the cross.

Wherefore God also hath highly exalted him and given him a name above every name: That at the name of Jesus every knee should bow, of things in heaven, and things in earth, and things under the earth; And that every tongue should confess that Jesus Christ is Lord, to the glory of God the Father.

Wherefore, my beloved, as ye have always obeyed, not as in my presence only, but now much more in my absence, work out your own salvation with fear and trembling.

For it is God which worketh in you both to will and to do of his good pleasure. [Philippians 2: 1-13; KJV]

I have been writing with many difficult thoughts to comprehend to break the story into many parts, so they can be reassembled in the simplicity of Occam's Razor. There are things I will miss explaining here, but I will address them in a deeper fashion as we move along. If I tell you everything up front in the simplest form I will have nothing to say later. Yes, I believe in the Occam's Razor format, but I also believe in dissecting words and thoughts to get the most I can out of each written perspective so each of us will have more input; to be in a position to help others as the occasions arise. If we never had to live with other people; if we were secluded on a deserted island, simplicity may be easier—Or Not!

Look again at the descriptive words for Truth:

Reality, validity, accuracy, authenticity, certainty, fact, legitimacy, principle, truthfulness, veracity, actuality, axiom, case, correctness, dope, exactitude, exactness, facts, factuality, factualness, genuineness, gospel, infallibility, maxim, nitty-gritty, perfection, picture, precision, rectitude, rightness, scoop, score, trueness, truism, verisimilitude, verity, factualism, gospel truth, honest truth, inside track, naked truth, plain talk, unvarnished truth, whole story.

Now, look at the descriptive words for consequences:

Result, outcome of an action, aftereffect, aftermath, effect, fallout, issue, reaction, repercussion, end, event, follow-up, outgrowth, payback, sequel, sequence, spin-off, upshot, waves, bottom line, can of worms, chain reaction, follow through.

Reality will cause valid or resultant outcomes; it will accurately authenticate that there will be fallouts or consequences in which the spinoff will be like opening a can of worms while expecting the truth of reality to display pleasantries.

INTERMEZZO

Rejoice in the Lord always: and again I say, Rejoice. Let your moderation be known unto all men. The Lord is at hand. Be careful for nothing; but in every thing by prayer and supplication with thanksgiving let your requests be made known unto God. And the peace of God, which passeth all understanding, shall keep your hearts and minds through Christ Jesus. Finally, brethren, whatsoever things are true, whatsoever things are honest, whatsoever things are just, whatsoever things are pure, whatsoever things are lovely, whatsoever things are of good report; if there be any virtue, and if there be any praise, think on these things. Those things, which ye have both learned, and received, and heard, and seen in me, do, and the God of peace shall be with you. [Philippians 4:4-9 KJV]

The Lord is my shepherd; I shall not want. He maketh me to lie down in green pastures: he leadeth me beside the still waters. He restoreth my soul: he leadeth me in the paths of righteousness for his name's sake. Yea, though I walk through the valley of the shadow of death, I will fear no evil: for thou art with me; thy rod and thy staff they comfort me. Thou preparest a table before me in the presence of mine enemies: thou anointest my head with oil; my cup runneth over. Surely goodness and mercy shall follow me all the days of my life: and I will dwell in the house of the Lord for ever. [Psalms 23 KJV]

Selah

A can of worms is a complicated matter, likely to prove awkward or embarrassing.

The bottom-line is, the principles of truthfulness, though sometimes offering us a paycheck where more deductions were made than were expected, will in the end be as though they were placed into a savings account for a welcome beneficial repository or storehouse, from which to receive increase at just the right time. Maybe we can think of a time when it seemed like we were being charged more for the amenities of life than we thought we should have to pay. Our thoughts at the time may have been more on the negative side of the things we were facing than understanding, "all things work together for the good for those who love God and know He has a purpose for their life, realizing that this may just be one of the costs to pay for His purpose to come to fruition for us on the personal side of things.

Faith isn't an abstract absolute; Faith is a subjective experience with God. It's full of mystery and messy variables. In our Faith we need not understand it to enjoy having it. But that's embarrassing for moderns; we want something more akin to scientific notation or legal code. Yet faith only rings true and makes sense if we interact with God on a heart level, not just investigate him objectively. When we approach faith too rationally, we lose something—the mystery, the wonder, the life faith affords—like dissecting a frog. [Gungor, Ed. What Bothers Me Most about Christianity: Honest Reflections from an Open-Minded Christ Follower. Howard Books. Kindle Edition.]

Once again we face reality when we analyze objectivity and subjectivity. Is it a one or the other scenario? Is objectivity always the only recourse we have in any discussion of and about reality? Is objectivity the only option we have when trying to convince someone about what we believe so strongly, about faith being the only entity we can use to access a true understanding about God? As I see it, we can have a greater trust factor if we see something in black and white. Black and white can be smudged or fudged to appear to be something they are not. Unless black and white are uncontaminated, they will never substantiate or authenticate the truth of anything. Our world is full of entities or options to make black look white or authentic. Deception runs rampant out there.

Does subjectivity have any part to play in the Faith Scenario? Another quote from Ed Gungor goes like this:

> An objective understanding and objective truth claims have great value, but so do other kinds of truth claims. Think of falling in love. You don't discover everything that is relevant about love when you try to examine it objectively. There are too many subjective and mysterious aspects to it. And it is the subjective, emotive, messy, mysterious parts of falling in love that capture the human imagination. [Gungor, Ed. What Bothers Me Most about Christianity: Honest Reflections from an Open-Minded Christ Follower. Howard Books. Kindle Edition].

We cannot grasp everything we want to know about faith; everything we need to know about faith; everything we think we know about faith; with a strictly objective mindset. While trying to convince someone about the necessity of faith to understand God, and even for us to come to grips with what faith is all about from start to finish; the challenge is huge. Those who try to fit God into a box of their own size or making, are the majority.

By looking at a Japanese Blow Fish [Fugu] one might perceive and assume it is edible by just removing the skin, the head, and the guts, and slapping it into the frying pan, just like one would do with any other fish. If you are unfamiliar with preparing the Fugu, Blowfish, Puffer Fish, and you bite into the first scrumptious looking morsel, this could be your last meal. Perception in this case can be subjective, based upon a feeling that everything is all right, but there needs to be objectivity involved in this evaluation or proposition.

Value—is it objective or subjective? What is the gap between the two?

In the scenario of the Blowfish the absence of objective truth is what is in the gap of life and death. You may have innocently gone fishing and caught a Fugu and expected to top off your day with a delicious meal of Fish and Chips. There is nothing wrong with all the good feelings you had about this adventure, but ignorance of the truth in this matter can be costly. The greater cost in this picture may be the cost of a life lost, and the funeral expenses, compared to the price of a good meal.

We can have subjective [emotive or euphoric or joyful] feelings in the 'Blow Fish' scenario, this may be the first thoughts we might have as we haul in this beauty. However, it should be only one of many thoughts as we participate going past the catching stage to the partaking stage of the catch [kind of like preparing for love and marriage; they go together like a horse and carriage; so I heard!].

Pastor, Author, Speaker—Ed Gungor mentions thoughts like these in the above quote, while addressing the faith issue:

There are too many subjective and mysterious aspects to it. And it is the subjective, emotional, messy, mysterious parts of falling in love that capture the human imagination.

Sometimes the chain-reaction of the Gospel Truth shows us the certainty of the perfect picture plan God has for us in the whole story as opposed to just a little blessing here and there. When we realize He has events lined up to follow through uniquely with the soundness of purpose, and because of His trustworthiness to keep His promises, we can accept some of the little inconveniences' life gives us as repercussions and or consequences.

The consequences we think of negatively when we 'feel' we are pursuing the Gospel Truth, go from looking like the waves of the sea as we sit in our little rubber raft on the sea of life, to that calm after the storm: An aftermath of tranquility rather than gloom and doom. As we sit on a rubber raft on the sea of life, we may see a calm outing, a storm, a hole in the raft, no rescue in sight.

If you are watching carefully at what I have been writing, you may see I have been using words from the lists of synonyms [descriptive words to tell the story of other words] to broaden the story of Truth and Consequences. Words by themselves will not enlighten and encourage anyone to keep on keeping on when the going gets tough; words can be a waste of time when heart stuff is needed. While thinking through this train of thought, I realize why people who write dictionaries, thesauruses, encyclopedias—and other resources like these, do what they do.

It is never a waste of time to scrounge and search for every possible resource to assist someone along on the path of life. Whether you believe as I do in God, in the Person of Jesus Christ, Who by His Holy Spirit guides us through the issues of life we experience, or not, helping someone along the way will not hurt.

I think of the scenario when an accident occurs; it may be a car accident, a mistake in judgement when dealing with other people. An accident is an unplanned event, not one perpetrated or enacted to look like an accident, and make people think and or believe strongly it was an accident—this is subjective.

When an accident happens, it is a truthful event. The objects are the participants in the scenario, making the accident an objective truth. God did not 'plan' for this accident to happen, although He may have allowed for it, to cause a participant to see the error of their ways and the mess of the consequences of the error and or accident may have been preventable. We cannot change what happen, but we can learn from it as a caution for another time when forethought may be the blessing of the day to prevent an accident.

For just a moment I wish to pull out a word which by itself, without its present context, is a word that can fit the subjective—objective situation. We can feel good about our choice to follow this path, but not be prepared for what lay ahead, because we have not considered the reality [the objective] side. The word I wish to input here is 'plan.'

My wife and I just watched a movie the other day: It was a heart wrenching story. The movie was the portrayal of the book: *Unplanned*. If you have the opportunity, watch it; whether you are Pro-Life or Pro-Choice, it will affect you.

I have a book start which is far from finished and been sitting on the 'To-Do-Shelf' for many years now—*Passion And People* is that book. I feel as though I am discussing reflections of this theme here in this book. I might not need to finish it, even if I had the time and energy left to do all the stuff which has taken priority on my 'To-Do-Shelf' to date.

Truth or Consequences—truth garners the ultimate possibilities, thereby producing actions; consequences describe or picture out the results of truth or error. We see that both truth and consequences have repercussions and benefits. Truth breeds impending or future actions in words and realities; knowing we will just scratch the surface with what I lay out before us all. Let's set a balance and or reality of both truth and consequence. We have looked at some words that describe 'Truth' and 'Consequences.'

Truth has an object, a purpose to assist positively; a consequence is the conclusion reached by a line of inference and or reasoning. [Re *Chapter 4*: *Book Value Reality: What Is Reality?*

The devaluations, reductions, and or depressions we often experience as we attempt to get through life and living without too many hurtful encounters, may be the harsh standards of the reality of the measuring system we see employed by the status quo [existing conditions] of society? Is there a more impartial [fairer] measuring rod than the status quo? Who is "President of The Status Quo? Is it our earthly bosses, or is there really a Higher Power in charge of this? There is a huge difference between the two. The contrast of life and death pictures it well.

Market Value—the amount for which something can be sold on a given market—often contrasted to book value. Who sets market share? Who decides what the market can bear—is it those who are only interested in higher profit margins, as opposed to allowing everybody fair access to a life free of hardship?

Who sets the book value? Is it the status quo? How far back into history should we go to find a system that is any different than the one we live with every day of our lives, and will live with while waiting for the 'when of change' to make a major difference to our personal status?

"Don't be afraid to give up the good to go for the great [boundless.]" These words are those of Rockefeller, who is somewhat entrenched in history, but still have a huge story to tell. [http://www.feelingsuccess.com/john-d-Rockefeller/.]

I often come up short as I insert a placeholder of a mental picture of myself alongside of this quote. Many of us get stuck in living life because we fear the challenge, we hesitate to move from our present reality because here we know what we have, but out in the boundless or ceaseless world of "The Theory of Everything Goes," we fear we will lose this solid hold on what we already have: We get satisfied with this. This is not a bad thing, unless it keeps us from expanding our vision to include the "Possibility of Everything That Matters," enough to extend a hand to someone else who is on the same journey as the one we are facing.

Rockefeller is trying to tell us to make sure, doubly sure, we do not miss out on our Greatest Life Purpose, to settle for the meaningless that comes from a lack of vision, or not seeing our "Mandate" [Jacob Bergen *The Mandate*] for a life that will allow for us to be the best we can be. This applies not only to the best we can be for our own book value, but for the value we can be to others who are also part of the whole world scene that affects everybody. What lies ahead may just be better than what we have in the present and especially in that eternal sense, this matters as well—how will we live in this life after death?

This could be anyone of us, on either end of the scenario I presented. What a great person it is who has a heart such as this, and it is an even greater person that gives his life for someone as poor in totality as the receiver in our story, as issued by Jeannie or Johnny Journalist [hypothetical]. There is such a man, guess who? J — — — —! [Excerpted from *Twin Towers of The Heart*]

"Don't be afraid to give up the good to go for the great."

The word 'envelop' comes to mind, as does the word 'envelope.' What a vast difference we see between the two while we walk through this story. One picture shows the reversing fortunes and hopes of other people. The other picture shows us something much different. Can you see the difference between the two?

One of the two more quickly splits my heart in two: Envelop does this. I will not say that the person who uses his ability to be charitable, humane, generous in the fashion of the word envelope, is not as good a person as the other is. Both of these apply at different times for each of us.

If we wish to pin a medal on someone's chest, is our first reaction to pin it on the chest of someone who envelops [gathers them as close as needed and then some, to themselves as to the matter of importance] someone or sees them in a way they want to put them [the problem] into an envelope and ship the out into "no-man's land"]. This is a picture I spoke of in *Twin Towers of The Heart*. It is too gigantic to see at a glance. The Whole Story is a heart matter. Sometimes we allow the pride of self-importance too much territory, as opposed to giving territory to others who deserve it more.

Twin Towers of The Heart, explores two separate facets of what and how we give, feel, and react to these life situations. Our responses may all differ; I do not even suggest we all go to the extent of the sacrifice proposed in the hypothetical story of a wealthy man who became poor for a season. It is even harder to believe someone could give it up permanently. Our world has many generous people with a heart of gold, and money displays this on their shirtsleeves. Their generosity turns great rewards back to them in ways we may not know. We all have a part in the story of the heart, and each story differs significantly.

I learned a lesson from Neil Young in the lyrics of his song *Heart of Gold*. I enjoy this song because of the theme that runs parallel to the theme of *TTOTH*. Our heart can be this heart of gold. We can never say we have had it long enough and quit using it to the fullest degree. My goal is to keep searching for this heart of gold—no, I am not there yet! Some say we are ever learning and never coming to the knowledge of the truth.

Now, let's give this story another twist. Imagine for a moment this vast wealth is in the hands of someone who was once the worthless part of society, what then? Now, what will be the rest of the story? Is this a good and fair question? When this person now looks out of his inherited ivory tower, the one that once belonged to John Doe Smith, what does he see?

How this benefactor managed his portfolio of life, was, he once placed himself where he felt and knew the stuff of life where it hurts so much, but one where the seemingly hopeless lived because the eyes of future vision were blind because of the hopelessness of the day-to-day. Is everything we face as a challenge in this life, regarding assisting someone else, as big as this? Many things are much smaller, but still relevant.

How does goodness like this come to reality? I read the book *Good Without God* by Greg M. Epstein. I agree that we can be good without God in the immediate sense. While perusing the information highway, many folks do not believe in God, and they have no use for the concept of God. I have read many of their journalistic offerings and buy their books—and not because of a lack of satisfaction where I am in my skin. Their books are valuable to discover what they use as the first cause source of the philosophy they carry on their sleeve.

Can an inanimate single cell molecule come from out of nothing to become a resource for goodness. I have been looking at my roasted laptop screen, one without batteries, without a plug into the power source called electricity. The power supply is gone, it has no hard drive, and it has no memory, it is 'dead!' The trick for me is to realize the power source which will bring good for me to use this still a nice-looking paperweight.

What would this require? To accomplish this task someone would need to refurbish this laptop. It would never be the same laptop, it would be rebuilt, and it would require a person to accomplish this. If I leave my dead laptop stashed in the box I have it in, for billions of years, it will rot before it ever shows signs of life again.

I need to locate the logic that makes this idea work: Something out of nothing. Maybe I am just naïve enough to believe, someone good could get the whole thing going, all by Himself. These are my thoughts, and they are not intended to harm or demean any who do not agree with my philosophy. Personally, and without prejudice, I can only see 'Goodness,' as coming from a root source of living matter.

Yes, it takes something hard to put together, and I call this something 'Faith.' I do not ask all the questions about where did the Someone who I say created everything, come from. I am just gullible enough, I guess, to believe this is God; maybe there is something to this 'Faith Thing.'

Yes, the target of faith for me is God. As I read the lives of others who do not think as I do, I look at them and try to understand where they are coming from, and why. Once again, I am not attempting to slight or demean anyone; we all have our thoughts and beliefs, and this by our own choice.

Books of any genre, fiction or non-fiction, love or hate, truth or consequence, tedious or exhilarating, penned by brilliant people, or composed by perceived nobody's, have no fundamental value, and project no life lessons without a Storyline. Would the New York Times Best-Seller List house a book written by whomever, if it had no real Storyline? Without the central theme relevant to the people, it is supposedly addressing, would it have any intrinsic value if it had no Storyline? I think not. [Twin Towers of The Heart page 25—]

At some the point I will be moving on into Our Personal Book Value. It is only a small part of the Book Value concept or reality of life that is 'us,' and us alone. The full currency [physical an or personal resource value] this involves is vast, like the vast fortunes of physical wealth many achieve is huge. If we judge personal worth on the money scale, then most of the world has no chance to be a SOMEBODY!

Remember, at no placement in this book, *Everybody: Everybody Is A Somebody*, will I intentionally try to tell you what to do, although I believe that I am telling you the truth of the whole story of life with truth and consequences, and life with erroneous or flawed 'truth with its consequences.'

I Am Looking Back To See "IF—"
"IF" You Are Looking Back To See—.
If You Are Looking Back To See If I Am Looking Back To See If You are Looking Back At Me Or Someone Else.

I often sing this line from a song of time already past, "I was looking back to see if you were looking back to see if I was looking back to see if you were looking back to me." [*Looking Back To See* as sung by Buck Owens and Susan Raye]

These words have huge credibility as we put ourselves into the scope of The Theory of Everything, where everything is possible, even that of little old me making a difference for the outcome of a part in the eternal tomorrow.

Susan Raye also sings a song called; *Everybody Is Somebodies Fool*.

Planning a journey?

We need:

"Sit A Spell Moments."

We Need:

"Thinking Time."

We Need:

"Evaluation of Time and Space."

There is a cost.

Count the Cost!

What To Do?

Be Open To Listen
Be Ready To Hear
Be Ready To Face Challenges
Be Ready To Make A Difference
Be Ready To LOVE!

Study to shew thyself approved unto God, a workman that needeth not to be ashamed, rightly dividing the word of truth.) [2 Timothy 2:15 KJV]

The Worth Of A One Genesis Scenario—One Choice Of Beginnings, says a *Sketch One Genesis: One Beginning* setting is the story of life. No story is without a beginning and or an end. The end is not yet in sight. However, we will gain from a few moments of reflection on this *Chapter Eight* title as we move forward. If we think the end result of Eternity is there under the guise of multifaceted beliefs, we need to think it over.

What Did I See, and What Does It Say To Me?

"Prepare To Launch!"

Beginnings have a 'Value Platform' from which we can Launch out from where we think we are entrenched or rooted. When we try to launch out from a situation where we know nothing of our history, we may have a difficulty understanding why we are what we are and how we react to some issues. For instance, people who do not know their parents, seem always to be wondering who and what they were, and seem to be on a never-ending search to find their birth parents. This is not always the case, but often, whether spoken or somewhat buried in their innermost part, what the rest of us do not see, they are wondering about that part of their life, and how their lives may have been different had they known and lived with birth parents.

Beginnings—I feel blessed to have known my birth parents. I can see how some of what they were, is what made me what I am. This can be good, however, sometimes, people wished they had never known their birth parents. Memories are not always great for some folks, this is unfortunate. Everything my parents did was not perfect for them and or for me, and my understanding of that time may be skewed, or slanted; my memories are still sweet.

When I dream, and I do so every night, I sometimes dream of my parents, who are gone now, but they bring back memories for me when I wake-up in the morning.

Beginnings: What should 'Beginnings' do for us? How I see it, is that beginnings will give us a platform from which we can launch out into the best out there for us to attain to!

—Some folks oppose everything opposite their belief; they may not read far enough into life to gather an understanding that different people exist, and everyone may believe what they wish. What our "Beginning" was on this earth produces differing matters for each of us.

—People who listen while watching others, often try to understand another person's belief long enough to check reliable facts for the truth issue; these folks may find there is a truth in this world that supersedes all other 'Perceived Truths.'

When confusion reigns, as it often does, because there are almost innumerable belief systems in our world, we seem to begin life from more than one kind of beginning—more than one platform. Though we should know where we came from, it is imperative to realize where we are now no matter if we know our history or not. As we get older there are so many resources for us to get ahead in life, at least in the affluent world which most of us live in, in which there are few excuses for not contending for or coping with life. There are exceptions; this is one of the sad parts of life.

Life As We Have It Now!

Each one of us can have a part of making life better for someone who does not have such an easy time of managing the life they have, that which seems unbearable. We need not watch too far into any news cast to see that life is not fair to or for everyone. This is part of what this book is about. This book is about trying to get us to realize that we each have a part to play; if we play it well, then there will be a lot fewer people out there who are left without hope! Can A Single Genesis Attraction satisfy the need of everyone, if everyone chooses the life God offers?

Try To Imagine A Sketch Of A Single Genesis Attraction

Is One Beginning, Which Is Value Packed, Enough For You!

7822295

Believe It Or Not

9th Chapter
Realization Can Produce The Courage Of Conviction

Truth is what? For the men and women of the FBI, bravery is reflected not only in the physical courage often necessary in the job. It can be seen in the courage of conviction, in the courage to act with wisdom in the face of fear, and in the courage it takes to admit mistakes and move forward. [Robert Mueller]

What Would It Be Like To Follow A Thoughtful Or Prayerful Viewpoint, With An Encouraging Attitude Towards Intently Knowing Other People's Intently!

In my previous book, *Bridging The Gap*, I began each Chapter with a Pre-Chapter Heading and somewhat of an overall recap, from a present situational sense, and with a forward look, as I do in all of my books. In *Bridging The Gap*, I called this segment *Looking Over The Horizon*. This not only gave me a jump on what I wanted to say going forward, but it allowed me to stay in context, rather than just jumping off a cliff and hollering, "Que Sera Sera" [Ka SA Ra SA Ra—Whatever Will Be Will Be].

Chapter 9
LIFE AS WE HAVE IT NOW!

A strange thing happens to me that I am sure happens to a lot of actors when the camera starts rolling, I'm not 'me' anymore. [Emily Browning]

There is nothing so uncertain as a sure thing. [Scotty Bowman]

Life Is A Sure-Thing, not in length of days; we are born to live: Life Has Overhead—or Not? Our Cast Iron Certainty Is A Safe Bet or Not?' Life gathers together its pivotal or key worth, thus constructing movements; penalties label the marks of truth or error reasoning. Questions and Sensitive Issues are Reality!

It is one thing for me to stand back on my patio and look towards the horizons around me, and wonder what lies beyond those mountains, open fields, hills, valleys, forests, creeks, streams, rivers —and surmise or imagine what is over the horizon which scales out in some distance calculator. If I step out from where I am, maybe a hundred steps, or even another mile towards those horizons, crests, peaks, or summits in the land before me, the bar rises again to become a new horizon. From where I am at present I need to set a benchmark or target to see a greater horizon than I see presently.

If I climb one mountain so I can get a good look, thinking, now I can finally see every horizon without ever facing the problem of being limited as far as knowing what lies out in every part of the world, and all the people in it, I may be wrong; I may still be limited in some capacity. None of us have it all! None of us are God!

The meaning of 'Horizon' is simply this, 'it is the limit' of someone's ability to see past a set boundary, physically, emotively, or spiritually. People rationalize to see, understand, or experience any interest segment of their lives, spiritually or otherwise. Anything beyond the physical items of life, requires a non-physical tool I call FAITH.

Faith is something akin to us looking into an oblivion [blankness], a perspective beyond the understanding we have at the moment. How do we begin to have a perspective which allows us to develop this Faith I speak of? Without seeming morbid, morose, or gloomy, I just wish to make antipodal or opposing statements that are a reverse of each other—horizons are there; oblivion, who knows about this. Is faith this much of an objective approach it cannot be challenged by questions of the emotion or the subjectivity of the humanity we all suffer from, endure, experience, or welcome with open arms to 'experience'—Not Endure.

Is what we think of as 'oblivion' actually out there somewhere? Is the horizon we cannot ever seem to get a look at physically out there somewhere? People on the other side of the world opposite to where we are see what we cannot see, they know what is beyond the horizon we cannot see; and verso [visa versa— an about face—the other side of the coin]. Oblivion is different, none of us can see this because it never seems to come to a visual point because it is a bottomless pit; somewhat like what we think of as eternity—if we do not acknowledge an eternity Maker!

Much of the time we are oblivious to the realities that other people face regularly. A case in point is someone living in a Third World Country; they may think of everyone else in the world as being wealthy. In a comparison to them, we in the regular world, if you will, the affluent world in comparison, are not only rich in resources, but in a better moment by moment state than are they.

This is also a visa versa situation from which they are trying to see over their horizons to know about what they do not seem to know about. Because there are negatively acclimatized people on our side of the high concrete wall or fence, these Third World People do not always understand us—they may, if, we let them into our world for a while. We have it better than many folks do, in many respects. When we think of our position in life, and the responsibilities we have to be our brother's keeper—are we fulfilling this measure yet? If we remain oblivious to their need we are really the ones to be most pitied. If we are, as I just stated, and I point no fingers, just thinking dangerously again, then, if we close our eyes to the rest of the world where the need exists, we are set as far apart as are horizons and oblivion to the real reality of intention that has always been in the making since creation.

If all we see is the oblivious entities of life, we cannot even say we are looking into a forgetfulness [obliviousness], because we have not yet seen this oblivion, and we are still as though falling into this bottomless pit. If we think of the potential of our horizons obliviously, as if being unconsciousness, then we will achieve nothing. We may not achieve unless we re-affix our perspectives on the right context of the present, and or our context of eternity. Don Richardson wrote a book called, *Eternity In Their Hearts*. As we live the present it ought to be with an eye on eternity.

Always having one hand on the throttle with an eye in the rear-view mirror, knowing where we are in the present, with one hand or foot ready for action at the 'brake,' is not a bad relationship to have with life. When life changes in the moment, and as quick as it does, we can prepare for most situations arising around us. Too often, I may have implied or suggested to someone, "all you need is faith." Just believe what you do not see about the reality of God, without all the questions. I have to ask myself the question, "Do I Have Faith like this?"

In a perfect world I should have this Faith which I examine and align with another word called 'Trust'—especially if I am referring to God. If I am referring to just another person, maybe I should not even imply I should be able to trust this way unless our relationship is as if faith and trust have become the building-blocks to bring us into a truthful trusting relationship. Building-blocks are not the foundation. Building Blocks are materials placed on and or fastened to the foundation. In *Chapter Eight* I wrote about beginnings [The Genesis] being the necessity for understanding the Best Eternal Results.

Believe It Or Not!

In the moment, as I am thinking through what this Chapter may look like, I feel as though I am about to step off a cliff titled 'Oblivion.' What I feel in my spirit makes me want to put on my seatbelt, as if I was just getting into my car to go somewhere. It is one thing to get into my car and know I am going to Tim Hortons; another thing entirely to get into my car and scratch my head and think, "where was I going to go?" I have done exactly this at times— more than a few times—any takers here?

This feeling can be much like as if I were standing at the edge of a cliff with a compulsion, impulse, or just an uncontrollable sensation to take one more step, not realizing there was no more ground under my feet where that next step would take me. It is risqué, salacious, rude—or risky to be so sketchy about how we are living, to where we leave ourselves so wide open to the dangers of wrong living, in-so-far as our eternity goes—we live in a Que Sera, Sera world which can turn on us in a moment.

'The Sky Is The Limit.' Where I stand on God's green earth is a strength I can depend on, when I trust this is where I should be. If I am sure God is enough, I am in good shape. If I am unsure there is something solid for me to put my trust in for all that lay ahead, I better be wearing a seatbelt because what lies ahead may just kill me. What is a safety-belt anyway? We can see a safety-belt—physically or instinctively. We know what a physical safety-belt is; do we know what our mental seatbelts are?

A safety-belt [seat belt] may be the difference between life and death. Fastening my seatbelt is a good thing. I may do it nonchalantly out of a force of habit because it is the law; breaking this law has its hazards or penalties. Or I may do it because I have actually bought into the philosophy, thinking mode, or theory that putting this safety measure into place when I get into my car is safe; for that reason alone, it can be the right thing to do!

Below is oblivion—below life's level of travel, the here and now, the day-today we are living and breathing in, which allows for us to take one more step of safety, or one into oblivion—here life is always a challenge. This is a concern to be concerned about [either a conundrum, or challenge], or an oxymoron [puzzle], or both! Although this need not be as dire as the word 'concern' suggests, it is often on the minds of the people we meet as we move through life.

Concern is not necessarily an apprehension or fear. Although we often affix the word 'Concern' to anxiety, fear, worry, alarm — many pleasantries fit well with the word 'concern.' When we check out the Thesaurus we learn that we cannot conclude there is nothing left in life with any value. If we have seen no value, we might think Jumping Off A Cliff Into Oblivion is the answer. This way we will have no more worries, unless there actually is a reality we will face after death, one which may not fit what we presently believe will be our eternal destiny—one way or the other.

It may be informative, even of great worth to look at some alternatives to worry and fear as we look at the word 'concern,' as one synonym of affection. It may be helpful to know it is beneficial to ourselves and others to be concerned about other people; how they handle life, and why they manage it differently than what we believe is the right way. Please take a walk with me through some other words:

Affection: [noun; strong fondness], amore [love], ardor [enthusiasm or passion], care [attention], desire [longing, craving], devotion [commitment], emotion [excitement], endearment [kind word], feeling [sensitivity], friendliness, friendship, good will, hankering [yearning], heart [core, sentiment, temperament, character], inclination [disposition], itch [eagerness], kindness [this speaks for itself, but sympathy, compassion, and gentleness comes to mind], liking, predilection [preference, or fondness], 'Puppy Love,' warmth—.

We could go on and on and end up at the same crossroads; we can be 'concerned' [fearful, apprehensive, troubled, anxious, disturbed, worried]. Or, we can have a built in trust level with someone who can help us with this in-so-far as it is possible in this life. We may still feel this is all that we can achieve or expect in this life and beyond, in the oblivion we do not understand. Knowing what lies behind us; what we have in the present; what we can expect ahead of us; these are factors to consider as part of tomorrow.

Or we can find the 'Someone' who can assure us enough to lift us out of this concern which leaves us fearful of everything not exactly in place as we planned for it to be. In the moment by moment level all of us live in, this is no easy task. In the grand finale it means the final frame of the picture of life, when there is nothing left but trusting in something beyond ourselves, we need to cry out for help—trust me, I do not have this one mastered yet!

Knowledge, wisdom, and faith, 'Yes Faith,' are workable ingredients in our story. Faith is the biggie. It seems Faith is like standing at the edge of that Cliff Called Oblivion. At times we are about to give it all up, what is left but faith? Who wants to take a chance on what they know little about, regarding anything they cannot hold in their hand and say, 'this is real, this is what I need, this is enough!' [*Take A Chance On Me*—ABBA]. Do I dare; is this sufficient?

Hey, you may take a chance on me when you are in the pickle you cannot swallow; the mess you cannot fix; or when your need for hope and resolution is so strong you cannot conceive of living anymore. But I may just go so far—then what? I may just let you down; I am only human; I am just like you. There are times for me as well, when I am in a mess; I cannot swallow the whole pickle; or I cannot see far enough anymore to where my next step will keep me on solid ground—what then?

Sometimes I am so confident or cocky; I find myself singing the Johnny Nash song [original composer] *I Can See Clearly Now*. As I watch the video right now and the song begins, I see Johnny looking down a long winding road with a tree down past the bend; the sky is filled with inclement [ominous gloomy or bad] clouds. This is the picture of how this sojourner seems to assess or weigh out what the future holds for them in the moment! Sometimes, when life is 'All Good,' I do not see these ominous conditions—I Only See Blue Skies.

While I am in the storm, while the thunder and lightening are in their extreme proportions, before the blue sky, it seems has no intention to show itself, I am in deep trouble. Sandra Bullock said in *Miss Congeniality* "You In Big Trouble." Yes, more than once when I was in big trouble, I was looking for the blue skies on a blue horizon I could not yet fathom.

Lou Christie sang relevant songs which I think of now as I write these words—*Beyond The Blue Horizon, I Can't Stop The Rain, Lightning Strikes, Two Faces Have I*—. Each of these has powerful thoughts that pertain to me so often when I am in big trouble emotionally. Then, with another song I hear him singing, he kinda wraps up the answer to all my troubles, when he sings *O Holy Night*. Listen to it now in your mind. As I write this, Christmas is just under a month away now in 2018:

> O holy night! The stars are brightly shining.
> It is the night of our dear savior's birth.
> Long lay the world in sin and error pining:
> Till he appeared, and the soul felt its worth.
> A thrill of hope, the weary world rejoices,
> For yonder breaks a new and glorious morn.
> Fall on your knees! O hear the angel voices!

O night divine, O night when Christ was born.
O night divine, O night divine, O night divine;
O Night Divine!

In *Beyond The Blue Horizon* Lou sings about the beautiful day awaiting, where joy is coming up, where life just began; once again the sun comes up after the storm; so it seems, as Lou Christie sings some of his songs. For me, I see The Wrap as he sings *O Holy Night*.

As Johnny Nash sings, *I Can See Clearly Now*, I see him saying he saw life and living a little clearer as the rain lifted; as the obstacles blocking his path disappeared, he said, the blinding clouds are gone, and the blue comes up on a horizon he had not seen for a while. Now he saw the rainbow he was praying for as being up there, bright and beautiful; Johnny says it will be blue skies from now on. Yes, when this all happens this way, on the bright sunny days, we foresee no more dark days.

Jimmy Cliff also sang *I Can See Clearly Now*. I wonder if he was ever at the Cliff of Oblivion, where the next step spelled doom; where the pain of life was full blown, where the answer was not blown in the wind of change for him? I see him also coming to the place where the pain goes away; all those bad feelings of the hurting times have dispersed to where they are no longer present.

In 1962 Bob Dylan wrote *The Answer Is Blown In The Wind*. He leaves me a picture of a person walking many roads in search of something they can finally latch onto as the answer he sings about as blown in by the wind. How many roads must women, men, and children travel before they find the peace which supersedes all the promised rainbows of life. He sings of a white dove as if being on a journey of many days and many seas before it finally rests on the seashore sand. Bob Dylan notices war has gone on far too long, wondering when the cannon balls will cease.

Is the answer to these and more, about the issues of life just blowing about in the wind? Then, as if by chance one day everything will be beautiful in its own way without the help of that Someone I spoke about. Dolly Parton and Willie Nelson sang *Everything's Beautiful (In Its Own Way)* in what I see as a special rendition; I like how they acknowledged God for the uniqueness we see in how He made everything and everybody.

Then, as if Dolly and Willie did not complete the program of God with their rendition, we have Ray Stevens, writing and singing another rendering of the same theme when he wrote and sang *Everything Is Beautiful*. Ray starts with an old Sunday School song many of us sang as we grew out from that innocence we had at birth, to where we could acknowledge God with these words:

> Jesus loves the little children, all the little children of the world; red and yellow, black, and white, they are precious in his sight; Jesus loves the little children of the world.

Ray writes and sings about some people who see the things God made beautiful in His own way, but they are blind to the wonder of it all.

The starry summer nights come alive under the heaven God made. Ray lets us know, as for him, God will make a way when the storm clouds and obstacles hinder The Good Life He desires, and always did desire for us to live in from the beginning. This changed because we were blind to God's initial desires; we went it alone. However, Mr. Stevens says God will find a way to right the ship [my words]. God already knows what way this was; the time will come for us to realize His way was the best way after all.

We let so many things deter God's plan, the color of someone's skin; the length of their hair; the places they came from, which represent a culture we have not lived; we do not even try to understand them. These are issues we all contend with. While grinding my way through the issues, I am writing, *Everybody: Everybody Is A Somebody—When All Is Said and Done*.

Sometimes I feel I am not the person qualified to address this telling title. Yes, I feel like packing it in because of this. I hope and pray I will have the God given stuff to tough it out in a way He has figured it out, instead of singing, "I'll Do It My Way." Frank Sinatra got a hold of something along these lines when he sang, *I Did It My Way*.

On and on we go, it seems so anyway, just to end up at the same crossing. We may be troubled [bothered, distressed, nervous] or we can have an already assembled trust in someone who can help us with this in-so-far as it is thinkable in our lifetime. He can sense this is all that we can accomplish or imagine in this world and beyond, in the obliviousness we do not yet recognize.

Or we can find the Someone who can and will guarantee us of being rid of those anxieties which find us scared of our own shadow, of 'the whole lot things' not panning out anything close to what we had envisioned for ourselves at the position of life we find ourselves. In the minute by minute moment all of us live in, it is no easy task; at the grand finale, the "Finish Line," when nothing remains of the dreams we had, but believing in something outside of ourselves, we need to cry out for help. Trust me, I do not have this one mastered yet either!

In 1945 Scotty Wiseman wrote and published *Have I Told You Lately That I Love You*. I think of that golden oldie now because of what I said a while ago "I am telling you now." Sometimes we go through life without the knowledge of some of the paramount or incredibly important facets of life, those which carry us when things get tough. When someone tells us about something or someone who can help us work through the stuff we may not understand, we are often grateful; or we may say, mind your own business!

Sometimes we know it all, or we think we do, fair enough. However, there are 'present factors,' and there are eternal factors. We may handle the present factors with ease—Great! The present we live in is the bird in the hand, if you will, who needs faith; we got a grip on this, what more is there? We may feel there is no eternity—dust to dust is all she wrote—this is the rest of the story. If we are right, so-be-it! What if we are wrong, and the eternity we think we will get is a far greater picture than we imagined.

Nobody loved and or loves more than God. A while ago I mentioned Ray Stevens and some of what he sang in *Everything Is Beautiful In Its Own Way*. Ray began this song like this,

> Jesus loves the little children, all the little children of the world; red and yellow, black, and white, they are precious in his sight; Jesus loves the little children of the world.

Another Sunday School song from the past is, *Jesus Loves Me, This I Know, For The Bible Tells Me So! Little ones to Him belong, they are weak, but He is Strong*. Compared to God, we are all "Little Ones." Another song I know is, *No One Ever Cared For Me Like Jesus*. This is the picture I like to present. I know not everyone agrees with me, and some may not appreciate me saying these things—so-be-it.

Oh, what a story this is; what a story this can be for each of us. Is the Answer to life's issues so fickle? Is it so thinly lined that it blows up onto the seashore with the tide? Where is this place where real peace resides: *When All Is Said And Done*? This peace cannot be shared with a note measured in a bottle, corked, and set out to sea for someone to find to hear the story? We may be made aware of it through one means or another; then comes the clincher: We need to believe the story! I call this 'Found Faith!' We may not think we believe in this faith thing; one way or another we all have faith in one thing or another about what lies ahead in eternity.

This is often beyond the hope I can give you. We talk about the value of everybody. How does this fit into life as we know it? Life's choices—are they the right ones or the wrong ones, and by whose rule do right and wrong even exist. In *Chapter Six* I wrote things about *The Golden Rule*; whose rule is that anyway? Much more can be said about The Golden Rule.

We travel from place to place: We walk, we run, we crawl, we ride bikes, we drive cars, we take buses, we take boats [ships]. We used to take trains—and for going great distances, and short distances, most often we take a plane to where we are going: It gets us there more quickly, and sometimes more safely. Then there are the other times. We can travel by many differing modes of transportation; each one can be precarious [risky] if the right precautions are not in place. Then, even when all things are figured out to the nth degree there is still the unknown; it is often the out of the blue entity which gives us the boot. The seat belt often saves lives. However, too often we think, "I Will Do Just Fine Without It Thank You!"

I am leading into the many differing struggles we all face. Not one of us has total immunity. Leaders such as we see and know them, have motives for wanting to be leaders, or they were thrust into the leadership position. Some motives are more honorable than are others. Some motives are right; some motives are plain wrong. I probably need not break this down for us. Right is right, and wrong is wrong; this just makes sense [well, it makes sense for me]. The Biggee we face today, more so than we did back in the day, the breakdown of right and wrong, that which God laid out in the Bible, falls under an undermining factor, other than what the Bible points out.

Tolerance is a good thing, YES! Forbearance is another word for tolerance, and it is a guiding principle of the Word of God. One scripture tells us to bear each others' burdens [the load they carry, when they may not be strong enough to do so].

> Bear ye one another's burdens, and so fulfil the law of Christ. For if a man thinks himself to be something, when he is nothing, he deceiveth himself. But let every man prove his own work, and then shall he have rejoicing in himself alone, and not in another. For every man shall bear his own burden. [Gal. 6:2]

What does it mean to live productively? When someone fails in our eyes, as per the relationship we expect everyone to have with and about God, we think we have to pound out the message till the other person either accepts our position or walks out feeling as if they have faced the onslaught of a speedy train. The Bible calls disobedience to God, 'sin.' The Bible says sin is the breaking of the laws of God. God's word is the last word, if we are truly believers in the purpose Jesus came to this world for.

Jesus came to save humankind from the penalty of non-acceptance of God for Who He is. All people, Christian or never having come to this belief, started on the same page. We were all born sinners; we were all born into a state of not knowing what the meaning of God was all about, and what He wanted for us, but we came to an age of understanding, where we came to know it.

When anyone is in a position which comes short of living life without regard for God, and who He is, we should try to help them realize they need God. We ought to do this without judging them because they believe differently than we believe, because before we came to believe we were in the same boat. Too often we forget where we ourselves came from. We who think we know it all, can be unkind in not accepting people for who they are as people.

How can we judge someone for something they are doing against God's law if they do not regard God's law as the ultimate word, the final answer on all issues—moral or immoral? However, the laws of humankind have always been broken down into two camps: moral or immoral; good or evil; right or wrong. Since the earliest beginnings of life as history tells us about, rules have existed. When we break those rules there are consequences. Good breeds good results: evil breeds the unpleasantries we often ignore.

The Golden Rule—this rule takes on different meanings for different people. The Golden rule is not our otherwise interpreted law to suit our selfish desire. The simple outlay of The Golden Rule is to treat others as fairly as we ourselves want to be treated. Maybe our mandate in life is largely to make sure we do everything within our power to live in this format. If we see someone breaking this rule, is it our responsibility to steer them onto the right course?

To explore life carefully is a part we should play as we live, no work can be done to change the plan, after we die. We ought to make our life's work about others. Our selfish wants need to take the back seat; we need to be less impressed with ourselves; more impressed with the concerns of others; we ought not to see ourselves as better than others. We all hold a responsibility to be fertile with our own lives, while considering others better than ourselves.

The rubric [red-letter emphasis, title, context, theme or word-formatted-scenario, or general direction] of *Everybody: Everybody Is A Somebody*, presents many differing pictures of actual life happenings. These 'happenings,' or issues and situations we all face, become a part of the schema, diegesis or storyline which brings about fulfilling my intentions in writing this book. My intent is that no-one in this universe should feel they are of no intrinsic, basic, inherent, or central value in what was God's original plan.

My subjectivity, penchant, or partiality for allowing a someone, or The Designer or Creator to be my focal point for a successful journey in life, is not hidden in this book. The conceptual [theory based] idea that a 'thing,' or inanimate substance [such as in the Big Bang Scenario] could allow for an emotional act such as love, to be a part of a full relationship, is out of context for me.

I Am Looking Back To See "IF—"
"IF" You Are Looking Back To See—.

We live in a precarious, dicey, chancy, or uncertain world. We never know what the next moment will spring on us. Look at all the terrorist acts, killing, weather patterns, leadership decisions. After we are born, we live for a while under the care and direction of someone more capable of handling the affairs of life for us. Then, There Is Life As It Daily and Moment By Moment Creeps Up On Us, Lifts Us Up At Times, and Overwhelms Us at Times.

Life is a sure-thing? It has overhead? Cast-iron certainty is a 'safe bet?' Life gathers together its pivotal or key worth, thus constructing movements; penalties label the marks of truth or error reasoning!

Questions and Sensitive Issues are Reality!

As I worked through this Chapter, I had many thoughts about life as it is for each of us in our own "Individually Ordered World." Our edition of life is inclusive of what happens around us as it incorporates the people that cross our path. These things are a 'given,' if we are breathing the air around us.

We do not live to far into life before we realize, that to have a safety-net in place when encountering some of those precarious or chancy moments which often jump out at us, is not so hard to accept. Safety-nets come in a huge variety of ways: family, friends, other people with a depth of resources—those which may carry the day for us when the day is burdensome.

When we are "Walking The High Wire" it only takes a little slip, and we are off the wire and into oblivion: If we have no net below us. When a home bursts into flame and traps someone in a place somewhere they cannot escape on their own, it is a "Godsend" when the firemen spread a net on ground level to allow for our escape to safety. 9/11/01 was such a case in point. However, life as it came to be because of things out of our control, did not offer a sufficient safety-net to give the desired hope that cried out loudly to everyone in earshot, and around the world via the media. Thus, the uncertainty life hands us occasionally, is 'hard to understand life,' when it turns on us!

What Did I See, and What Does It Say?
"Prepare to Launch!"
Let's Think About It!

Differing manner of people will read this book:

—Some folks contend against everything that does not suit them in the moment, possibly because of how they were raised, whether it could change them for the better or not. These people may not read far enough in this book to harvest an understanding about what God has suggested.

—Some people are open to attending to observing and trying to understand another person's belief long enough to check reliable facts, and this book; these folks may find there is a truth in this world that supersedes all other perceived truth.

—Some folks may read and be on the same page as the author of *Everybody: Everybody Is A Somebody* and say Amen!

> That we henceforth be no more children, tossed to and fro, and carried about with every wind of doctrine, by the sleight of men, and cunning craftiness, whereby they lie in wait to deceive; [Ephesians 4:14 KJV]
>
> The wind bloweth where it listeth, and thou hearest the sound thereof, but canst not tell whence it cometh, and whither it goeth: so is everyone born of the Spirit. [John 3:8 KJV]
>
> And there went forth a wind from the LORD, and brought quails from the sea, and let them fall by the camp a day's journey on this side, and a day's journey on the other side, round about the camp, and two cubits high upon the face of the earth. And the people stood up all that day, and all that night, and all the next day, and they gathered the quails: he that gathered least gathered ten homers: and they spread them all abroad for themselves round about the camp. [Numbers 11:31-34 KJV]

When the wind blew and or the waves of life churned and tossed about the stuff of the lives of these people in these scriptures, an action was begun.

IS EVERYBODY A SOMEBODY?

Believe It Or Not

10ᵗʰ Chapter

As we observe the life we have before us, it is fairly evident we are still living with inequities and injustices— 'I Get This!'

Truth is what? It is possible to become discouraged about the injustice we see everywhere. But God did not promise us the world would be humane and just. He gives us the gift of life and allows us to choose the way we will use our limited time on earth. It is an awesome opportunity. [Cesar Chavez]

'Frustrations!' The frustrations of this world are in a continual mode of being invective, ranting, being on a diatribe, driving an onslaught or tirade. What once was historically or politically correct, or just a nice thing to do, faces the haranguing, soapbox delivery of being an intolerant issue. Should we allow this to continue for this our generation, the next, and the future we cannot envision—by annihilating the strength of past experiences? [Psalms 23; 1-6 makes it inviting to participate with The God of the past].

I am all for treating everyone equally in life. However, we may have too much free time on our hands or too much liberty at the hands of the understanding and or deciphering [interpreting] of our 'Constitution.' Will we eventually get rid of the color scale—that which allows for us to dress up to enhance a context—not to demean any particular entity. If we do, and never allow for any one color to share its engraved [inbred] speciality with the rest of the world, what color will we have to dye everything, including people, so we do not cross the barriers within tolerance issues. One day we may all be 'Robotic' in nature, or all commandeered to accept a certain government orchestrated way to present our beliefs to allow for an everything goes system of life.

Every time we turn another corner on the road of life as it has always been, we have to stop and say it was not good enough to get us over the barricades of understanding one another enough to get along. Time has built for us a belief system, saying, 'unless we change what God made us to be we will never survive this life.'

Chapter 10
THE ANSWER IS BLOWN IN THE WIND!

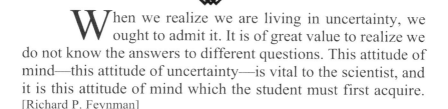

When we realize we are living in uncertainty, we ought to admit it. It is of great value to realize we do not know the answers to different questions. This attitude of mind—this attitude of uncertainty—is vital to the scientist, and it is this attitude of mind which the student must first acquire.
[Richard P. Feynman]

Reality Issues Seem To Insert Themselves Into Life!

Abraham Lincoln and others opened the door of communication and tolerance enough to say we can live with each other lovingly, and productively if our heart condition says, 'everybody is equal.' God never created our hearts so we would discriminate based on color. He created us to follow the path He had laid out for us to have any chance of survival. There was no hesitancy on God's part about what was best for us!

In the 'First Place,' people, because of disobedience in The Garden of Eden, got it all wrong about life and living. Rather than real Peace and Prosperity at the hands of God's plan, people chose the knowledge in which they set their own plan in place; we can see where that got us. No one it seems, has had a moment of peace "Since That Fateful Day!" God's intent was far richer in resource power, and satisfaction with who and what he created us to be, than what we settled for. When people go on strike in the work force they often lose more than they settle for. By the time all the costs are tallied, satisfaction might have been the better recourse to have taken [especially in a lengthy strike].

I do not for a moment think anybody is inferior because of how they believe. In The Beginning, did God think, 'because He was not obeyed,' He would get out the whip and teach us a lesson we would never forget? Did He therefore hesitate to give us any good thing to help us out of our mess?

Did we come out of the Garden of Eden Naked? Of Course Not! Instead of God giving us what we did deserve, the heavy lash, a bleeding back, and the nakedness which might have had us face the chilling nighttime's without a warm blanket, He provided for us a decent start with a wardrobe sufficient for the day Adam and Eve lived in. Too often we only see God as being a heavy-handed ogre, a giant monster who only wants to crush us like Goliath planned to do when he faced David, the little shepherd boy. Is this what God had in mind before He carefully, lovingly, uniquely, and purposefully fashioned us in the foreground of Eternity past?

Because our hearts are all wrong, we have the issues we have today. Because the 'Takeoff' of the blueprint of and for life was all wrong, Adam and Eve gave out the wrong parameters for sending out a proper value-based quote for acceptance, to the humanity, which was to come after them. We misunderstood what God said initially. We still do! The schematic of what kind of power source best suited life in the day of these folk—this is the reason we needed resistors, capacitors, inductors—to allow for the fluctuations that frustrate life. We thought ourselves more powerful than we were.

Oh, if only life were so simple we could figure out every problem we ourselves concocted because of our unbelief. Please realize, God already had it all figured out before He picked up the handful of soil which is the make-up of our existence. God used a special soil; we know it as clay to make things like the pottery we see today and patterned after the things of the past our ancestors grew up with. He was the Potter then; He formed the clay to fashion us; He can still change us from what we are without Him in our lives; but it is His Way, or The Highway in the opposite direction! We never seem to learn, it ain't over until the cows come home!

Is The Answer Blown In The Wind?

One scribe came, he heard people reasoning together, perceiving he had answered them well, he asked, 'Which is the first commandment of all?' Jesus answered him, 'The first commandments is, Hear, O Israel; The Lord our God is one Lord: You shall love the Lord thy God with all thy heart, and with all your soul, and with all your mind, and with all your strength: This is the first commandment.'

Secondly, you shall love your neighbor as you would love yourself. No commandments are greater than these. The scribe said to Him, well, Master, You have spoken the truth: Yes, we know there is one God; and there is none other than He: And to love Him with all the heart, and with all the understanding, and with all the soul, and with all the strength, and to love his neighbor as himself, this is more than all whole burnt offerings and sacrifices. Jesus, when He saw the scribe answer discreetly, said unto him, You are not far from the kingdom of God. After this, nobody dared ask him any more questions. [Mark 12: 28-34 JBI]

Is the answer blown in the wind of Time, or Time Change? Sports is one entity which presents a differing picture today than it once did, in how people dissect everything differently than the populace did "Back In The Day!" The 'Whiteout Phrase' [Re The Winnipeg Jets Games], this is offensive to some cultures because it does not present a picture of tolerance towards other cultures, and or a picture of Inclusion. While being sympathetic, I wonder if we might not find something offensive in nearly every word in the Thesaurus, or at least in many other words; might we suggest changing every dictionary, Bible, and every book written, at least those that were written in a certain context, and a proper intention!

Other teams, like the Cleveland Indians, the Boston Red Socks, other teams, and other things like black or white—with these things in their names, are being expected to change all of history from which they chose certain names because of a variety of reasons, and that's not because of race, etc. I wonder, 'Are There Not Any Defining Issues' which are considered acceptable? Are there things which are stated with innocent intent in the language we have grown up through, without someone taking personal offense, because they feel assaulted! Are we so sensitive to every aspect of life, where we leave no room for 'Grace and Mercy?'

What once was acceptable, is not good enough or compelling enough to save the day. I believe we will rue the day we changed what was once right and good enough [this part of history], because God set it in place and looked back at what He had done, and said it was good; in effect saying, "What I Have Made Is Good Enough To Carry The Day!"

And God saw everything that he had made, and, behold, it was very good. And the evening and the morning were the sixth day. [Genesis 1:31]

We can readily see there are cries for self gratifying satisfaction all around us, and across the whole earth that God declared "Very Good." This satisfaction is often out of our reach, so we think, because of one incident in The Garden of Eden. I say huge; others say, "What's The Big Deal:" "God Said What?" *"So God said, Thou shalt not—partake of one of the two special trees in the middle of The Garden of Eden; He just didn't want us to have any fun!"* Yet, having now gotten our way, we the people continue the cry, "we are not having fun yet, we want more for ourselves." So, God gave people everything they needed; this should have been 'satisfying,' but it did not suffice well enough for us. The more we've gotten, the less satisfied we are, and the weaker we became!

Liberalism is capturing the political agenda across our countries to the degree our leaders and their personal agendas are being entrenched into the law of the land to the degree that our personal freedoms of speech, even in proper context, are being challenged in the courts. Our constitutions are still in place as they were written a long time ago, to declare as if written in stone, that we are all created equal and we can believe what we wish, under moral guidelines [my interpretation].

And they took their journey from Elim, and all the congregation of the children of Israel came unto the wilderness of Sin, which is between Elim and Sinai, on the fifteenth day of the second month after their departing out of the land of Egypt. And the whole congregation of the children of Israel murmured against Moses and Aaron in the wilderness: And the children of Israel said unto them, Would to God we had died by the hand of the LORD in the land of Egypt, when we sat by the 'flesh pots' [in the context, are simply feeding stations], and when we did eat bread to the full; for ye have brought us forth into this wilderness, to kill this whole assembly with hunger.

Then said the LORD unto Moses, Behold, I will rain bread from heaven for you; and the people shall go out and gather a certain rate every day, that I may prove them, whether they will walk in my law, or no.

And it shall come to pass, that on the sixth day they shall prepare that which they bring in; and it shall be twice as much as they gather daily. And Moses and Aaron said unto all the children of Israel, At even, then ye shall know that the LORD hath brought you out from the land of Egypt: And in the morning, then ye shall see the glory of the LORD; for that he heareth your murmurings against the LORD: and what are we, that ye murmur against us? And Moses said, This shall be, when the LORD shall give you in the evening flesh to eat, and in the morning bread to the full; for that the LORD heareth your murmurings which ye murmur against him: and what are we? Your murmurings are not against us, but against the LORD. And Moses spake unto Aaron, Say unto all the congregation of the children of Israel, Come near before the LORD: for he hath heard your murmurings. [Exodus 16:1-9 KJV]

Psalms 106 is said to be anonymously written, but I like to think of it in the guise or picture of The Shepherd boy David as he is tending sheep on the hillside and in the quiet meadows, while feeling the flow of Psalms 23:

The LORD is my shepherd; I shall not want.

He maketh me to lie down in green pastures: he leadeth me beside the still waters.

He restoreth my soul: he leadeth me in the paths of righteousness for his name's sake.

Yea, though I walk through the valley of the shadow of death, I will fear no evil: for thou art with me; thy rod and thy staff they comfort me.

Thou preparest a table before me in the presence of mine enemies: thou anointest my head with oil; my cup runneth over.

Surely, goodness and mercy shall follow me all the days of my life: and I will dwell in the house of the LORD for ever.

Within this picture of solitude in the presence of God, Who has our best interest in mind, from before time as we know it, we see Psalm Twenty-three, credited to, 'Anonymity.' I do not want to be accused of 'pseudepigraphy' [suggestively false] or anything the like of it that resembles me saying something out of context. I try to keep context in mind as I write, even when I play on words at times.

Here I am again, using words that hardly anyone can understand, and 'methinks' you will fall in line and say, "Wow" are you ever smart, and "I like how you put it." "Pseudepigraphy, this sure strikes a cord with me—oh, by the way, what does it mean?" I just discovered 'Pseudepigraphy' early this morning before I was awake enough to think the word, let alone write it—I didn't even know this word existed. I have many sleepless nights because I am 'Word Conscious' twenty-four-seven. Life hits us regularly with the issues we would like to delete from life's vivid blackboard.

Pseudepigraphy: Spurious writings, especially writings falsely attributed to biblical characters or times—A body of texts written, between 200 BC and AD 200 and spuriously ascribed to various prophets and kings of the Hebrew Scriptures. [Falsely crediting someone else's writing to the wrong source].

How could a God that loved us so much even think to add the load of what is carried in the words of this Mr.—Mrs.—Ms.—'Anonymous' on us just because we wanted more than He thought would be good for us! Listen to what 'Anonymous' says from out of their wild blue yonder in Psalms 106: [KJV], especially verse 15, while listening to how people treated God while expecting all the benefits of life]

'Anonymous' says, Praise ye the LORD. O give thanks unto the LORD; for he is good: for his mercy endureth for ever. Who can utter the mighty acts of the LORD? Who can show forth all his praise?

Blessed are they that keep judgment, and he that doeth righteousness. Remember me, O LORD, with the favor thou bearest unto thy people: O visit me with thy salvation; That I may see the good of thy chosen, that I may rejoice in the gladness of thy nation, that I may glory with thine inheritance.

We have sinned with our fathers, we have committed iniquity, we have done wickedly. Our fathers understood not thy wonders in Egypt; they remembered not the multitude of thy mercies; but provoked him at the sea, even at the Red sea. Nevertheless he saved them for his name's sake, that he might make his mighty power to be known.

"We need to get a hold of the power of God, 'Then and now!"

He rebuked the Red sea also, and it was dried up: so he led them through the depths, as through the wilderness. And he saved them from the hand of him that hated them and redeemed them from the hand of the enemy. And the waters covered their enemies: there was not one of them left. Then believed they his words; they sang his praise.

They soon forgot his works; they waited not for his counsel, but lusted exceedingly in the wilderness, and tempted God in the desert. And he gave them their request; but sent leanness into their soul.

They envied Moses also in the camp, and Aaron the saint of the Lord. The earth opened and swallowed up Dothan and covered the company of Abiram. And a fire was kindled in their company; the flame burned up the wicked. They made a calf in Horeb and worshipped the molten image. Thus they changed their glory into the similitude of an ox that eateth grass.

They forgat God their Saviour, which had done great things in Egypt; wondrous works in the land of Ham, and terrible things by the Red sea. Therefore he said that he would destroy them, had not Moses his chosen stood before him in the breach, to turn away his wrath, lest he should destroy them. Yea, they despised the pleasant land, they believed not his word: But murmured in their tents and hearkened not unto the voice of the Lord.

Therefore, he lifted up his hand against them, to overthrow them in the wilderness: To overthrow their seed also among the nations, and to scatter them in the lands. They joined themselves also unto Baalpeor and ate the sacrifices of the dead. Thus, they provoked him to anger with their inventions: and the plague brake in upon them.

Then stood up Phinehas and executed judgment: and so the plague was stayed. And that was counted unto him for righteousness unto all generations for evermore.

They angered him also at the waters of strife, so it went ill with Moses for their sakes: Because they provoked his spirit, so he spake unadvisedly with his lips. They did not destroy the nations about whom the LORD commanded them: But were mingled among the heathen and learned their works.

And they served their idols: which were a snare unto them. Yea, they sacrificed their sons and their daughters unto devils, and shed innocent blood, even the blood of their sons and of their daughters, whom they sacrificed unto the idols of Canaan: and the land was polluted with blood. Thus were they defiled with their own works and went a whoring with their own inventions.

Therefore was the wrath of the LORD kindled against his people, insomuch that he abhorred his own inheritance. And he gave them into the hand of the heathen; and they that hated them ruled over them. Their enemies also oppressed them, and they were brought into subjection under their hand.

Often did he deliver them; but they provoked him with their counsel and were brought low for their iniquity. Nevertheless he regarded their affliction, when he heard their cry: And he remembered for them his covenant and repented according to the multitude of his mercies. He made them also to be pitied of all those that carried them captives. Save us, O LORD our God, and gather us from among the heathen, to give thanks unto thy holy name, and to triumph in thy praise.

"Blessed be the LORD God of Israel from everlasting to everlasting: and let all the people say, Amen. Praise ye the LORD." [Psalms 106; KJV]

There was a spirit of repentance in verse six, in this another generation of people than the words of verse fifteen addresses. And we wonder why God is so nasty, or is He nasty? Is He not just trying to point us to our errors, while pointing to what we could have had, had we listened to Him. We can still have the best of the best in some ways today, and then on into the eternity we cannot yet understand. In the Gospel of John 11:35, Jesus wept out of compassion, for us who did not understand His heart.

Macbeth, Act Three, Scene Six expresses a cry of despair.

Lennox said something like this, "Was Macduff told to return to Scotland? [Lennox: Sent he to Macduff?]

A British lord said: He did, and with an absolute "Sir, not I," The cloudy messenger turns me his back, and hums, as who should say "You'll rue the time that clogs me with this answer." [Take note of "You will rue the day"]

Lennox speaks again: "And that well might advise him to a caution, t' hold what distance his wisdom can provide. Some holy angel. Fly to the court of England and unfold his message ere he come, that a swift blessing may soon return to this our suffering country under a hand accursed!"

The British lord: "I'll send my prayers with him."

"You'll Rue The Day!"

These are harsh words if some other person says them to us, as if they are formed to be a threat against us continuing to mess up their plans to keep on keeping on along a path that does not fit their normal. These are harsher words yet if we believe in God, expecting Him to always ditto our best laid plans with a huge amen as we continue along our merry way to our own demise. Is God that 'Nasty' when out of a heart of love He says 'no' to us when we load up for ourselves instead of reaching out to the suffering?

Then, after this stark reminder, we cannot continue to disobey God and expect His blessings to pour all over us, soaking us always with the goodness of Psalms 23; so, someone tells us that the answer is blowing in the wind. Such is the superficial or shallow replies we get when we present our case to some philosophers of our time—philosophy, psychology, religiosity, secularism, humanism, and every ism known to the gods of this world, and humankind, about our cry of pain and suffering all around us, still leaves us oblivious to reality. Will we not repent of our sin and seek after God with everything we have within us; we struggle with this part of life.

I cannot say life differed in the history we left behind, one which, for the most part we do not want to remember for the morality it suggests for every person ever born. When we see the sin of Noah's day, which he was told to prepare to escape by building The Ark, it is a scary thing when we think of it keeping us from God! What measuring stick do I use as I look at the pictures of life and the people around me? Without a benchmark or standard to measure life, we are on the wrong track.

What measuring stick should I use?

What objective measuring stick exists without my input, one which will be well able to determine the rights and wrongs of all life, and the people in it?

Is this item which I call 'sin,' up for grabs? Is that which The Bible calls 'sin,' ready for a do-over? Does this, which many good and proper people [whatever this means] say, hold enough weight to upset the apple cart, because they say, "The Times Are A Changing?" Should we keep up with the times as they are changing on every moral issue, because we fear we will lose ground to those people who seem to make progress while flipping on everything once considered sacred? So, back to the context of this paragraph: Is it time we pull every book in print and every publication of every sort and remove the word 'sin.' If so, we will be in the same position as was the case when there was a crisis in Germany, of whether to burn books which held words we thought were unacceptable for our people to sort out for themselves.

Kathy Benjamin, a freelance writer wrote a piece called, *11 Book Burning Stories That Will Break Your Heart* [April 2013]. I read some of her stories on a website publication called Mental Floss; it also has or had a print magazine as well. According to the "About" section on the bottom of the page, the information is freely shareable, because they wish to share the intensity of some issues, which often get hushed up: I gathered this from the seriousness of these 11 stories. (http://mentalfloss.com/article/50038/11-book-burning-stories-will-break-your-heart).

What I will share here of Kathy Benjamin's writings is not intended to demean or hurt anyone, even those who are on the side of the burning of books and information which has life changing and informative resources to aid the world's cry for help.

I do not condone or excuse these sentiments, but folks, we were all equal at birth. People who handle history in these devastating manners may someday get their reward, it may not measure up to what they expected; they may "Rue The Day" they were in this destructive mindset. However, I do not intend to go about searching out what I consider their unacceptable stuff and begin the mass destruction of their stuff.

"ThinkStock: Recently, society has become more creative in the ways it shows displeasure for particular books, doing everything from banning them to using them as toilet paper. But the classic method is still a good old-fashioned book burning. Here are some of the worst, but a warning to all bibliophiles: Reading this might hurt a little."

The Burying of Scholars

For over 500 years, Ancient China experienced a golden age of writing and ideas. Despite the wars and power struggles from 770 to 221 BC, scholars came up with some of the most fascinating philosophies of all times, including Confucianism and Taoism. Then, in 221 BC, the wars stopped, and all power was consolidated under Emperor Qin. Qin and his advisors didn't trust the scholars, and, starting in 213 BC, ordered thousands of priceless books burned. All history books were destroyed so Qin could write his own version where he came out looking the best. This carried on for three years, until Qin buried over 1000 scholars alive, while burning their works. No one knows how much irreplaceable information was lost.

Nalanda

For 600 years, Nalanda was one of the best universities in the world. In India, it attracted students from as far away as Greece who came to study in one of the greatest libraries the world had ever seen. It extended over three buildings up to nine stories high. The hundreds of thousands of books inside those buildings covered subjects as wide ranging as grammar, logic, literature—.

But many of the most precious texts were among the most important in Buddhism, and those religious tomes may have been what Bakhtiyar Khilji and his Muslim army were intent on destroying when they sacked the university in 1193. According to legend, there were so many books, they burned for three months. Losing the religious texts effectually ended Buddhism as a major religion in India for hundreds of years.

Heretical Books

The Spanish Inquisition, especially under Tomas Torquemada, is famous for its use of torture to discipline people suspected of following the 'wrong' religion. When they were burned at the stake, often any books they had that were not the Catholic Bible were burned with them. The Inquisition was especially on the lookout for any books written in Hebrew or Arabic. But Torquemada also arranged for book burning festivals where thousands of heretical volumes were destroyed, and the atmosphere was like a party.

These three are only a few of the eleven stories that Kathy Benjamin placed on this site. The other eight stories are also a worthy read, if one wishes to grasp the evil of injustices in the world while suppressing the forward movement of knowledge, intending to open the world to only new theories and doctrines, which are largely erroneous. As I have said often, I have my steadfast or even dogmatic belief in One God, who displays Himself to us in The Three Persons of The Godhead: Father, Son [Jesus], and the Holy Spirit of God. If I did not have these as my benchmark, I would not have a leg to stand on for the eternal future I cherish. An unknown future lies ahead, unseen as yet; it is the best hope on the planet?'

However, there are certain seemingly new things which are really not new, they are just reworked to sound new; they challenge me to look again at the facts of history and The Bible to find the proper balance—there is always a proper balance. Just as in the measurement of weight, the scale of justice, over the period of eternity, will not fail to give an accurate account. Might we need to look over 'Our Accounts' [our beliefs] for another internal look.

The words of the Preacher, the son of David, king in Jerusalem. Vanity of vanities, saith the Preacher, vanity of vanities; all is vanity. What profit hath a man of all his labor, which he taketh under the sun? One generation passes away, and another generation cometh: but the earth abideth for ever.

The sun also ariseth, and the sun goes down, and hasteth to his place where he arose. The wind goeth toward the south, and turneth about unto the north; it whirleth about continually, and the wind returneth again according to his circuits. All the rivers run into the sea; yet the sea is not full; unto the place from whence the rivers come, thither they return again.

All things are full of labor; man cannot utter it: the eye is not satisfied with seeing, nor the ear filled with hearing. The thing that hath been, it is that which shall be and that which is done is that which shall be done: and "there is no new thing under the sun." Is there any thing whereof it may be said, See, this is new? It hath been already of old time, which was before us. There is no remembrance of former things; neither shall there be any remembrance of things that are to come with those that shall come after. [Ecclesiastes 1:1-11 KJV]

Just as it was initially in the Bible, in The Garden of Eden, where people disobeyed God and ate from the Tree of The Knowledge of Good and Evil, it is today. It could not be stopped by human hands then, and history itself proves it has been unstoppable. So, why would we think we can solve all the problems for which the general answer to all the questions, 'Is Blowing In The Wind.' Curious thought— 'Blowing In The Wind.' It carries a pejorative [harsh and disapproving] tone in one sense and hope in another sense. If I experience a favorable wind in my sails, I will do okay. If I see a 'Red Sky' in the morning, and I look for favorable winds for my sailing pleasure, I may be in for a rude awakening.

The pejorative view, the harsh and often disapprovingly verbiage we get when we acknowledge only God as the ultimate answer, seems impossible to convey to a person on the opposite side of our view. The sufficient source to keep us from floundering along in the wind to catch up to the Twenty-Dollar Bill that caught our eye as we were simply living life as we knew it, is still "Blowing Around In The Wind." We may never get the fair winds we so desire until Jesus comes back into the picture to help us out.

Do we need to question this 'sin' entity. What is sin anyway? Does it lay open on the table as being, disobedience, lying, cheating, stealing, hating, being unfaithful, committing adultery, inappropriate sexual sins, murder—? I am against sin; however, I fall into a category of sinfulness when I do not obey God's word; I continue doing wrong; being unholy—sin is the breaking of God's law—are we diminishing God's law?

The story of sin has been, and always is, one of such contention, dispute and or debate, it seems the universe cannot come to grips with it or come up with an answer fitting every description of it. I do not know if enough books could be written to help us get it right; I mean about what is sin and what constitutes not sinning. I cannot include enough information in this short book to guarantee I will have given every right answer to the questions which abound.

However, there are a few hard and fast rules we can use to get the picture fairly close to being right—be objective, not subjective. If we are to solve the problems of life, and the intrinsic or basic value of each person ever born [came into this life with], we might need to recognize what value is and demands of us—how we manage our lives as we age—day by day, moment by moment.

We can look at the many belief systems, be it one promoting issues of morally, relativity, or dependence [believing that right and wrong are not a matter of objectivity, (absolute values) but based on subjectivity (our personal viewpoint) because of our particular circumstances or because of the culture we were born into], or not. When it comes down to bottom line scenarios, we balk at anything that does not line up with 'our' subjective slant of life. Try claiming God is all we need, in a theater of people: 'You will need God's help to survive the onslaught!'

One of the many belief systems is 'secular humanism' [materialistic or temporal, as everything made by human hands will perish at some point]. This belief says, human reason and ethical, philosophical, or moral issues are not based upon any belief system that espouses or adopts God as the authority on the subject. Do we need to follow these guidelines to be in an absolute right position with life and or the universe; for our decision making process to sustain life and eternity, whatever that may be?

Atheism is the old term we got used to. It and its close relative, New Atheism, are big-ticket items more so today than ever before. Hence, we have gone from plain old atheism [believing there is no God], to the New Atheism. New Atheism maintains the old but goes further by saying there can be no respect for anybody who believes in God; thus they try to take away the right of freedom of conscience and belief, as ensconced in our constitutions. Their distain has increased to say that religion is not 'simply wrong,' religion of any kind is evil in its very inception, no matter when and where it comes from.

Being an agnostic simply says that you are not sure about anything, besides what is physically before our eyes; that which we can feel or touch. Admittedly or not, 'they are saying they are unsure about being unsure.' The bottom-line is, Agnostics are really saying there are no reasonable grounds for a belief in God or the non-existence of God.

Another issue which has been with us for eons, is the one of Evolution. The Big Bang Theory is a big topic of this belief. Many atheists are in this camp; there are also some Theistic Evolutionists, they believe God may have used evolution to bring about all of what we have in our universe. I am not trying to discredit anyone in these camps, I am just proposing my own biases of beliefs as I see them.

Evolution in its basic form says the evolvement [evolving] of everything began from a single cell, which came from nothing. It just appeared. Some say this happened from the entity of gravity, which seems to have existed before or along with the nothing that preceded everything that came to be. What a 'Power Packed [my attempt at some humor]' cell this must have been. Yes, again, some Christians believe in an evolutionary process where God is still involved, differing from the many atheists who passionately believe that anything like a God or Supreme Designer had nothing to do with Creation or the appearance of everything. Accordingly, 'Time and Chance' alone, were the progenitors [forerunners] of all we see. It all falls into the hands of Mister, Madame, MS, It, They— [to try to be politically correct, tolerant], and I am not sure what tomorrow's name for gender will be, we will figure it out: I guess, or not? If not, we will be more troublesome to each other.

Christianity: As a Christ Follower I look at the Bible for my reference to all we know of as Christianity. However, to come to a debate on the above subjects like I read about in *Can We Be Good Without God*—by Paul Chamberlain, and this being only one resource, is also theory based because it requires faith. All other belief systems require faith; nobody was there at the inauguration of the very beginning of everything to see it coming into existence. However, when Paul Chamberlain finishes with his conversations with the participants of his book, the results show reasonable doubt being cast on the other belief system, because of the balancing act of Moral Objectivity and Moral Subjectivity.

The whole matter of debate between people who hold differing views about anything, and everything is one which only asks everyone to take an unbiased look at the topic; look at the Pros and Cons and see which one makes the most sense from a logical platform. The Occam's Razor Principles suggests that the 'Simplest Answer' most often proves to be the most efficient way to garner the truth on any matter to decide anything.

The God scenario requires only faith to believe God is Who He says He is; He will do what He said and or says He will do; accept Him personally as their Guide for life; with the expectation of there being an everlasting life after death; the one He provided for us because 'Jesus' paid off the full debt of us living our lives for ourselves, and the temporal desires of the flesh.

Many of the other Belief Systems say they are not faith based. They feel they can decide on all of what many expect after they die, by using Common Sense Reasoning, based on the feeling we have within our psyche, spirit or being—'subjectivity,' as opposed to 'objectivity' [trust and faith based, detaching ourselves from the entity of feelings, and entrusting ourselves to The God Who offers Love as the avenue of eternal life; not feelings].

You may say "Love is a feeling." Love is not a feeling; love is a fact. If love is evident in life, it produces more than feelings to determine an action. We love God because He showed us how to love. We access this belief system through the acceptance of Jesus Christ as God in the flesh, having come in human form to guide us through the rough spots of life. I highly recommend reading, *Can We Be Good Without God?* [Paul Chamberlain].

One man I appreciate most highly with Apologetics, is Ravi Zacharias. From what I suggest as my short list, people who I can trust to tell it like it is, no matter whom he is speaking to, Ravi and his team discuss everything I may feebly try to express, while he would do proper justice to his presentation because of his calling and knowledge base. Paul Chamberlain is also a trustworthy mentor.

The Answer is Blown In the Wind: OR NOT?

I Am Looking Back To See "IF—"
"IF" You Are Looking Back To See—.

There is such a spirit of flippancy, almost a boldness to say, "Who Cares About This God Thing" which the preachers are propounding. Our world grasps at everything that is blown into our space in this wind of time we live in, for all things it feels are new and will finally satisfy that insatiable inner craving that only the initial life giver could supply.

A life-force which propels us on, day by day to keep reaching for that something that just seems to blow around in the wind, is part of a tangled mess that includes every belief system concocted by humankind—'some god, or some other entity which may yet be unknown,' is the answer. The morality, which was once the norm, is *Gone With the Wind!* Methinks the answer we are looking for is not just blown in by any wind of doctrine, rule, principle, or dogma.

What Did I See, and What Does It Say To Me?

"Prepare to Launch!"

Cast thy bread upon the waters: for thou shalt find it after many days.

Give a portion to seven, and also to eight; for thou knowest not what evil shall be upon the earth.

If the clouds be full of rain, they empty themselves upon the earth: and if the tree fall toward the south, or toward the north, in the place where the tree falleth, there it shall be.

He that observeth the wind shall not sow; and he that regardeth the clouds shall not reap.

As thou knowest not what is the way of the spirit, nor how the bones do grow in the womb of her that is with child: even so thou knowest not the works of God who maketh all.

In the morning sow thy seed, and in the evening withhold not thine hand: for thou knowest not whether shall prosper, either this or that, or whether they both shall be alike good.

Truly the light is sweet, and a pleasant thing it is for the eyes to behold the sun:

But if a man live many years and rejoice in them all; yet let him remember the days of darkness; for they shall be many. All that cometh is vanity.

Rejoice, O young man, in thy youth; and let thy heart cheer thee in the days of thy youth, and walk in the ways of thine heart, and in the sight of thine eyes: but know thou, that for all these things God will bring thee into judgment.

Therefore remove sorrow from thy heart and put away evil from thy flesh: for childhood and youth are vanity. [Ecclesiastes 11 KJV]

PART THREE

HUMAN VALUE

And

"IF AND WHAT IF?"

I was not born into wealth: "What If I Was?" I was not born as a "Person of Differing Color From Yours:" "What If I Was?" I was not born with any "Disabilities:" "What If I Was?" I was not born as a "White Person." "What If I Was?"

These are open-ended questions.

You get the message! I have tried to be as kind as I know how to be in the words, I have chosen to say what it is I am trying to say. Everyone is born with a "Value Added Clause Attached," albeit, in an invisible, yet non-disclosed, and unbeknown to our way. Our future lies before us; depending on the circumstances of our upbringing, we will begin to be more than what we were at birth; or we may become less than what we were at birth, in another way: We may not remain as innocent as what we were at birth; dare I say most all of us will be guilty of this deficit; excluding people with a disability they have no responsibility for because this is how they were born.

"What If I Was" born into wealth?
"What If I Was" born "Colored Different From You?"
"What If I Was" born as a "White Person?"
"What If I Was" born with "Disabilities?"

I have laid out four questions so each of us can look at them and try to figure out what our lives would look like today if we were born different than the way we were born. "What If" I had faced different circumstances, met different people, had wealth—? "What If?" What would I value you as today? What would you value me as today?

In this life, "This Story Never Ends!"
Stay Tuned!

Part Three—Human Value And "If And What If?"

While processing the direction for *Part Three* of this book, *Our Value As Human Beings—If And What If*, I am reflecting on the Chapter Approaches I have used in *Part One*, and *Part Two*. In *Part One*, I titled this part *The Approach Shot*. In *Part Two*, I titled this part, *Believe It Or Not*. The reason for these openers is to present an Entrance into what the Chapter to follow will Present.

In *Twin Towers of The Heart* I used the theme of an *Overture* in each Chapter Intro. Overture means, proposal, proposition, offer, advance, approach—. As I wrote *Twin Towers of The Heart*, this format became a theme of sorts because I often referred to the Movie *Music of The Heart*. Because of this book title [TTOTH], this theme was appropriate because 'Heart' was the operative word [Re The Thought OPERA]. Waiting for the grand entrance creates anticipation and a sense of apprehension. The implication is not to present a Fear Factor, but to introduce what lay ahead with an Anticipation or a Looking Forward Stance to enhance the words of the Chapter to follow.

In *Bridging The Gap*, my most recent book, I used an 'Intro' called, *Looking Over The Horizon*. The intention being, as the book title *Bridging The Gap* suggests to be an Entrance to connections of two or more themes of thought. The intro suggests going forward, being a preface for what comes [preamble, prologue, prelude, front matter to the Chapter, not the book], and or 'Lead-in.' *Looking Over The Horizon* was an insertion in *Bridging The Gap*, to take us 'Into' the Chapter, which was to come, to offer a look past where we are at presently with the hope of a better tomorrow. Who of us does not want a better tomorrow?

Horizon: One definition is, it is the limit of a person's mental perception, experience, or interest. The inference here is to get a better picture of this perspective if we look at the physical horizon in the scene of the physical horizons of the earth, we will get a better idea of how life lays out before us—Real Life! Horizon, Outlook, Perspective, Scope, Perception, Compass.

In *Everybody: Everybody Is A Somebody*, the 'Saga of Entrances' continues with, *The Neutral Zone. Chapter 11—The Domino Stories Of Life Affect Everyone* and lead us to *Chapter 12— The "IF" Factor*, and so on through *Chapter 16*.

The Neutral Zone

11th Chapter

Moving Out of The Defensive Zone, To Advancing the Cause

—Moving Into The Neutral Zone—

—Why? And Because! —

Life presents us with many options: Inequities, Injustices and or Prejudices; These Will Not Change In Our Lifetime.

God always knew what He was doing. Before He ever laid out the step by step plan of creation, He already had us, people in mind. Yes, even before He spoke the physical Universe into existence, God formed or profiled [predestined or predetermined] those folks who would believe in Him as they were presented with the message [obedience to what God said He wanted for people] He presented as early as in the Garden of Eden; to fit the Imagery of His Son, Jesus Christ. From all the understanding I have about God, Him allowing us to choose if we would serve Him, allows for me to think God knew who would accept His Son Jesus.

Predestined or predetermined for me, does not mean certain 'Goody Two Shoes' would get into His Kingdom, but those who follow John 3:16, "God so loved the world that He gave His only begotten Son, that whosoever believes in Him, would not perish, but have everlasting life." [In His Kingdom; Heaven] 'Whosoever,' is a big word; it suggests a huge story: The Story is messaged out to all of creation. These, who accepted the Message of God, in Jesus Christ, would enter a process whereby they would become more like Jesus. These folks were and or are not accepted into the kingdom of God because they were good when they came to God. They came as filthy as filthy could be, the process after they believed cleaned them up. [JBI—Jacob Bergen Insight Re Romans 8:28-29]

IS EVERYBODY A SOMEBODY?

Chapter 11
THE DOMINO STORIES OF LIFE EFFECT EVERYONE

The domino Effect is a chain reaction which occurs when a small change causes a similar change nearby, which then causes another similar change, and so on in linear sequence. The term is best known as a mechanical effect and is an analogy to a falling row of dominoes. It typically refers to a linked sequence of events where the time between successive events is relatively small. In chaos theory, the butterfly effect is the sensitive dependence on initial conditions in which a small change at one place in a deterministic nonlinear system can cause large differences in a later state. [Wikipedia]

'In the moment,' I feel Subjectively—Impulsively prompted to open the drapes. So I am doing this; the first thing filtering into my mind is, *Open Up Your Heart and Let The Sun Shine In*. As I look out the window for a moment I see the sun is overtaking the fog permeating the horizon, which moments ago I could not see past. God does work in mysterious ways His wonders to perform.

So, as we advance the cause of life and stuff in this Chapter we may be asking 'Why Questions.' My initial answer is, 'Because.' we already addressed part of the 'Answer' in *Chapter Ten—The Answer Is Blown In The Wind*—not in the simplicity of saying, 'this Is The Answer' to every one of life's issues. By the time I am done, I will have told you 'The Because,' and the 'cause' is, we are all looking for 'Answers.' By the time I am finished writing this book I will have addressed many reasons 'Why' we are looking for answers; the short answer is that it is because we have so many questions about 'Who' and 'What' is right. Our world is not always an easy place to live in.

'Because' this is an open-ended subject; 'because' there are so many people, so many belief systems, and so many perceived avenues to find the 'Answers' we are so desperately searching for. 'Opinions' run rampant [wild], where we have so many people across the spectrum of this world. Because we have so many 'Opinions,' we have so many 'Belief Systems:' These lock us into 'So' many perceived avenues to find "THE ANSWER!"

Somehow amidst the whole mess of things in this world which we toss into the sorting bin, lies the horrendous task of laying everything openly on the Big Table of This World, and settling on the 'One' entity that can settle all our, 'Who's, What's, Where's, When's Why's and How's.' Measuring our value as human beings—with all the 'If's and 'What If' questions, is an unsolvable challenge unless we settle on one entity, "Who." He has the Power and Authority to land the Answers–The Big Catch of All Eternity.

Chapter 11—The Domino Stories of Life Effect Everyone, is slated to address some of these things. The closer I get to the end of this book, the harder it is for me to dot all the "i's" and cross all the "t's." If I miss some of the important stuff which may be on your mind, things I have not anticipated, I apologize in advance. If *When All Is Said And Done* in this book, I have not covered all the bases, watch for my next book. I do not have a title or any thoughts for that yet! [Maybe it will be, *"Are The Old Accounts Settled?"* We will probably all have to "Wait For It!]"

Appreciation [Increase] and Depreciation [Decrease] are always a part of determining estimated market value, as we set to achieve a certain mark as in moving forward in our efforts to achieve—corporately, physically, and spiritually. Knowledge depreciates us because it drains us—it inputs or contributes to a weariness in our bones.

God knows when we are not at our best—!

God knew best in the garden!

Every passing day attempts to derail us from the path we set out for the course of our day. Then, for our lifetime, the physical and the spiritual intersect with each other regularly. Ordinary intersections are often panic driven without traffic lights; then they added Traffic Circles! Some of the Traffic Circles I have maneuvered are okay; then there are others! When I come to an area like a city I have not frequented often or ever, I may struggle here.

'Tomorrow' never comes without having had a 'Today.' We never manage a day, without setting a well-defined course; we need to set parameters or boundaries. We play a part in providing for tomorrow, this defies somewhat what we read as part of James 4:13-15; [The Bible]. Boundaries—in our day people care little for limitations, when liberalization offers so many more choices. We live in an "Everything Goes Society!" However, we do have the responsibilities to hear what God says on the matters of our lives.

From whence come wars and fightings among you? Come they not hence, even of your lusts that war in your members? Ye lust, and have not: ye kill, and desire to have, and cannot obtain: ye fight and war, yet ye have not, because ye ask not. Ye ask, and receive not, because ye ask amiss, that ye may consume it upon your lusts. Ye adulterers and adulteresses, know ye not that the friendship of the world is enmity with God? Whosoever therefore will be a friend of the world is the enemy of God. Do ye think that the scripture saith in vain, The spirit that dwelleth in us lusteth to envy?

But he giveth more grace. Wherefore he saith, God resisteth the proud, but giveth grace unto the humble. Submit yourselves therefore to God. Resist the devil, and he will flee from you. Draw nigh to God, and he will draw nigh to you. Cleanse your hands, ye sinners; and purify your hearts, ye double minded.

Be afflicted, and mourn, and weep: let your laughter be turned to mourning, and your joy to heaviness. Humble yourselves in the sight of the Lord, and he shall lift you up. Speak not evil one of another, brethren. He that speaketh evil of his brother, and judgeth his brother, speaketh evil of the law, and judgeth the law: but if thou judge the law, thou art not a doer of the law, but a judge. There is one lawgiver, who can save and destroy: Who art thou that judgest another?

Go to now, ye that say, To day or to morrow we will go into such a city, and continue there a year, and buy and sell, and get gain: Whereas ye know not what shall be on the morrow. For what is your life? It is even a vapor, that appeareth for a little time, and then vanishes away. For that ye ought to say, If the Lord will, we shall live, and do this, or that.

But now ye rejoice in your boastings: all such rejoicing is evil. Therefore, to him that knoweth to do good, and doeth it not, to him it is sin. [James 4:1-17]

Out from amongst this *Chapter 4* of James, I need to clarify my position of saying we need to plan for tomorrow.

"We play a part in providing for Tomorrow. This defies somewhat what we read as part of James 4:13-15;" [The Bible].

If we do not look at the context of life, the things it pertains to, we will always get it wrong. It may have been yesterday, it may be today, or it may be the tomorrow not here yet, but the one we hope and pray for. If we do not properly evaluate the context of life and the eternity or infinity of the time element we may not yet understand, we will not be living in the 'Heaven' God promised to those "Who Get It!" The context of life is God first; our neighbor second, and ourselves next. The approaches of all other entities will fail because life has only One Source—find it and live! Though most everybody wants life to be all that it can be on the positive side; negatives come, they cause the grief we can best live without.

Look at what James 4:13-17 means when we break it out in plainer words: [JBI Insight Version (Jacob Bergen Version)]

There is a substance or an ingredient of the real truth of knowing how to plan for tomorrow for those of us who think we can make up our bucket list and expect to see it fulfilled exactly as we have listed it in our Best Laid Plans of Mice and People. Now, this very day, or by tomorrow for sure, we are headed to the place where all our dreams on the bucket list will become reality—wrong. Then we will find our name on the Forbes List—The Rich and getting Richer [or poorer], and The Famous Now, who also fit the category of one day losing credibility because of their brazen lifestyle: Wrong Again!

Foolishly, we are on shaky ground if this is our motif, theme of life, and or our Mandate. If we think we will determine our tomorrows, however many they may be, by our bold claims of success, we do not have a clue. Life is just a breath of wind, not the full force of a guarantee of still having a whole day or greater piece of time to do it. Ed Gungor, Pastor, writer, author, wrote a book called, *One Small Barking Dog*; I recommend this read.

The bottom line is that we can and should prepare for 'Tomorrow,' but there is a qualifying caveat and or quantifying or calculating process we need to consider. We are not our own, we did not self-create ourselves, we owe our existence to some force outside of ourselves. Therefore, we need to say, "if it is in the plans of that Force," we will complete our bucket list. It may not be as lavish or extravagant as we planned; it may not get us onto "The Forbes List;" but it may just give us all the satisfaction of a plan best executed by that Someone we do not always wish to acknowledge: God! We may just realize what God will give us is 'Enough' to get us beyond the fork in the road which 'we' need to journey, not the one we thought we should have taken: Second-guessing ourselves. Second guessing always leaves us to deal with a guilt factor we cannot sustain indefinitely without the greater cost of peace of mind, and maybe even life.

So shall my word be that goeth forth out of my mouth: it shall not return unto me void, but it shall accomplish that which I please, and it shall prosper in the thing whereto I sent it.

For ye shall go out with joy and be led forth with peace: the mountains and the hills shall break forth before you into singing, and all the trees of the field shall clap their hands.

Instead of the thorn shall come up the fir tree, and instead of the brier shall come up the myrtle tree: and it shall be to the Lord for a name, for an everlasting sign that shall not be cut off. [Isaiah 55:11-13 KJV]

Wow—who does not want this guarantee for the present and the end result of the portion of their earthly time—the time spent and paid for with our lives? Or who does not want a reward for what they thought they expended or exhausted—personal resources. Oh, what a plus, when we realize our resources are a gift for making life better for all concerned, not a right to exploit selfishly. What Is the Domino Effect? How will it change the course of our lives?

The reality of our worth is garnered within the, Who, What, Where, When, Why and How of life. Who was involved? What Happened? Where did it take place? When did it take place? Why did it happen? How do these things make any difference to life as we now know it?

Dominoes, Not The Game, But The Realities We Know, Have An Impact On The End Result—The Bottom-Line.

While prepping my heart for this Chapter my mind turned to the theme of Dominoes. No particular reason was responsible, because I never play dominoes, I do not even know the rules. I have heard about dominoes; I have seen dominoes; they have numbers on them; most of the regular ones are black with white dots on them; it is a game. I think that I played Mexican Train Dominoes once, so do not ask me to explain the game to you! You might say I am naive as far as playing Dominoes goes.

I said there was no particular reason for my choice to branch out on the theme of dominoes, but there is always a reason. Most often I need to dig deeper for the reason, and at other times it comes as if out of the blue. To one person my reason may not be relevant; for another person, the reasons I give for my thoughts may be 'Just What The Doctor Ordered.' I believe that in "the scope of everything," anything left out of life measures out in what each of us lives out. Some of it measures out for the right things and weighs out for the good; some events measure out in wrong actions with adverse results, better lived without, but they can be character builders.

'Who' was involved in the inner and outer workings in and of our lives? Personally—this is the case for everyone; the first bit of input was from the people who caused our entrance into this challenging world we live in. The evolutionary route suggests that we came from nothing; I do not say this to suggest these folks are of no intrinsic, inherent, fundamental, basic, essential, or central importance in the Creator's Master Plan because of their theory.

However, we all, or at least those of us born in what we know as the free world, have an innate, distinctive or inborn ability to choose what that initial value will amount to as we live on into the big world; the challenge is how do we incorporate 3rd. World Peoples into our answers page. Our immediate value may decrease and or disintegrate because of how we choose to treat others; it may be those who are our immediate neighbors, or those worlds away from us.

Hypothetically, let's consider removing one of the dominoes God lined up in His plan for each of us. God does not eliminate the domino [person] that matters most in each our own lives and say, "I do not like you as much as I like other people. You are on your own, tough it out on your own!" If God did this as part of His Grand plan for all time yet to come, methinks, by taking out the one domino, God would be advocating uncertainty in His overall plan.

If we take out a 'Double Six Domino' [bone, cards, tile, ticket, stone, or spinner] from a huge row of dominoes set to fall as they hit each other, from the first to the last, [the color of which does not matter], and replace it with a 'Double One Domino,' the end effect does not change. If we take out one domino, the action of falling down halts immediately; our life cycle forms a gap.

In the evolutionary model, the missing domino, the 'Missing Link,' happened without an Intelligent Designer as the 'First Cause,' leaving us with uncertainty as the norm. If something did pop out of nothing we would have no chance of knowing anything; we would have more of an excuse. Unless that nothing was intelligent, 'how could this be;' it would then be an equal to God's Plan. [as above]

So, getting back to the first 'W' Who, I must go farther back in time than the seed a man planted into a woman. Or we could in todays world, with cloning procedures—take the seed that a man gave up to be placed in a test tube, vial, flask, bottle, ampoule, or container, to be joined by carefully placing the fertile cell [egg] of a woman into that test-tube scenario. We might end up with you or I as a well-developed anthropological specimen—Or Not? Or the doctor or whatever practitioner, expert, or GP they were, may just have shaken the container vigorously till they assumed it was well-done. Or, we could go the route of surrogacy or artificial insemination, because of the difficulty couples have in trying to conceive of having children and see how that works out.

Hey, if you did not notice, I have not gone back far enough yet to determine the overriding Who; the one which supersedes or replaces the other means of forethought and procedure required to bring about you or me: Girl or boy, female or male, male or female, Y and X YX and XX, DNA and RNA—. It seems there is no end to the details and explanations of how we came from the First Cause Source which got us all started. First Cause is relevant no matter what scenario we present.

It is evident, I'm not a Scientist, or a knowledgeable source with enough smarts to put it all together in my own mind, let alone getting to where I can convince anybody else about how we got here: My brother thinks I am the smartest person in the world, or at least smarter than he is [said tongue in cheek]. Sometimes he phones me about an issue he wants some input to, he says, because I am so smart. I never told my brother I was smart, he just thought he had that part figured out on his own—maybe because I am the older brother, and older people are supposed to be smarter, or just because of how I conduct myself?

I figure, without Y and X in proper balance with one another, we will never produce 'another,' another [another person]. According to the resources I have searched out, 'we,' [you or I], would not be here to write or read what lies here on the pages of *Everybody: Everybody Is A Somebody*. Something Very Important, or SOMEONE VERY IMPORTANT was the only COG IN THE WHEEL.

We not only have the XY chromosome scenario to produce us 'Beautiful People,' we have what seems likened to an XYZ scenario; meaning we are the finished product, and one that has all the capacity and or capabilities of fitting the DNA and RNA Scenario. DNA is DeoxyriboNucleic Acid; this is like a blueprint of biological guidelines that a living organism must follow to exist and remain functional—like building anything, we need a plan or a blueprint. It may not be blue, but it is a printout [blueprint] we can use to follow the direction we need to accomplish the building process. The 'Who' revolves around The Architect. We do not get far into life before adversity challenges us. If there are no guidelines, advancement stops; ruin may be the result.

Downhill ski racecourses are often marked by ribbons of blue spritzed across the white, snowy surface. The simple curves might be an interference for audiences, but prove to be effective for the triumph and care of the competitors. The paint helps as an attendant would, to help maneuver the racers to be positioned to the fastest route to the bottom of the hill; added to this, the distinction of the paint against the snow suggests depth awareness to the racers, which is paramount to their physical well being when traveling at such high rates of rapidity.

What is the RNA? For a long time I only knew about The DNA. If we want the whole picture we need both factors. Now I Know 'The ABC's of RNA, Ribonucleic Acid [DeoxyRiboNucleic]. The RNA is like the builder and or contractor who needs the DNA [blueprint] to fashion whatever construct they are intending to construct. Between the two, the 'DNA and the RNA,' the RNA can perform many differing jobs on a job site, while The DNA is more secure, the constant or unchanging planner [God initiated], it holds more complex information and for longer periods of time than does The RNA [likened to a contractor, subtrade].

'Deoxy—' defined as follows, is a merging system telling us that something is being removed to form its own word so when we put them back together as one word we will understand the process that the whole of life and existence is trying to teach us. 'Deoxygenated:' We use the concept here in the formation of compound words, to get a fuller understanding of the whole of a thing.

Every word has syllables [1, 2, 3—]. We divide a larger word into sections called 'syllables.' 'About,' is an example, it has two syllables, 'A' 'Bout' ['fit,' is a synonym of bout]. A 'bout' is an event that tells a story 'About' something. A 'bout' is a story about a wrestling match, a tournament, a boxing match, a contest.

So 'deoxy' divides DNA and RNA but allows us to put the syllables back together again to tell the whole story. It is like oxygenate and deoxygenate, oxygenating gives life; deoxygenating takes life from us, as if creating a vacuum. 'Deoxy' takes away the some of the unity to express its individual character. It also expresses a willingness to be a part of a team which does the job. Conformity is traditionalism— never wanting to change because we have gotten used to a certain pattern; anything that does not 'fit' into our own personal preconceived mold is a falsehood, or a false theory—or so we think!

We assemble the pieces of a jigsaw puzzle to renew the big picture idea—the big picture was the time before it was punched out into pieces to make a puzzle. The individual pieces lost no value by being chopped up by some cutter wanting to make life difficult for us; we retained our equality and or importance. A Jigsaw Puzzle with missing pieces is useless. When I did puzzles, I got aggravated if there was a piece missing, because it was a no-brainer to complete the picture. The pieces by themselves are of no value [DNA and RNA].

The 'Domino Effect' affects all of us. Remove the oxygen from our existence, as supplied by The First Cause of life, and we die. Confiscate love from our existence and we end up with nothing, no relationship! Love is a prerequisite or a necessity essential to begin with. 'Love' demands a 'Who,' as we contend for a starter in the usage of the '5WS.' Right behind 'Who,' 'What' must follow in order to meet relationship head on. The Domino Effect is an extreme visual, an extreme story of a one small change in a moment of time in our lives, it can change for better or for worse the direction our lives took, and the placement of life in our present term of life.

'When' and 'Where' can interchange without much of a loss of value. However, I suggest that 'When' may take the lead because of an immediacy and or nearness factor, because of 'how' it might affect our safety in the area of 'how' soon I need to take an action to be safe or fix a problem. 'Where' becomes vital here as well, if a danger, whatever it may be, is lurking in my neighborhood, or presenting in the time factor, 'When,' miles away is safer from 'where' I am at in the immediate sense, because I have more time to prepare for the pronounced danger. We have almost come to a place where these W's are like tongue twisters.

'Why' kind of wraps it up with a motive for what's stated. Although, when we are suffering a difficulty and discussing it with someone, because the adversity we bear seems to harsh, we often look upward and ask "WHY?" Kris Kristofferson wrote and sang *Why Me Lord?* Though, Kris uses the same word 'Why,' addressing the same God with the 'Why Question,' his perspective is opposite what we usually mean when we talk to God about our problems. Most often we use the "Poor Little Old Me" setting. Kris Kristofferson asks God 'Why' he is so blessed. He asks 'What' can I do Lord to make it up to You for all the stuff I did against You LORD?

Too often the 'why' of the 5W's takes priority over the 'Who' factor in the story. What did I do to deserve this punishment? Most often the 'why' is describing 'my' desperation for the 'Me' factor as opposed to the importance of the main component of the story. The songwriter [Fanny Crosby] wrote, *Tell Me the Story of Jesus*, this is the main entity the story history tells us is the news of a day—the birth of Jesus. However, the highlight of the story surrounds Christ's suffering, not ours, and that because of 'Love.'

Fanny Crosby was born March 24, 1820. Six weeks into life, she developed an eye infection. Her family doctor was not available, so an available doctor was called, and he treated Fanny's eye infection by using hot mustard poultices and her eyes were permanently burnt leaving her blind from near birth. [I am very familiar with hot mustard plasters; whenever we got a chest cold as kids, this was the treatment we received (it was hot alright, it burned the skin). I am thankful I did not have an eye infection, although I do not think my parents would have used this on our eyes. But, knowledge, being yet untried in many areas, including in medicine, was experimental. Such was the case, I suppose, in the case of Fanny Crosby].

Sixty years later, having lived life blind from six weeks old, Fanny wrote *Tell Me The Story of Jesus* in 1880. Her priority and perspective of life, still, after years of blindness and the difficulties it must have caused for her, did not write *Why Me LORD?* Fanny left this idea behind; I guess she left it for Kris Kristofferson in nineteen-seventy-two. Did she ever consider writing this song; maybe, no one will ever know.

When Fanny was eighty years old, she wrote, *Balm In Secret Prayer*. Balm is an ointment; it is even a healing ointment in the right usage. Balm, hot mustard plaster, and the list of ointment [camphor], all have their place. However, used wrongly each and every one of them can be dangerous. We need to be careful 'Who' and 'What' we rely on for healing and or guidance.

Tho the cross is hard to bear, there is balm in secret prayer. Go and tell thy sorrows there and leave it 'all' with Jesus. [the words of Fanny Crosby in 1900 at eighty years of age]

If you read anything I write, you will find me in song at some point. If you were hovering over me in secret, like an invisible angel, you would often hear my outburst of song. I think Fanny Crosby had a song in her heart twenty-four-seven. I would not be surprised to hear her singing many of her waking hours—she probably sang in her sleep [just me thinking out loud]. Fanny is credited for some nine thousand songs, and they say, 'Blind Folks Cannot See!' Sometimes we sighted folks see so much less with the blessing of sight we have. What if one day we lost this blessing after having had it much of our lives—What Then? I am humbled as I write these words.

Part Three—Human Value And "If And What If?"

Pull 'One Domino' in life, and 'What Do We Get?' Change! In Journalism, 'Who? What? When? Where? Why? and How?' are the bread and butter tools for telling a story—along with, S-V-O sentences, Subject, Verb, Object. Set up a journey of dominoes, no matter the design of the complex, or the complexity of the nature of the build, and pull out just one little old domino and all the all the best laid plans come to a halt. In a Story, remove 'Context,' and you have nothing.

You may have had in mind to set a Guinness Record, when someone begins to pull some dominoes, wrecking your plan. Oh, if you had replacements you could add in new ones. If there were no replacements and the record to beat was one million dominoes, and you had to rework all the dominoes to make the run from beginning to the end, it would change the result. You would no longer have a million and one set up to break the record. Removing one domino would change the planned action—hence we have The Domino Effect.

When we add 'How,' to the mix of Ws because of the 'Why' questions we all have, every time someone expounds on a theory— our mind is fickle one moment and at other times it is as sharp as a tack. Depending on our emotive [subjective status] position, we can flip-flop on what we say and do; this presents us being two-faced or just plain crazy. If we could control our emotions we may come close to being perfect in the things we say and do; we could be consistent enough to handle the ups and downs that will come.

So, when we add a 'How' to a conversation we are having with someone on any topic they may be trying to get us to come to grips with, 'Why' is a counterpart or equal of the scenario we are in. If and when we or anybody else is trying to convince someone else about the relevance or truth of a theory of something, or just a plain explanation of an event, those who try to do the convincing or explaining needs to be cognizant or mindful of where the target person is at in life; before they use someone as a garbage dump. This is not always a life and or death scenario, but it can be.

How life came to be and 'why' life came to be 'what' it is, are uppermost in our minds 'when' we think about deciding about God: His existence; His Nonbeing or Nonexistence. So, 'where' we fit each of these 5WS and 'H' is not always about the sequential, chronological, linear, or progressive order; they can come up at different times and in differing situations because of differing circumstances. 'Who' must always be a part of the mix.

Herein, we check the emotive factors too often coming into play when looking to solve an issue. This is 'Why' we need to focus on 'The Who,' when dealing with life and death matters. On minor issues, 'The Who' may not always be first in the line of necessity, but equally relevant to the whole story. Every story presents as part of another, in the quest of knowing the whole story.

I will be surging in and out of the 5W's and 'H' in this chapter and others, while trying to stay true to this Chapter Title: *The Domino Stories of Life Effect Everyone*. Life is a conundrum, puzzle, or poser, and pans out like relational experiences. The initial purpose, and one intended to be the norm according to the Master Plan, was not meant to be a conundrum, a puzzle or poser. The First Cause for some folks, is God; for some it is No God. Can any 'cause' stand on solid ground without a Who or a What? Did someone pull out a Domino?

Motive is a TV Series which aired for Four Seasons [2013-2016] with fifty-two Episodes. A team of detectives tries to determine motive after they have a dead body, while they do not know the killer's identity, they begin with certain persons of interest to find the killer and the *Motive*. We, the viewing audience, are told who the victim will be and who will be the killer. We the people who are the watchers, get a heads' up right away as to who is the victim and the killer. So, we only need to figure out the Motive.

It is often not too hard for us to figure out the motive because movies and tv shows often leave us hints along the way, in the Title and The Storyline—the participants of the Movie or TV Show are involved without the outcome on display, so they are as if 'In The Dark' for a while. However, certain people's skills allow for them to be detectives, while others in the law enforcement grouping are not so skilled but are better equipped to be the 'Beat-Cop,' where their interpersonal skills may better allow them to be relational with the people along their walk. In this way these Beat-Cops may be in a position to get ahead of a crime by showing people a better way than doing the crime, instead of having them doing the time!

When we are in a position to get relational with someone via a conversation or in a partnership of living—motive, although important in other situations, may not be so important. During differing circumstances from those of some other scenarios, certain matters may be hugely paramount—life and death are paramount.

INTERMEZZO

Motive, the TV Series, presents many situations for the viewing audience; there are many reasons that people take someone's life in this way. The killer is often the most unlikely person, at least to us the viewer. I rarely watch anything which does not present purpose as part of life as I know it. I watch for learning curves in the Movies and TV shows so I will be prepared to pass it on throughout My Mandate for living—writing is this for me.

When amongst family [first party concern] and friends [second party concern], motives may differ. Sometimes there may be, and likely will be, differing matters to discus; those with motives attached to the decision-making process of how to handle the affairs of the target person—elderly or infirm. I will allow you the latitude or liberty to link what these motives may be, and whether each their own are justified, right or wrong in their placement.

There is seemingly no end to TV shows about crime— murder, heists, robbery, lying in a criminal investigation, border crossing issues, perjury [lying] in a court case—. The FBI, Columbo, Dragnet, Murder She Wrote, Leverage, Motive—are but a few in a long list of TV Shows and Movies I like to watch. When we google the internet to list all the crime related shows we need to get ready to be in it for the Long Haul, or *In It For The Whole Ride.*

Sometimes we need to pull out a domino to halt a disaster; at other times we need to be careful what we do to halt the direction someone is taking, because according to our smarts, they are off course. As we look at life it is often difficult to decipher what life will be like tomorrow, based on how things are lining up for us in the today we have before us. As we look at the past we had in our history, life made more sense back in the day—so it seems. Back in the day it was as if the domino's lined up enough so we could plan for the present and for the future with more hope and assurance that our children would be born into the good life we all envisioned.

As we look at the line-up of options life presents for us at the hands of our leaders, no matter what position they hold [politicians, religious leaders, teachers of our educational facilities—and even at the level of where we live, the 'you and me' relationships], we need more of an assurance of getting the Good Life. Too often we set the wrong parameters for what the "Good Life" really is.

If this is true, which Domino do we pull out of the line-up so we can be a part of making this happen, and where do we find the resources we need to have, for the strength and fortitude for each of us to do what is needed to help make life happen?

Is this the Numero-Uno issue [domino] which needs to be pulled from the line-up, tagged as The Selfie Mode Domino? It seems this domino has become the paramount or a principal motivator or entity for life to be as good as we want life to be. In overall reality, 'How' can we envision or foresee life being the best for us if we do not give-it-up for our neighbor—who is my neighbor? The Bible says to 'give-it-up' for those who do not necessarily carry our handle. The Bible points out at least two guidelines.

One guideline is the Golden Rule; treat others in the fashion you would like for them to treat you. This principle is true in most every context it is quoted.

> Therefore, all things ye would that men should do to you, do ye even so to them: for this is the law and the prophets. [Mathew 7:12 KJV]

Another guideline is found in the Bible as well; it says about the same thing. It does not say we should neglect to look after ourselves too.

> Look not every man on his own things, but every man also on the things of others. [Philippians 2:4 KJV]

Important to note for these things to be possible to the fullest extent, there is a resource we need to consider for the Golden Rule to even be possible like this: This is the pattern of The Bible, which is generally considered God's Word as transcribed or recorded by people: Or so it used to be! Sometimes this becomes problematic because people are human, and people do not always hear things as they were once heard and applied. Listen to three declarations, from three writers in The Bible:

> And thou shalt love the Lord thy God with all thy heart, and with all thy soul, and with all thy mind, and with all thy strength: this is the first commandment. And the second is like, namely this, Thou shalt love thy neighbour as thyself. There is none other commandment greater than these. [Mark 12:30-31 KJV]

And he answering said, Thou shalt love the Lord thy God with all thy heart, and with all thy soul, and with all thy strength, and with all thy mind; and thy neighbour as thyself. [Luke 10:27 KJV]

Master, which is the great commandment in the law?

Jesus said unto him, Thou shalt love the Lord thy God with all thy heart, and with all thy soul, and with all thy mind. This is the first and great commandment.

And the second is like unto it, Thou shalt love thy neighbour as thyself. On these two commandments hang all the law and the prophets. [Matthew 22:36-40 King KJV]

Based upon the words of these writers, I find the principle thoughts and words for us are for us to 'get it right,' at the outset of our plan to succeed in life. If this is not how we handle the process of life, adversity or consequences affect the results at journey's end [after we leave this world and enter the next]. There is a 'Who' we need to consider before we consider the 'What' of our actions, and or what seems largely to be our desire.

Master, which is the great commandment in the law?

Jesus said unto him, Thou shalt love the Lord thy God with all thy heart, and with all thy soul, and with all thy mind. This is the first and great commandment.

These words start by saying we need to be in a position of submission [yielding to a Superior source] to someone other than what seems to be the norm in our day. The questions come from people; the answers come from The Provider [Jesus, God in The Flesh]. Jesus says we need to start off any question and answer session in this fashion: "Love God with all which could possibly be in the confines or border of your intent." Jesus says this is Priority Numero-Uno [Number One].

These texts say the Number Two command [some of us think of this as only a suggestion] is to Love Everyone Else like we want to be loved. It is an automatic, or a given for us to get the Second command right if we have the First command right. Before we ever get to take two steps while learning to walk, we need to get the first step. Before we get to the first step we need to get up on our feet and take an action which requires a step of faith—moving our legs.

Before we realize our neighbor is as important as we ourselves are, we need to recognize God is more important than the rest of us! I've talked about people, songwriters who worked through issues of the importance of others above themselves. They saw the blessing of what their lives had become, rather than fixating on the matter of how poorly they were affected by a domino of life which was pulled in some way. Thereby they were adversely challenged in the life they lived as opposed to the life they thought they might have had, had life given them the same chances others received.

The main dialogue, and or the main intent I wish to convey in *Chapter 11* is, we need to have an initial and a prioritized entity on which to place the purpose and perspective of our lives upon. The choice for each of us remains in 'this life,' the one that continues for as long as we have the breath of life; the choice is ours to make; no one can force us to make the right choice. There are always two choices—the right one and the wrong one, in the eternal journey or perspective. How I understand this conundrum as it appears to us as being, is, there is God, or there is no God!

The story is ongoing for now, as long as time as we know it is intact. The row of Dominoes will have spaces which make life become many stories in one sense. In the other sense, it is always only one story. On the one side, it is God's Story, God's Story as told by Him through History, through Creation; through the folks He Created; this will carry the day from an initial source with only God—on the other side it is another story! I have spoken much about the story on the other side of where I am at. It may be "Hell or High Water" for these folks. Here it is without God forever! After death, there is no choice.

We can wait, see, and hope for the best, or we can choose to take a chance and change. Simply rationalizing anything in life, as far as we can rationalize what we cannot see, by assumption or supposition, always leaves us a little short of being in charge all by ourselves in the selfie mode in an action-packed thriller, or as a selfie all about me photo as posted on Social Media. Life Is All About 'Who?'

I Am Looking Back To See "IF—"<br>"IF" You Are Looking Back To See—.

Think about our time here as if it were a journey. We come to some disaster or storm and we need to decide, 'do we keep on going and hope all will be well, or do we go back to where we were safe and wait out the storm.' We know the road we just travelled, so this sounds like the most logical and wise decision to make. Think also about our safety on the roads in precarious situations where it is best to seek out someone who can help us through the storm—like a semi driver and his big rig being the best path finder to follow on the winter roads in a winter snowstorm, or a deluge of rain.

Living in the present and hoping for a bright tomorrow will not always require a retrospective look at the history of events behind us. Much of the stuff we are living in is great; in this windowpane of time we just need to Keep On Keeping On. Day to day stuff can be managed successfully by the things 'at the ready' in our mind's eye, because we should not always be looking over our shoulder for everything which may hound us if we do not have the fortitude to live in the present. It is not always easy to live through some stuff—all things are possible with God.

However, as we look at the choices we make as always being based on chance alone, neglecting the changes we need to make to negotiate for a better tomorrow, a look back over our shoulder at history past may not be such a horrible thought or consideration to assist us in managing life towards the brighter future of tomorrow, which lasts forever. We struggle with the concept of yesterday, we are often in a skirmish today to figure it all out; we are not cognizant or acquainted with what the future will hold in a visual format.

Looking Back to See can actually enhance our perspective or viewpoint if we 'get it right' in our focus on 'Who' is the most important entity of all time. History will help us to come to grips with how life does follow a pattern—it always has, and it always will. Living with a helter-skelter perspective as opposed to a solid-ground-focus on Who can help us through, makes more sense. I may not always 'get it right,' but I find justification in following the course set out in the Bible; following the lead of the main entity— Love God, Keep His Commandments, and Love the people He created.

What Did I See, and What Does It Say?
This is the good question of the day.

Prepare to Launch!

My son, forget not my law; but let thine heart keep my commandments: For length of days, and long life, and peace, shall they add to thee. Let not mercy and truth forsake thee: bind them about thy neck; write them upon the table of thine heart: So shalt thou find favour and good understanding in the sight of God and man.

Trust in the LORD with all thine heart; and lean not unto thine own understanding. In all thy ways acknowledge him, and he shall direct thy paths. Be not wise in thine own eyes: fear the LORD and depart from evil. It shall be health to thy navel, and marrow to thy bones. Honour the LORD with thy substance, and with the first fruits of all thine increase: So shall thy barns be filled with plenty, and thy presses shall burst out with new wine.

My son, despise not the chastening of the LORD; neither be weary of his correction: For whom the LORD loveth he corrected; even as a father the son in whom he delighted.

Happy is the man [person] that findeth wisdom, and the man [person] that getteth understanding. For the merchandise of it is better than the merchandise of silver, and the gain thereof than fine gold. She is more precious than rubies: and all the things thou canst desire are not to be compared unto her. Length of days is in her right hand, and in her left-hand riches and honour. Her ways are ways of pleasantness, and all her paths are peace. She is a tree of life to them that lay hold upon her: and happy is every one that retains her.

The LORD by wisdom hath founded the earth; by understanding hath he established the heavens. By his knowledge, the depths are broken up, and the clouds drop down the dew. My son, let not them depart from thine eyes: keep sound wisdom and discretion: So shall they be life unto thy soul, and grace to thy neck. Then shalt thou walk in thy way safely, and thy foot shall not stumble.

When thou liest down, thou shalt not be afraid: yea, thou shalt lie down, and thy sleep shall be sweet. Be not afraid of sudden fear, neither of the desolation of the wicked, when it cometh. For the LORD shall be thy confidence and shall keep thy foot from being taken.

Withhold not good from them to whom it is due, when it is in the power of thine hand to do it. Say not unto thy neighbour, Go, and come again, and to morrow I will give; when thou hast it by thee. Devise not evil against thy neighbour, seeing he dwelleth securely by thee. Strive not with a man without cause, if he have done thee no harm. Envy thou not the oppressor and choose none of his ways. For the froward is abomination to the LORD: but his secret is with the righteous.

The curse of the LORD is in the house of the wicked: but he blesseth the habitation of the just. He scorneth the scorners: but he giveth grace unto the lowly. The wise shall inherit glory: but shame shall be the promotion of fools. [Written by a "Wise Guy" Solomon a long time ago in a Book called [Proverbs, Chapter 3 KJV]

What Did I See, and What Does It Say?

The answer is not blown in the wind; the answer comes in part by what has already been lived by others and prescribed as being sufficient to carry the day today, because of "The WHO" they knew to be enough, to help us carry the load of life—God is The Way, The Truth and The Life.

I was reminiscing a few days ago; I do this often, and I thought to myself, "What If" when I was going through some of the stuff [events of life which were not so pretty], I had made just one different major choice for the direction of my life, "What Then?" My wife and I would not be together today. I would have married someone else, and who knows how life for me, and others would have differed compared to what I am living today. As I talked this over with my wife later in the day, I did so with a thankful heart. Thankfully, because of what I know about the life I have with her, and all she brought into our relationship, I have enough—Not Stuff, but Satisfaction. Who but God knows where my life with Him might have gone? My life may have had an eternity of a different nature than the life I am drinking in so abundantly.

1785 saw Robert Burns write a poem called *To A Mouse*. Here is Verse 7 of this poem in Robert's words; they may be hard to understand:

But, Mousie, thou art no thy-lane,
In proving foresight may be vain.
The best-laid schemes o' mice an' men
Gang aft agley,
An' lea'e us nought but grief an' pain,
For promis'd joy!
The Best laid plans of Mice and men

"The Best Laid Plans of Mice and Men" means:

We are all in the same position as The Mouse. We plot and plan for today long before today arrives. Spring and Summer are days of preparation for Fall and Winter. If these are not prepared for, then winter hits us exceptionally hard. However, even if we strive with all the might we have, winter [the difficult times of our lives] may cause us to take a turn in the road of life we had not expected to take, changing the course of our lives on the road before us because it may have a fork in the road at which we need to decide which fork to venture out on as a continuation of the 'Whole Journey of Life!'

The Road Not Taken

[Robert Frost 1916]

Two roads diverged in a yellow wood,
And sorry I could not travel both
And be one traveler, long I stood
And looked down one as far as I could
To where it bent in the undergrowth.

Then took the other, as just as fair,
And having perhaps the better claim,
Because it was grassy and wanted wear.
Though as for that the passing there
Had worn them really about the same,

And both that morning equally lay,
In leaves no step had trodden black.
Oh, I kept the first for another day!
Yet knowing how way leads on to way,
I doubted if I should ever come back.

I shall be telling this with a sigh
Somewhere ages and ages hence:
Two roads diverged in a wood, and I—
I took the one less traveled by,
And that has made all the difference.

There is much we can read into this poem by Robert Frost. Many are the varied explanations and or interpretations of Robert's words in this poem. I have used this poem more than once in my books.

If I take the left fork over the right fork I will experience life in a different way than if take the right road. If I take the 'Right Road' I might be the better for not having taken the 'Left Fork.' We decide, and yes, as far as we can figure out the whole story, it is we ourselves that determine the end result of all the issues we have been challenged with. Yes, we chose in the immediate sense.

However, "What If" in the big picture the direction was laid out by some faction of thought, or by some overall authority for life, or some overall power, maybe even a 'Divine' force or power simply being played out to its best-case scenario—one we may never understand until Eternity comes! Question: What Do We Do? Stop life or continue to become the best we can be in this sense?

"What If" I say God is this Power and or Force; am I suggesting God is both good and evil? And IF HE IS GOD, 'Why' would He be like this? Remember, as the poem suggests, we can only travel one road of life and it may present many more forks in that road on which we will again need to choose. There are difficult issues I may never understand enough to give an affirmative answer. Someone said, my part is not to reason 'WHY.' My part is not necessarily to figure out the "Best Laid Plans" of all of present life in the eternal aspect of things.

Neutral can be a good place to be if we do not have any plans to get somewhere. On a car the gear shifter has markings which allow us to make decisions about whether we want to go forward or backwards [Drive and Reverse]. If we are not planning to drive anywhere we can have the shifter in Park or Neutral. If we are in Park mode, we cannot freely push the car if we need to move it because it won't run. In Neutral mode, it simply means we cannot drive anywhere in that notch, but we can push it if we need to.

If we have a car we should probably train ourselves to better understand the gear shift lever, and the best practices of when to use which gear. Life is like this as well. To maneuver life, we need to train ourselves in the practice of when to go forward, and when to go in reverse [back off]. If we just start the car, slap the shifter in gear, no matter which gear we choose, and put the gas peddle to the floor, we may not extend our time for living too far. This is somewhat akin to having a bull in a china shop!

The Neutral Position or the Neutral Zone in Hockey is where the puck often changes hands because the defenses of either team are trying to stop the offensive team from entering the offensive zone and shoot the puck at the goalie and score a goal. There are two Neutral Zones: Each team has one on either side of the Center Line. Just when we think of why there are even dividing markers on the ice at all, instead of just one big sheet of ice with Goal nets at each end, we need to realize it is all about Rules and Regulations to make the game safer for everybody, and fair in the attempt to set parameters for a professional event: Such as The NHL. When we played scrub hockey, we never had lines we just went roughshod up and down the ice, no offside or anything else; we just tried to score goals—Oh The Poor Goalie!

In the world around us there are Neutral Zones, sometimes we call them No Man's Land. No man's land is land which is uninhabited or is two sides quarrel over because they are uncertain about each other's motives, and or they fear some aspect of the others forces. Originally the phrase was used to identify a queried region or a dumping ground for refuse between fiefdoms [Kingdoms]. In modern times it is commonly associated with World War I to describe the area of land between two enemy trench systems, which neither side wished to cross nor seize due to fear of being attacked by the enemy in the process. The term is also used to refer to ambiguity, an anomalous or indefinite area, in regard to an application, situation, or jurisdiction.

In life we have times where we need to take a Neutral Stance in order to keep peace in one scenario or the other. This is hugely important in the age in which we live, because of the many tolerance issues which come to the fore every day in one category or another. This said, we should never be on Neutral Ground about what we believe in the spiritual sense, and why.

Part Three—Human Value And "If And What If?"

We can run, or practise defending our faith, and or we can move forward as if we were putting our car into the Drive Slot on the gear shift. There are times and seasons where we need to step back and survey life, and how we fit into it in regard to what God wants to do, and it may be we do not always agree with His tactics or purposes. If we do not believe in God, the rules are different for us as we 'DO' life, but the consequences follow God's Rule. I could write a whole book on the topic of The Neutral Zone—but for now, I am just saying some things about it so as to find a way of defending the theme, which is the Title of this book, *Everybody: Everybody Is A Somebody*!

The Neutral Zone

12th Chapter
If', And's, Or But's
—If; And What If? —

—Questions Are the Challenge—
Yes, If', And's, Or But's Will Always Be With Us:
In This Life!
Challenges in The Neutral Zone

Truth is: A loser doesn't know what he'll do if he loses, but talks about what he'll do if he wins, and a winner doesn't talk about what he'll do if he wins but knows what he'll do if he loses. [Eric Berne—Brainy Quotes]

Truth is: You must come to your closed doors before you get to your open doors. What if you knew you had to go through 32 closed doors before you got to your open door? Well, then you'd come to closed door number eight and you'd think, 'Great, I got another one out of the way.' Keep moving forward. [Joel Osteen—Brainy Quotes]

There is at least one reason God says those who come to Him [for understanding—salvation—] must simply believe 'He is!' This spreads out or expands in its source:

> But without faith it is impossible to please Him: for He that cometh to God must believe that He is, and that He is a rewarder of them that diligently seek Him. [Hebrews 11:6 KJV]

In the Garden of Eden, the choice was between *The Tree of Life*, and *The Tree of the Knowledge of Good and Evil*. God's directive for the first created humans was to take His words at face value. At the core of all God was saying, was the issue of faith. By faith in what He said, Adam and Eve would never need to go the route of figuring out all the confusing issues which would present themselves if they chose *The Tree of The Knowledge of Good and Evil*.

Chapter 12

THE IF FACTOR!

Epistemology is the philosophical study of the nature, origin, and limits of human knowledge. Epistemology is the investigation of what distinguishes justified belief from opinion. It is somewhat like the difference between subjectivity and objectivity. Ontology, is a branch of metaphysics—the branch of philosophy dealing with the first principles of things, such as being, knowing, substance, cause, identity, time, and space; dealing with the nature of being]—we may be discouraged, frustrated, and confused at the outset of these studies. However, if we want to come to terms with the many explanations of tough theology and science, it is beneficial to at least get a picture of these Big Words in our mind, and let those pictures open the eyes of our understanding.

Because one step of knowledge always leads to a demand for the next step of knowledge, this search for the ultimate knowledge would be a never-ending search—one which gives a final and independent [not dependent on the feeling of subjectivity (emotion)] affirmative answer to rule over subjectivity [emotion]. How can we possibly think we can get our hands on the hundred-dollar bill blowing in the wind; scurrying faster than we can travel; no matter what method of transportation we use.

How can we come to grips with an infinity through a knowledge base increasing at an accelerating pace? With simple words, God trained [guided] us to the only solution to getting the specific 'hundred-dollar bill' blowing in the wind; are we chasing it to no avail? For us to get to an infinity [eternity, future] without always understanding the limitlessness of the past, faith is necessary. We like to see things clearly with our physical eyes; yet, how much more can we see in the eyes of faith!

Before the foundation of the world, from the past we did not know, to the present—God had our best interest at heart all the time, He offered everything He had, by His foreknowledge—'via us needing to trust His judgement.'GOD Himself was offering His Best as a command for our understanding of the life before us; in effect, demanding our attention to duty regarding parameters we would never successfully travel beyond without consequences—yes, this is so, but in the big picture it was not so much a command, but a Present—A Gift.

> "And the LORD God took the man and put him into the garden of Eden to dress it and to keep it. And the LORD God commanded the man, saying, Of every tree of the garden thou mayest freely eat: But of the tree of the knowledge of good and evil, thou shalt not eat of it: for in the day thou eatest thereof thou shalt surely die." We will never grasp enough knowledge to sustain ourselves for eternity future, in and of ourselves—we need to look around us at how the world is churning, and turning from the morality God commanded we adhere to—we need to realize only God can satisfy completely. [RE Genesis 2: 15-17]

It's one thing to study Epistemology, Ontology—for interest sake, it is another thing for us to study these items and all the other belief systems of the world so we can find the best alternative. Any alternative to God, 'will' fail—believe it or not! Someone said, "The Arm of Flesh 'will' fail you!" God, in The Bible told us up front, if we wanted the 'only' sustainable source for life which would be 'enough,' we would only attain to it by FAITH. [Hebrews 11: 6]

> But without faith it is impossible to please Him: for He that cometh to God must believe that He is, and that He is a rewarder of them that diligently seek Him. [Hebrews 11:6; KJV]

What will be evident to us in *Chapter 12* is *The If Factor*. We can also follow this theme beyond here. Let's take one step at a time to move into *The If Factor* as far as it can take us in this life—in the next life There Will Be No 'IF's,' And's, or But's.' We are not slaves; we are pilgrims in search of 'Crown Lands.' We are not enslaved to the boarding houses of the present! This world's methods of fashioning right and wrong do not have to limit us for God's purposes. God's will for humanity supersedes our wants.

We are moved to sedentary [in action], or to action by emotion, but we are not enslaved or enraptured by subjectivity.

Objectivity is the solidity [fact bearing] shouldering the weight of the day for us to get the eternal results we think are ours for the having. This said, I suggest there cannot be enough strength to begin any project, no matter what the 'what' is, if our foundation does not have a beginning, one able to withstand every test we throw at it. No matter how big or how small a ship, boat, or any floating device is, ballast, displacement, shape, packaging type, weight—are part of the package for stabilizing whatever the entity is. The factor or issue of staying on the water as opposed to sinking to the bottom, is "The Knowing—" this we should not ignore.

Hence, we enter the "IF FACTOR" stage.

If one entity or thing in any scenario is out of whack, "Houston, We Have A Problem." If the weight of a boat is too huge for the size of the boat, and we place it into the water, it will sink on contact. If the thing we are calling a boat, is a 'three-foot by three-foot by three-foot concrete block' [27 cubic feet], it would weigh about 4000 lbs. If it was not on the proper floatation device, and we place it in the water, it will sink—guaranteed! If we place the concrete boat [block], as I call it, on the proper pontoons the concrete boat will not sink if it meets the weight bearing criteria to hold this amount of weight. Right now, I am not smart enough to lay out all the variables. However, if we do everything right, everything will come out right in the end.

Methinks—had I not done this, that, or the other—if this, that, and the other had not hindered a perfect existence for me, I would not have any problems living life perfectly. "Why," is much like "If," while we look at the variables which are the difference between facing a consequence of unbearable weight.

Had I listened to those folks inhabiting planet earth before I arrived via the Starship Birth, I would be in a better position to help other folks. Whether or not those who will come into my life via "Birth" are my family or simply those with whom I meet daily, I can be a Godsend "IF" I follow basic guidelines for life. The major determiner is, 'I need to know' "Whom" or what I have believed in, knowing this will be enough to get me to where I want to end up.

As I look through the stages of my authoring of books, I covered life and how it works. *It's Jacob! My Name Is Jacob! What's Yours?*—is about beginnings; how the sequel of life displays how we are alike in the basic factors of living. The Preface of this book goes like this, Some of the 'If Factors' are noticeably clear when we read *It's Jacob! My Name Is Jacob! What's Yours?* Jacob was a considerably basic person, he wanted to get everything he could for himself for a measure of his life. Oh, he did care about some of the others in his life; he was almost a complete person in so many of the physical ways we use to determine "wholeness." Jacob discovered it was not enough to satisfy the inner something which most of us crave. Yes, life is surprisingly Good! Yes, I am happy, I guess! Yes, I am doing well: BUT!

If only Jacob had done a better job of the things in which he messed up supremely, life would have been different! Yes, things would have been different. However, there is an answer for life when we mess up on the 'IF Factor' of our lives.

The Mandate—moves on to help us realize we are all important. Most of what I write has the theme of all people everywhere each being as valuable in the big picture of life as is the next person. We tend to lose sight of this as we move up the ladder. Let's look at the *Introduction* of *The Mandate*, and see how the 'IF Factor' would have made a difference in our lives:

This book is part of My Mandate: What is yours?

If I had quit writing; If I had quit doing much of what I did in my life, what would my life have looked like—this is a two-way street.

Twin Towers of The Heart—helps us understand; we are involved in how our lives pans out, by the heart choices we make. Reading *Twin Towers of The Heart*, can be a huge helper.

The IF FACTOR: What if the stories of *Twin Towers of The Heart* had been read into the life of our ancestors; what if the story laid out differently in the life you have lived; what if the story line for me would have changed the course of history had I just done it right—or did we do it right? These are huge questions and I for one cannot answer them all, but I know God can; I know God will one day give us the answer to all the questions, like it or not; I am praying it is the right answer for me and He will say:

Well Done You Good And Faithful Servant; Enter Into The Joy Of Thy Rest!

Bridging The Gap—shows us many variables in life and it speaks to how the stuff in the gap we do not like so much, sometimes has to happen for something else to work out in our favor. Ifs, ands or buts—and yes WHYS, are part of the big picture. This is my most recent book, the one just before this one; for me it *Bridges The Gap* to this one as a Four Book Package with its Finale of sorts. Let's browse the end of the *Introduction* to *Bridging The Gap*:

"So, most of the book is preparatory for the ending to have the most durable, long-lasting, eternal reaction for each of us. Someone said, 'Life is short, eat desert first.' If that is our path we may be in trouble. This philosophy makes me think we are in selfie mode. You are not in Church; you can close the book at your whim or dislike; I try not to be the Preacher, although I am not against this; sometimes it is necessary. However, my hope is, 'you will think this book to be an invitation' to considerations you may have overlooked."

Are Understanding, Comfort, and Compassion, some of these bridges? Stay Tuned!

Often, we do not realize the upshot of the overall plan of God as He directs the Movie of Life for us in ways He sees best. He does not arbitrarily stop us in our tracks when we choose our own way over His way. The IF FACTOR, be it 'IF' I had done it His way, or 'IF' I had not done this, that, or the other—would it really have changed anything?

Back to the ongoing scenario of *Everybody: Everybody Is A Somebody*; Back to the Chapter Twelve Scene of,

THE IF FACTOR

Seemingly, there's no end to TV shows about crime, murder, heists, robbery, lying in a criminal investigation, border crossing issues, lying under oath [perjury] in a court case—. The FBI, Columbo, Dragnet, Murder She Wrote, Leverage, Motive—are but a few in a long list of TV Shows and Movies. When we google the internet to list all the crime related shows we need to get ready to be in it for the "Long Haul," or be "In It For The Whole Ride."

Part Three—Human Value And "If And What If?"

As detectives investigate, they are looking for clues to point toward to, 'The Who Done It.' Even clues, not in and of themselves, which are direct pointers to the culprit they are on a search to apprehend for an offense, are important enough to be considered for the eventual arrest they anticipate. A detective is a person who has a keen sense of the awareness of things around them, which can be significant factors in solving the case in question.

The investigation may be slow in getting to the finalizing positions before the motive is determined, but as they say, 'Leave no stone unturned' while looking for the big clues which will come to direct conclusions that 'So and So' is guilty. As the search begins, the detectives ponder what they see at the crime scene, and during the processing of facts they think, 'if this was the case, or if this was the motive; 'if'—then, this seemingly insignificant person may be the one who committed said crime.

Often, especially with murders, the DNA factor comes into play for them, enough so, to say they have enough evidence to make an arrest, for the District Attorney to charge said offender with the offense, and to set a Court Date. If small pieces of hair on the scene, those which seemed to be of no consequence, are held as evidence, so that, 'if all else fails' for the conviction to proceed, they can break down the DNA to see if it matches the victim's DNA with the perceived guilty person's DNA: The DNA is proof positive.

Forensic Files is a TV Series I watch occasionally. Often, the police believe they have the right *Person of Interest*, but they do not have the final nail with which they can nail down the lid of the coffin and put the case to rest. If everything points to said Person of Interest, a Jury's verdict of guilty will nail it down, and the sentence is passed on the accused.

'If,' is not only important in criminal cases, it is the deciding factor in how we live life itself. If I get everything I want out of life I will be happy and satisfied. If my parents treat me right, I have a good chance of becoming successful and make a lot of money.

The 'What If Scenario Analysis' (WISA) differs from 'What You See Is What You Get' (WYSIWYG). The WISA demands that 'If' be considered to determine if it is prudent, sensible, or wise to carry on with a projection or estimate in the business sector to make the business more money this year than it did the year previous. The list of possible scenarios is endless.

When all the 'IFS' weigh out, and the facts are gathered and sorted out within the demographics of a setting, the project at the ready, is Ready Set Go! On Your Mark, Get Set, Go gets the prospective business to the starting line to present the product to the public market and the For-Sale Sign is raised.

As I look at the differences in many purposes for comparison sake, between WISA and WYSIWYG, my reasoning tells me 'If' does not play the same part in "WYSIWYG" as it does in "WISA."

I Am Looking Back To See "IF—"
"IF" You Are Looking Back To See—.

If we are so melodramatic or overdramatically enslaved to the history we came from, to the point of not realizing life changes as we move from one generation to another, then we never realize throughout 'this' 'History,' change has always been inevitable! Slaves [no matter what the skin color is] are in bondage; the Children of Israel under Pharaoh's rule knew this all too well. In Abraham Lincoln's day the African Americans [then, most often called the Negro People], were slaves. When I use the words "Negro, Blacks, or African American" I am on a pilgrimage [Journey] to find what exactly I should be using as words to describe a person and their inherent values. As most people are quite aware of, it is increasingly difficult to always use the right terms in the world in which we live: Especially in North America!

Pilgrims [wayfarers, travelers, wanderers—] are explorers in search of what they may not yet know or know about. I think of the slaves of Abraham Lincoln's Day, not simply as the slaves they were made to be after they were stolen from Africa, but also as Pilgrims in a strange land. They were not simply seeking Crown Land [Free Land], but something and someplace where they could put down roots, work hard, and buy "Their Little Piece of Heaven on Earth." Heaven on Earth, "What A Concept!"

We are moved [encouraged, stimulated, and motivated] by emotion [subjectivity] but we are not captured [enslaved] or enraptured [beguiled, hypnotized, or mesmerized] by subjectivity.

What Did I See, and What Does It Say?
"Prepare to Launch!"

What is behind us in life cannot only be good to make life what we had back then [stuck in one place, and that without hope]. If this were the case we would never have discovered new lands and or new potentials. Yesterdays potentials as they are for us as we look back, were once histories "Tomorrows." This left open to them the potentials or possibilities for making the life ahead of them, and for their offspring, better in the many ways those living at the time found to be arduous or difficult. I don't hesitate to look at my "Yesterdays;" there is always something to be learned.

But seek ye first the kingdom of God, and his righteousness; and all these things shall be added unto you.

Take therefore no thought for the morrow: for the morrow shall take thought for the things of itself. Sufficient unto the day is the evil thereof. [Mathew 6:33]

Though this scripture is very relevant to us, especially when we worry about tomorrow, it is not saying we should never plan for tomorrow. Remember, if we ignore context, or the picture the whole story is trying to tell us, we will be in big trouble insofar as or while we expect to have a very present hope, which we can accomplish someday, to make life better for our children, ourselves, and firstly for The Kingdom of God on Earth.

All The Way My Savior Leads Me, this song has mega messages for us to be encouraged from. I think about how we got into Lakeview Manor 2011. The story behind it is, I was getting a bit older, getting ready to retire—and the list of other things in the scenario of my life at the time. After my first knee replacement [and yes there was a second one four years later] I did not have the same incentive to keep on doing what I was doing in the workforce. I was not incapacitated by the knee replacement, but I might have been, had I not retired six months early.

IF this had not happened; IF that had not happened; IF, IF, IF; then all the things following this time of my life, would have changed. Yes, I know God would have made up the difference for my insufficiencies, but I always have a sense of thinking I am part of the package God uses to make the nest step be the right one!

"THE IF FACTOR"

298

The Neutral Zone

13ᵗʰ. Chapter

If', And's, Or But's Before We Hit Center Ice
Now What?

Truth is, I can't change the direction of the wind, but I can adjust my sails to always reach my destination. [Jimmy Dean–Brainy Quotes]

Truth is, we have two options when we approach a hostile checkpoint in a war zone, and each is a gamble. The first is to stop and identify our-self as a journalist and hope that we are respected as a neutral observer. The second is to blow past the checkpoint and hope the soldiers guarding it don't open fire on us. [Lynsey Addario—Brainy Quotes]

Not everybody is a Hockey Fan, I am from this perspective. I wish to prepare the way for the 'toughies' of living life on the whole plane. I am not referring to the New Age, Buddhist, or any of the other concepts of the different 'Planes' of life, which these and others proport [claim] to be the phases of life in which we live. I am simply trying to use the analogy of what happens on the Hockey Ice, as the players move about from the starting point of the game at 'Center Ice.'

The changes taking place from 'Puck Drop' to the 'Final Whistle,' after sixty minutes of playing time [plus the overtime segments needed if the game is tied after sixty minutes], are a picture of unending metamorphoses [changes] in momentum and in the results of the 'Whole Game.' The Neutral Zone offers miniscule moments of time in which huge decisions need to be made—in the Blink of An Eye.

What does the playing field look like?

That ye may be the children of your Father which is in heaven: for he maketh his sun to rise on the evil and on the good, and sendeth rain on the just and on the unjust. [Mathew 5:45 KJV]

Chapter 13
OBSERVABLE METAMORPHOSES

It becomes an invigorating experience to discover the life cycle of a butterfly—pointedly or purposefully. In this endeavor, we get a 'wide zoom lens' glance at what we can become; even when other people think we will never amount to much! By looking at all four stages of the life of the butterfly we see how fully transformed they become—they are converted from being 'yucky' or wormy—or is it an unsightly mess? When the complete metamorphosis takes place, we see how value comes full circle from something we might have 'thought to be worthless.'

So, which came first: The Butterfly or The Egg? This is basically the same question as is, "Which came first, the chicken or the egg?" All egg laying species fit into the same box. Either the egg came first and then the animal in question, or the animal in question came first and through a process of conjugal interaction [spousal setting], or simply an attractive process formed between an XY [male] chromosome and an XX [female] chromosome, which resulted in forming the same end result—A Child; not a nice little kitty cat, a ferocious lion, a dog, a bird or any other species of animal. I know of no XX or XY interaction that produced an offspring outside of their gene pool.

Can we put our hand in the box of a concoction of a ratio of 3 X's to 1 Y, say multiplied by a hundred, and pull out precisely what we have always wished for or intently prayed for? The choices are all in the box, so we will come out with something in our grip! Or do we need some form of an orderly pattern, put in place by Someone Who knew exactly what they were doing, to get anywhere close to pulling out a girl or a boy? Can we come to any conclusion based on adding up the two female XX's and the one male Y?

Without some kind of prior determination, such as the design and creation of how to mix things together proportionately enough to get just the perfect result we were aiming for, we are sure to fail in our expectations—like putting our hand in the box and expecting to pull out a child. If we started out to create a "Wacky Cake," and we forgot to put in the chocolate substance [cocoa] we would surely have a WACKY CAKE! It would not be brown, because the cocoa was not added. We can make a "Chocolate Cake" without eggs and milk by substituting apple cider vinegar for the eggs, and by using water instead of milk—this is what we call a 'Wacky Cake." [Thought to have been created during the WWII, when milk and eggs were scarce]. So, stages in building, creating, fashioning, cooking, baking—are important to get "Just the Right Result" we planned for. I guess, if we forgot the 'cocoa' we would end up with an off-colored cake we might call a 'white cake.'

It gets perplexing when we try to calculate the process of forming any life form without their first being a replica, copy, imitation, or model—of the species in place before an egg ever came to be. Now, back to the butterfly—to grow into an adult butterfly we first need to begin with an adult butterfly. The process follows like this; the female butterfly is impregnated by the male of the species in the mating process [no need to explain fully this procedure]. Next, the female lays the eggs in a certain place, and the continuation of the four-stage process [not counting the mating], is the eggs turn to larva, the larva turns to the pupa, and the final result is that we end up with a fully formed adult—the baby butterfly is the egg. Talk about change, metamorphosis. I know of no other living species, plant, animal, or human, which begin as adult copies, as do the butterfly.

Each stage has a different goal—for instance, caterpillars need to eat a lot, and adults need to reproduce. Depending on the type of butterfly, the life cycle of a butterfly may take anywhere from one month to a whole year. I am no expert in the reproductive processes of plants, animal, or humans. I have raised tropical fish, plants, dogs, and children; each of these began at a place I call the "Planting Season," or an act of beginning a process of preparation to begin another relational entity: Humans and animals [in varying forms] are the two most relational species. The Bible says Human beings take first prize, because they are made in the "Image of God!"

History holds the depth of our story of the day. Without yesterday we have no story. Think about it! Even if we came out of a test tube concoction, through "In Vitro Fertilization" (IVF), there is a history which made this possible (DNA). So, what is history? History is what came to us before our 'now.' History holds the resource pool of our Genesis or Beginning. So, what came first—the Chicken or The Egg?

This is an age-old question which still confuses the issue whenever someone has the nerve to even ask this question. Two factions or groups say the answer is finally solved—no more questions about this question! 'Two Wrongs Make A Right!' This often-debated claim is like the question about the chicken and the egg. Finding the one and only right source is essential to solving the issue about these questions. Someone is Right—Who?

A)- And God blessed them, saying, be fruitful, and multiply, and fill the waters in the seas, and let fowl multiply in the earth.

Which came first—the chicken or the egg? Well, I'm happy to report that this—dilemma has finally been solved. It was the chicken that came first—something that creationists have known all along. The Bible tells us God created every winged fowl and gave them the ability to reproduce after their kind. (http://www.creationmoments.com/radio/transcripts/chicken-or-egg-which-came-first)

B)- Which came first, the chicken or the egg? Evolution has the answer.

Science does, in fact, have an answer to the oft-repeated conundrum, which came first, the chicken or the egg? This, of course, means that you should never let anyone offer this as a riddle ever again without correcting them: The Egg! (According to Science Writer Kyle Hill, https://sciencebasedlife.wordpress.com/2012/03/10/which-came-first-the-chicken-or-the-egg-evolution-has-the-answer/)

How Deep Will We Go?

All the preamble, preface, introduction, forward, overture, prelude—prior to what I will say here, has to do with presenting a picture of how everything changes [metamorphoses (Plural), metamorphosis (Singular)] from its source, to become the entity of value it was initially intended to be.

Part Three—Human Value And "If And What If?"

Life itself presents natural changes in the Four Seasons of the year; I am tempted to call the changes in these seasons a 'Metamorphosis of The Four Seasons.' Although for the most part 'metamorphosis' relates to issues dealing with Biology, Pathology, Botany—, while perusing or examining many things in this book, I think much about how things change in relationship to the 'Ifs, Ands, or Buts;' how they change our existence, as in the context of how our lives change.

I am rolling towards the latter part of this book; I feel somewhat like being at The Old 13th. Golf Hole [Skerries] at Royal Portrush Golf Course, as I was writing these words: "SCARY." Tee off for the 'Open' will be on July 18, 2019: I Love It!

While not trembling in my boots, I say it is scary as I proceed. The subject matter I am dealing with involves 'People,' and the precious importance each person has rights to as they begin their journey. People change from 'The Starting Line' as they move along their piece of the path on which they each have a piece of the lay of the land of this world of ours. I see so many divisions of morality, so much so, it seems the battle to keep a proper perspective of the value of each person as they make their way through life, is huge.

A 'Military Division' numbers between 10,000 to 20,000 soldiers. When we pit one or more divisions against each other, the battle is intense. The diversity of cultures in this world is huge; definitions of morality are so mingled [like in a melting pot], it is hard to find a dividing line which holds the context of the source meaning of right or wrong. What can we use as a plumbline to gauge whether we can, or will, all end up at the same eternity? If we do all end up at the same 'Heaven' and or 'Nirvana,' we would only experience the same battles all over again; we may then not have the promise of an Eternity where all will be Peace; this could never be—Heaven would be a "Pandemic"—a sinners attempt at holiness.

If Tolerance Rules are in full force [as we know them today], white will be black, black will be white, right will be wrong, wrong will be right, good will be evil, and evil will be good. If there was, and is, a differentiation between these entities in the manner they were in the past; if we cannot live without rules of right and wrong today, how can we expect to live without having had a celebration of the same in the life we now live, to live an eternity with each other in Heaven—unless we all end up in a heaven of our own making.

If 'If,' means anything, then what?

As Pilgrims in search of a new country, or an experience we may not yet have encountered or practiced, we might be excited about the prospect of what lies ahead of us. We are stirred [inspired, encouraged, and driven] by passion [desire, hunger, thirst—], but the ultimate passion does not capture or ensconce us as if we are imprisoned for a crime; rather, this passion emboldens, buoys, or maintains us, while challenging us to be something specific in the Plan God has for us!

'If' has a sentiment, opinion, attitude, or passion all its own. 'If' immediately becomes more than a suggestive word to cast doubt on a positive word and or action taking us into the position of not accepting a challenge. Instead of leaving us in the negative position of being lifeless, ineffective, or lethargic, we can accept the position of endearing ourselves to the prospect of an expectation of something good, which will change us from the inside outwards [A 'metamorphosis' of sorts]. 'If' works through our opinions, attitudes, and passions; the challenges we are drawn to attending to may be daunting. However, 'if' our heart is in search mode for a resource we may not yet have access to, I suspect we will not come up short in our effort to be the best we can be.

Someone said that a picture is worth a thousand words. This is so true, isn't it? If someone at a podium is teaching, preaching, or conversing, and they are using hard to understand analogies or parallels to get their point across, I may get it sooner or later. I generally remember what they have said, but it may not sink in immediately. I may have to mull it over for awhile. A few lines back, I asked the question, "How Deep Will We Go?"

Many folks are geared to hear a speaker and grasp quickly what they mean, because they have a good understanding of the verbal or written delivery of a certain speaker. But not everyone is built the same way. Usually, a picture will clarify something more quickly than words will do. If an artist came to the podium along with the speaker and painted a picture of what they heard the speaker saying, we may 'get it' right away. As I read the poem "IF—"by Rudyard Kipling, I see a clear picture before my eyes; it becomes as if this were an artists rendering or a delivery of sculpting or shaping written words into a living picture show.

IF—

If you can keep your head when all about you
Are losing theirs and blaming it on you,
If you can trust yourself when all men doubt you,
But allowance for their doubting too.
If you can wait and not be tired by waiting,
Or being lied about, don't deal in lies,
Or being hated, don't give way to hating,
And yet don't look too good, nor talk too wise:

If you can dream—and not make dreams your master;
If you can think—and not make thoughts your aim;
If you can meet with Triumph and Disaster
And treat those two impostors just the same;
If you can bear to hear the truth you've spoken
Twisted by knaves to make a trap for fools,
Or watch the things you gave your life to, broken,
And stoop and build 'em up with worn-out tools:

If you can make one heap of all your winnings
And risk it on one turn of pitch-and-toss
And lose, and start again at your beginnings
And never breathe a word about your loss;
If you can force your heart and nerve and sinew
To serve your turn long after they are gone,
And so hold on when there is nothing in you
Except the Will which says to them: 'Hold on!'

If you can talk with crowds and keep your virtue,
Or walk with Kings—nor lose the common touch,
If neither foes nor loving friends can hurt you,
If all men count with you, but none too much;
If you can fill the unforgiving minute
With sixty seconds' worth of distance run,
Yours is the Earth and everything that's in it,
And—which is more—you'll be a Man, my son!
[Rudyard Kipling 1885]

The Bible Book of Ecclesiastes is a 'Homerun Hitting' picture of how much of life lays out before us. We see here a picture of someone trying to teach us about the facts of life; how they may involve us, better yet, how they 'Will' affect [change, influence—] us. By saying "Homerun Hitting" picture, I simply mean it has a way of getting our attention. However, to get the full impact of this Book of Ecclesiastes, we ought to step back to the previous Book of The Bible: The Book of Proverbs.

Why? Well, it always holds true, what happened before where we are at today, always had Lessons For Living for today; nothing has ever changed. My yesterday is influencing me for what I have been involved in today; it will continue to do so as I face the remainder of my day. It may be in the actual physical way I activate the events of my day; it may just be in the thoughts I had about yesterday and what happened there. The lessons of yesterday will impinge on me for something I experience in the Now! Now, is an increasingly more powerful entity for us 'Today,' more so than ever before. There is an evidential or a visible sense out there as we passage, channel, or route our way through each day—The 'Selfie Mode' is in plain view everywhere we go!

So let's step back for a moment to reflect on the value of The Book of Proverbs, to see why the same writer, Solomon, prefaced Ecclesiastes with The Proverbs. Proverbs are 'sayings,' mostly shorter than a whole book: Words of wisdom, catch phrases or mottos. Here, The Book of Proverbs has us looking at the advice, such as a Father has for his son [and the strength of these words apply to daughters as well]. The picture this artist, Solomon [not that he was an artist, but he pictures it out as if he was an artist, so we could more clearly understand], has for us, is one where he is addressing his son. So, in this sense, because it is his story, I will use the applicable male gender words. From here, each reader can think in the broader sense and apply the gender they wish to reflect on to grasp the whole meaning of The Book of Proverbs.

The opening instruction of Solomon, in The Proverbs allows for us to grasp the heart of Solomon, as he attempts to prepare his son for the life before him—this includes the life he talks about in The Book of Ecclesiastes. This brief insert from Proverbs is just an invitation for us to read it for ourselves as we prepare to look forward to the rest of the story.

INTERMEZZO!

To know wisdom and instruction; to perceive the words of understanding; To receive the instruction of wisdom, justice, and judgment, and equity; To give subtilty to the simple, to the young man knowledge and discretion. A wise man will hear and will increase learning; and a man of understanding shall attain unto wise counsels: To understand a proverb, and the interpretation; the words of the wise, and their dark sayings. The fear of the LORD is the beginning of knowledge: but fools despise wisdom and instruction. A Father's Exhortation: Acquire Wisdom [we get to see here the heart of the intent of this Father]. My son, hear the instruction of thy father, and forsake not the law of thy mother: For they shall be an ornament of grace unto thy head, and chains about thy neck. My son, if sinners entice thee, consent thou not. [Proverbs 1:1-10 KJV]

"Everything Is Meaningless" [This is an addon by the editing team to reflect on the scripture here] Vanity of vanities, saith the Preacher, vanity of vanities; all is vanity. What profit hath a man of all his labour which he taketh under the sun? One generation passeth away, and another generation cometh: but the earth abideth for ever. The sun also ariseth, and the sun goeth down, and hasteth to his place where he arose. The wind goeth toward the south, and turneth about unto the north; it whirleth about continually, and the wind returneth again according to his circuits. All the rivers run into the sea; yet the sea is not full; unto the place from whence the rivers come, thither they return again. All things are full of labour; man cannot utter it: the eye is not satisfied with seeing, nor the ear filled with hearing. The thing that hath been, it is that which shall be; and that which is done is that which shall be done: and there is no new thing under the sun. Is there any thing whereof it may be said, See, this is new? it hath been already of old time, which was before us. There is no remembrance of former things; neither shall there be any remembrance of things that are to come with those that shall come after. [Ecclesiastes 1 KJV]

Through these thoughts I want to express thoughts and pictures from "IF—."

> If you can keep your head when all about you
> Are losing theirs and blaming it on you,

How often have we experienced situations where the blame game someone else is playing comes so forcefully into the actual moment of the day we are trying to live—like Solomon is trying to get us to see so clearly so many years ago, to see how we are affected and or overcome so badly, we lose our peace of mind. If I am having a 'Bad Day,' stand clear of me! I might get over it as quickly as what may seem to you should be my response to this adversity of the moment, or the hardship may be ongoing for an extended time. Or, you could take another course of action, including me in your day, to say, "I am going to try to understand your predicament and see if I can be a help and or be a comfort to help you get through this interruption to your peace of mind." As we begin to make headway in the matter of understanding the issues other people experience, the ones we may not have experienced on the intensity level they have had to live with, we get a step closer to where God wants us to be.

Often, we blame others for the hard times we experience; the story gets blown out of proportion because—why should we ourselves take responsibility or blame for what may have been in part our own fault. Remember, how Eve, in the Garden of Eden said, "The Devil Made Me Do It!" The Devil played the blame game, he said, "IT WAS GOD'S FAULT." He was passing the buck for his own consequence of being tossed out of God's presence because he was rebelling; trying to take the other angels with him—The Devil still plays that blame game.

I clearly recount a situation of my own story, one of many, where I got a call from out of the blue, saying I had said something that reflected badly on the integrity of another person closely related to themselves. At first, I vehemently or passionately denied the accusation as not being true. Though it was false in the sense that what I had said in confidence to someone else closely related to this other person, and more closely related to me; the context was misconstrued along the way. I was in a position of trying to encourage this person closely related because they felt themselves as being unloved and unwanted by everyone around them. I was trying to bring comfort.

"IF—" we never try to be there for someone else in their time of need, we may be committing the greater error. "IF—" we stand back and watch someone trying to get through a mess they might have caused on their own, but they feel they are innocent, even though their fault may have been caused in part by the actions of another, we may be committing the greater error because "Everybody Needs Somebody" during their tough time.

My son, hear the instruction of thy father, and forsake not the law of thy mother: For they shall be an ornament of grace unto thy head, and chains about thy neck. My son, if sinners entice thee, consent thou not. [Proverbs 1:8-10 KJV]

Please let me pull out one verse to set us straight. *For they shall be an ornament of grace unto thy head, and chains about thy neck.* We all need grace and mercy. "IF—" we wear this truth of Grace around our neck like a cherished diamond necklace, the harsh realities of the mistakes each of us are guilty of, will not be so much like the harsh winter storms we struggle to dig out from under. Digging out from under a mess is most always a major production.

All the rivers run into the sea; yet the sea is not full; unto the place from whence the rivers come, thither they return again. [Ecclesiastes 1:7]

Even though life seems like a never-ending story of grief, there are Bright Spots Too! We ought to Remember Them As Well!

"IF—" you can trust yourself when all men doubt you,
But make allowance for their doubting too;
"IF—" you can wait and not be tired by waiting,
Or being lied about, don't deal in lies,
Or being hated, don't give way to hating,
And yet don't look too good, nor talk too wise:

"IF—" you can trust yourself when all men [others] doubt you—." I wonder, what is Rudyard talking about here when we are sure of our purpose; about when we carry the integrity of the purpose and the honor of our heart into this context of life; when we are at peace with ourselves and the world around us. I wonder "IF—" Mr. Kipling is suggesting if our patience has the strength of the purpose we propound or advocate, we will become the better person for it.

I the Preacher was king over Israel in Jerusalem.

And I gave my heart to seek and search out by wisdom concerning all things that are done under heaven: this sore travail hath God given to the sons of man to be exercised therewith.

I have seen all the works that are done under the sun; and, behold, all is vanity and vexation of spirit.

That which is crooked cannot be made straight: and that which is wanting cannot be numbered. [Ecclesiastes 1:12-15 KJV]

"IF—" our strength of purpose is the purpose of God for our lives, our outlook as it is laid out by Solomon as fruitless and or empty, may give us a better outlook on life than Solomon is projecting. Yet, this journey will not be trouble free because we are not only dealing with our own issue, we are intersecting our lives with that of the lives of others.

The key ingredient I see is one of 'wisdom.' This is a good projection or plan of life to seek after. "IF—" we can continue to trust in our focus on God when people lie about us and our intent, and they doubt we are genuine; or they hate us; or we think that they do not look so good, and they are not really too wise in their action; remember, they are facing the same struggles of life we are enduring. We are all in this life with a string of events in which we are as if chained together; often, we pull in opposite directions. A tug of war is one way to try to settle things, but physical strength is not the answer to the problems of life.

Life seems to be a Tug of War. "IF—" we ever get on the same page; "IF—" we ever all pull in the same directions to pull down the problems life itself has, we may just realize that *Everybody: Everybody Is A Somebody*. "IF—" we do not give in to disunity, or the mistrust of others when their intent may be like ours, to give a hand up, not a push down or a put down, we may yet make a difference in and for the well being of our planet.

Let Us Remember and Remember Well:

Everybody: Everybody Is A Somebody

If you can dream—and not make dreams your master;
If you can think—and not make thoughts your aim;

Part Three—Human Value And "If And What If?"

Dreaming and setting goals is not a bad thing. "IF—" we have no dreams or aspirations to get out from under the pressures of life overtaking us at an accelerating pace, we will never get on the right track to run a race as if we are running with the wind and not against it. Eugene H. Peterson wrote a book called *Run With The Horses*; he got this theme from Jeremiah 12:5; KJV.

> If thou hast run with the footmen, and they have wearied thee, then how canst thou contend with horses? and if in the land of peace, wherein thou trustedst, they wearied thee, then how wilt thou do in the swelling of Jordan? [Jeremiah 12:5 KJV]

"IF—" we cannot weather the storms of winter on our own; "IF—" we cannot build the dikes high enough to keep out the Flood Waters of life that overflow us; "IF—" when we face the smaller issues of life we cannot seem to cope, how do we expect to keep up with the bigger issues. If we are so easily trodden down when it's cloudy now and again instead of sunny all the time, we can never run well enough to run a solid race.

Saturday, May 4th. 2019 my wife and I watched The Kentucky Derby, which was run in Louisville Kentucky. This event is a big item in the horse racing world. Many of the best horses in the country participate in this Mega Event. There is much "To-Do" for days and hours before the actual race of about Two Minutes.

The 145th running of The Kentucky Derby had a host of 21 picks, of which 19 horses actually ran. Maximum Security, the favorite, came in first, but lost to Country House [a 65-1 longshot], because of disqualification. "IF—" projected security means anything in this life, then this was shot down because of 'Stuff That Happens' as we live life. I am sure that Maximum Security trained as hard as anyone, to be the best, and the horse was the best in the race, but just a slight infraction, maybe even an unintentional one, cost Maximum Security the prize. Country House also trained hard but was not considered anywhere close as being the best but picked to be near the back of the pack. "IF—"?

"WHAT IF" everything had gone right according to all the predictions of which horse would finish where, then, there would it seem, also be no surprises in life. There would then be nothing coming into the picture of our daily lives to appear to be as if Out Of The Blue!

The horses in the 2019 Running of The Kentucky Derby trained hard to be the best they could be. They all ran faster than any person could have run the race. However, not one horse, their owners, or their jockeys knew for sure who would be the ultimate winner. What is predictable is that "IF—" I you or I ran the length of the track in Louisville, Kentucky at the pace these horses ran, [The site of The Kentucky Derby] we would have become weary [*If thou hast run with the footmen, and they have wearied thee, then how canst thou contend with horses?*]. "IF—" in this world of ours, there is a plot of land in any country where the people can say they have Maximum Security, where they have a peace in their hearts, and nothing, nada, can disturb this peace, they are under strong delusions of false hope [*and if in the land of peace, wherein thou trustedst, they wearied thee, then how wilt thou do in the swelling of Jordan?*]

If you have a "Country House" near the Brahmaputra, Ganga, Yamuna—Rivers in India, you are more prone or exposed to being flooded—how can anyone be guaranteed to manage these onslaughts without adversity. Out of the top fifteen countries in the world more prone or disposed to flooding, India is ranked the worst. Results from the World Resources Institute give us these statistics about world flooding issues:

"We ranked 164 countries by the number of people shaken by river flooding. We found that the top 15 countries account for nearly 80 percent of the total population affected every year. These countries are all considered least developed or developing. Roughly 167,000 people in the United States, the highest-ranked high-income country, are affected every year." [https://www.wri.org/]

"If you can meet with Triumph" [triumph allows for the possibility of ups and downs; what about reality in life] "and Disaster" [we do not embark on a disaster intentionally]

"And treat those two impostors" [triumph can become an imposter, if all we envision is a triumphant journey of success in whatever venture we have embarked upon] "just the same;"

> If you can meet with Triumph and Disaster
> And treat those two impostors just the same;
> If you can bear to hear the truth you've spoken
> Twisted by knaves to make a trap for fools,

Triumph and Disaster are direct opposites. We do not think of triumphing on an adventure of disaster. If a disaster is scheduled to be an adventure, please let me stay home. It could be an adventure will be disastrous. However, when I think of an adventure I think in terms of pleasantries. We can experience disaster while we are on an adventure, when everything we have planned just seems to go awry; then, I will tag it as an unwelcome guest, with phrases such as these, "Go Home; Get Out of Here—". So, you can see we can use the play on words scenario and make everything to become that which it is not.

How can we treat a triumph and a disaster the same? If we focus on them as if we are looking at a blank page, then anything is possible [we fill in the blanks]; if we are the artist or writer, possibly we can determine the outcome and we can be prepared to face either of these: Triumph and or disaster. If we are looking at a scene of beauty just before the horizon, at a calm, clear lake on a sunny blue-sky day, as it is, 'the foreground,' we may feel this is how it will be over the horizon beyond the immediate. However, as the wind shifts, and clouds roll in, everything changes. If we are cautious about our expectation, we can treat circumstances with respect.

If only my niece and her husband and a friend had seen the dangers of triumph and disaster having the same capacity to show themselves on the same page on the same day, on what was to be an adventure, so many years ago now, as they sailed on a lake in Manitoba. My niece's daughter had almost sailed with them. That day on which the storm lay out over the horizon caused them to capsize, leaving them unable to cope with the condition. If they had not taken a chance that everything would be okay. If their expectations for a pleasurable adventure had been satisfied with waiting for a better day to venture out, they would probably be alive today—saving their children from the uncertainties of life which would come upon them down the road. My sister, would not have had to raise her grandchildren, as opposing to the way grandparents are supposed to be, doting on their grandchildren.

> If you can bear to hear the truth you've spoken
> Twisted by knaves [swindlers] to make a trap for fools,
> Or watch the things you gave your life to, broken,
> And stoop and build 'em up with worn-out tools:

Oh, the vigor this poem by Rudyard Kipling strikes us with. Reality lays out open on the table of life before us everyday. Not to say every perceived 'Triumph' runs the gamut or extent of adversity. The charlatans seem to wait at every street corner of life, simply to waylay us of our right to the good life.

If we prepare for adventure wisely, with aforethought, observing the conditions in the right perspective, the chances of a triumphant run are much better. Just as the wind can switch suddenly, so can the circumstances of life change in an instant, demanding a staying power we may not know we have until Triumph and Disaster confront us on the same page. Hope of triumph misplaced can be an imposter looking the same as the disaster we try to evade.

Often, once life is broken badly, we do not know where to turn to regain the strength we once had to get up from the ground we have been tossed to, our fate for the victory we so badly wanted is dead in its tracks or halted for an unplanned season of life.

> Or watch the things you gave your life to, broken,
> And stoop and build 'em up with worn-out tools:

Kipling has a way with words to make us look at life from both sides. Many poets do so, with fewer words than what I use to tell a story much the same as they tell in such a summarized fashion. Maybe, if we the elongated book writers had the exact same vision of life as do the poets, who tell the story of life in small segments, we could spend so much less time writing our stories of life. However, I believe it takes people with giftings of many genre to get the whole story out there so those folks who do not grasp the short story, can observe through the lengthy entourage [train] of words it takes to teach the depth of life.

> If you can make one heap of all your winnings
> And risk it on one turn of pitch-and-toss
> And lose, and start again at your beginnings
> And never breathe a word about your loss;
> If you can force your heart and nerve and sinew
> To serve your turn long after they are gone,
> And so hold on when there is nothing in you
> Except the Will which says to them: 'Hold on!'

If you can talk with crowds and keep your virtue,
Or walk with Kings—nor lose the common touch,
If neither foes nor loving friends can hurt you,
If all men count with you, but none too much;
If you can fill the unforgiving minute
With sixty seconds' worth of distance run,
Yours is the Earth and everything that's in it,
And—which is more—you'll be a Man, my son!

"IF—" [Rudyard Kipling 1885], is used as an insert into our lives, and about our lives, as the run of our day takes its course. As I looked at this poem I thought long and hard about how Solomon portrayed life in the 'IF' scenario. Solomon saw so much of life as Vanity; we see it as somewhat hopeless [vain] to expect perfect results, with the imperfect tools that Kipling speaks of. The tools of use for us to present our lives so people will read us well, and right in the context of how we want them to see us, are easily waylaid.

Or watch the things you gave your life to, broken,
And stoop and build 'em up with worn-out tools:

Looking Back To See—
How often is "IF" in the Bible?

According to *E-Sword* the word 'If' appears 1,595 times in 1,420 verses of the King James version of the Bible. Similarly, a search revealed that the word 'If' appears: 1,673 times in the English Standard Version; 1,588 times in the American Standard Version; 1,670 times in the Modified King James Version, and there are dozens upon dozens of other versions of the Bible.

Observation can be a beautiful thing if we see it through the eyes of our creator. What God saw as the best case 'scenario to be' for all He set out in His plans for all of eternity, was indeed 'A Beautiful Thing!'

Methinks, apart from the 'People Thing,' 'Creation' would have been just that, "A Beautiful Thing." As I see it, everything got messed up when we showed up. The first thing we wanted to do was to 'Morph' [alter, change or doctor] the original plan for *Everything Is Beautiful In Its Own Way*.

Our plan to doctor the plan of creation to fit our own way, because we did not want to adhere to a few regs and regulations required for life to be 'Beautiful' in its 'Own' way, was not what the main 'Doctor,' God, designed to be the 'Way To Go.'

Observation by choice is a 'Two-Way Street.' Change requires obedience to a set of rules: One street is 'Obedience,' and the other is 'Disobedience.' Chapter Thirteen is part of the picture of life as it plays out in its "Observable Metamorphoses" process.

Observable Metamorphoses: Are they manageable? In the "Changing Times" we live in, the moralities of the past did not disappear with the changing times of today, all by themselves. Our desires changed as we tired of a lack of a "New Toy" for every "New Day," so we looked for "New Moralities." We were and are still today, so sure life will always be good, even if we think we have changed the rules of life in the "Face of God!"

During the "Changing Times," In the Throes [struggles] of staying afloat in the Sea of Immorality and looking for peace in the midst of the storms of life all around us, God is still God. He says He loved us from the beginning, and He still loves us today. However, to get to the Heaven we often imagine as all for one and one for all, anything and everything goes, no matter how we treat God in our Day-To-Day, we need to form a "Relationship with this God over all time," one which will change or morph the picture we have of God.

Observable Metamorphoses: The changing of the times began long ago, from the very physical existence of humanity on this earth. We always wanted more than what God was offering. He offered Himself, and we chose "US!"

Everybody: Everybody Is Still A Somebody!

The Neutral Zone

14th Chapter
The Who, What, Where, When, Why, and How
Of Center Ice
—Now What? —

Truth is: A leader is one who knows the way, goes the way, and shows the way. [John C. Maxwell–Brainy Quotes]

Truth is: Who we are makes us special; we do not need to change this; we were made in God's Image. What lies ahead on our journey is and will always be a mystery at this juncture, one we need not fear to explore. When life knocks us down, we need to get up and get going again. Where we meet the crossroads of life, we can choose to make choices we will not need to fret over. Why things happen to us, this may never be certain; we should at this crossing, 'Keep On Keeping On!' How is it possible to follow these principles of the Five W'S and H? We need to keep our eye on the goal of 'God First,' and the rest will pan out!

If my people, which are called by my name, shall humble themselves, and pray, and seek my face, and turn from their wicked ways; then will I hear from heaven, and will forgive their sin, and will heal their land. [Chronicles 7:14 (KJV)]

At some point in life we need to Centre on The Point of Life! We are headed for Part Four of this book, this is where we will pick up more on this position of where each of us fit into God's plan, and how we deal with it, as we move towards the Finish Line of this book. Do we Begin with God, so we can end [The Game of Life] with God, or do we push all this aside and maintain what began in the Garden of Eden: Our Penchant For Living In The 'Selfie Zone!' however, we still have some ice to cover, on which we often find ourselves on thin ice—The Slippery Zone.

Chapter 14
THE FIVE W'S AND HOW: THEN WHAT?

Six Honest Servers—Slaves they are not, servants, they well may be. To serve is no shame; to take a request, to ask how we can help, this is truly a gift that not all will effectively use.

Pain: The Gift Nobody Wants [by Philipp Yancey and Paul Brand], presents us with scenes of how we can become real or active even when we suffer this 'PAIN.' We may even become the better person through pain. The Gift of Servitude is spearheaded by LOVE.

I know of a story about two ladies who were both servers. On a certain occasion Jesus was a guest at their home. The guest list included the closest followers of Jesus [His disciples]. The dinner was at the home of Lazarus the brother [and host] of the ladies, and Mary and Martha, the hostesses.

Comedian Red Buttons made famous the saying, "Never Got A Dinner." Many famous people "Never Got A Dinner." When I retired, just shy of my sixty-fifth Birthday, my employer at the time gave "Me A Dinner." The wife of one of my fellow workers asked me how I came to work for this company. My boss was first to reply to this question before I got to share the answer; his reply was, "God brought Jacob here." It was a special time for me to be honored in this way. Not that I was such a special person on the world scene, like many others seem to be. The great thing about it was, I was appreciated for just who I was.

To be appreciated for Who We Are, is a special thing. Being a part of creation should be a value in and of itself—not only for the 'great things we did.' This does not always seem to be the case in this world in which we live. Being appreciated for our achievements is not a bad thing. Everybody likes to know they are of value!

When we ourselves take the credit for what God allowed for us to become, we are in error. At 'My Dinner' I said to my fellow workers, and other friends through association at the firm I worked for, yes, God brought me here to play my part in the plan everyone else could also choose to play a part in—"God's" Plan For Them. One of the Five W's is 'Why;' this is the question I ask, 'Why Would The God of The Entire Universe Make Me Special!' If He made me so special, then He did the same for You. 'What' possible reason could God have had to make us special? I think He wanted us to be relational as are friends. In ways we may not understand, He seems to have wanted us to be partners in all that He planned the Universe to be!

God, just for 'Who' He is, GOD in The Person of Jesus Christ, this is 'Who' we know because we have seen Him. No, we have not seen Him physically, but history has recorded "His-Story" clearly enough for us to get a good look at, enough so, we can acknowledge Him for Who He Is! But, as history also records, "We Hid our faces from Him," because we lacked using Faith; just believing in God for 'Who' He Is!

But without faith it is impossible to please Him: for He that cometh to God must believe that He is, and that He is a rewarder of them that diligently seek Him. [Hebrews 11:6; KJV]

'When' He needed us the most to acknowledge Him; 'when' He, GOD in the flesh, Jesus Christ, The Son of God, was hanging in 'what' seemed to be a helpless state; because He hung with the weight of our sin on the cross, we denied knowing Him! Oh, it was Peter we single out, but everyone else did the exact same thing by their distance from Him. Even we, denied Him at the time, by our birth into humanity; we take on the guilt of denial because of our association with all humanity.

Here's where the value of what Jesus did that day on the cross of Calvary comes full circle. All the power of Heaven and or earth was available to Him if only He used it to avoid the humiliation of such a death. Jesus could have used all these resources to call the host of Caesar's army, and the whole host of the angels of Heaven. Even if Caesar's army were not willing to come, and or, join the angels of Heaven, to defeat Satan in the battle over the sin we were born with—But He Did Not!

"Jesus Got A Dinner!"

Around the time of The Passover, which is a time of remembrance of when the Children of Israel marched out of Egypt, from under The Pharaoh's rule, Jesus seemed to prepare His disciples and the others at the dinner for the time He would sacrifice Himself on The Cross, via The Via Delarosa, The Way of The Cross, giving us all a chance to be His disciples.

As we prepare to look at the Five W's surrounding the dinner Jesus got, let's also look at other words beginning with 'W,' to see how they also work in and through the context of the event of 'The Dinner,' to tie in 'the 'value' of each person at 'The Dinner.' Listen as 'we watch' together the scene of Jesus at His Dinner:

> Then Jesus [the main 'Who' of our context], six days before the Passover ['when'] came to Bethany ['where'], where Lazarus [another valuable 'who'] was, 'which' [points to one of the key elements of this story (context)] had been dead, whom he raised from the dead; 'Which [not a regular of the 5 W's]' is an important 'W' it adds 'Value' to people other than Jesus, showing 'Why' [not in actual words, but by 'How' the story is told] Jesus came to earth: "To seek and to save that 'Which' was lost". There they made him [Jesus] 'a supper' ['What']; and Martha ['Who'] served: but Lazarus ['Who'] was one of them that sat at the table 'with' him. Then took Mary ['Who'] a 'pound of ointment of spikenard ['What'],' very costly ['Value' is created again, in the context (story)], and anointed the feet of Jesus, and 'wiped' his feet [highlighting the 'What' scenario] with her hair ['How']: and the house was filled with the odor of the ointment. [John 12: 1-3 KJV]

If we look carefully at how many of the words and phrases take their place in the context of John 12: 1-3, we see just a 'small' picture forming, one 'which' 'will' enhance our interest level enough to keep us wanting more! As we know, and it is readily evident, it is not only words beginning 'with' 'W' 'which' are important, though they lead us clearly through the story; every word a writer uses is there so as to capture the story, epic, context—of every conversation, 'written' or spoken. In Journalism, The Five W's and How, are vital to any story the Journalist produces for print.

Part Three—Human Value And "If And What If?"

The name of *Chapter 14*, is *The Five W'S and How: Then What?* We looked thinly at the first part of the title; now, the last part comes to light as it says, "Then What." The next three verses maintain the story [context, epic], by beginning 'with,' 'Then.'

'Then,' brings 'when' back into the picture 'with' an extension to include another person of 'worth' into the story. As we listen to the whole story of the life of Judas Iscariot, we struggle in ourselves to approve Judas as a person of 'value,' because he was a key character in the plot to kill Jesus. 'Then,' saith one of his disciples, Judas Iscariot, [another 'who'], 'which' should betray him ['What'], said, 'why' was not this ointment ['What'] sold for three hundred pence, and given to the poor? This he said, not that he cared for the poor; but because he was a thief, and had the bag, and bare 'what' was put therein. [These three verses are all about 'What,' 'Who's,' 'Why's,' 'When,' was happening at the supper (dinner)]. The opening context of the whole story still picks up the 'Where [Bethany]' of the 'What' was happening throughout.

If we miss any part of the 'Whole' Story, we leave some very important 'context' flopping in the wind—we did this just by not mentioning two ladies 'who' were very important to the story, yes, but they were also very important to Jesus. Mary and Martha have a story all their own, yet inclusive to the mix of the rest of the story. Jesus addresses this insert, yet more than an insert, because John 11 tells us about the interaction of Jesus 'with' Mary and Martha. If we are ever to get a grip on the context of any story, we need to [I think of the Cole Porter song "Begin The Beguine (it does not mean the beginning)," as I play 'with' a dance of Words—in the context of my writing here] begin where the story of these girls begins. In one verse, Jesus gives the ladies, Mary and Martha, the recognition other folks sometimes withheld from the women. Jesus never failed to acknowledge people who had a pure heart. The plan and purpose of God was for us to have a "Pure Heart!"

Then said Jesus, Let her [Mary] alone: against the day of my burying hath she kept this.

Lazarus, Mary, and Martha are equally part of the story of the dinner for Jesus, but the heart of 'Mary' is singled out here.

Just so we can get the whole picture of what John was talking about in *Chapter 12* of John, I will present the verses 'without' breaking down each word and or phrase. Each of us can take the time to do this for ourselves—it can be done by most anyone; it just takes some time spent 'With' Jesus; this is not so bad! The true 'Value' of a relationship 'With' God only comes full circle 'When We Make Time, Even In Our Busy Schedule!'

For the poor always ye have with you; but me ye have not always.

Much people of the Jews therefore knew that he was there: and they came not for Jesus' sake only, but that they might see Lazarus also, whom he had raised from the dead. But the chief priests consulted that they might put Lazarus also to death; because that from him many of the Jews went away and believed on Jesus.

On the next day many people that were come to the feast [Passover]. When they heard that Jesus was coming to Jerusalem, took branches of palm trees, and went forth to meet him, and cried, Hosanna: Blessed is the King of Israel that cometh in the name of the Lord. And Jesus, when he had found a young ass, sat thereon; as it is written, fear not, daughter of Sion: behold, thy King cometh, sitting on an ass's colt.

These things understood not his disciples at the first: but when Jesus was glorified, then remembered they these things were written of him, and that they had done these things unto him. The people therefore that was with him when he called Lazarus out of his grave, and raised him from the dead, bare record. For this cause the people also met him, for that they heard that he had done this miracle.

The Pharisees therefore said among themselves, Perceive ye how ye prevail nothing? behold, the world is gone after him. And there were certain Greeks among them that came up to worship at the feast: The same came therefore to Philip, which was of Bethsaida of Galilee, and desired him, saying, Sir, we would see Jesus. Philip cometh and telleth Andrew: and again Andrew and Philip tell Jesus. And Jesus answered them, saying, The hour is come, that the Son of man should be glorified.

'Watch for The Five W's and H; especially the rest of the W's through this exercise of reading The Gospel of John 12.'

Verily, verily, I say unto you, Except a corn of wheat fall into the ground and die, it abideth alone: but if it die, it bringeth forth much fruit. He that loveth his life shall lose it; and he that hateth his life in this world shall keep it unto life eternal. If any man serve me, let him follow me; and where I am, there shall also my servant be: if any man serve me, him will my Father honour.

Now is my soul troubled; and what shall I say? Father, save me from this hour: but for this cause came I unto this hour. Father, glorify thy name. Then came there a voice from heaven, saying, I have both glorified it, and will glorify it again.

The people, therefore, that stood by, and heard it, said that it thundered: others said, An angel spake to him. Jesus answered and said, This voice came not because of me, but for your sakes. Now is the judgment of this world: now shall the prince of this world be cast out. And I, if I be lifted up from the earth, will draw all men unto me. This he said, signifying what death he should die.

The people answered him, We have heard out of the law that Christ abideth for ever: and how sayest thou, The Son of man must be lifted up? who is this Son of man?

Then Jesus said unto them, Yet a little while is the light with you. Walk while ye have the light, lest darkness come upon you: for he that walketh in darkness knoweth not whither he goeth. 'While' ye have light, believe in the light, that ye may be the children of light. These things spake Jesus, and departed, and did hide himself from them. But though he had done so many miracles before them, yet they believed not on him: That the saying of Esaias the prophet might be fulfilled, which he spake, Lord, who hath believed our report? and to whom hath the arm of the Lord been revealed?

Therefore they could not believe, because that Esaias said again, He hath blinded their eyes, and hardened their heart; that they should not see with their eyes, nor understand with their heart, and be converted, and I should heal them. These things said Esaias, when he saw his glory, and spake of him.

Nevertheless among the chief rulers also many believed on him; but because of the Pharisees they did not confess him, lest they should be put out of the synagogue: For they loved the praise of men more than the praise of God. Jesus cried and said, He that believeth on me, believeth not on me, but on him that sent me. And he that seeth me seeth him that sent me.

I am come a light into the world, that whosoever believeth on me should not abide in darkness. And if any man hear my words, and believe not, I judge him not: for I came not to judge the world, but to save the world. He that rejecteth me, and receiveth not my words, hath one that judgeth him: the word I have spoken, the same shall judge him in the last day. For I have not spoken of myself; but the Father which sent me, he gave me a commandment, what I should say and what I should speak. And I know that his commandment is life everlasting: whatsoever I speak therefore, even as the Father said unto me, so I speak.

In John 12, Jesus was at the house of Lazarus, Martha, and Mary, and He was the guest of honor. Here the Dinner was made for Jesus after Jesus had raised Lazarus from the dead. Jesus seemed to have an intimate relationship with this family. 'This time' at the 'Dinner' for Jesus seemed to be a time of duality. There seemed to be a 'dual purpose.'

For some, at least for Mary, it was a time to sit at the feet of Jesus in a time of worship—simply to honor Him for Who He was. Martha and Mary had a great load lifted from off their shoulders because Jesus raised their brother from the dead, leaving their family intact for the immediate future in which they had probably expected life to be all that they had anticipated it to be as they were growing up and for a long time. So, yes, in part the Dinner may have been orchestrated.

I see another aspect of the reason for this Dinner at the home of these, friends of Jesus. Though the Dinner was prepared by Jesus's friends, and He was the Guest, not The Host, Jesus also saw past the immediacy of the moment, given He was continuing to prepare these His disciples, and others for 'the time' He had spoken of as early as 'the time' of the feeding of the five thousand. Many of the folks 'who' came, did so only to get a free meal.

I thought Mary got a glimpse and or a grasp of this part of what I see as a 'duality' of eating and socializing. Mary is singled out as the only one 'who' captured the meaning of what Jesus had spoken after the feeding of The Five Thousand.

> And they did eat and were all filled: and there was taken up of fragments that remained to them twelve baskets. And it came to pass, as he was alone praying, his disciples were with him: and he asked them, saying, whom say the people I am? They answering said, John the Baptist; but some say, Elias; and others say, that one of the old prophets is risen again. He said unto them, but whom say ye that I am? Peter answering said, The Christ of God.
>
> And he straightly charged them and commanded them to tell no man that thing; saying, The Son of man must suffer many things, and be rejected of the elders and chief priests and scribes, and be slain, and be raised the third day. And he said to them all, If any man will come after me, let him deny himself, and take up his cross daily, and follow me. [Luke 9: 17-23 KJV]

In John 12, in verse 7 we see the inference that The Dinner was in part at least, more than for what Jesus had done, because Jesus says that Mary was washing His feet, maybe this was because she actually understood more than did some of the others.

> Then said Jesus, Let her alone: against the day of my burying hath she kept this. For the poor always ye have with you; but me ye have not always.

Jesus was and is The Son of God. Jesus was and always remains to be God, He made that clear more than once! The scribes and the Pharisees took this to be blasphemy, when Jesus referred to this. People have not always understood this, and yes, to explain every aspect of this belief is not an easy matter because it requires a somewhat huge measure of faith.

We more easily understand the fact of God, or for some, the notion of God; we struggle to equate Jesus, the son of man [the presentation of a physical being from the union of a man and a woman] as being anything more than just that. Jesus was not concocted or brought onto the scene of this life as a 'physical' person by the input of any human.

The residency of God, in physical form on this plot of land He called earth, is not something easily understood by the average person. The requirement for this is 'Faith,' and 'Faith' comes from first hearing about God from someone who already has; Faith.' The Holy Spirit of God did all the work, Joseph and Mary were only partners in this birth, because to be real to humankind, Jesus had to come through the physical birth process of coming out from the womb of a woman.

The difference, which is hard to explain to the understanding of all, 'because it requires' Faith, is that Jesus was declared by God The Father to be The Son of God. Scripture tells us that He, Jesus, was Immanuel, which means GOD With Us! At Jesus baptism a voice was heard from heaven, watch for it in these verses to see what it said,

> In those days John the Baptist came preaching in the wilderness of Judea," repent, for the kingdom of heaven is at hand." For this is he who was spoken of by the prophet Isaiah when he said,

"The voice of one crying in the wilderness: 'Prepare the way of the Lord; make his paths straight.'"

> Now John wore a garment of camel's hair and a leather belt around his waist, and his food was locusts and wild honey. Then Jerusalem and all Judea and all the region about the Jordan were going out to him, and they were baptized by him in the river Jordan, confessing their sins.
>
> But when he saw many of the Pharisees and Sadducees coming to his baptism, he said to them, "You brood of vipers! Who warned you to flee from the wrath to come? Bear fruit in keeping with repentance. And do not presume to say to yourselves, 'We have Abraham as our father,' for I tell you, God is able from these stones to raise up children for Abraham. Even now the axe is laid to the root of the trees. Every tree therefore that does not bear good fruit is cut down and thrown into the fire." "I baptize you with water for repentance, but he who is coming after me is mightier than I, whose sandals I am not worthy to carry. He will baptize you with the Holy Spirit and fire.

His winnowing fork [fan] is in his hand, and he will clear his threshing floor and gather his wheat into the barn, but the chaff he will burn with unquenchable fire."

The Baptism of Jesus

Then Jesus came from Galilee to the Jordan to John, to be baptized by him. John would have prevented him, saying, "I need to be baptized by you, and do you come to me?" But Jesus answered him, "Let it be so now, for thus it is fitting for us to fulfill all righteousness." Then he consented. And when Jesus was baptized, immediately he went up from the water, and behold, the heavens were opened to him, and he saw the Spirit of God descending like a dove and coming to rest on him; and behold, a voice from heaven said, [Mathew and Luke]

"This is my beloved Son, with whom I am well pleased."

Someday, all who receive Jesus as The Savior He is, through the process of 'Faith' to believe what God clarified in Hebrews 11:6, will "Get A Dinner." Not for all the service they did, all the good works; these we will cast as crowns at the feet of Jesus, but for accepting Him, Jesus, as their 'enough'—the propitiation or satisfaction for a seat at the table of the Marriage Dinner [Supper] of The Lamb. This will be one of the greatest events taking place after The Rapture: In Heaven.

But without faith it is impossible to please him: for he that cometh to God must believe that he is, and that he is a rewarder of them that diligently seek him. [Hebrews 11:6]

Out of about 25,000 English words beginning with 'W,' I found myself wondering 'Why,' these five words, "Who, What, Where, When, Why" became the benchmark of communication in the world of trying to get 'The Message' out there. Out of the 5 W's all writers and journalists, preachers—have determined that these have enough clout [influence] to cover the basis of getting the message out there—The Message of faith to believe.

The yardsticks or tape measures of communication or interactions which are able to enlighten and convince people about a subject is contained within the parameters of everything—"Who, What, Where, When, Why," are sufficient.

Merriam Webster tells us that there are about three-thousand core words which begin with 'W.' Where do we begin when we wish to determine the value of words, and 'Then What' about the value of the people they relate to and how these words affect the outcome of people's lives—Oh how the story comes alive 'When' we take the time to acknowledge the value of every person in the whole of all God created. Have we got the eyes to see this reality—the 'Eyes of Understanding' which can only come through 'Faith.'

> Through faith we understand that the worlds were framed by the 'WORD'[A 'W' Word] of God, so that things which are seen were not made of things which do appear.
> [Hebrews 11:3 KJV]

"Word, With, Which, Walk, Water, We, Wage, Welfare, Well—" these and many more play out on the 'playground' of our lives each moment of every day. Then, as if this isn't enough to tell the story of life, and 'Why' we even exist, we add 'How' to the mix of the Five W'S. We could ask how many words there are beginning with H. It is near impossible to put a number to this question, because it depends on who is counting. It also depends on how many more words are concocted each year, maybe even each day, to add to the list, to explain what is really simple when we narrow it down to "Who, What, Where, When, Why and How." As we answer these simply put questions, we have enough to go on to make life good for every person on Planet Earth!

This has been kind of a preaching chapter—it is what it is! If someone does not preach it from the housetops, from a podium with a mega-phone large enough to speak to the whole world, every moment of every day, we will not get the message that Jesus Christ came to save sinners, such as all who were born—hey, that's all of us! This message is in the hands of most people today via our cell phones, tablets, computers—but the readership is low, because people say they can handle life 'All By Themselves!' It is what it is for now—Then What?

Chapter 14 is titled, *The Five W'S, and How: Then What?* This not only leaves us with a challenge, it allows us to get to know The God of The Universe, The God of all eternity past, present, and future! We miss the mark when we center on ourselves instead of Who made everything possible for us on the personal level.

"IF" is the first word; it is not only effective or the operative word we deal with, but it is imperative, insistent, or essential to the 'faith word' of importance, one we should not dare to neglect or cast off as slight or inconsequential. We covered this word fairly intensely in *Chapter 13*, but, let's just peek back at it as a refresher as we move on to stage two of this *Chapter 14*:

> If you can make one heap of all your winnings
> And risk it on one turn of pitch-and-toss
> And lose, and start again at your beginnings
> And never breathe a word about your loss;
> If you can force your heart and nerve and sinew
> To serve your turn long after they are gone,
> And so hold on when there is nothing in you
> Except the Will which says to them: 'Hold on!'
>
> If you can talk with crowds and keep your virtue,
> Or walk with Kings—nor lose the common touch,
> If neither foes nor loving friends can hurt you,
> If all men count with you, but none too much;
> If you can fill the unforgiving minute
> With sixty seconds' worth of distance run,
> Yours is the Earth and everything that's in it,
> And—which is more—you'll be a Man, my son!
>
> Or watch the things you gave your life to, broken,
> And stoop and build 'em up with worn-out tools:

"IF—" [Rudyard Kipling 1885], sends a huge message with the simple lines of a poem. Most often, simplicity [Occam's Razor] is a better fixer than the complicated means we expound, illustrate, or even 'preach on,' if you would. We all need fixers, or people, who are at the ready to help us with what we may think as simple, but unintelligible or garbled to them—yes, in the simple things, but also in the things of life where they have no place to turn; but possibly to us! As I looked at this poem I thought long and hard about 'how' Solomon described living in the 'If' state. He saw so much of life as Vanity; we see it as somewhat hopeless [vain] to expect perfect results, with the imperfect tools that Kipling speaks of.

The tools of use for us to get our lives in proper placement with the rest of the world, so people will read us well; right, in the context of 'how' we want them to see us—this can be a chore. Life was created to be simple, but it got a little messed up.

I Keep Six Honest, Serving Men

I KEEP six honest serving–men; (They taught me all I knew) Their names are What and Where and When And How and Where and Who. I send them over land and sea, I send them east and west; but after they have worked for me, I give them all a rest. I let them rest from nine till five. For I am busy then, As well as breakfast, lunch, and tea, For they are hungry men: But different folk have different views; I know a person small —. She keeps ten million serving–men, Who get no rest at all! She sends 'em abroad on her own affairs, From the second she opens her eyes—. One million How's, two million Whereas, And seven million Whys! [Kipling, Rudyard. The Elephant's Child (Illustrated) . Laverock. Kindle Edition].

If we think of this whole God Thing as a vain attempt to rack up Brownie Points in the Good Works Column of our walk with Christ, so we make sure that we "GET A DINNER," we are living in the world of Vanity like Solomon ranted about in Ecclesiastes. "Hear Ye The Word of THE LORD:"

And you hath he quickened, who were dead in trespasses and sins; wherein in time past ye walked according to the course of this world, according to the prince of the power of the air, the spirit that now worketh in the children of disobedience: among whom also we all had our conversation in times past in the lusts of our flesh, fulfilling the desires of the flesh and of the mind; and were by nature the children of wrath, even as others.

But God, who is rich in mercy, for his great love wherewith he loved us, even when we were dead in sins, hath quickened us with Christ, (by grace ye are saved;) and hath raised us up together, and made us sit together in heavenly places in Christ Jesus: that in the ages to come he might shew the exceeding riches of his grace in his kindness toward us through Christ Jesus.

For by grace are ye saved through faith; and that not of yourselves: it is the gift of God: not of works, lest any man should boast. For we are his workmanship, created in Christ Jesus unto good works, which God hath before ordained that we should walk in them. [Ephesians 2:1-10 KJV]

Now, let's do a back flip reflectively to a place we talked about earlier in this Chapter; about 'Who' Got A Dinner.

And the Jews' Passover was nigh at hand: and many went out of the country up to Jerusalem before the Passover, to purify themselves. Then sought they for Jesus, and spake among themselves, as they stood in the temple, What think ye, that he will not come to the feast? Now both the chief priests and the Pharisees had given a commandment, that, if any man knew where he were, he should shew it, that they might take him.

Line this up with the Six Serving Men; Jesus had 12 Serving disciples at His side, where we also will be accredited for being His Disciples. We are servants, yes, but we are known as FRIENDS.

IF My People—called by My name will—? Then What?

If my people, which are called by my name, shall humble themselves, and pray, and seek my face, and turn from their wicked ways; then will I hear from heaven, and will forgive their sin, and will heal their land.

Now mine eyes shall be open, and mine ears attent unto the prayer that is made in this place. For now have I chosen and sanctified this house, that my name may be there for ever: and mine eyes and mine heart shall be there perpetually.

And as for thee, if thou wilt walk before me, as David thy father walked, and do according to all that I have commanded thee, and shalt observe my statutes and my judgments;

'Then' will I stablish the throne of thy kingdom, according as I have covenanted with David thy father, saying, There shall not fail thee a man to be ruler in Israel.

But if ye turn away, and forsake my statutes and my commandments, which I have set before you, and shall go and serve other gods, and worship them;

'Then' will I pluck them up by the roots out of my land which I have given them; and this house, which I have sanctified for my name, will I cast out of my sight, and will make it to be a proverb and a byword among all nations.

And this house, which is high, shall be an astonishment to everyone that passeth by it; so that he shall say, Why hath the LORD done thus unto this land, and unto this house?

And it shall be answered, Because they forsook the LORD God of their fathers, which brought them forth out of the land of Egypt, and laid hold on other gods, and worshipped them, and served them: therefore hath he brought all this evil upon them. [Chronicles 7:14-22 KJV]

What Did I See, and What Does It Say?
"Prepare to Launch!"

What will we center on in Life? We can focus our lives on getting to know Jesus for Who and What He was throughout eternity past. We can seek to know Him in the present, in a way which can guide our lives to the best possible future. How do we do this? To do this, is what I have been talking about in this Chapter—the short answer is, 'If' we learn what it is to serve others like Jesus did, we will know How to enjoy life to the fullest. 'IF' our penchant [desire] for Centering Jesus as our focus, our heart cannot help but to guide us to be a 'Server—a Servant.

Who can I serve? I can begin with my neighbor. Who is my neighbor? Anyone can be my neighbor, family, friends, strangers, others—anybody to whom we can be a hand up in their time of need; anyone with whom we can share our lives, from a list of so many ways to do this; all it takes is 'True Love.'

'What,' is the subject of what the 'Who' needs. 'Where' can I serve? Wherever the need presents itself. 'When' can I serve best? When the need comes, be it morning, noon, or night; be alert and ready at a moment's notice. 'Why' should 'I' be the one to take up the challenge of "Servitude?" Because Jesus did, and 'IF' we do what Jesus did, we cannot be far from the Kingdom of God! 'How' can I be of the greatest value to the Kingdom of God? We can keep an open mind, an open heart, and cast all our cares or anxieties on Jesus, and when we feel we cannot go another mile, we could start by taking just a few small steps of faith to get us going.

The Neutral Zone

15th Chapter

Inquires; Ignorance; Responses; Resentment!

Truth is: Beware of false knowledge; it is more dangerous than ignorance. [George Bernard Shaw–Brainy Quotes]

Truth is: The truth is incontrovertible. Malice may attack it, ignorance may deride it, but in the end, there it is. [Winston Churchill]

And ye shall know the **truth**, and the **truth** shall make you free. [John 8:32 KJV]

But he that doeth truth cometh to the light, that his deeds may be made manifest, that they are wrought in God. [John 3:21 KJV]

Pilate saith unto him, What is **truth**? And when he had said this, he went out again unto the Jews, and saith unto them, I find in him no fault at all. [John 18:38 KJV]

Inquires are questions which can be our desire to know the truth we are ignorant about; inquiries can be a means for us to acquire someone else's knowledge about an issue, for the sake of becoming better equipped to help someone else. However, inquires can be in play so as to gather information so as to fit it into 'The Gossip Column,' to keep a story unwinding, whether it be true or false, always leading to harm someone.

Responses to inquiries are guardians of action—right actions are the positives required to build relationships; wrong actions will always tear down relationships which may have been years in the making, and resentment will be one of the major reactions or consequences to come out of illegitimate or dishonest intentions to demean another person, who is also created in the image of God!

Chapter 15

INQUIRIES, IGNORANCE, RESPONSES, RESENTMENT!

We are not slaves; we are pilgrims in search of crown lands. We are not enslaved to the tenements or boarding houses of the present—those which will cause regrets, a place of homelessness within the placement of truth, and will in the end, bring only 'Death!'

We might be moved [encouraged, stimulated, and motivated] by emotion [subjectivity], but we are not captured [enslaved] or enraptured [beguiled, hypnotized, or mesmerized] by subjectivity—unless we choose to be. Often, it seems we cannot shake the tentacles which wrap themselves around us with emotions we feel are the truth, as if they will not ever let go of us, leading us to no-mans-land; here we will find ourselves alone, when we most need the help of the others we have shunned [rejected] for so long!

Every good question deserves a good answer. The Canadian Broadcasting Corporation (CBC) hosted a segment in their daily programming called: *The Good Question.* Over the years, I have often listened to this segment of their broadcasting day. Sometimes I heard rational questions, and sometimes I heard questions sounding like they had no answer. Usually, the host searched long enough to facilitate an answer.

I am not sure, but there were questions, which appeared not to have an answer. One question someone asked is, "Where did the term Curiosity Killed the Cat come from?" There did not seem to be an obvious answer. All I can find is, it has its origin in international English. My question was, "What if there was no finish line." I never phoned to ask the question.

Part Three—Human Value And "If And What If?"

R.C. Sproul wrote *Defending Your Faith*. It is about answering questions. Josh McDowell is a prolific writer on questions and answers. Books like: *Right from Wrong, More Than a Carpenter, Evidence That Demands a Verdict, New Evidence That Demands a Verdict*—and more are part of his portfolio.

Another author, Lee Strobel, once lined our bookshelves with, *The Case for Christ, The Case for Faith, The Case for a Creator, The Case for Christmas* and more. To the other thousands I have not mentioned, I apologize. Lack of time and space, and a lack of necessity to include every manuscript written to answer our questions, is in part my reason. Please find and read their books. I am sure many will answer some of your good questions. Each person seems to have more questions than I could possibly ever answer, because as soon as I think I have answered them all, a new batch of questions enters their mind or psyche.

Are the answers these books provide, enough to satisfy our questions or inquires? Possibly, if I literally piled every book ever written to give us the answer to our asks, on a pile within the boundary lines of the Former World Trade Center, they would surpass its height and boundaries. I am talking not only about titles, but also every printed, audio, or video copy. Maybe the titles alone would do the trick. The age of information is staggering. We need more than a billion trees each year, to supply our paper needs. Look at just a little information I found.

Some people calculate that the world flow of book titles; it is staggering to keep up with the newbies each year which we add to the already staggering amount of books published in the past. It matters not so much who we ask, the numbers differ hugely—who really knows?

Every year many new books come on the scene. Stephen Hawking in his recent book *Brief Answers to the Big Questions*, suggested, "if you stacked the new books being published next to each other, at the present rate of production you would have to move at ninety miles an hour just to keep up with the end of the line." Being Stephen is a Scientist, a renowned one at that, he seems to have resources by which he feels he can give us numbers like this. It is astounding when we think about it; we will never catch up with every thought people have. People are 'thinking thoughts' [they may think of as new thoughts] faster than we can imagine.

340

UNESCO (United Nations Educational, Scientific and Cultural Organization) is said to keep track strategically or purposefully, the number of books published by country. Their estimation runs in numbers surpassing two million titles a year of new book titles published each year. [Statistics from 2013]

Book City, World; is there a city by this name? I cannot find it. The closest thing I can find resembling this name is an internet site that gives access to many books. Book City, World; how big would it be if it were an actual place? If Book City was, an actual place and it housed every book ever published and printed, how big would it be. What if Book City was a tourist attraction because it was the only place you could read books to get the answers to life's questions.

I just showed a few statistics about books and data. I am not sure that covers every book ever put into print. Looks like the statistics I show above are dated; so how many books does that add to the list? Are there ten billion books? If there were, how much physical space would it require to pile them? Not all the answers to accommodate everyone's need are in Book City. To me, the Bible has all those answers; we just do not want to access those answers. Therefore, what does that leave us if Book City, and the Bible, which houses all those books in one volume, cannot satisfy all the answers? All that is left is Jesus. When Jesus comes back He will have all the answers, and we will then know that God has all the answers; but until then—then what?

Then comes the questions, what are my gifts, what does God want from me, and what is my vision, dream, goal, or mandate? I wonder where the answer is. Yes, I know it is in the Bible, and in many other publications.

Where there are a million people, we can expect at least a million questions at the very least. Individually, each of you, my readership, can each come up with a dozen questions about things, life, and faith. In my book *The Mandate*, [Location 2925] *Chapter 14, Questions and Answers*, I started this chapter with my *"My Good Question,"* "What if there was no finish line?" It is hard to imagine running a race with no finish line, but sometimes we flail away doing the things we think will get the job done, without ever consulting our LORD. The longer we try fixing life for eternity, on our own, the farther we travel in the wrong direction.

The Marathon is the longest official race in which anyone participates, hundreds of people run this race at the same time to. It is 26.2 miles. I have never considered this challenge, to prove my endurance level on the physical side—I would never consider it. If a Grizzly Bear was chasing me, I could not endure for this length of time in a run of Marathon Proportion. I would be "One Dead Dude" long before the 26.2 miles were finished, even if I could run faster than the grizzly.

Philippides ran the first marathon in 490 B.C. The Athenians, greatly outnumbered, urgently needed the assistance of Sparta's military to help the Athenians against an enemy too powerful for them to attend to on their own. The Athenian chain of command sent Phidippides to Sparta for reinforcements. The route Philippides had to manoeuvre took a course though the mountains and so it was not an easy task. Phidippides was a trained runner and he ran the distance in approximately 36 hours. The Spartans had to delay their assistance to the Athenians because of some beliefs they had about the moon, and how it reflected on their religious commitments. Therefore, the Athenians had to engage the Persian Army with no help. Phidippides bore the bad the news in the 140-mile trek.

Pheidippides and the Athenian Army set their sights on the Plains of Marathon to fight to the death if necessary. They were outmatched 4 to 1 but initiated a sneak attack that by all appearances was indistinguishable from suicide. The death toll was huge, but the thing of it was that the heavy losses were on the side of the Persians. Sixty-four hundred Persians died, while under two-hundred Athenians died.

Those Persians who remained made their way to Athens to endeavor to topple it before the victorious Greek Army could re-assemble there. Again, Phidippides had to run to Athens (26 miles away) to deliver news of their victory at The Battle of Marathon. He also had to break the bad news that Persian ships were on the way to Athens to take the city. Phidippides was physical wreck. This being the case was not enough to keep him from this challenge. He was thinking there was no finish line in this race. About three hours later, he arrived at Athens, delivered the news, and died. Eventually the Spartans and others came to help, and they won another victory.

This is a vivid picture of someone trying to manage life when the trouble of each day is almost unbearable in the quest to fulfill their God breathed mandate. From the story we looked at it is easy to understand what it takes to be victorious in any fray. If there were no finish line, would Phidippides still be running? His finish line was death, but the cause, or the mandate lived on. He did his part so others could finish well!

Sometimes we pay the price. I guess the thought of martyrdom in today's culture is not a pleasant thought. I would much rather do my job, get my cheque, and get on with my life. For the Christian there is no loss if they give it up for Jesus. His Mandate—to bring everyone whom the Father had foreseen would want His plan, to salvation, this is the important factor.

Just doing life for a long time without seeing an immediate personal accomplishment, is a tough task. To keep doing what I know for sure is my mandate, day after day without knowing if I will have a publisher interested in giving you a chance to read this book—this is not always easy.

If we only keep what we want as an accomplishment as our focus, we might get discouraged when the results do not come quickly—even though it may be God's plan for our lives. The reason for this is, in these between times, I have some living to do. Here God is trying to get my attention to the fact I need to put others first. It is His intent, and mine, that's what I do as my mandate—this is not really for my accomplishment. Influencing others is always the main plan. God is "Semper Fidelis," always faithful. He brings me to these times where I think I have run the race without a finish line because He does not want me running indefinitely.

So, what is a finish line? Well, death is a finish line. I believe 'hope' is one of the greatest finish lines that anyone of us can rely on. God is always faithful in providing hope when I have run too long. People often say that God has not been there for them when the chips were down. I guess my thought is this, have I been there for him when it was imperative I listen to what he is saying. J.F. Kennedy's inaugural speech often comes back. "Ask not what your country can do for you, but what you can do for your country." Some of the people of the past spoke some powerful directive words in an effort to help us along the way.

God never speaks just to hear Himself say words. When He spoke the world into existence, He was speaking for creative purpose. When Jesus spoke to the troubled waters as the disciples fretted because of a storm, they thought, was uncontrollable, He was speaking for purpose. I believe He was speaking to instill hope into the hearts of the disciples. Hope Is The Final Frontier. Space is not The Final Frontier, as Star Trek would have us believe. We are encouraged to look for the Blessed Hope. There is no guessing as to who this is. It is Jesus.

I have written about Martin Luther King Jr. And Rosa Parks. There is an even longer list of Civil Rights Activists than this. Daisy Bates, Ella Baker, Jessie Jackson, and the list is long, of people who saw it as the God given right to pursue a vision that saw all men and women have equal rights. Although we have not yet eradicated prejudice from the American or world culture, many victories have their success stories. Many people played out their parts so a few small victories would lead to major victories in the Civil Rights movement. Civil Rights is not the only area of life in which we see accomplishments. Every day there are victories for somebody—somewhere.

What is a victory? What is an accomplishment? What is competition? What is a task well done? 'How' can anyone achieve these? Questions—it seems as if this is all there is. There are more questions than there are answers—so it seems. For every answer, likely a hundred questions have preceded the answer. Before the answer comes, we question, 'why' the answer is not forthcoming? Why did it happen like this?

Today I may ask, "Does God not care any more?" It may mean that I saw him care more directly for my situation at one time. Now it is dark again and I am having trouble seeing again—why? We are never convinced God is always on his throne. Is God always in power. If He is in power, He does rule capably. The questions are unending for all of us.

If I tell you I received an answer to my prayer about the new car I needed, would your only reply be, 'GREAT?' I suspect not. If you were anything like my wife, you would begin by asking: What color is it? What does it look like? Does it have four wheels? Does it have a motor? These are just a few questions I hear when I talk about 'one specific answer.'

When I finally get to respond to the array of questions and say the car is black, this does not settle the question. Is it light black, is it dark black, is it shiny black, or is it a dull faded black? If my answer was, 'the car was white,' the question would be, 'is it pure white, is it off white—?' However, for every question, is there only one right answer? Intellectuals tell us everything is relevant. Truth is relevant! So, is there only one answer to every question?

How can I get from Canada to The U.S.A.? Well, you can take this highway or that highway, depending on your startling line. You can walk, or you can drive. You can fly a plane, or you can go fly a kite. One way or another you can get there. With one question, how many answers are available? There is no end to the dilemma of finding 'The Finish Line.'

How can I get from earth to heaven? Well, you can take a jet, or you can take a rocket. No, I mean, how can I transition from earth to "Heaven?" How can I get from this life to the next life? Well, you have to die first, and then you will wake up in Heaven. Someone else will tell you space is The Final Frontier; if you travel space long enough you will find Heaven. If it is out there, we'll find it. If we cannot find it, then there is no Heaven. Did you ever hear this conversation about Heaven? Randy Alcorn wrote *Heaven*—all about what Heaven may be like.

Questions and answers are a confusing game. If I ask you, are you happy? You may say yes, or you may say no, but you may say, relatively. Relatively simply means, sort of. If I ask you what you want to do with your life, will you say, 'well, I do not know'—sometimes I want to be a police person; some may even say they have thought of becoming a high-tech thief. Now there is a conundrum. This is like saying this paper is black when I ask you what color it is. There might be black on the page, but the paper is white. To say I might be a police person or a crook, simply means I will never amount to anything, because I have not determined to make a positive difference.

I realize, sometimes we need to check our options; survey what we actually want to do with our lives. Eventually we need to decide on something. Life is too short to wait to decide what to do about making a difference in this life. It's a sad day if we don't care about making a difference.

There is a finish line. In the job I worked at, I needed to give an account for the time I spent at the office. If I went in every day and put in my eight hours, and the pile of work on my desk kept getting higher, and no paper work ever left my desk, I need not be very smart to realize I would not have had this job for long. I would not have cashed many pay checks from the company before I ended up with no pay checks.

Life is like that. If I put nothing into my 24/7, then it will not be long before I get nothing out of my 24/7. I have 24 hours every day, it happens 7 days every week. That means I have 365 ¼ days every year I live, to make a difference in someone's life. If I only ever make a difference in one person's life, and they make a difference in another person's life, Wow! The law of multiplication will take charge and the results are grand.

This is not really a book about whether you or I are doing enough religious things. I am not so concerned about whether you are doing enough things because you call yourself a Christ Follower. Should I be? I am not so sure. What I am concerned about though, is whether you or I want to get the best for ourselves by way of God's mandate for our lives. If we are doing this, then everything we can and should be doing for the Lord, via works, will happen through God's strength alone. If we know God is enough for every situation we encounter, we will get along pretty well, in so far as the end result goes.

A while ago I asked some good questions. Here they are again. What is a victory? What is an accomplishment? What is competition? What is, a task well done? How can anyone achieve these?

What is a victory? The answers is, defeat of an enemy or opponent, success attained over a difficult situation or opponent. Some synonyms are, conquest, triumph, win and success. Some of today's superlative actions for victory are; "Yeh (with a pumped fist in the air)," another is, "Alright" (with a similar hand pump). The thought expressed by these words is excitement. Who is not excited when relief comes from a stressful situation to a feeling where stress is relieved from the body and mind? If for instance, I am a PGA. Golfer, playing in the highly esteemed British Open, and I win, "Yeh:" "Alright" is my response.

When we experience the Olympics, and the athletes arrive, each of them believe they have as good a chance of winning gold, as do the other athletes. Going with any other attitude leaves a person with an excellent chance of not getting a metal. What each athlete goes to the Olympics for is to be victorious in their particular sport: 'It Could Happen.' Any other aspirations, such as just getting to some place you have never been, and enjoying the atmosphere of this place, is not a good enough reason for people to support your trip to the Olympics.

When the athletes come back home after the gruelling efforts he or she exerted, they do not quit training unless they are too old to compete in another Olympic games. The metals they win are great, the victory is sweet, but soon, they are busy planning their next strategies. The next Olympics are only four years away. If they won a bronze last time, they want gold the next time. If they won a silver metal last time, they want gold next time. If they won a gold metal last time, they want gold again next time. They strive to win the gold; the ultimate victory is what they reach for.

Victory of any kind always brings with it an expression. Hand and arm pumps are the most expressive ones we see. If you win, you just have to release what you fought hard to achieve. It is not just about sports; victory is associated with many other facets of life. Achievement is what it is about for me as I write. I write to compete in the mandate I feel God laid out for me a long time ago. I cannot quit trying to be the best I can at writing. If my last book was not a success, as I classify success, then I want this book to be a success.

I need to be careful, as to what I call success. I may not have a bestseller yet; if this does not happen, I must look for where the success lies. If God asked me to write, He had a reason; it was more than just giving me an exercise in linguistics or word play. If I write, I need people to read what I write. It does not require a million readers to make me successful; if one life is changed, success is evident! At the finish line I will know where my successes were. Will it be a feather in my cap, or will it read as a success which changed a life—Yours or Mine? There is a huge difference between the two.

We do not get a second chance when we come to the finish line of our lives. There are no guarantees; no assurances of having the resources to make an 'Eternal Life Decision,' when the lights dim at the 'End of the Tunnel' of this life. If we have an illness which lingers, and the doctor gives us a prognosis, which says we have 'X' amount of time left, this is a hint, it is time to put our house in order; if we have not yet done so. Many folks just lay themselves down to sleep [thinking there is another proposed tomorrow in which they can get the details of eternity readied or prepared for], and never wake up. The Bible does say, "Now is the day of Salvation." How many tomorrows are left for any of us—Do You Know?

'We know,' 'if We Do Not Know,' 'about such things'—'inquiries [questions]' are not a bad idea. When a person has lived all their lives without spiritual things on their priority list it might come as a shock when they find out that they are on the short list of remaining time to get it all done. Many folks do not believe eternity is a big deal; you live, and then you die; that's all she wrote. Many folks believe there is something beyond this life, and they know they should really do something about it while they are still breathing, but they feel the price is too great; they may miss out on the self-fulfilling pleasures of life. They may think time will allow for the necessary preparation 'when the time comes;' after all, the thief on the cross beside Jesus, had a second chance—why not us?

Inquiries, Ignorance, Responses, Resentment.

'When nature calls,' it often does so with the 'Caveat [red flag]:' Now! My intent here is not to be lewd, indelicate, tasteless, or crude in any way; my only hope is to exhibit a 'call to urgency' which is 'way overdue!' Another way to express this call, is to say, "IT IS HIGH TIME!" 'It is High Time' we got the message, "LIFE IS SHORT;" we will not live forever in this state of "Humanhood." To my knowledge I have never used this word before. However, we tend to live each day without ever realizing there is 'A Red Flag' of urgency in our world, saying, 'we do not love each other so much any more;' we cannot agree on much any more in some of the most important realities. Life—'Here Today and Gone Tomorrow!' As sudden as a wind gust can come in, so might be the tenure of life.

To achieve, we need to recognize the urgency of some events on the horizon; we may not have forever to achieve or accomplish our dreams or goals, those we may have set early in life. It is not always, only, about us [in the selfie mode], in fact, if proper life etiquette, customs, or good manners are intact within the parameters of our goals, because of our giftings, we should always make the journey of life about 'how' we can reach out and touch someone outside of our comfort zone!

Inquiries, Ignorance, Responses, Resentment.

So, If Inquiries [questions] are in order in context with the subject of conversation, ask them. Don't be like the person who is lost in a big city or small community wandering about endlessly because they are too stubborn to ask for directions—LIKE ME!

To wander around in ignorance makes no sense, but it is commonplace amongst those of us who feel we 'have it all together.' Once again, I raise my hand in acknowledgement! I would rather search Google than to broach a difficulty, such as a question about something I am struggling with, by placing the burden of finding an answer, on another person, to see if they can help me. I do not wish to appear ignorant!

Yet, there is a saying going like this, "Ignorance Is Bliss!" It means, if I do not know about something, it is easier to shirk the responsibility of answering 'The Call' to manage life, to take care of a danger which is lurking around the next bend in the road of life. I am not suggesting we should have knowledge about every conceivable entity in life; suggesting that those who do not have this sort of understanding are 'ignoramuses or nincompoops.'

However, the signs of the times in the world we live in are dire. Within the country of Canada, the place I call home, there has been for many years, one part of the country which has threatened to separate from the whole of Canada, because nobody has the mental resources to come to consensus or harmony on most any subject. If the rest of Canada says 'White,' it is offensive to the other Province, and they say 'Black.' What I am saying is simply a clear example of how we differ on everything. What I am saying here, is not intended to make anyone different than I am—feel slighted or inferior by my standards.

Now, it seems that some of Western Canada wants to separate from The Whole of What we have called Canada since Confederation, July 1st. 1867. This, at the present, suggests we could end up with Three different sections of what we call Canada: Western Canada [or whatever we would call it], Quebec [or what we would call it], and The rest of what we have called Canada since Confederation [or what we would finally end up calling it].

The USA and every other country, I think, are having the same problems; they may call their problems by different names, but the core problem is that we are all ignorant of 'how' to get along in this life—because we did not ask the right question 'In The Beginning,' when life was presented to us, we didn't 'inquire' by saying, "why are we so blessed GOD?" We Responded much differently!

Inquiries, Ignorance, Responses, Resentment.

In The Beginning, we said, God, what You made for us is not good enough. What did we know, we just arrived, and we had no clue what was good for us, but we thought we would like to "Take A Chance" on 'Chance!' Well, it seems as though we have not yet 'arrived;' we are still floundering around looking for the answer which was always there from The Beginning! A Rolling Stone Gathers No Moss:

> A rolling stone gathers no moss is an old proverb, credited to Publilius Syrus, who in his Sententiae, states, people who are always moving, with no roots in one place or another, avoid responsibilities and cares. A common modern meaning is that a person must stay active to avoid stagnation.

Ignorance Is Bliss: I guess. We grow up and we want everything that comes along. Men want women; women want men; men want men; women want women; some folks do not know what they want. Some want *Love and Marriage* [Frank Sinatra]. He said they go together like a 'Horse and Carriage.' Some don't want this because it requires 'Commitment [Responsibility].' If we have Love and Marriage in the original context, we cannot have 'Our Cake and Eat It Too!' So we opt out and make our own rules, and now nobody really knows what they want. When we get what we think we want, like that favorite toy at Christmas, we tire of it before long!

We have all these 'Responses' to what once was 'Good, Right, and Proper' and we replace it with 'Resentment.' We hate people when they say God doesn't know what He is doing, if there even is a God. Then we resent those same people when they say, "If there is a God, and you believe in Him, why do you not do what He says to do?" We harbor Resentment [dislike] when other people do not see things our way. Then, when they concede and look for consensus or a path which can lead us to walking together on a path where we can love each other respectfully, we think they have ulterior motives—ulterior motives are often a part of the package. It seems we fear stagnation because we may not get everything we want—A Perfect Life! Eat Dessert First! Eat Only Dessert! We do not want Children; they are too much work! The list is endless!

Steven Hawking has a book called *Brief Answers To The Big Questions*. [October 16, 2018] Steven Hawking died on March 14/2018. Looks like this was his last book.

> Stephen Hawking was regularly asked for his thoughts on the "big questions" of the day by scientists, tech entrepreneurs, senior business figures, political leaders, and the general public. Stephen maintained an enormous personal archive of his responses, which took the form of speeches, interviews, and essays. This book draws from this personal archive and was in development at the time of his death. It has been completed in collaboration with his academic colleagues, his family, and the Stephen Hawking Estate. A percentage of the royalties will go to the Motor Neurone Disease Association and the Stephen Hawking Foundation. [Hawking, Stephen. Brief Answers to the Big Questions (p. vii). Random House Publishing Group. Kindle Edition].

> 1 IS THERE A GOD? [Hawking, Stephen. Brief Answers to the Big Questions (p. 23). Random House Publishing Group. Kindle Edition].

Chapter One: It seems *Chapter One* captured 'The Number One Inquiry' of all other questions which people addressed to Mr. Hawking, and if I am right when it comes to Questions and Answers about Atheism, Christianity, Beginnings Endings—methinks this is one question which has been asked by every interested party in the context of 'How' It All Began? 'How'—is a big part of what we question about life—how did it all happen?

I have just stepped into the early part of this book, on my eBook Version of the book *Brief Answers To The Big Questions* on my Kindle; and a few lines I will quote are,

"Science is increasingly answering questions that used to be the province of religion. Religion was an early attempt to answer the questions we all ask: why are we here, where did we come from? Long ago, the answer was almost always the same: gods made everything. The world was a scary place, so even people as tough as the Vikings believed in supernatural beings to make sense of natural phenomena like lightning, storms, or eclipses. Nowadays, science provides better and more consistent answers, but people will always cling to religion, because it gives comfort, and they do not trust or understand science." [Hawking, Stephen. Brief Answers to the Big Questions (p. 25). Random House Publishing Group. Kindle Edition].

I direct no disrespect towards Mr. Steven Hawking; I do not hesitate to call him MR. In one of the Introductory portions of the book, *Why We Must Ask The Big Questions!*, Steven says,

"I was always very interested in how things operated, and I used to take them apart to see how they worked, but I was not so good at putting them back together again. My practical abilities never matched up to my theoretical qualities. My father encouraged my interest in science and was very keen that I should go to Oxford or Cambridge. He himself had gone to University College, Oxford, so he thought I should apply there. At that time, University College had no fellow in mathematics, so I had little option but to try for a scholarship in natural science. I surprised myself by being successful." [Hawking, Stephen. Brief Answers to the Big Questions (p. 7). Random House Publishing Group. Kindle Edition].

In *Chapter Fourteen* of *Everybody: Everybody Is A Somebody, The Five W'S and How: Then What?*—some answers were clear—do you think so? As I close in on the ending of all I will say in this book, part of what I wish to present is "THE HOW FACTOR!" Steven said, "I was always very interested in "HOW" [emphasis mine] things operated, and I used to take them apart to see "HOW THEY WORKED" [emphasis mine], but I was not so good at putting them back together again.

Inquiries, Ignorance, Responses, Resentment.

If any subject in this world has been more aligned, and or misaligned, appropriated, misappropriated, and straight out hung out in the wind, looking for an exacto place to land, than has, The Big Bang, Creation, God, No God, Atheism, Christianity, Islam, Buddhism—and all related isms concerning "HOW" we got here, I WOULD LIKE TO HEAR ABOUT IT!

IT WOULD BE GREAT TO KNOW FOR SURE HOW WE GOT HERE!

What Came First: The Chicken of The Egg?

Inquiries, Ignorance, Responses, Resentment. What are Inquiries?

Simply, questions about anything and everything. Often, in some of these matters where we inquire about everything, we just mean to remain aloof, so we do not need to get too involved in anything! Somewhat like 'Pleading Ignorance.'

What is Ignorance?

Ignorance is a noun, and it simply means we have no knowledge about the specific entity, when we are asked about it— we can plead ignorance if we are truly unaware of something, or we can plead ignorance when we just wish to get off the hook. When we break it all down, we can learn a lesson in honesty and integrity: In our day, this is a challenge because knowledge is so readily available. A few synonyms for ignorance are—unawareness, lack of knowledge, unfamiliarity, unconsciousness, nothingness, blindness, innocence—then we have disregard or disrespect [this can be for others we meet], insensitivity, oblivion [we look at this earlier in the book]:

If we fail to include God in the landscape of lives or on the waters of the seas of our journey, like someone being born as a functioning human, while shrinking moment by moment into an oblivion of nothingness in eternity, all it leaves us is nothing to show for our lives in this Eternal Sense. It is challenging to surrender to God's purpose.

Someone said, "Ignorance concerning a matter can be said to be 'sensible,' if the outlay for this education costs more than it is worth, if we were to make a ruling which might cause us a loss of beneficial comeback. This bears weight if we are more inclined to be selfish, than we are to be charitable or giving. If we are of this ilk, why should we waste our time on the matter—this is the conclusion of said issue."

What are Responses?

Responses, in the short answer mode are just actions of words or deeds to either Pay Forward to help another person, or to neglect an action which may benefit someone else in their quest to challenge life, and go out and make a difference! Why would we want to make a difference in someone else's life when there is "ME" to look after?

What is Resentment?

Resentment goes much deeper than simply working through Inquiries, Ignorance, Responses, and the like. Resentment takes us to the deepest feelings of hatred—a clear picture of subjectivity, emotive actions of the heart, which are not easily healed. The direction which resentment can take can lead to wars—World wars or simply wars with each other about issues which when addressed empathetically, could be resolved, but too often, they are lifelong deterrents to forming a peaceful relationship again with a party who has wronged us in some way. The thesaurus gives the following synonyms for resentment:

Annoyance, grudge, ire, antagonism, fury, rage, irritation, bitterness, rancor, malice, acrimony, passion, animus, displeasure, cynicism, outrage, animosity, exasperation, indignation, huff—.

Resentment has a cure and an accommodation akin to reconciliation [compromise], but it only remains as a settlement for a certain reason. We can work around it to make it appear as if resolved, by making agreements which are best for everyone, so everyone will benefit from the resolution, but the underlying distastes still fester, but we learn to bite our tongue, while never really settling the emotional stir within our being.

Resentment has a sure cure, but it takes "FORGIVENESS," and this is the toughie. This often requires making a Divine Appointment with God, for a lasting Resolution to be in place. The Cure requires a Love we as humans do not seem to have without a meeting with God, Who best describes this cure in John 3:16;

For God so loved the world, that he gave his only begotten Son, that whosoever believeth in him should not perish, but have everlasting life.

This means, requires SACRIFICE, it requires us to sacrifice our subjectivity, our emotional feelings about someone, and FORGIVE them, so it will be like the offense never happened. More often than not I have not seen 'This Cure for Resentment' work too often without God's Help!

The Neutral Zone
16th Chapter

Truth is: People Groups seem to demand we all adhere to the same belief system. If we have a morally sound belief, based on our religious belief, on the Biblical principles of history, and we express said belief publicly to someone about what we believe, we can be prosecuted or ostracized.

Truth is: We are expected to be fearful of using words like "White, Black, Normal, Challenged—and much more," because society has become too cautious of not offending anyone. Whatever happened to "Sticks and stones will break my bones, but names will never hurt me!"

Truth is: Just this morning a popular singer who supports a certain popular way of life, said they would cancel their appearance at a certain venue, unless a certain charitable ministry to the homeless made a public statement affirming they would change their belief system, one they held for about a hundred and fifty years, to say in effect, they support a certain lifestyle other than what they have always believed, they would lose major support systems. This ministry group to the homeless makes no distinction about race, creed, lifestyle—never has, and always will minister on the basis of compassion for the needs of others, regardless of their choice of lifestyle.

Even God, when He created people, allowed them to choose on their own, Who they would serve, and How they would manage their own lives. However, though God set certain parameters; this being His right to choose to have, because this is what He always was, announced in a multitude of ways that He created people in love far advanced than physical attraction. As far as human value God has never denied anyone who came to Him for help!

The following invitation is to, "Everyone, ever born;" it's an open display that *Everybody: Everybody Is A Somebody*, in the eyes and heart of God; if it is not enough, then nothing ever said beyond this, will ever clarify the human value of People:" As Far As God Is Concerned!

There was a man of the Pharisees, named Nicodemus, a ruler of the Jews: The same came to Jesus by night, and said unto him, Rabbi, we know that thou art a teacher come from God: For no man can do these miracles that thou doest, except God be with him.

Jesus answered and said unto him, Verily, verily, I say unto thee, except a man be born again, he cannot see the kingdom of God. Nicodemus saith unto him "HOW [highlight is mine JB]" can a man be born when he is old? Can he enter the second time into his mother's womb, and be born?

Jesus answered, Verily, verily, I say unto thee, Except a man be born of water and of the Spirit, he cannot enter into the kingdom of God. That which is born of the flesh is flesh; and that which is born of the Spirit is spirit. Marvel not that I said unto thee, Ye must be born again.

The wind bloweth where it listeth, and thou hearest the sound thereof, but canst not tell whence it cometh, and whither it goeth: so is every one that is born of the Spirit. Nicodemus answered and said unto him, "HOW [highlight is mine JB]" can these things be?

Jesus answered and said unto him, Art thou a master of Israel, and knowest not these things? Verily, verily, I say unto thee, we speak that we do know, and testify that we have seen; and ye receive not our witness. If I have told you earthly things, and ye believe not, how shall ye believe, if I tell you of heavenly things?

And no man hath ascended up to heaven, but he that came down from heaven, even the Son of man which is in heaven. And as Moses lifted up the serpent in the wilderness, even so must the Son of man be lifted up: That whosoever believeth in him should not perish but have eternal life.

For God so loved the world, that he gave his only begotten Son, that "WHOSOEVER [highlight is mine JB]" believeth in him should not perish but have everlasting life. For God sent not his Son into the world to condemn the world; but that the world through him might be saved ['saved from what,' insert is mine JB].

"He that believeth on him is not condemned: but he that believeth not is condemned already, because he hath not believed in the name of the only begotten Son of God. And 'THIS IS THE CONDEMNATION,' [According to the parameters of GOD, Who claims to have created us (People), and thereby has the authority to lay down the rules of the everlasting life He speaks about. This address is an open one, sent forth to all people who have and will ever live, before He God, in the Person of Jesus Christ, comes back to bring in the kingdom He talks about here]" that light is come into the world, and men loved darkness rather than light, because their deeds were evil. For everyone that doeth evil hateth the light, neither cometh to the light, lest his deeds should be reproved. But he that doeth truth cometh to the light, that his deeds may be made manifest, that they are wrought in God." [John 1:1-21 KJV]

Choice is and always has been ours.
Choice against God's laws or rules, if you will, always have had consequences, as are the consequences of breaking 'The Laws of Nature.'
The consequences of breaking God's Laws are not because He Gave Up On Us, But Because We Gave Up On HIM!

Chapter 16

THE HOW FACTOR

I am in the final stages of writing *Everybody: Everybody Is A Somebody*. Before I do a final edit, I want to make sure I have done it all right. I want to make as sure, as I, as a piece of mud with skin on, which God thought enough about to say we were created in His Image, to get it as right as a human being can get anything right. Knowing myself, I admit this is a challenge.

From the very outset of the thoughts I have had concerning the topic of this book, the Number One Value in my mind is, *Everybody: Everybody Is A Somebody*, Everybody, as a human being, is "Valuable!"

Not long ago, my wife and I came across a movie called, *Temple Grandin*; it was here I first heard the words, "*I Am Different; Not Less*." I do not know if the phrase is exclusive to Temple Grandin, did she first coin these words in the fashion they are recorded in the movie; if they are, I acknowledge her here.

If someone else first said these words, and that is possible, I acknowledge this person here. The person who first said these words; the people along the way who have said these words; all speak truth. What is most important—the people who said the words—or the inherent value of the words in and of themselves. Value, what an amazing concept.

Are these words, "*I Am Different; Not Less*," just an inert set of words which dictionary writers or someone else first defined in a conversation. If so, we need to take a notice of the people around us! Are phrases simply a set of dormant, immobile, inactive, listless, motionless, paralyzed, passive, powerless, apathetic words someone defined in the way they did just to fill in space in this world of words contained in dictionaries, encyclopedias, thesauruses—?

From the beginning of understandable history, the utterance or display of words may have been a picture on a cave wall; an expression by mouth; or possibly spoken by GOD Himself! Who knows but God Himself! Every word which God spoke as per the record we find in The Bible, and in other viable resources of history, which attribute God as The All In All, has 'value.' Even words which are as I spoke of as inert, have a place—hard to believe, I know; but stay with me.

Let me put it this way, even words tagged as inert, dormant, immobile, impotent, inactive, listless, motionless, paralyzed, passive, powerless apathetic—words, have some value. If we attribute these as the handles we put on other people, we should be careful; these folks may outshine us in the value they attribute to the world scene. The offshoot here might be to put us who think we are so smart, in our place. These words, when applied to someone who has the audacity to suggest they are on the top of the heap articulately or eloquently, may fall flat on their face because their own ignorance of the significance of every created person.

> For beautiful eyes, look for the good in others; for beautiful lips, speak only words of kindness; and for poise, walk with the knowledge that you are never alone. [Audrey Hepburn Brainy Quotes]

These are eloquent thoughts as expressed by Audrey Hepburn in this Brainy Quote. These thoughts are almost Biblical. Maybe they are Biblical.

> Finally, brethren, whatsoever things are true, whatsoever things are honest, whatsoever things are just, whatsoever things are pure, whatsoever things are lovely, whatsoever things are of good report; if there be any virtue, and if there be any praise, think on these things. [Philippians 4: 8 KJV]

So, are these words, *I Am Different; Not Less*, inert, or are they inherent from the character of God Almighty? We attribute the Bible as being God's Word to us—well, not everyone does, but there is a huge part of the populous which does. Even people who are not directly followers of Jesus give some credence to the Bible as being God's Word!

Today, as I am writing these words I am also somewhat engaged in watching some of the Impeachment Hearings on CNN. As a rule I do not like to watch much of the news broadcasts because someone is always casting aspersions on someone else—abuses, defamations, libels, a rap, a put-down, a slander, a backhanded compliment, a smear, a black-eye, or a dirty-dig. Someone said, "No News Is Good News;" it is almost getting to this place in life.

Again yesterday, as so many times in recent years, another school was attacked by a shooter. This time it was a sixteen year old boy, who on his birthday celebrated by killing at least two people, injuring others, and then shooting himself in the head. Last I heard, the shooter was in critical condition.

It is no secret President Donald John Trump has been in the news since before he was selected to lead the Republican Party of The United States of America, which are anything but united. Check out the book written by him and about himself, if you are curious enough to try to find out more about him than the news media has already presented us with. Methinks there are not many secrets left as unknown incidents about President trump anymore.

Today, a few days into the Impeachment Hearings, stuff is coming out of the woodwork via witnesses of every level. I cannot give you a Blow by Blow, nor do I care to. However, I just wish to bring in one part which I briefly watched this morning. I will only say it simply; the former Ambassador of The Ukraine shows signs of being adversely affected by words said about her during some of the goings on between The Us and Ukraine. At some point she was removed from her post. It is on TV, so it is no secret, killing words were and are being directed at her now during the Hearings; it seems this is something she will have to endure for an unknown amount of time yet.

Worth—at what point in every one of our lives do we lose esteem, or do we? Where in time does this happen. I liken 'Where' to 'When' in our life do we come to the place where we no longer seem to have 'The Importance of Innocence?' When we were first born babes, seemingly only knowing how to eat, sleep, cry and dirty our diapers, we still had Value. These things we did as babies were not such that cost us anything. Mommies and Daddies did their duty in the daytime, the nighttime, and every time in between; it was tiring, but when they got that first smile [or gas], it seemed worth it!

When we got a little older, and began to understand what 'no' meant, did it deter us from doing the 'dirty deed' again—that which we were told not to do? No! When we were children we kept breaking the 'no' rule. Did we lose our significance as people? 'No!' When we got older, still being a child of those same parents; when we disobeyed willfully because we just wanted our own way, we knew full well the consequences were harsher now than when we were in the 'Terrible Two's;' we still seemed to do everything worse; it seemed everything they could get their hands on was a 'No, No.' Now at the older age, when we the children were beginning to rebel, thinking we could rule our own lives, did we lose our created worth as a Person, created in The Image of God? Did we become unimportant to God at any time in life?

Okay, it is not getting any easier to stay focused on 'If.' Is it right to even look for, and then think we have found a breakpoint in the matter of Where, When, or 'If.' Do we begin to lose brownie points as we live our lives, and things begin to churn inside of us to where we begin to get off the track people expect of us. The more I watch people in the news, the more I feel I have found justification to think of some folks as Anathema—To Be Cursed!

Let's take the time to try to find a platform on which we can justify anathematizing [hating, censuring, loathing, cursing] someone because we see how they are handling life and the people around them. Please look at the meanings of Anathema:

> noun, plural a·nath·e·mas.
> a person or thing detested or loathed: That subject is anathema to him.
> a person or thing accursed or consigned to damnation or destruction.
> a formal ecclesiastical curse involving excommunication.
> any imprecation of divine punishment.
> a curse; execration.

This is a pretty nasty list of calculations we can use to level someone as having lost their God given right to what they had when they were just little bitty babies. Huddie William Leadbetter, better know as Lead Belly seems to have written *Cotton Fields*. [in and about 1940]

Quite a number of different singers sang this oldie, including Johnny Cash, Creedence Clearwater Revival, The Beach Boys, The Highwaymen—

Lead Belly released *Cotton Field*s in 1947. At the time it must have created quite a bit of interest; *Cotton Fields* had immense credibility. Many other singers must have thought so; as you see above, some of the people who revived this song were popular singers in their time. The operative words here may be, "In Their Time!"

> When I was a little bitty baby My mama would rock me in the cradle, in them old cotton fields back home—.
>
> Oh when those cotton balls get rotten, you can't pick you very much cotton, in them old cotton fields back home.

"Little Bitty Babies" are priceless. Then, "When Those Cotton Balls Get Rotten," when the folks get older; when they get a little out of style; they seem to lose their priceless worth. They were still babies with value once; they grew up and held their desirability—for how long? Well, they are still profitable for some folks, but most people do not even know they ever existed. How soon we forget!

What's the saying, "Value Is In The Eye Of The Beholder." Oh, I think the saying goes like this, "Beauty Is In The Eye Of The Beholder." I guess it is the critical eye within us that has no clue 'how' to judge merit. Remember the words of Audrey Hepburn:

> For beautiful eyes, look for the good in others; for beautiful lips, speak only words of kindness; and for poise, walk with the knowledge that you are never alone. [Audrey Hepburn Brainy Quotes]

To form a continuance with what once was Beautiful, it may take a bit of remembrance from time to time. We may need to *Walk Down Memory Lane* once and awhile. If we do this we may have a chance to stop loathing the things of the past. I hear people say, "I Hate Country Music." "I hate—!" Doing so devalues those who were once so valuable they were easily recognized, for 'who' they were on the open market! We talked much of Book Value, Market Value; everyone should have a chance to excel.

"I Am Different; Not Less"

Temple Grandin was autistic, she had quite a battle to become someone of 'Value' in the eyes of the beholders. When she looked at situations, she didn't just see a bunch of words describing the situation, she saw pictures in her mind as she viewed situations. Now she was able to see in those mind pictures, 'how' to solve the problems other so called 'Value People' could not seem to get a handle on. This is not to say, 'So Called Value People [As I have phrased it] are not of equal value. There needs to be a consensus or unanimity to be able to make the whole world work as one unit of equality across the board.

As I see it, we often see those things that do not really matter so much; things off in the distance of time as being so much closer in merit to our peace of mind than are those things which are right on our doorstep. I am thinking for the moment in terms of 'Space Exploration.' I guess I am thinking about this because I am reading *Brief Answers To The Big Questions*, by Steven Hawking.

Stephen William Hawking was an English theoretical physicist and mathematician. He was born in Oxford. In 1950, he moved to St Albans, Hertfordshire. He was one of the world's leading theoretical physicists. Hawking has written many science books for people who are not scientists. Steven Hawking was a very smart man. He said, "I have spent my life travelling across the universe inside my mind. Through theoretical physics, I have sought to answer some of the great questions. At one point, I thought I would see the end of physics as we know it, but now I think the wonder of discovery will continue long after I am gone. We are close to some of these answers, but we are not there yet." [Hawking, Stephen. Brief Answers to the Big Questions (p. 3). Random House Publishing Group. Kindle Edition].

What a mystery unfolds as people like Steven Hawking begin a search out life through adversity. Maybe its not because of the adversity, maybe it is, but there are people who somehow feel they need to explore—thank God for people who use ingenuity and insight to go way beyond where many of us go, because they cannot sit on todays accomplishments. This said, in another sense, we miss the mark God intended by always reaching so far into the past to see the future.

Steven seemed to have telescopic vision, as he himself said, he traveled the universe in his mind. He looked for clues, and he found what he calls 'Black Holes.' For him it meant more than most of us can envision with all the smarts we have—speaking for myself. Astronomy opened up the heavens for Mr. Hawking. It seems, until his death, he was looking for the builder and maker of the whole of what it seems he was looking for: The Answer to all of his search. Steven Hawking said,

> We are close to some of these answers, but we are not there yet. [Hawking, Stephen. Brief Answers to the Big Questions (p. 3). Random House Publishing Group. Kindle Edition].

We are not there yet. For a while, I want to 'Zero In' on the issue of 'Black.' According to the definition of 'black,' it is,

> Comparative adjective: Blacker; comparing one noun in a modifying or descriptive sense against one other noun. Superlative adjective: blackest; Comparing one noun in a modifying or descriptive sense against a group of other nouns.
> Definition: of the very darkest color owing to the absence of or complete absorption of light; the opposite of white.

So, is 'black' what it is because 'white' has zeroed out to its most infinitesimal size, absolute 'Zero,' so we can say this is where the universe and everything in it allowed for the Big Bang to formulate everything we know? Is this the *Theory of Everything*, as per Steven Hawking? Is 'black' the most source color, and black because of the absence of white or light.

Mr. Hawking initially had one view about 'Black Holes,' and since then he has changed his mind about his initial prognoses. This does not mean he was 'Out To Lunch,' because he said one thing at one time and then he changed his mind. I think everybody has this proclivity or tendency to change their mind about a belief or issue, because as learning increases we often come to a deeper understanding. All this means is, when we didn't understand everything we thought we understood as a perfect understanding, we were wrong; leaving open the chance we may yet come to a perfect or true understanding. This can be true in Science, Christianity, and Everything Else—I guess, because I don't know everything.

Faith is such so it requires us to conclude or assume something when we have never seen the noun [In this case, the noun Science] and its conclusions about beginnings, and the noun God, which we are describing or suggesting as factual—we can say, 'I Believe!' These to me seem to be fair assessments about both parties. Maybe if Science did not make conclusions about beginnings, and Christianity did not make conclusions about beginnings, the whole package of 'Beginnings' would be a non-issue, in our search for the meaning of life!

If this were the issue [a non-issue], we would not be so concerned about 'Beginnings' but more concerned with accepting what we have in the immediate sense. Using 'Faith' to come to the acceptance of the most logical conclusions of 'how' in the light of what a fact should be, "Nothing comes from Nothing," but we still have something—everything not man made! Knowing what we know about 'everything' tangible we have ever seen come onto the playing field of life, logic tells us "Somebody" had a hand in it coming into being! May I be so bold as to suggest the "God" idea as being the most logical choice.

I know it is good to know what is going on. Thinking back over history does not change what is happening today and it will not change what will happen tomorrow. It could though, change what will happen down the pike from our immediate tomorrow [twenty-four hours from now] because of 'how' our yesterdays show us pictures of what happens when we go it our own way on morality, negating what God said was the best course for us to take. If our choice was to follow what seemed to work better [morality wise], and then used the wisdom of listening to good advice rather than wanting so much to say, *I Did It My Way*, we might be the better off.

No matter which logical conclusions we come to about the past and or beginnings, how will my day get better by trying to find out if black holes existed? How will my day get better when I get more information on 'How' everything came to be? 'How' are all these things helping our peace of mind. If 'Science' stuck to the resources of finding new cures; finding out what will make us healthier, so we can better serve the needs of others—I think 'Science' will have done the job it was intended to do. If 'Christianity' stuck with the job of, "Going into all the world and making disciples—" I think 'Christianity will have done its job!

What do I know about all this stuff? Life and living do leave a few clues behind for us to *Know Whom To Believe In*, instead of "Knowing So Much, 'What' To Believe." "Whom" gives us a source, to depend on, if it is the right source. 'What:' What is a tangible entity; it can blow up in our face at a moments notice. Give me substance every time. 'How' looks like the following:

Now faith is the substance of things hoped for, the evidence of things not seen. [Hebrew 11:1 KJV]

If Science stuck to Science [physicality] and Christianity stuck to Spiritual [Eternal] things, we might have a more cohesive world. If we used The Bible as the main source for life, opposed to what so-and-so said, we would all be better off. In order for the Bible to be the most useable source for life and living, one would need to believe the Bible is true: This Is 'One Big If' in the minds of people!

If we want to know about "The Heavens," God, in The Bible, says, "The Heavens declare The Glory of God!" So, what are the heavens about, and for? Are they there to fill our minds with empty black holes which have not yet settled any answers for us about where we came from—what are they there for anyway? The Bible tells us what they are there for. The heavens are there to tell us about the magnificence of God, and to give us the assurance He will always be as stable and dependable as are the Sun, the Moon, The Stars, and all the constellations.

What about the 'Weather,' do we need to know what the weather will be like tomorrow? Well, it is a nice thing to know, but how often are the 'Weather Persons' right in their prognosis? Anyway, what can we do to change any of the predictions about the weather? We cannot change what only God has the controls for. What we can change is our attitude about God and accept the fact He is 'Trustable.' God can look out for our 'Tomorrows.' To have an assurance about these things we need Faith!

I know, I have my bailiwick [place and or belief], and you have yours! Steven Hawking says, when zero gets so infinitesimally small it exploded as the Big Bang to give us everything! I checked out Google on this matter, as I always do, after having read these beliefs in *Brief Answers To Big Question*, [by Steven Hawking], and I found someone calling themselves *The Master Imagineer*, saying the following, in part of their piece:

An infinitesimally small point, area, matter, volume or whatever has a very, very, small value and I believe it is not quite right to just assume a discrete value such as zero. The center of the black hole may have zero progression of time, but as you move an infinitesimally small distance outwards, then time progression would have an infinitesimally small value, not zero. But in the case of Hawking, he seemed to be determined to prove that God did not exist, and that made him assume that a very small value (since it is very close to zero) to be zero because that would support his belief.

I like this quote because it comes to the main point of all I have been trying to get across. It says all I have been saying, by bringing in the word 'value.' If everything we know in life as it has been from the beginning of whatever amount of time is attributed to our existence, is of so little value, that it had a 'ZERO' beginning, we may as well have come from first being 'APES,' because we often act like them.

The Bible, taken to be The Word of God, never, ever said we came from a source of 'NOTHING." The Bible says we were in the heart of God long before we materialized from a handful of dirt— by the way, God made the dirt too! It was a Special Concoction, not a helter-skelter splash of water mixed with some unintelligible shovel of dirt causing a hole from which 'Something' made a mountain out of a mole hill. [Re my own thoughts from reading *Brief Answers To The Big Questions*, by Steven Hawking]. I am enjoying the book, but for me, it presents a work of "Science Fiction," not a non-fiction [reality] publication.

Ex nihilo, is what we usually think of as creatio ex nihilo, (creation out of nothing), in the theological sense. Along side of this we have one contrasting view seeing it like this, creatio ex materia, (creation out of a pre-existent, eternal matter). Another example is creatio ex deo (creation out of the being of God). Then we have creatio continua, meaning, the ongoing divine creation.

I will not try to sort out all of this. When too many options present themselves, apart from what the Bible physically says, I tend to believe the simplest explanation is the best one to follow.

'HOW' was tacked on to the end of the Five W's to make the guideline for Journalism 5W's and H. Who, What, When, Where and Why, it seems, never quite finishes addressing the quandary people are in to finally get all the facts. To me, even after asking the 'Big Why' question, something is always still missing. One would think 'WHY' would I answer most questions satisfactorily.

When we think of the word 'HOW,' as in looking for the final something to nail down a question about God, for instance, the never-ending thought might be, "BUT HOW" could God exist, if He did not come from some other entity. The question is often asked, "Who Made God? How Did God come to be? For me, unless we have a structure which begins with an eternal factor, we always come up short to complete an answer.

As best as I can, I will try to begin to narrow down some of the obstacles in a structural way. I am closing in on the end of this book, not an end as such, to answer all the question which can ever arise. Within, this *Part Four*, I expect to conclude. My intention for *Everybody: Everybody Is A Somebody* addresses the hope I have to help people realize the 'INHERENT VALUE' of all of humankind, without saying, 'it does not matter' 'HOW' we live. So, let's move along into a few briefer Chapters, to lay out some brief structure on which I base the entirety of my life.

Finally, brethren, whatsoever things are true, whatsoever things are honest, whatsoever things are just, whatsoever things are pure, whatsoever things are lovely, whatsoever things are of good report; if there be any virtue, and if there be any praise, think on these things. [Philippians 4: 8 KJV]

PART FOUR

BLUEPRINTS—SCHEMATICS!

RESISTORS—POWER!

Part Three of *Everybody: Everybody Is A Somebody*, set my thoughts in motion to think through the scenario of an NHL Hockey Game. What I came away with at this time, was the pattern of the markings on the ice. I have dealt with The Neutral Zone because it is the place where we set up the play to attack the focus of the game—Score Goals. However, the Game does not begin at the blue line [the marker line which separates the Neutral zone and the Offensive [or Defensive Zone, depending on which team is attacking] Zone.

Four zones divide the playing surface on an ice hockey rink. One of these zones is only applicable to the goalie. To explain the zones we will imagine ourselves to be playing for one team. We will start with the end that our goalie defends. The end of the rink to the first blue line (75 feet) is the defensive zone—obviously, because we are defending our own goal in this zone. In between the two blue lines and including the center line (50 feet) is the neutral zone. The remaining 75 feet beyond the second blue line and where the opposing goaltender stands is the offensive zone.

At some point in life we need to Centre on The Point of Life! We are headed for Part Four of this book, this is where we will pick up more on this position of where each of us fit into God's plan, and how we deal with it, as we move towards the Finish Line of this book. Do we Begin with God, so we can end [The Game of Life] with God, or do we push all this aside and maintain what began in the Garden of Eden—Our Penchant For Living In The 'Selfie Zone!' However, we still have some ice to cover, on which we often find ourselves on thin ice—The Slippery Zone.

BLUEPRINTS AND SCHEMATICS

are simply directions or plans to build from. Without plans nothing can be accomplished. Without plans, I would say everything happens by accident, or by chance. In "The Good Old Hockey Game," it would not make much sense for professional hockey teams to show up in front of thousands of fans in hopes of entertaining them with hopes of coming out as the "Grand Winner," which culminates at "The Stanley Cup—or the trophy which a team receives at the end of the season game, no matter if it is professional or amateur, without a "Game Plan." When we played "Scrub Hockey," street or pond hockey—, it was not so much because someone made a game plan for winning a prize; it was just a bunch of kids out to have a good time.

Resistors are controllers in a system of Power Sources, which distribute just the right amount of energy, of whatever sort it is, so just the right result is achieved at the end point of the system, where we use the power in so many ways—ways too numerous to highlight here; one example is, the electricity in our homes.

In the "Good Old Hockey Game," and in life, we are introduced to many plans for our future. Many resistances [resistors] fall into the category of those we do not like so much, because they may change the blueprint we had outlined for ourselves. Then there are those power sources which kind of flow into our lives in good ways, so as to propel us forward onto the best builders plans we could imagine.

Sometimes, bad things happen, in fact "Bad Things Do Happen more often than we want them to, as if we ever want them to show up." If we manage these situations well, life may end up the better for having experienced the bad times. At other times, if we get too much of the "Good Life," we may be detracted from being any good to anybody but ourselves—in the end we die with hordes of stuff but condemned to Eternal Damnation—Go Figure!

IT WOULD BE GREAT TO KNOW FOR SURE HOW WE GOT HERE!

Thus the heavens and the earth were finished, and all the host of them. And on the seventh day God ended his work which he had made; and he rested on the seventh day from all his work which he had made. And God blessed the seventh day and sanctified it: because that in it he had rested from all his work which God created and made.

These are the generations of the heavens and of the earth when they were created, in the day that the Lord God made the earth and the heavens, and every plant of the field before it was in the earth, and every herb of the field before it grew: for the Lord God had not caused it to rain upon the earth, and there was not a man to till the ground. But there went up a mist from the earth and watered the whole face of the ground. And the Lord God formed man of the dust of the ground and breathed into his nostrils the breath of life; and man became a living soul. And the Lord God planted a garden eastward in Eden; and there he put the man whom he had formed. And out of the ground made the Lord God to grow every tree that is pleasant to the sight, and good for food; the tree of life also in the midst of the garden, and the tree of knowledge of good and evil. And a river went out of Eden to water the garden; and from thence it was parted and became into four heads. The name of the first is Pison: that is it which compasseth the whole land of Havilah, where there is gold; and the gold of that land is good: there is bdellium and the onyx stone. And the name of the second river is Gihon: the same is it that compasseth the whole land of Ethiopia. And the name of the third river is Hiddekel: that is it which goeth toward the east of Assyria. And the fourth river is Euphrates.

And the Lord God took the man and put him into the garden of Eden to dress it and to keep it. And the Lord God commanded the man, saying, Of every tree of the garden thou mayest freely eat, but of the tree of the knowledge of good and evil, thou shalt not eat of it: for in the day that thou eatest thereof thou shalt surely die. [Genesis 2: 1-17 KJV]

God simply said, "Do not eat from the Tree of The Knowledge of Good and Evil. IF you do, you will surely die."

The "Neutral Zone" can be a place where we step back and take a 'Selah' moment [respite, rest] to just think things over and settle personal issues so we gain strength to "Go The Distance." There is a "Neutral Zone" in medical terminology; there is a "Neutral Zone" in football terminology; there is a Neutral Zone [demilitarized zone] in war; there is a Neutral Zone in the area of resistors and power systems [Re Voltage Regulators—in some power substations there are regulators that keep the voltage within certain predetermined limits, but there is a range of voltage in-between during which no changes are made, such as between 112 and 118 volts (the deadband is 6 volts), or between 215 to 225 volts (deadband is 10 volts)], and the list extends to other areas.

What about Life?

—There Is No Neutral Zone—

17th Chapter

TRUTH IS: There is no neutral ground in the universe. Every square inch, every split second is claimed by God, and counterclaimed by Satan. [C.S. Lewis]

TRUTH IS: We are not living in a world where all roads are radii of a circle and where all, if followed long enough, will therefore draw gradually nearer and finally meet at the center—rather in a world where every road, after a few miles, forks into two, and each of those into two again, and at each fork, you must make a decision. [C.S. Lewis]

Chapter 17
NEUTRAL OR NOT NEUTRAL?

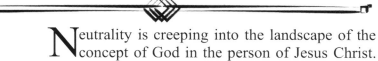

Neutrality is creeping into the landscape of the concept of God in the person of Jesus Christ. This perspective of spirituality has actually been in play for a long time—I want to say fifty to sixty years now. We have grown up to believe "Neutrality" was God's Plan.

'Neutrality' suggests we are not helping the concept of the "Reality of God!" I might rather say from my perspective, it seems the majority of folks do not support the Reality of God as a very present intimacy of the very moment we breath in the air someone gave us to keep us existing in the physical capacity. One definition puts it this way:

Neutrality is the state of not supporting or helping either side in a conflict, disagreement, etc.—impartiality.

The space, or The Gap, between 'agreement' on an issue and 'disagreement' of said issue, is spreading wider every day. This is where 'neutrality' often sets in; if neutrality is not the order of the day, we often see 'Intentional Resistance' to what was once more of a considered fact in a larger part than it is today—The Existence of GOD! As we get farther afield [in distance] from our roots, and farther back even into what we think of as "Ancient Days," we become more intent to accept the 'New' rather than the seemingly ingrained [established, unshakable] truths of the past, to accept most anything—Atheism, and New Atheism are front runners in this race towards an 'Eternity" of one sort or another.

Let's look for a few moments at '*The Gap*' between 'agreement and disagreement.' "Neutrality, or plain out "Intentional Resistance," are the participants of our race of time to get through life.

I defined 'Neutrality' as being "the state of not supporting or helping either side in a conflict, disagreement—impartiality." To better fully understand 'Neutrality,' let's look at some further expressions of the word—"disinterest, non-interference, non-partisanship"—the story gets even more complex as we add words associated with these, please look with me at some of these:

Detachment, disinterest, dispassion, equitableness, fair-mindedness, impartiality, justice, objectiveness, rightfulness!

Depending on the context of what we are expressing, these suggestive words are miles apart from each other in the gap between 'agreement and disagreement.' On the one hand, they suggest we are partners in the race through life, to find solutions to our issues. Some words that are associated with 'Neutrality,' are detachment, disinterest, dispassion. I keep looking; I see the words, fairmindedness, objectiveness—and I say, if we are interested in finding a resolution [neutral], how can we say we are disinterested or dispassionate? If we are disinterested, how can we say we are Objective? How can we say we have a goal or purpose in mind? If there is no Object [reason], how, may I ask, does this put us on Neutral Ground?

While in a state of neutrality we are not helping any situation. When we encounter someone who is expressing their view of God, and we say we are neutral, are we not in effect saying, "Don't Count On Me!" ''I am not interested!' 'I am Dispassionate!' When we are here on "Neutral Ground" we lose effectiveness—we do not lose our Inherent Worth. Inherent worth always leaves us with a chance of increasing our Book Value, by how we handle life and its issues— for ourselves and for others.

While we are in a state of Neutrality we still have a 'chance' to make a difference. If we make the right moves; if we take the chance of thinking through the whole picture of Reality from beginning to the end, we have a chance to increase our Market Value, as opposed to decreasing it and going Bankrupt!

Sometimes other people ask us to help them with or through a situation, or just help them with a task, this can put us into a state of neutrality. While here, we can be a part of the problem, saying, 'Don't count me,' leaving us far from agreement. On the other hand, we could say, *You Can Count On Me*! It is time to decide.

Songwriters—Ari Levine, Peter Hernandez, Philip Lawrence, wrote *You Can Count On Me*; Ari Levine along with Bruno Mars and Philip Lawrence were a part of The Smeezingtons. I looked at a few of their songs and they are kind of down to earth, not neutral about how they feel for the folks they sing about. What a concept—someone asks for help, and we say, *You Can Count On Me.* Better yet is, if we see someone in need, we let them know by our actions, they can count on us!

Another group which were my 'Favs' at one time was Abba. One song, especially, which has crossed my path in memory, more often quite often—more often than not, is, *Take a Chance On Me.* This pictures for me a scene of someone inviting us [me] to step into The Gap and cancel out 'Neutral Ground!' I hear a little voice saying to me, 'Count On Me,' this is definite 'I Am Enough!' In my previous book, *Bridging The Gap*, this is the theme of the book. In *Everybody: Everybody Is A Somebody*, this theme comes across as inserts; in reality, it could also be the theme here.

So, how does Neutrality help us in the Game of Life? Does it stay out of the path, to find solutions. Is it an area we can bend towards thinking time, to where we can come to consensus of being there for our neighbor—who ever this may be!

The lyrics of *You Can Count On Me*, suggest, if we are lost, as if out on the sea of life, we can know there is Someone who is searching to find us. The Songwriters here, suggest, they are that someone. I am talking about a different Someone. You may get the drift, but if you don't, it is Jesus! The Bible is like this song suggests. Psalm 139, a favorite, talks about being there for us in this way:

> O LORD, thou hast searched me, and known me. Thou knowest my downsitting and mine uprising, thou understandest my thought afar off. Thou compassest my path and my lying down, and art acquainted with all my ways. For there is not a word in my tongue, but, lo, O LORD, thou knowest it altogether. Thou hast beset me behind and before, and laid thine hand upon me. Such knowledge is too wonderful for me; it is high, I cannot attain unto it. Whither shall I go from thy spirit? or whither shall I flee from thy presence? If I ascend up into heaven, thou art there: if I make my bed in hell, behold, thou art there.

If I take the wings of the morning, and dwell in the uttermost parts of the sea; even there shall thy hand lead me, and thy right hand shall hold me. If I say, Surely the darkness shall cover me; even the night shall be light about me. Yea, the darkness hideth not from thee; but the night shineth as the day: the darkness and the light are both alike to thee. For thou hast possessed my reins: thou hast covered me in my mother's womb. I will praise thee; for I am fearfully and wonderfully made: marvellous are thy works; and that my soul knoweth right well. My substance was not hid from thee, when I was made in secret, and curiously wrought in the lowest parts of the earth. Thine eyes did see my substance, yet being unperfect; and in thy book all my members were written, which in continuance were fashioned, when as yet there was none of them. How precious also are thy thoughts unto me, O God! how great is the sum of them! If I should count them, they are more in number than the sand: when I awake, I am still with thee. [vs 1-18 KJV]

Search me, O God, and know my heart: try me, and know my thoughts: And see if there be any wicked way in me, and lead me in the way everlasting. [vs 23-24 KJV]

It is no easy matter to capture the story of the Neutrality of Life. By the time we go around in circles for a while, trying to come to grips with it, we may get frustrated because we cannot figure out how to get the job done. Though it's not easy, if we each do our part, as small as that may be, we can make an impression in the frame of life around us. This creates a 'Pay It Forward' approach to go beyond what we may grasp—if everybody does a little. Sadly, this will not happen in this life. It could, if we all began at the same 'Starting Line.' We need to begin at the same Starting Line to Finish at The Same Finish Line—this is The Bottom Line!

Everybody: Everybody Is A Somebody, laid out for us in such a way so as for us to get a grip on life's intended purpose to be fulfilled. I am nearly in that groove. I have yet a few more words—for your sake, hopefully not too many [I could go on indefinitely, or so it seems]. To get my message across to my reading audience, I have thought it important to include many aspects of life, this book began with thoughts on Book Value and Market Value, and how we can make a Spiritual connection by thinking in these terms.

Book Value is the actual worth of an asset of the company, whereas Market Share is just a projected value of the firm's asset's worth in the marketplace. Book Value is akin to the value of the firm's equity. On The Other Hand, Market Value shows the current market value of the firm or any asset.

Is book value the same as market value?

Book value is not necessarily the same as an asset's market value, since market value is based on supply and demand and perceived value, while book value is simply an accounting calculation.

Somewhere in the whole story we all fit into, we need to calculate how we fit into it, and why we were slated to be in a particular niche of the whole story. Too often we are not satisfied to be in the particular place created for us by our Maker. Don't get me wrong, being in that particular place 'Does Not Have To Limit Us!' There are borders within every scenario of life, and these can keep us on track, so we do not get messed up. However, there are mega opportunities within these parameters, enough for a lifetime—if God is allowed to be in charge. I know, not everyone will buy into what I say, but when I think in The Eternal Sense, and what it is God has planned for this to be, and how we are all uniquely planned to be an integral part of this plan, I just wish to accentuate or heighten our expectations for this Eternity.

Can I ask you to take another look at how I began this *Chapter 17?*

NEUTRAL OR NOT NEUTRAL?

Neutrality, or plain out "Intentional Resistance.

It is creeping into the landscape of the concept of God, in the person of Jesus Christ; in fact, this perspective of spirituality has been in play for a long time; I want to say, fifty to sixty years now.

I have talked at some length about 'Neutrality,' albeit, maybe not a sufficient portion to cover all the bases. However, I feel the need to move on so we can 'Do This Thing!'

—Plain out Intentional Resistance—

Resistance—What is this? It comes in many forms. Let's begin by checking out what this means:

"Resistance is a noun. It is the act or power of resisting, opposing, or withstanding some other issue or belief—it is the opposition offered by one thing, force, etc., to another thing.

Electricity also has to do with resistance; it is called ohmic resistance. It is one of the properties of a conductor by virtue of which the passage of current is opposed, causing electric energy to be transformed into heat: Equal to the voltage across the conductor divided by the current flowing in the conductor: usually measured in ohms: Abbreviated by the R factor. It's a conductor or coil offering such opposition: Resistor.

Psychiatry: Has an opposition to an attempt to bring repressed thoughts or feelings into consciousness [often initial capital letter]. There are underground organizations composed of groups of private individuals working as an opposition force in a conquered country to overthrow the occupying power, usually by acts of sabotage, guerrilla warfare—the resistance during the German occupation in World War II."

There is a resistance level in the Stock Exchange:
Resistance in a technical analysis, is a price level that a rising stock cannot seem to overcome. Once a stock reaches its resistance level, it often stalls and reverses. Resistance is caused by heavy selling that overpowers buying, and typically occurs at specific resistance price levels.

The Bible speaks to the issue of resistance in many ways and in many contexts. One passage which addresses this issue is in the Book of James: *Submit yourselves therefore to God. Resist the devil, and he will flee from you.* [James 4:7 KJV]

The context suggests resistance is a prerequisite; a necessary requirement for keeping On The Straight and Narrow! When we begin by serving God because we have formed a relationship with Him, and He with us, we are called to 'Submit' to Him because of the love factor of getting to know Him. If we fail in submitting to God, we end up yielding to the devil instead of 'Resisting' him.

Now, getting back to 'Intentional Resistance,' yes, what I have just stated is an act of staying close to God. However, when we put the same words to use in another context, it has an entirely different look. When we 'Resist' God, as in when He calls us to serve Him and Him only, the Intentional Resistance we display by our actions, is an opposition to Who and What God is—The Creator of all that ever was or is. This is like when we get 'In The Face' of someone physically, over an opposing view we or they may have. This can get messy, and the stronger party usually wins—God is the stronger party, when it comes down to the bottom-line. Make no mistake, there is always a Bottom-Line!

Pride goeth before destruction, and a haughty spirit before a fall. Wherefore he saith, God resisteth the proud, but giveth grace unto the humble. [Provers 16:18 KJV]

There is a considerable amount said in the Bible about proper resistance, and there is much said regarding Improper, Intentional Resistance, and God also talks about another scenario of these things—*God Resists The Proud*! Two can play the 'Resistance Game.' Us resisting God will come at a great cost: An eternity without His presence; an eternity where we will never have access to Him in any relational way that will change our eternal consequence; this is by the choice we make about God!

Neutrality is the state of not supporting or helping either side in a conflict, disagreement—impartiality.

There is an emotional, spiritual, mental, psychosomatic, or self-induced 'No-Man's-Land' sandwiched between 'accord or consensus,' and 'discord or conflict'—It is 'Neutrality!' While living in this zone of Neutrality we never seem to find the means to bring any issue to resolution. The 'Old' way of things seems to be anathema or loathing to us, while the 'New,' the conflicting mindset, is to fight anything which once was, because it no longer satisfies; this is because our desires are farther and farther away from what God wanted for us "In The Beginning!" Every time we escape, leave one room through one door, we enter another room, and that one of another character or makeup.

"Every exit is an entry somewhere else." [Tom Stoppard, British Playwright; Brainy Quotes]

Part Four: Blueprints—Schematics! Resistors—Power!

The Neutral Zone is central to moving through life from one position to the next: For God—Against God; For Peace—For War; For Neutrality—For one-sidedness, or indifference. If we remain neutral we never make up our mind about an issue. If we are non-neutral, we make up our mind about an issue, we are one-sided, possibly indifferent—leaving no room for coming to a consensus. The neutral zone presents us with a transition route of travel emotively, moving us between an old way to a new way. The old may have left, but the new us has not come to grips with everything in our new environment. I am speaking in the approach of making internal emotional decisions.

When we are in the Neutral Zone of life we take heavy losses—possibly, in the area of our self-confidence. Maybe we do not produce as well or feel we are as Valuable to Life as much as we once thought we were. Neutrality has it's deficits.

The Neutral Zone gives us options: Face danger, or Face Adventurous Prospects. The adventurous opportunities come because much of the old baggage we were carrying is dumped off, allowing for us to add the new tenets, principles, or precepts to our repertoire or range of living, so we can once again produce meaningful life in us and others. Within this zone there are dangers as the possibility arises that we may go the overkill route and forget there are borders to every opportunity life offers us. There is a tendency for us to try to fast-track our hope and dreams; this may lead to depressive counterparts or emotional colleagues if things do not pan out as quickly as we expect them to come to fruition.

As we transition from one generation to another we may be left in a zone of involuntary resistance. We may not want to be left behind to live life only and always in the fully framed mentality of everything we have or had, as being the only thing worth living for. Someone [Doris Day] sang, *The Future's Not Ours To See—Ka Sera Sera*. It speaks of when we were little. we grew up a certain way, and had to look at what lay ahead, and wonder if it would be something we could come to terms with.

When we look at the picture thoroughly, we come to where we need to step out of the Neutral Zone and begin to look for some of the positives which can lead us to the future with hope and a vision for the future, without giving up the morality and comfort level of what we had in the past. Life can still be Good!

I was just accosted by "Memories." Some years ago now, Gordon Lightfoot sang a song called, *Ribbon Of Darkness*, and moments ago this song came to mind as I was writing these thoughts just past. When we think too much about what might have been, without seemingly any concept of a future hope because of what we appear to have lost, we may be like the words of the song portray for us. There are clouds of darkness hanging over any chance to experience the 'The Good Life' ever again. What a horrible place for any of us to live, or might I say, "EXIST," but it happens all the time. I see people in this dilemma fairly often.

There is no "Neutrality in DNA or RNA. These entities tell us exactly where we fit into the life cycle of our individual heritage. DNA and RNA tell it like it is. The evidence of our makeup, heritage or ancestry tells us where we came from within the gene pool [source and surroundings of a population of which each of us is a part of] we arrived from. But DNA and RNA cannot define who we will become. They give us a picture of the inherent value of the past parentage we came from; they tell us much in relationship to forensic investigation on the crime scenes which are often left without clues, until a deeper investigation takes place. I like watching Forensic Files on TV.

I'm not a Scientist, or a knowledgeable source with enough smarts to put it all together in my own mind, let alone getting to where I can convince anybody else about how we got here. My brother thinks I am the smartest person in the world, or at least smarter than he is [said tongue in cheek]. Sometimes he phones me about an issue he wants some input on, he says, because I am so smart. I never told my brother I was smart, he just thought he had that part figured out on his own—maybe because I am the older brother, and older people are supposed to be smarter, or just because of how I conduct myself?

I figure, without Y and X in proper balance with one another, we will never produce 'another,' another [another person]. According to the resources I have searched out, 'we,' [you or I], would not be here to write or read what lies here on the pages of *Everybody: Everybody Is A Somebody*, without these things. Something Very Important, or SOMEONE VERY IMPORTANT was the only COG IN THE WHEEL.

We not only have the XY chromosome scenario to produce us 'Beautiful People,' we have what seems likened to an XYZ scenario; meaning we are the finished product, and one that has all the capacity and or capabilities of fitting the DNA and RNA Scenario. DNA is DeoxyriboNucleic Acid; this is like a blueprint of biological guidelines that a living organism must follow to exist and remain functional—like building anything, we need a plan or a blueprint. It may not be blue, but it is a printout [Blueprint] we can use to follow the direction we need to accomplish the building process. The 'Who' revolves around The Architect. Life does not go far before adversity challenges us. Without guidelines, advancement stops; ruin is the result.

Downhill ski racecourses are often marked by ribbons of blue spritzed across the white, snowy surface. The simple curves might be an interference for audiences, but prove to be active to both the triumph and care of the competitors. The paint helps as an attendant would, to help maneuver the racers to be positioned to the fastest route to the bottom of the hill; added to this, the distinction of the paint against the snow suggests depth awareness to the racers, which is paramount to their physical well being when traveling at such high rates of rapidity.

What is the RNA? For a long time I only knew about The DNA. If we want the whole picture we need both factors. Now I Know 'The ABC's of RNA, Ribonucleic Acid [DeoxyRiboNucleic]. The RNA is like the Builder and or contractor who needs the DNA [Blueprint] to fashion whatever construct they are intending to construct. Between the two, the 'DNA and the RNA,' the RNA can perform many differing jobs on a job site, while The DNA is more secure, the constant or unchanging planner [God initiated]; it holds more complex information and for longer periods of time than does The RNA [likened to a contractor, subtrade].

'Deoxy:' Defined as follows, is a merging system telling us that something is being removed to form its own word so when we put them back together as one word we will understand the process that the whole of life and existence is trying to teach us. 'Deoxygenated,' we use the concept here in the formation of compound words, to get a fuller understanding of the whole of a thing. [ibid—(spoken elsewhere)]

DNA and RNA cannot define who we will become. All of us were of huge Value when we were born. It matters not at all if we were rich or poor; black or white; it matter not at all if we had slanted eyes or round eyes; it matters not at all if we were born in the ghetto, or we were born in the fanciest, most well equipped hospital in the world—our Value as being a Person, is unmatched by anything else in the world. God said so, and this is good enough for me!

> For God so loved the world, that he gave his only begotten Son, that whosoever believeth in him should not perish, but have everlasting life. [John 3:16 KJV]

I have covered much territory with a word count over one-hundred and sixty-thousand words; which if you have read up until this very place in *Everybody: Everybody Is A Somebody*, you will have read most of the thoughts I have expressed surrounding the "VALUE OF HUMAN LIFE!"

We were not all born with some of the amenities which allow for others to become more successful because of their ease of access to the tools necessary to attain to degrees of success which suggest they must have come through the most predominant education facilities of the world. Not everyone has this access, this is not too hard to see as we look out across our world. Hey—even the community we live in, big or small, has folks who do not have the resources to become famous. However, within the parameters of where we live, we can have an equivalent value as those who headline the media of whatever sort it is. All of us can make a difference; sometimes, those who have more of the necessary tools to assist others, just need to lend a helping hand so the less privileged in the area of earthy goods, and or the mental capacity—to enable change for themselves, can still present themselves at FULL VALUE as HUMAN BEINGS!

> There was a man of the Pharisees, named Nicodemus, a ruler of the Jews: The same came to Jesus by night, and said unto him, Rabbi, we know that thou art a teacher come from God: for no man can do these miracles that thou doest, except God be with him. Jesus answered and said unto him, Verily, verily, I say unto thee, except a man be born again, he cannot see the kingdom of God.

Nicodemus saith unto him, how can a man be born when he is old? Can he enter the second time into his mother's womb, and be born? Jesus answered, Verily, verily, I say unto thee, except a man be born of water and of the Spirit, he cannot enter into the kingdom of God. That which is born of the flesh is flesh; and that which is born of the Spirit is spirit.

Marvel not that I said unto thee, Ye must be born again. The wind bloweth where it listeth, and thou hearest the sound thereof, but canst not tell whence it cometh, and whither it goeth: so is every one that is born of the Spirit. Nicodemus answered and said unto him, How can these things be? Jesus answered and said unto him, Art thou a master of Israel, and knowest not these things?

Verily, verily, I say unto thee, We speak that we do know, and testify that we have seen; and ye receive not our witness. If I have told you earthly things, and ye believe not, how shall ye believe, if I tell you of heavenly things? And no man hath ascended up to heaven, but he that came down from heaven, even the Son of man which is in heaven.

And as Moses lifted up the serpent in the wilderness, even so must the Son of man be lifted up: That whosoever believeth in him should not perish, but have eternal life. For God so loved the world, that he gave his only begotten Son, that whosoever believeth in him should not perish, but have everlasting life. For God sent not his Son into the world to condemn the world; but that the world through him might be saved. He that believeth on him is not condemned: but he that believeth not is condemned already, because he hath not believed in the name of the only begotten Son of God. And this is the condemnation, that light is come into the world, and men loved darkness rather than light, because their deeds were evil. For every one that doeth evil hateth the light, neither cometh to the light, lest his deeds should be reproved. But he that doeth truth cometh to the light, that his deeds may be made manifest, that they are wrought in God. After these things came Jesus and his disciples into the land of Judaea; and there he tarried with them, and baptized. And John also was baptizing in Aenon near to Salim, because there was much water there: and they came, and were baptized.

For John was not yet cast into prison. Then there arose a question between some of John's disciples and the Jews about purifying. And they came unto John, and said unto him, Rabbi, he that was with thee beyond Jordan, to whom thou barest witness, behold, the same baptizeth, and all men come to him. John answered and said, A man can receive nothing, except it be given him from heaven.

Ye yourselves bear me witness, that I said, I am not the Christ, but that I am sent before him. He that hath the bride is the bridegroom: but the friend of the bridegroom, which standeth and heareth him, rejoiceth greatly because of the bridegroom's voice: this my joy therefore is fulfilled. He must increase, but I must decrease. He that cometh from above is above all: he that is of the earth is earthly, and speaketh of the earth: he that cometh from heaven is above all. And what he hath seen and heard, that he testifieth; and no man receiveth his testimony.

He that hath received his testimony hath set to his seal that God is true. For he whom God hath sent speaketh the words of God: for God giveth not the Spirit by measure unto him. The Father loveth the Son, and hath given all things into his hand. He that believeth on the Son hath everlasting life: and he that believeth not the Son shall not see life; but the wrath of God abideth on him. [John 3 KJV]

Chapter 17 leaves us with questions to answer to The Higher Power we may never fully understand in this life. God, in The Person of Jesus Christ, has the answer to all our questions. If we are willing, God in The Person of The Holy Spirit will help us through to all the understanding we need to fully satisfy our greatest need. However, many people cannot understand the simplicity of the whole matter of Who God is, and what He wants for every person; every person has had and still does have the INHERENT RIGHT to be a part of the Family of God—the invitation was, always has been, and still is open to EVERYONE.

Many are the opportunities, and many are the resources which have and still present the opportunity to know about God, and to know Him personally. Not a day goes by that we are not told in media sources of every sort—God Loves Us!

Now faith is the substance of things hoped for, the evidence of things not seen. For by it the elders obtained a good report. Through faith we understand that the worlds were framed by the word of God, so that things which are seen were not made of things which do appear.

By faith Abel offered unto God a more excellent sacrifice than Cain, by which he obtained witness that he was righteous, God testifying of his gifts: and by it he being dead yet speaketh. By faith Enoch was translated that he should not see death; and was not found, because God had translated him: for before his translation he had this testimony, that he pleased God.

But without faith it is impossible to please him: for he that cometh to God must believe that he is, and that he is a rewarder of them that diligently seek him.

If we confess our sins, he is faithful and just to forgive us our sins, and to cleanse us from all unrighteousness. [1 John 1:9 KJV]

For by grace are ye saved through faith; and that not of yourselves: it is the gift of God: Not of works, lest any man should boast. [Ephesians 2:8-9 KJV]

For all have sinned, and come short of the glory of God; [Romans 3:23 KJV]

For the wages of sin is death; but the gift of God is eternal life through Jesus Christ our Lord. [Romans 6:23 KJV]

But what saith it? The word is nigh thee, even in thy mouth, and in thy heart: that is, the word of faith, which we preach; that if thou shalt confess with thy mouth the Lord Jesus, and shalt believe in thine heart that God hath raised him from the dead, thou shalt be saved. For with the heart man believeth unto righteousness; and with the mouth confession is made unto salvation.

For the scripture saith, Whosoever believeth on him shall not be ashamed. For there is no difference between the Jew and the Greek: for the same Lord over all is rich unto all that call upon him. For whosoever shall call upon the name of the Lord shall be saved.

How then shall they call on him in whom they have not believed? and how shall they believe in him of whom they have not heard? and how shall they hear without a preacher? And how shall they preach, except they be sent? as it is written, How beautiful are the feet of them that preach the gospel of peace, and bring glad tidings of good things! But they have not all obeyed the gospel. For Esaias saith, Lord, who hath believed our report? So then faith cometh by hearing, and hearing by the word of God. But I say, Have they not heard? Yes verily, their sound went into all the earth, and their words unto the ends of the world. [Romans 10: 8-18 KJV]

PART FIVE

UNDERSTANDING THE "REAL:"

THE VISIBLE!

AND THE INVISIBLE!

"TRUE REALITY!"

The Realities of Life live out before us more vividly at times than we may wish they did. Often, we do not get far into our day before one unwanted episode after another crowds our day to where we do not believe we will make it through the day! The Episodes of the different topics or themes of a any 'Season of Life' are so numerous we cannot number them from one to ten; many times these 'episodes' figure out consecutively, 'not necessarily coordinately, but this is another picture'— if we picture these thoughts in the same order or degree; equal in rank or importance.

However, these infractions and or interruptions swarm around us to inhibit or inhabit our regular space [whatever this means]; what seem like the spatial [three or four dimensional] zones we all live in the reality of every day, but we also have openings in our day to live—Really Live!

The 'Seasons' of our lives may look different in make-up, depending on age, surroundings, and a host of other entities—each 'Season' presents the same scenarios. We get up in the morning, we eat, work, play, sleep—and do it again 'Tomorrow' [the physical tomorrow or the eternal tomorrows, which show up 'Consecutively or serially, and carry on 'Concurrently,'] through every Season of life. The calendar year presents us with Four Seasons, but life and living may produce a few more—like The Television Series we watch, they often run what seems to be 'Endlessly.'

Someone said, "If you can't do the time, don't do the crime!" When we go to court the Judge may remind of us of this if we balk at the sentence he pronounces for our episode of criminal activity. We each owe our term of life some due diligence. If there is a "Creator," as I believe there is, and He made everything while only thinking of us as being His main interest, 'and He did,' then does it not fit that we honor His wishes and not have to end up in His courtroom at the end of OUR TERM. Life does not need to be like a Prison Sentence, often this is how we view life; this is a sad picture of living for anywhere from one nanosecond of life to anywhere upwards from that, to even over a hundred years for some.

We looked at some of the Seasons of Life, those times when not everything runs smoothly. Then we have those times when everything run so smoothly we don't even notice what we often think of as the loud clanking of the clock's ticker as we plod through life [LG]—Life Is Good! We all want this to be the case. It can be, but there will always be some of the [LB] Life is Bad situations—count on it! We need to handle life within a set of parameters which incorporate 'all of life' and its failures and promises.

The Bible often speaks in "Parables." Parables are simply stories which lay out the examples of the Realities we all face.

> —What woman having ten pieces of silver, if she lose one piece, doth not light a candle, and sweep the house, and seek diligently till she find it? And when she hath found it, she calleth her friends and her neighbors together, saying, Rejoice with me; for I have found the piece which I had lost. Likewise, I say unto you, there is joy in the presence of the angels of God over one sinner that repenteth. [Luke 15:8-10; KJV]

In the Garden of Eden we lost one of the two coins, so to speak; Adam and Eve saw to that. There were two trees in the middle of the garden; there were many more trees, but two tree in particular sealed our fate for this life, until we found the other coin, which brought back what we lost during the realities of this life at the time—they were set apart for us to experience as the fruits of searching for the lost coin, as life continued. Adam and Eve chose the path of tomorrow for us, as they did for themselves. We know this as the journey we have all experienced. Let's not judge them too harshly; had it been Jacob and Rebekah; had it been you or I; the story would have been the same.

The parables [stories] of The Bible give us clarity, and Jesus carried on the practise of telling a story to get a point across. Please allow me to pass on one of the greatest parables—it gives us an image to help us understand how we can finish The Final Chapter of life, so as to glean the results we all want—Eternal Satisfaction.

> Jesus said: A certain man had two sons; the younger of them said to his father, Father, give me the portion of goods that falleth to me. And he divided unto them his living.

And not many days after the younger son gathered all together, and took his journey into a far country, and there wasted his substance with riotous living. And when he had spent all, there arose a mighty famine in that land; and he began to be in want. And he went and joined himself to a citizen of that country, and he sent him into his fields to feed swine. And he would fain have filled his belly with the husks that the swine did eat: and no man gave unto him. And when he came to himself, he said, how many hired servants of my father's have bread enough and to spare, and I perish with hunger! I will arise and go to my father, and will say unto him, Father, I have sinned against heaven, and before thee, and am no more worthy to be called thy son: Make me as one of thy hired servants.

And he arose, and came to his father. But when he was yet a great way off, his father saw him, and had compassion, and ran, and fell on his neck, and kissed him. And the son said unto him, Father, I have sinned against heaven, and in thy sight, and am no more worthy to be called thy son. But the father said to his servants, Bring forth the best robe, and put it on him; and put a ring on his hand, and shoes on his feet: And bring hither the fatted calf, and kill it; and let us eat, and be merry: For this my son was dead, and is alive again; he was lost, and is found.

Now his elder son was in the field: and as he came and drew nigh to the house, he heard music and dancing. And he called one of the servants, and asked what these things meant. And he said unto him, Thy brother is come; and thy father hath killed the fatted calf, because he hath received him safe and sound. And he was angry, and would not go in: therefore came his father out, and intreated him. And he answering said to his father, Lo, these many years do I serve thee, neither transgressed I at any time thy commandment: and yet thou never gavest me a kid, that I might make merry with my friends: But as soon as this thy son was come, which hath devoured thy living with harlots, thou hast killed for him the fatted calf. And he said unto him, Son, thou art ever with me, and all that I have is thine. It was meet that we should make merry, and be glad: for this thy brother was dead, and is alive again; and was lost, and is found. [Luke 15:11-32; KJV]

All of our Seasons of Life are not invisible; some seem to be invisible, like a devilish or spiritual spirit sometimes cropping up within us; others, the visible ones, have names [titles] which allow us to address them more easily. "Physical Pain" caused by a physical blow, like the whack of a hockey stick in the face of an opposing player, these try to impede our attack mode to score a goal against a goalie. This not only pains the player who got the stick in the face, the whole team feels the impact. It does not stop here, the player who raised his stick in his attack, also suffers in the penalty box, and or a suspension from the game. Now, his team also hurts from the incident. We all affect others by our infractions against life.

The turmoil of the mind over the many things we face in life are often hidden beneath the surface. When someone speaks harsh words to us, those which are underserved, we feel the emotional pain I just spoke about, but often, we suck it up on the outside, but it festers on the inside. This kind of pain is often felt more deeply, and the pain and suffering often lasts much longer than the 'whack of a stick in the face.'

The seasons of life entertain both of these scenarios, and many more. I could develop a whole book around this topic alone, but I will spare you this pain. I am just setting the stage for some of the pains of life, some of the seasons we live through, which not only involve us, but they pain God. When we deliberately go against His wishes, when He has given so much, and we continually break His heart, how do you think He feels. One place in the Bible Jesus said,

> "Oh Jerusalem, Jerusalem, how often did I want to cradle you in my arms, but you refused me, as being able to help you when you were going astray, or you were in pain [JBI Insight, my words of paraphrase]."

If, and when God was visible to us [when Jesus walked amongst us], did we have any easier time understanding Him? When He proposed, commanded, taught—that we should do more than consider Him, but obey Him, so as to get the best of the reality situations we would encounter. Did we acknowledge Him? Remember this chapter has to do with GOD, more than us: Who He is, why He was not recognized when He came [Jesus], and why He isn't recognized today.

Who, or What Will Be Left Behind:

[Not God: That's For Sure!]
Looking Forward To God!

18th Chapter

TRUTH IS: When we concentrate on our 'Leftovers' [Yesterday], we are always falling backwards, opposed to moving forward. Leftovers get stale quickly; tomorrow can be a brighter day, because there is hope for a freshness we can more easily digest. Any hope of 'Yesterday' [leftovers] is dead, if not properly kept; 'Tomorrow' [everything after today] has not yet arrived, so hope keeps our aspirations alive: New Birth is always exciting!

Therefore, if anyone is in Christ, he is a new creature; the old things passed away; behold, new things have come. [2 Corinthians 5:17]

Because he who is blessed in the earth will be blessed by the God of truth; and he who swears in the earth will swear by the God of truth; because the former troubles are forgotten, and because they are hidden from My sight! [Isaiah 65:16]

So also we, while we were children, were held in bondage under the elemental things of the world. But when the fullness of the time came, God sent forth His Son, born of a woman, born under the Law, so that He might redeem those who were under the Law, that we might receive the adoption as sons. [Galatians 4:3-5]

For He rescued us from the domain of darkness, and transferred us to the kingdom of His beloved Son, in whom we have redemption, the forgiveness of sins. [Colossians 1:13-14]

Do not call to mind the former things, or ponder things of the past. [Isaiah 43:18]

Brethren, I do not regard myself as having laid hold of it yet; but one thing I do: forgetting what lies behind and reaching forward to what lies ahead, I press on toward the goal for the prize of the upward call of God in Christ Jesus. [Philippians 3:13-14]

Chapter 18

THE FORGOTTEN ONE: GOD!

orget Me Not! If I read anything into these opening three words, it is this, "It is a cry of hope; it is a desperate heart rending cry for hope, which says, 'I want to have a Relationship with You!'" If we do not read well, and we think the suggestion here is a physical, sexual relationship, it is not. Within the guise of this world, if we talk like this without first framing a context which explains what we are suggesting, we can get into "Big Trouble." We need to look long and hard if necessary, to get the context of what I have just said,

"It is a cry of hope; it is a desperate heart rending cry for hope, which says, 'I want to have a Relationship with You!'"

In this world, if we go to where the 'UN-Christ Follower' subsists, we do not need to cry too long and hard to get the satisfactions of our desires. Just look around; physical attractions are everywhere; they are more prevalent today than they have ever been in history. The degree to which physical attraction goes, has "NO" Bounds!

When I plead with someone, and I say, "Forget Me Not," I suggest there are places outside of the parameters of physical pleasure. When our hearts cry out for the kind of "Relationship" I am talking about, there are caveats which stand out front and center for me: Love God; Love your neighbor. One scripture I refer to often is, Matthew 22: 36-40, the short versions says,

If you only do one thing well, do this, "Love God with all your heart, mind, body and soul—this is absolutely first if you want to find true "Love and Peace."

Secondly, and always second, there is no option for true 'Relationship:' Love your neighbor as you love yourself!

The true "Forget-Me-Not Flower" (Myosotis scorpioides) grows on tall, hairy stems which sometimes reach 2 feet in height. Charming, five-petaled, blue blooms with yellow centers explode from the stems from May through October. Flower petals are sometimes pink. Forget-me-not plants often grow near brooks and streams and other waters which offer the high humidity and moisture that is desirable to this species. [https://www.gardeningknowhow.com/ornamental/flowers/forget-me-nots/growing-forget-me-nots.htm]

Before I "Forget," and so I can follow through in some semblance of order, let me just show us where we are coming from, to get to where we are going—Make Sense? *Part Four* is called *Blueprints—Schematics! Resistors—Power! Chapter Seventeen*, is called *Neutral Or Not Neutral*; from here it is my plan to present God as the only "Blueprint" worth the effort for life. I boldly declare God to be The Only Power Source worth its weight in Gold! Added to this, I discussed "Neutrality and Non Neutrality."

God is fair, never has He been unjust; if we did not or do not follow the direction He laid out, and continues to lay out, then "Judgement" is all we can expect. There are no Eternal Bonuses apart from this if we "Forget God!"

The only caveats [qualifications] are, we need to be a sinner to have access to the promise of Salvation [and we are all born in this condition]; we need to be sorry we rejected God, in the Person of Jesus Christ; we need to ask God for forgiveness and believe He will be true to His Word. All of this requires faith. If we have no access to faith as yet, listen to what other Christ Followers are saying about God, and "Faith" will begin to build to where you can believe in God for Salvation. The Rest is up to God, through the Mercy and Grace He willingly and lovingly [believe it or not] extends. He would not have had to do any of these things, He is God, He could have nipped us in the bud when we failed to accept Him in The Garden of Eden.

'Neutrality' suggests we are not helping the concept of the "Reality of God!" I might rather say from my perspective, it seems the majority of folks do not support the Reality of God as a very present intimacy of the very moment we breath in the air someone gave us to keep us existing in the physical capacity.

404

One definition puts it this way:

Neutrality is the state of not supporting or helping either side in a conflict, disagreement—impartiality.

The space, or *The Gap*, between 'agreement' on an issue and 'disagreement' of said issue, is spreading wider every day. 'Neutrality' often sets in; if neutrality is not the order of the day, we often see 'Intentional Resistance' to what was once more of a considered fact in a larger part than it is today—The Existence of GOD! As we get farther afield [in distance] from our roots; farther back even into what we think of as "Ancient Days;" we become more intent to accept the 'New' rather than the seemingly ingrained [established, unshakable] truths of the past; to where we accept most anything—Atheism, and New Atheism are front runners in this race towards an 'Eternity" of one sort or another.

Forget Me Not!
Ramifications

Ramification: A means, consequence, development, complication, consequence, upshot, bifurcation, branch, branching, breaking, divarication, division, excrescence, extension, forking, offshoot, outgrowth, partition, radiation, result, sequel, subdivision, and subdividing.

Some of these words are easy to grasp, others need further investigation. Let's simply highlight even just a few of these words to come to consensus on what "ramification" means—complication, consequence, breaking, outgrowth, partition, radiation, result, sequel, subdivision, and subdividing. These synonyms make muddy waters quite clear. I will not go into the physical methods of making muddy water clear enough to drink, but there are possibly more ways than we know off hand. So, if our understanding of words, in this case, is a bit murky, there is hope. Writers, authors, and communicators of every sort, do this, or rather, they should do this— bring clarity. If 'we, those just mentioned,' muddy up clear water [make your life more difficult than it already was], then how do we make sense of our claim of being "Communicators!"

In 1954 The Louvin Brothers released a song entitled, *If We Forget God*. I was about ten years old when I first heard it. I haven't listened to it for a long time now, however, just the other day I was writing this *Chapter Eighteen* when these words came to me: "If We Forget God." I thought to myself, there is a song by this name, and my mind moved into search mode as I realized The Louvin Brothers [Charles and Ira] had sung this so many years ago. This is quite fitting for me here.

If we forget God, as far as we are concerned, there is no God; if there is no God, rulership [leadership] disintegrates [this is obvious in every facet of life]. If we forget God our Country faces doom and gloom. The narratives of the day, the photos in newspapers, magazines, and every communications outlet, displays what once was a criminal act—nudity, sexual acts—. A whole lot of other stuff is allowed full access to broadcast every conceivable act that once was considered a "SIN," even by those who did not believe Sin was as bad as "Christ-Followers" made it out to be. Children are bombarded with things even adults should not see and hear. Then, when life goes awry, we wonder why!

If we forget God, or believe He does not exist, we should not expect His mercy and grace when life turns on us—or we think the God we do not acknowledge, should do a better job. We say, "Why Would God Let This Happen!" If we forget God, His opposite, the Devil will have his party and he will "Have Us For Lunch."

The evil of this world is the theme of so many songs, people get a thrill out of this degeneration; if we sing about Jesus [God], they are ashamed to be near us. Often, people are offended by anything called God, Jesus; the person transmitting this message is considered to be as though forcing an ideology on someone against their will. No one needs to believe what is being said or sung; they can reject it; no one is forcing religion down their throats.

If We Forget God!
What Then?

Only take heed to thyself, and keep thy soul diligently, lest thou forget the things which thine eyes have seen, and lest they depart from thy heart all the days of thy life: but teach them thy sons, and thy sons' sons; [Deuteronomy 4:9 KJV]

We go through life in a state of thinking everything is "CONSTANT!" We have the tendency to 'feel as if feelings are objective:' "REALITY; REALLY!" We wakeup every morning as if we are in the movie *Groundhog Day*, where we wakeup at six o'clock because the alarm goes off, and the song comes on the radio, *I Got You Babe*—. Sonny and Cher made this a big hit.

Some of the words are reworked by me to say the equivalent. The thoughts expressed are exposed in the song by Sonny and Cher, but the words Origin came from farther back than we can really calculate. Origin: What does this suggest? Well, it tells me clearly, something or Someone got life as we know it started, and that, with an end in sight—as far as "Physicality" goes.

Some of the "words" say 'we are still young, and we do not understand—other 'words' say in effect we will not understand until we grow older—they say they do not know if they can believe what they do not know could be real, but this they know, "THEY HAVE EACH OTHER!" Please listen to the irony of the scenario of Sonny and Cher. A few of the "Words" of *I Got You Babe*, go something like this,

> You are wearing my ring on your finger [this suggests another song to me *Does My Ring Hurt Your Finger* by Charlie Pride], when I get afraid, you are always around, they are sure of the spring flowers, they suggest that with each other, they cannot go wrong, as long as they have their hand in each other's hand, no mountain is too hard to conquer—. The whole story of this song is beautiful! Thank You, "Sonny and Cher!

Problem: Well, Sonny and Cher were no longer enough for each other—they Divorced. Sonny died in 1998 after hitting a tree while skiing at [get this] "Heavenly Ski Resort at Lake Tahoe, at the age of 62. Cher was born May/1946, just shy of four months before my Big Day [My BDAY September/1946]. The moral of the STORY is this, "It Appears That Nothing Bearing The Name 'Physicality' will last forever. Did God know all about this? Psalm 139 is one of the Scriptures which assures me of this; I have used it in this book already, so because of time and space I will not repeat it here, except to say this, "O lord, thou hast searched me, and known me [vs 1]. Search me, O God, and know my heart: Try me, and know my thoughts [vs 23]: " And To This I Say," DO IT AGAIN LORD!"

This morning, as I thought about "WORDS," I thought about the scripture in John 1: 1-5;

> In the beginning was the Word, and the Word was with God, and the Word was God. The same was in the beginning with God. All things were made by him; and without him was not any thing made that was made. In him was life; and the life was the light of men. And the light shineth in darkness; and the darkness comprehended it not. [John 1: 1-5; KJV]

This did not come out of the wild blue yonder for this author. Genesis 1 begins the story for us in a "PHYSICAL" way, when it says,

> In the beginning God created the heaven and the earth. And the earth was without form, and void; and darkness was upon the face of the deep. And the Spirit of God moved upon the face of the waters. And God said, Let there be light: and there was light. And God saw the light, that it was good: and God divided the light from the darkness. And God called the light Day, and the darkness he called Night. And the evening and the morning were the first day. [Genesis 1: 1-5; KJV]

Can you see the connections the author of The Gospel of John made? John refers to God as, Light, Darkness, Life; he goes on to elaborate saying in effect, we did not understand; even though the Word was written so long ago in Genesis 1, where it also speaks about God as, Light, Darkness and suggests "LIFE!". Here, we have the Origin in-so-far as what we have in the Reality of the physicality of our world.

However, the author refers back even farther than Genesis to recognize there was another Author Who made even the Physicality of Genesis possible. John calls Him, The "WORD," he Calls Him God, he calls Him The Light. God is able to, if we chose right [Adam and Eve chose wrong], to give us understanding of everything we could not grasp on our own. How was this going to happen? This part of the story is huge—requiring someone to share the Word, but Someone other than us would share with us first, it was Jesus. When Jesus left earth He sent part of the 'Whole of What God Is,' back to this earth we subsist on, and this is The Holy Spirit of God! Genesis introduced us to Him when the Author of Genesis said,

And the Spirit of God moved upon the face of the waters. [I see this somewhat like The Waters of Time we never seem to understand.] The important part, as it was written, says, "The Spirit of God" was at work. John says without The Word [JESUS], Not nothing physical existed. Scripture goes on to teach us that there is more than the physicality we see, and the scripture refers to this as "The Spiritual."

The "Bottom Line" is, because we cannot seem to understand past what we see, we need to understand everything which we do not see, through something we most often ignore: "FAITH!" [Hebrews 11:—]. John goes on to talk about the water and The Spirit later in John Chapter 1—.

So, *When All Is Said And Done,* "What Is Constant Anyway? I don't really need to explain this, except to say, it is "CONTINUANCE!" Check your thesaurus if you need a wakeup call on this.

What do I think of when I say words like, "Author, Word, God, Jesus, Holy Spirit, Light, Life—I think, 'CONSTANT, CONTINUANCE!'

When I hear the word "Darkness," I think of it as being everything GOD IS NOT! God spoke light into existence to rid us of the Darkness! Then, when we still did not get it, God became flesh, the son of man, JESUS, THE SON OF GOD. The Bible speaks of this as Him being EMMANUEL, "GOD WITH US! ALL OF WHAT GOD IS HIMSELF! What a Gift this was to us; well, it can be!

"I Think, Let's Not Forget GOD!"

PLEASE; PLEASE, DO NOT MAKE HIM THE FORGOTTEN
GOD IN YOUR LIFE!
"The Unknown God!"

Have Mercy Oh God!

Have mercy upon me, O God, according to thy lovingkindness: according unto the multitude of thy tender mercies blot out my transgressions. Wash me thoroughly from mine iniquity, and cleanse me from my sin. For I acknowledge my transgressions: and my sin is ever before me. Against thee, thee only, have I sinned, and done this evil in thy sight: that thou mightest be justified when thou speakest, and be clear when thou judgest.

Behold, I was shapen in iniquity; and in sin did my mother conceive me. Behold, thou desirest truth in the inward parts: and in the hidden part thou shalt make me to know wisdom. Purge me with hyssop, and I shall be clean: wash me, and I shall be whiter than snow. Make me to hear joy and gladness; that the bones which thou hast broken may rejoice. Hide thy face from my sins, and blot out all mine iniquities.

Create in me a clean heart, O God; and renew a right spirit within me. Cast me not away from thy presence; and take not thy holy spirit from me. Restore unto me the joy of thy salvation; and uphold me with thy free spirit. Then will I teach transgressors thy ways; and sinners shall be converted unto thee.

Deliver me from bloodguiltiness, O God, thou God of my salvation: and my tongue shall sing aloud of thy righteousness. O Lord, open thou my lips; and my mouth shall shew forth thy praise. For thou desirest not sacrifice; else would I give it: thou delightest not in burnt offering. The sacrifices of God are a broken spirit: a broken and a contrite heart, O God, thou wilt not despise. Do good in thy good pleasure unto Zion: build thou the walls of Jerusalem.

Then shalt thou be pleased with the sacrifices of righteousness, with burnt offering and whole burnt offering: then shall they offer bullocks upon thine altar.

[Psalm 51 KJV]

EPILOGUE

Each of us has a story—lecturing others with our personal beliefs, putting pressure on them to do their story our way, does not usually work. To hesitate to share thoughts and information about what may be good and morally truthful, can imply we are not true to ourselves or the God we believe in. The resources of the Bible can be enough to make it all work. Many people think of The Bible as out of date and irrelevant to life's situations. Looking at the stories in The Bible, and placing them alongside the situations of life today, may prove more relevant to real life than we know.

Many folks do not grasp what the Bible says and may never get it, but we have a chance to change this by our lives of openness with them. Sometimes the grasp of understanding slips past us because of the many views people have about what the Bible means; the Bible is trustworthy. The representative picture is clearer once we accept God by faith. Just believe what He says He is for us in our day-to-day issues. We can be safe in His care because of what faith presents as the dawn of existence.

Why did I write *Twin Towers of The Heart* [two books ago]? Each of us is on one side or another of the differing topics of living life to the full. Divided hearts keep us aloof from total usefulness in the global sense because of the absence of concern for others, and this may be evident in how we think about and care for ourselves. We might have a strong mandate for self-survival; external survival owns part of this book's message. We need to articulate the long and the short answer; the short answer comes first. The short answer embraces our remembrance of 9/11.

Nine/Eleven still beckons us to remember some of the past so we can live in the present to reflect from our lives, all God wants from us for the benefit of other people who are of equal value to the rest of the world. How we live on and why we all have a legitimate place in life, this makes the whole story come alive. These feelings are like a merry go round in our heart of hearts. These images are flaming arrows to show us how to evaluate our position to make some right choices in living our book of life; this is challenging.

Each of us are but a small measure of the reality of the book of life. Some of us might just be a word in the book of life, others may be a note; others will be full-scale novels in the book of the living. However, each of has the capacity to be a sentence, a paragraph, a chapter, but none of us are the whole book; we do this together. Like it or not, we accomplish life with each other and our Creator, for some folks, this is an evolution of sorts.

As part of a book, we illustrate ourselves as words, full line sentences, paragraphs, pages, and chapters—fifteen, twenty, or thirty chapters or more in length. It will be colossal when our final chapter shines as brightly as a spotlight of importance and becomes a major lesson of life and learning. If this light is a massive laser beam in front of the world to point out what made this hour and final nanosecond of our lives available to us, then our value level increases with everyone else. To accept that God is all we need, sounds unreal; might this be a valid choice to consider?

Fantastic, if we could say this is possible for everybody. Life often offers too many options for our lives. It is hard to find one truth in the whole melting pot of humanity that will serve adequately enough for everyone. We would all like to understand thoroughly how and why the whole universe is as we see it. This does not seem possible with so many offerings of personal conscience and the desires that have built up over the many years of our tenancy on this earth.

Whether we accept God as true or choose evolution, one way or another we hold to a belief system. We need to hear what is shouting at us from all corners of the ring. Our determinations become pains of survival (WYSIWYG). However, one way or another faith becomes the tool we use to get where we think we are going.

Either way, we need faith because faith is the belief in the unseen or unknown. Choosing God is an option and we will all decide for ourselves which option we will follow. It takes less faith to understand someone, not something, always takes credit and responsibility for all the beauty we see in people or things—in living and in dying. When we put our trust in someone with this kind of power and He shows it to us through love, the rest of the story develops understandingly. People wrote about God from as long ago as written records exist; this is history: HIS-STORY.

Only a glimpse of the total magnitude of God appears before us as it nestles inside this visual picture of the short answer. This image of the heart within the heart of God, or the heart of hearts, pleads for enlargement, and this comes to focus in the long answer. Every idea has a tendency towards good or evil and becomes part of our story. The whole scenario plays a significant role in highlighting the best and the worst segments of our journey. Hope allows the best to win out through the yesterday's within our today, as the tomorrows of life live out in us. Getting up in the morning seems a little bit easier when life has a great measure of importance. An energetic reason for living each day offers belief and expectancy.

The long answer begins with an insatiable propensity for the written word as the starting point. People who read avidly gain knowledge. The Good Book tells us we are chapters of thought that come alive in and through other people. Those who make time to observe life and other people are those who see our journey as a gift. We are live video presentations to all who observe us. Those of us who are words come to life are cinemas presenting full-length screen productions to an audience of the world, other folks learn from us in the process. As we evaluate our inadequacy to make a difference, we often reflect too much on our past failures.

The long answer continues as long answers always do in a continuous or near endless way. Because of an insatiable craving for journaling about nearly everything seen and read, brevity becomes an enemy. Sometimes I think the biggest mistake anyone ever made was to invent the pencil or pen. It might even go back to as far as when our ancestors used lead, coal, or a flint stone as writing tools to etch out their feelings, to move thoughts from their mind into the mind of others in this antiquated way. Maybe it was the cave man's idea or maybe it was God's idea; dare we say it?

Trusting in the facts in so far they go, can show us clearly God is, and has always been in charge of every situation. This is something everyone must decide individually. A thorough search of the universe may imply mere chance may not be the best option. It is tough to explain the how's, and especially the why's of life's situations so everyone is fully satisfied; another story could come alive here. The pioneer of all of the creation, the Builder of all time promises to be ready for us, we also need to be willingly ready for Him; danger is not an enemy when we trust Him.

Part One of *Everybody: Everybody Is A Somebody*, is called *The Launching Pad*. If we are familiar with NASA and the many times they sent rockets into space, we will be aware of the term "Launch Pad." Without the framework for sending Space Vehicles into space, there would be no Space Program. We cannot just insert a bunch of dynamite or nitroglycerin under a rocket the size of NASA's Rockets, and expect to get them airborne far enough to get them into the upper atmosphere. The stage has to be set in particular fashion for the safety of all concerned, and so the USA can boast success for the exploratory venture of finding out more about what lies out there which may be of help in some of what needs to be set in stone on our earth.

The reason I named Part One, *The Launching Pad*, is to give us a picture of how one process or the other sets the stage for what is yet to come. No matter what we 'build,' not concoct out of thin air like the magicians try to make us believe is what magic is, but "BUILD," like when someone is building a house or any other edifice—there is always a blueprint or a plan in place to follow. We dealt with some of this previously when we spoke about DNA and RNA.

Moving on from *Part One, The Launching Pad*, so as to "Build" a pattern of thinking through the rest of *Everybody: Everybody Is A Somebody*, I moved on to write about many things which determine Value. By putting forth pictures in words concerning how accounting and stock market issues point us to a reality which concerns our physical day-to-day activities, it leads us to understand the necessities we all need to survive life. Along with these thoughts we mount a portrait in our mind of how these thoughts help us understand that we are all Valuable in the eyes of God, even if no one else thinks we are all of Equal Value.

The first five chapters led us through things like, '*The Value of Life, The Golden Rule, Balancing The Book of Life, What Is The Reality Within The Book of Life, and Finding and Dealing With The Market Value of Life.*' From my perspective it always comes down to Where and How it all began—Life. I have now, and have not for a long time now, ever hesitated to believe God did it all. Everything had a beginning. Many will dispute my beliefs to suggest everything just happened the way it did, and it all happened somehow, by some accident or unplanned way through what many call "The Big Bang.

What a Bang it must have been to fashion the intimacy portrayed in every facet of what we think of as Creation, or Existence of all that is. This takes us to another part of the plan and implementation of *Part Two* of this book.

Part Two was titled *Who Believes What? And Why?* Here we find another five chapters looking somewhat like this, '*Evolution Figured It Out: Or Not? Christianity Figured It Out: Or Not? Sketch One Genesis: One Beginning! Life As We Have It Now! The Answer Is Blown In The Wind.*' There is an interesting 'LOT' of info and assumption, surmising, and what in my perspective, are "The Facts of Life," as we know them, and our assumptions about "The Facts of Life!"

If and when we come from a Christian and or a Christ Follower Perspective, we deal with some of life differently than those who do not hold our view or set of beliefs. Sometime we think everybody should grasp Life and Eternity just exactly the way we do—this is not happening. Just because I see something one way, does not mean everyone will see it my way and follow my fully intended loving intentions to help them find the Truth which will one day become fully evident—at least, this is how I see it!

The flip side follows the same pattern which I have just alluded to, but it may just be the complete opposite of what I say is my perspective and belief system; it might very well be the antonym [opposite] of the beliefs many of us have. This is life as it is. Nothing will ever change in this life because life has taken a meandering course over many eons of time, because we decided to do things our own way. We think we have the Golden Rule fully handled in our lives, and we may have, but we may just have left out an entity which might just knock us down—The Truth of The Someone Who got life going in the first place—I Call Him God! I call Him Jesus!

Part Three moved us along a little farther in hopes of helping us along with understanding more of what was said earlier, and what would be said as we ventured on to where we are now in *Everybody: Everybody Is A Somebody.* Chapters Eleven through Sixteen look something like this, '*The Domino Stories Of Life Affect Everyone, The If Factor, Observable Metamorphoses, The Five W'S and How: Then What? Inquires; Ignorance; Responses; Resentment, and The How Factor.*' If we had stopped here, many questions may have been settled in your mind, or not?

By now I have written about a hundred and sixty- thousand words, quite enough by any standards, to present the greater message about life—I Guess? I titled *Part Four, Blueprints, Schematics, Resistors, Power—! Part Four* housed *Chapter 17, Neutral or Not Neutral. Part Five* is called, *Understanding The Real: The Visible! And The Invisible! Part Five* challenged us with the last numbered Chapter, and it was called *Chapter 18, The Forgotten One: God!*

What followed is what you are reading—The *Epilogue*. It capped off what has been said throughout. I am sure of at least one thing, and that because I have lived a considerable part of life now, and this makes me sure not 'Everybody' will jump to the pump and say, "Fill My Cup LORD!" This saddens me.

If you ever wanted to be invited to a major event, or a party, and were not included in the guest list, do not feel bad! I will send you an "INVITE" If I have not yet Invited you to the Greatest Event In History here-to-for, rest assured, I will be sending out The Invitation ASAP.

For now, I will conclude the bulk of this book with the words of this *Epilogue* by Saying, Stay Tuned!

Please Look Forward to—
THE FINAL CHAPTER

RSVP—THE INVITATION

Everybody Is A Somebody: in The Eyes of God
GOD HAS A WILL, A PLAN, AND A PURPOSE
GOD ALWAYS HAD A WILL, A PLAN, AND A PURPOSE
GOD ALWAYS WILL, HAVE A PLAN, AND A PURPOSE
FOR EVERYONE
UNTIL HIS PLAN FOR EARTH AND ALL THAT IT IS NOW,
IS COMPLETE.
UNTIL THAT TIME WE CAN CHOOSE TO GET ON BOARD
WITH HIM:
ONCE THAT DOOR CLOSES OUR CHOICE TO GET ON
BOARD WITH HIM IS OVER.
HERE IS YOUR
R.S.V.P
YOUR INVITATION
"THE INVITATION"
GOD IS WAITING FOR YOUR REPLY!
R.S.V.P
WHO GOD IS

In the beginning was the Word, and the Word was with God, and the Word was God. The same was in the beginning with God. All things were made by him; and without him was not anything made that was made. In him was life; and the life was the light of men. [Gospel of John 1: 1-4 KJV]

There was a man of the Pharisees, named Nicodemus, a ruler of the Jews: The same came to Jesus by night, and said unto him, Rabbi, we know that thou art a teacher come from God: for no man can do these miracles that thou doest, except God be with him. Jesus answered and said unto him, Verily, verily, I say unto thee, except a man be born again, he cannot see the kingdom of God. Nicodemus saith unto him, how can a man be born when he is old? can he enter the second time into his mother's womb, and be born?

Jesus answered, Verily, verily, I say unto thee, except a man be born of water and of the Spirit, he cannot enter into the kingdom of God. That which is born of the flesh is flesh; and that which is born of the Spirit is spirit. Marvel not that I said unto thee, Ye must be born again.

The wind bloweth where it listeth, and thou hearest the sound thereof, but canst not tell whence it cometh, and whither it goeth: so is every one that is born of the Spirit. Nicodemus answered and said unto him, How can these things be? Jesus answered and said unto him, Art thou a master of Israel, and knowest not these things?

Verily, verily, I say unto thee, we speak that we do know, and testify that we have seen; and ye receive not our witness. If I have told you earthly things, and ye believe not, how shall ye believe, if I tell you of heavenly things? And no man hath ascended up to heaven, but he that came down from heaven, even the Son of man which is in heaven. And as Moses lifted up the serpent in the wilderness, even so must the Son of man be lifted up: That whosoever believeth in him should not perish but have eternal life.

For God so loved the world, that he gave his only begotten Son, that whosoever believeth in him should not perish, but have everlasting life. For God sent not his Son into the world to condemn the world; but that the world through him might be saved. He that believeth on him is not condemned: but he that believeth not is condemned already, because he hath not believed in the name of the only begotten Son of God. And this is the condemnation, that light is come into the world, and men loved darkness rather than light, because their deeds were evil. For everyone that doeth evil hateth the light, neither cometh to the light, lest his deeds should be reproved. [John 3:1-20 KJV]

Let not your heart be troubled: ye believe in God, believe me too. In my Father's house are many mansions: Were it not so, I would have told you. I go to prepare a place for you. And if I go and prepare a place for you, I will come again, and receive you unto myself; that where I am, there ye may be also.

Where I go ye know, and the way ye know. Thomas saith unto him, Lord, we know not whither thou goest; and how can we know the way? Jesus saith unto him, I am the way, the truth, and the life: no man cometh unto the Father, but by me. [Gospel of John 14:1-6]

For by grace are ye saved through faith; and that not of yourselves: it is the gift of God: Not of works, lest any man should boast. For we are his workmanship, created in Christ Jesus unto good works, which God hath before ordained that we should walk in them. [Ephesians 2:8-10 KJV]

For all have sinned, and come short of the glory of God; [Romans 3:23 KJV]

For the wages of sin is death; but the gift of God is eternal life through Jesus Christ our Lord. [Romans 6:23 KJV]

That if thou shalt confess with thy mouth the Lord Jesus, and shalt believe in thine heart that God hath raised him from the dead, thou shalt be saved. For with the heart man believeth unto righteousness; and with the mouth confession is made unto salvation. [Romans 10: 9-10 KJV]

Lord Jesus: I understand that I am a sinner. I do not want to be a sinner anymore. I want to serve you, and you alone. Please forgive me from all my sin of unbelief and make me a child of Yours. Teach me how to live for you.
Thank You

X.

HOPE FOR TOMORROW

Throughout *Everybody: Everybody Is A Somebody*, we have seen pictures of life as it is; pictures of where hope can be the answer to the skewed pictures of life, and we have illustrations of the full scope of what life can be. I have always presented scripture because it has been and will always be my intent to offer Jesus Christ, God, as the only Hope For Humankind to experience eternity as many folks expect eternity to be for them. I always present in a way that allows for everyone to see that there is only one way for this to be the case.

THE CHANNEL OF HOPE
IS
JESUS!

To grasp this Hope and to see the Promise of Tomorrow, let's wind up where the Bible finishes; it finishes with a Big Bang of its own, compared to the promise of the Big Bang Theory. I have never told this part of the story in all the words of *Everybody: Everybody Is A Somebody*, as clearly as The Bible itself can in Revelation 19-22. I will never be able to tell this part of the story better than The Bible.

THE FINAL CHAPTER

[Revelation 19, 20, 21, and 22 KJV]

"Salvation, and glory, and honor, and power, unto the Lord our God: For true and righteous are his judgments: for he hath judged the great whore, which corrupted the earth with her fornication, and hath avenged the blood of his servants at her hand.

Again, they said, Alleluia And her smoke rose up for ever and ever. And the four and twenty elders and the four beasts fell down and worshiped God that sat on the throne, saying, Amen; Alleluia.

And a voice came out of the throne, saying, praise our God, all ye his servants, and ye that fear him, both small and great. And I heard the voice of a great multitude, and as the voice of many waters, and as the voice of mighty thundering's, saying, Alleluia: for the Lord God omnipotent reigneth.

Let us be glad and rejoice and give honor to him: for the marriage of the Lamb is come and his wife hath made herself ready. And to her was granted that she should be arrayed in fine linen, clean and white: for the fine linen is the righteousness of saints.

And he saith unto me, Write, blessed are they which are called unto the marriage supper of the Lamb. And he saith unto me, these are the true sayings of God. And I fell at his feet to worship him. And he said unto me, see thou do it not: I am thy fellow-servant, and of thy brethren with the testimony of Jesus: worship God: for the testimony of Jesus is the spirit of prophecy.

And I saw heaven opened, and behold a white horse, and he that sat upon him was called Faithful and True, and in righteousness, he doth judge and make war. His eyes were as a flame of fire, and on his head were many crowns; and he had a name written, that no man knew, but he.

And he was clothed with a vesture dipped in blood: and his name is called The Word of God. And the armies in heaven followed him upon white horses, clothed in fine linen, white and clean. And out of his mouth goeth a sharp sword, that with it he should smite the nations: and he will rule them with a rod of iron: and he treadeth the winepress of the fierceness and wrath of Almighty God. And he hath on his vesture and on his thigh a name was written, KING OF KINGS, AND LORD OF LORDS.

And I saw an angel standing in the sun; and he cried with a loud voice, saying to all the fowls that fly in heaven, Come and gather yourselves together unto the supper of the great God; that ye may eat the flesh of kings, and the flesh of captains, and the flesh of mighty men, and the flesh of horses, and of them that sit on them, and the flesh of all men, both free and bond, both small and great.

And I saw the beast, and the kings of the earth and their armies gathered together to make war against him that sat on the horse, and against his army. And the beast was taken, and with him, the false prophet that wrought miracles before him, with which he deceived them that had received the mark of the beast, and them that worshiped his image. These both were cast alive into a lake of fire burning with brimstone. And the remnant was slain with the sword of him that sat upon the horse, which sword proceeded out of his mouth: and all the fowls were filled with their flesh.

20]And I saw an angel come down from heaven, having the key of the bottomless pit and a great chain in his hand. And he laid hold on the dragon, that old serpent, which is the Devil, and Satan, and bound him a thousand years, and cast him into the bottomless pit, and shut him up, and set a seal upon him, that he should deceive the nations no more, till the thousand years should be fulfilled: and after that, he must be loosed a little season.

And I saw thrones, and they sat upon them, and judgment was given unto them: and I saw the souls of them that were beheaded for the witness of Jesus, and for the word of God, and which had not worshipped the beast, neither his image, neither had received his mark upon their foreheads, or in their hands; and they lived and reigned with Christ a thousand years. But the rest of the dead lived not again until the thousand years were finished. This is the first resurrection.

Blessed and holy is he that hath part in the first resurrection: on such the second death hath no power, but they will be priests of God and of Christ and will reign with him a thousand years. And when the thousand years are expired, Satan will be loosed out of his prison, and will go out to deceive the nations in the four quarters of the earth, Gog, and Magog, to gather them together to battle: the number of whom is as the sand of the sea.

And they went up on the breadth of the earth, and compassed the camp of the saints about, and the beloved city: and fire came down from God out of heaven and devoured them. And the devil that deceived them was cast into the lake of fire and brimstone, where the beast and the false prophet are, and will be tormented day and night forever and ever.

And I saw a great white throne, and him that sat on it, from whose face the earth and the heaven fled away; and there was found no place for them. And I saw the dead, small and great, stand before God; and the books were opened: and another book was opened, which is the book of life: and the dead were judged out of those things written in the books, according to their works. And the sea gave up the dead in it, and death and hell delivered up the dead in them: and they were judged every man according to their works. And death and hell were cast into the lake of fire. This is the second death. And whosoever was not found written in the book of life was cast into the lake of fire.

21]And I saw a new heaven and a new earth: for the first heaven and the first earth were passed away; and there was no more sea. And I John saw the holy city, new Jerusalem, coming down from God out of heaven, prepared as a bride adorned for her husband.

And I heard a great voice out of heaven saying, Behold, the tabernacle of God is with men, and he will dwell with them, and they will be his people, and God himself will be with them, and be their God. And God will wipe away all tears from their eyes, and there will be no more death, neither sorrow, nor crying, neither will there be any more pain: for the former things are passed away.

And he that sat upon the throne said, Behold, I make all things new. And he said unto me, write: for these words are true and faithful. And he said unto me, it is done. I am Alpha and Omega, the beginning, and the end. I will give unto him that is athirst of the fountain of the water of life freely.

He that overcometh will inherit all things, and I will be his God, and he will be my son. But the fearful, and unbelieving, and the abominable, and murderers, and whoremongers, and sorcerers, and idolaters, and all liars will have their part in the lake which burneth with fire and brimstone: which is the second death.

And there came unto me one of the seven angels with the seven vials full of the seven last plagues, and talked with me, saying, come hither, I will shew thee the bride, the Lamb's wife. And he carried me away in the spirit to a great and high mountain, and showed me that great city, the holy Jerusalem, descending out of heaven from God, having the glory of God: and her light was like unto a stone most precious, even like a jasper stone, clear as crystal; and had a wall great and high, and had twelve gates, and at the gates twelve angels, and names written thereon, which are the names of the twelve tribes of the children of Israel:

On the east three gates; on the north three gates; on the south three gates; and on the west three gates. And the wall of the city had twelve foundations, and in them the names of the twelve apostles of the Lamb. And he that talked with me had a golden reed to measure the city, and the gates thereof, and the wall thereof. And the city lieth foursquare and the length is as large as the breadth: and he measured the city with the reed, twelve thousand furlongs. The length, the breadth, and the height of it are equal. And he measured the wall thereof, a hundred and forty and four cubits, according to the measure of a man, that is of the angel.

And the building of the wall of it was of jasper: and the city was pure gold, like unto clear glass. And the foundations of the wall of the city were garnished with many precious stones. The first foundation was jasper; the second, sapphire; the third, a chalcedony; the fourth, an emerald;

The fifth, sardonyx; the sixth, sardius; the seventh, chrysolite; the eighth, beryl; the ninth, a topaz; the tenth, a chrysoprase; the eleventh, a jacinth; the twelfth, an amethyst. And the twelve gates were twelve pearls: every several gate was of one pearl: and the street of the city was pure gold, transparent as glass.

And I saw no temple: for the Lord God Almighty and the Lamb are the temple. And the city had no need of the sun, neither of the moon, to shine in it: for the glory of God lightened it, and the Lamb is the light thereof.

And the nations of them which are saved will walk in the light of it: and the kings of the earth bring their glory and honor into it. And the gates of it will not be shut by day: for there will be no night there. And they will bring the glory and honor of the nations into it.

And there will be in no wise enter it anything that defiles, neither worketh abomination nor maketh a lie: but they which are written in the Lamb's book of life.

And he shewed me a pure river of water of life, clear as crystal, proceeding out of the throne of God and of the Lamb. In the midst of the street of it, and on either side of the river, was there the tree of life, which bare twelve manners of fruits, and yielded her fruit every month: and the leaves of the tree were for the healing of the nations.

And there will be no more curse: but the throne of God and of the Lamb will be in it; and his servants will serve him: and they will see his face, and his name will be in their foreheads.

And there will be no night there; and they need no candle, neither light of the sun; for the Lord God giveth them light: and they will reign for ever and ever. And he said unto me, these sayings are faithful and true: and the Lord God of the holy prophets sent his angel to shew unto his servants the things which must shortly be done.

Behold, I come quickly: blessed is he that keepeth the sayings of the prophecy of this book. And I John saw these things and heard them. And when I had heard and seen, I fell down to worship before the feet of the angel which shewed me these things.

Then saith he unto me, see thou do it not: for I am thy fellow-servant, and of thy brethren the prophets, and of them, which keep the sayings of this, book: worship God. And he saith unto me, Seal not the sayings of the prophecy of this book: for the time is at hand. He that is unjust, let him be unjust still: and he, which is filthy, let him, be filthy still: and he that is righteous, let him be righteous still: and he that is holy, let him be holy still.

And, behold, I come quickly; and my reward is with me, to give every man according to as his work will be. I am Alpha and Omega, the beginning, and the end, the first and the last.

Blessed are they that do his commandments that they may have the right to the tree of life and may enter in through the gates into the city. For without are dogs, and sorcerers, and whoremongers, and murderers, and idolaters, and whosoever loveth and maketh a lie.

I Jesus have sent mine angel to testify unto you these things in the churches. I am the root and the offspring of David, and the bright and morning star.

And the Spirit and the bride say, Come. And let him that heareth say, Come. And let him that is athirst come. And whosoever will let him take the water of life freely.

For I testify unto every man that heareth the words of the prophecy of this book, if any man will add unto these things, God will add unto him the plagues written in this book:

And if anyone will take away from the words of the book of this prophecy, God will take away his part out of the book of life, and out of the holy city, and from the things written in this book.

He which testifieth these things saith, Surely I come quickly. Amen. Come, Lord Jesus.

The grace of our Lord Jesus Christ is with you all. Amen."
[Revelation 19-22; KJV]

If you have skipped to the back because you wanted to find out how
the story ends,
"PLEASE GO BACK,
If you don't, you will have missed
"THE STORY OF A LIFETIME!"

ABOUT THE AUTHOR

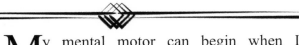

My mental motor can begin when I am supposed to be starting my night to sleep. This eventually leaves me tired. And most of the time I misplace the "My Remote—The Off Button" for this until midnight of that day, and then it begins again. The Lord usually puts me to sleep when he knows that I need to shut down, so I get my rest, but sometimes I push the envelope!

In this book before you, imagine me as a person walking along a highway with a divider up the middle, like the Promenade on the Brooklyn Bridge in New York City. From here I can go one of two directions. On this promenade, I am not in danger, but I may see things and distribute the thoughts I have within me, without living on the edge. Now, if I am walking in the center place, on either side of the guardrail, on the Grand Central Parkway, it is a different story. Sometimes my writing will have you thinking I am walking dangerously, like in the perspective of the Christianity I espouse. Danger lurks near because my enemy tries to deter my progress.

Yet, the greater danger remains when it is as if I am walking on an undivided freeway, only marking about a six-inch marker line separating the two directions of traffic. Sometimes you may see me in one scenario, but know this, if you stay with me, you will see what I am trying to pass on to you. On these roadways, I can go the wrong direction, from what the best-case scenario of life will give me; I have the choice of turning around because I see the danger of going the wrong way, cautioning me to make a mid-course change of direction because of the dangers before me.

My name is Jacob Bergen, this is no secret. I am retired from my day-to-day job as a Floor Covering Salesperson and Estimator: It is now six months to the day past my seventy-third birthday at the time of this writing. This, as your author of *Everybody: Everybody Is A Somebody*, is the basic starting point of who I am. I am a year and a half short of three quarters of a Century old.

About The Author:

My fifty-fifth birthday sometimes referred to as Freedom Fifty-Five, was one day after the fateful 01/09/11. Though this does not allow for celebration in the immediate sense, it allows for a capsulation of fifty-five years of reasons to be thankful. I am thankful I live in the country of Canada, on the continent of North America; this also gives me a reason to be thankful for my neighbor to the South of me: The United States of America. Though the USA does not always show unity in their actions towards others, just as my country Canada is not always united, both give me reasons to have a sense of overall security, at least in the day-to-day sense.

I am a Christian in the Judeo-Christian Perspective. I believe in what The Bible says; there is one God Who has and shows Himself active in Three Persons of equal authority. These Persons are The Father, The Son Jesus, and The Holy Spirit.

I am a writer. If I could "Have A Do Over" this is what I would do from my earliest formative, productive years. However, a retraction to this declaration is in order. Why or how can I say this, without causing an enigma or muddling the waters?

I believe everything in our lives as we have lived them and live them, are placements in time for us to learn from and become better people at what we do and how we involve others in our lives.

I am a firm believer that everything in my life has been a time of preparation for something else which has happened in and through me: Throughout my journey. Therefore, if I had been a writer from an earlier time, I may have been unprepared for today and unready to face tomorrow.

I am married, have three stepsons, and one son by blood connection, and we have twenty grandchildren, and we have two great-grandchildren [both boys]. All our grandchildren Are Great, but in proper context or order they are still 'grandchildren.'

In the mix of life as we all face it, we have all experienced life from many different situations: Many good, and some of the adverse nature. This really is the same as all the rest of you, apart from the children, grandchildren, and situations—we have.

I have lived in Steinbach Manitoba, Winnipeg Manitoba, Belleville Ontario, Vancouver BC, Saskatoon Saskatchewan, Prince Albert Saskatchewan, Calgary Alberta, and now live in Invermere BC Canada. I was born in Steinbach Manitoba Canada, September 12, 1946.

My family was nominally Christian; by this I mean my parents believed in God, but did not always serve Him in the strictest sense of the word 'Christian.' By the time I was twelve my folks changed this part of their lives; they accepted Jesus Christ as their day-to-day companion and friend in all this means according to what the Bible says about these things. My conversion was at age twelve, although some interruptions were on this course until I was thirty-five years old.

How did I become a Writer? From as far back as when I was about fifteen or sixteen I made little notes trying to explain what I believed and how I felt about what I believed. At one time, I wrote awful little notes and put them in places for people to read because I thought this was funny. At another time in my life, I wrote nice and invitational notes for people, in trying to share my faith in different ways. One of these ways was to write notes and go out after midnight when most people were sleeping and put them in their mailboxes; I was fearful, and an arrest for prowling might have been my fate, but not thinking things through, I did it this way.

I was young once and sometimes I displayed this youth in wrong ways. However, I had a writer's heart in me; I had to get it out. For much of my life since then I have written things like articles and eventually in book format; even this *About the Author* segment is almost in book format, as a life story. I have a writer's heart and anyone with a writer's heart knows this is hard to contain.

To date, I have self-published four books: *It's Jacob! My Name Is Jacob! What's Yours? (2002)*, *The Mandate (2006)*, *Twin Towers of The Heart (2016)*, and *Bridging The Gap* (2018). All of these are in Paper Back, one in Hard Cover [*The Mandate*], and all in E-Book format. Google Jacob Bergen Books and these show up on Amazon and other places.

Well, there is much more than meets the eye, in the life of Jacob Bergen. Yes, my physical historical make-up is mud, the same stuff as anyone else's make-up; this is by design at the Hands of God: With the dirt he created. My heart and hopes are that *Everybody: Everybody Is A Somebody* captures some of your heart. We cannot trust our heart; take that to the bank. The heart can turn on us in a moment; often the heart is hard to pin down. [Jeremiah 17:9; (JBI)]

Me, just a little old farm boy to begin with;

About The Author:

Can This Be?
Go Figure

Jacob Bergen

Notes:

NOTES:

NOTES:

THE END
IT HAS BEEN MY PLEASURE
GOD HAS BEEN MY HELPER
HE IS MY STRENGTH
MOMENT BY MOMENT!

EVERYBODY: EVERYBODY IS A SOMEBODY

Bible Study Guide

TOOLS FOR GETTING the picture of what we can learn from reading *Everybody: Everybody Is A Somebody*! It is one thing to read a book of the volume of four-hundred and seventy pages, as is this book, it is yet another thing to be able to walk away from the last page and say, "The Distance I Travelled Made A Difference in My Life."

—Use the illustrations throughout the book as Perks to look for something in your day that you can relate to a spiritual insight: A God Thing!

—Use the scripture of each Chapter as Devotional Reading, along with the path you feel you are to walk in God's Light.

—Ask God how He wants to use what you read to give you a better insight to the World Around You!

—Stay in God's Word, Pray, and Open Your Ears to Listen.

Stop, Look, and Listen!

Look Over The Horizons Ahead of You!

Do Not Be Fearful and or Unbelieving:

God wants His Best For YOU!

I am planning to Do A Book and Bible Study For This Book:

EVERYBODY: EVERYBODY IS A SOMEBODY
Sometime In 2020

To God Be The Glory

Verse 1] To God be the glory, great things He hath done;
So loved He the world He gave us His Son,
Who yielded His life an atonement for sin?
And opened the life-gate that all may go in.

Praise the Lord, praise the Lord,
Let the earth hear His voice!
Praise the Lord, praise the Lord,
Let the people rejoice!
O come to the Father, through Jesus the Son,
And give Him the glory, great things He hath done.

Verse 2] O perfect redemption, the purchase of blood,
To every believer the promise of God;
The vilest offender who truly believes,
That moment from Jesus a pardon receives.

Verse 3] Great things He hath taught us, great things He hath done,
And great our rejoicing through Jesus the Son;
But purer, and higher, and greater will be
Our wonder, our rapture, when Jesus we see.

—In The Midst of The Ultimate God! —
Praise The LORD!

Amen!